HIGHWAY  61 REVISITED

HIGHWAY  61 REVISITED

Bob Dylan's
Road from
Minnesota to
the World

Colleen J. Sheehy and Thomas Swiss, Editors

UNIVERSITY OF MINNESOTA PRESS
MINNEAPOLIS · LONDON

Published by the University of Minnesota Press
111 Third Avenue South, Suite 290
Minneapolis, MN 55401-2520
http://www.upress.umn.edu

Library of Congress Cataloging-in-Publication Data

Highway 61 revisited : Bob Dylan's road from Minnesota to the world /
Colleen J. Sheehy and Thomas Swiss, editors.
    p.   cm.
  Includes bibliographical references and index.
  ISBN 978-0-8166-6099-5 (hc : alk. paper) — ISBN 978-0-8166-6100-8
  1. Dylan, Bob, 1941. 2. Singers—United States—Biography. 3. Dylan, Bob, 1941– Criticism and interpretation. 4. Hibbing (Minn.)—History. I. Sheehy, Colleen J. (Colleen Josephine), 1953– II. Swiss, Thomas, 1952–
  ML420.D98H54   2009
  782.42164092—dc22
  [B]   2009003358

Printed in the United States of America on acid-free paper

The University of Minnesota is an equal-opportunity educator and employer.

15 14 13 12 11 10 09   10 9 8 7 6 5 4 3 2 1

FOR
B.J.
ROLFZEN

Highway 61, the main thoroughfare of the country blues, begins about where I came from . . . I always felt like I'd started on it, always had been on it, and could go anywhere from it, even down into the deep Delta country. It was the same road, full of the same contradictions, the same one-horse towns, the same spiritual ancestors . . . It was my place in the universe, always felt like it was in my blood.

—BOB DYLAN, *Chronicles, Volume 1*

CONTENTS

Introduction
Colleen J. Sheehy, John Barner, and Thomas Swiss

A Place Called Riddle

In Todd Haynes's film *I'm Not There* (2007), two of the characters who play oblique versions of Bob Dylan—Billy the Kid (Richard Gere) and a young (black) Woody Guthrie (Marcus Carl Franklin)—converge in the small frontier town of Riddle, Missouri. While the action at first seems to take place in the nineteenth century, viewers slowly recognize that time is conflated with more modern times: Riddle's future is threatened by the imminent prospect of a six-lane highway coming straight through town, and its residents are evacuating. Some scenes of Riddle are reminiscent of those depicting the amiable, democratic citizens portrayed by nineteenth-century painter George Caleb Bingham; others suggest a ghoulish quality to frontier living, more murder ballad than ballot box. An Ophelia-like beauty, dead by her own hand, is displayed upright in a coffin onstage, her eyes wide open, as a ragtag Salvation Army band plays a dirgelike "Goin' to Acapulco."

Haynes's Riddle, Missouri, is surely the capital of what Greil Marcus has called an "old, weird America." Indeed, riddles themselves—that is, enigmatic questions or statements—emerged early in Dylan's career and were in full swing by the time of his 1965 press conference in San Francisco, when Ralph Gleason introduced Dylan to the gathered press corps, saying, "He's here to answer questions about everything from atomic science to riddles and rhymes." Dylan proceeded not to answer questions so much as to confound his questioners with more puzzling statements to decipher. When asked how he would define folk music, he responded, "As a constitutional replay of mass production."[1]

The riddle of Dylan in Haynes's film, with multiple characters playing multiple Dylans in overlapping narratives, speaks to the complexity of interpreting the singer and his songs. Haynes's work argues that Dylan embodies a Whitmanesque breadth of American culture and history that can only be understood as embodied by different races, genders, religions, eras, and figures both legendary and historical. In a related way, Dylan's physical and artistic geographies migrate from his

Todd Haynes, *I'm Not There,* 2007. Photograph by
Jonathan Weak, The Weinstein Company.

place of birth and upbringing in northern Minnesota into the vast reach of the nation and beyond. Dylan's own song and album *Highway 61 Revisited* tie his work to
the historic blues road that runs through his hometown of Duluth, Minnesota, and
parallels the Mississippi River south through St. Louis, Memphis, and on into New
Orleans. Hence Dylan's road to the wider nation, in spatial as well as cultural terms
(he has called himself "a musical expeditionary"), posits Highway 61 as a route of
geographic and artistic odyssey, and his song of the open road suggests it as a
metaphorical space of encounters, tests and tricks, fantastical experiences, and
reinventions. On this important route, Dylan writes in *Chronicles, Volume 1,* "I always
felt like I'd started out on it, always had been on it and could go anywhere from
it. . . . it was my place in the universe. . . ."[2] Our efforts to "revisit" this highway serve
as an organizing metaphor for the work of this volume.

Dylan's resistance to easy exegesis offers some reasons for the fact that followers
and fans, fellow musicians and admiring artists, as well as journalists and scholars
have demonstrated ongoing fascination with the singer for more than forty-five
years. Ever since Robert Shelton's first *New York Times* review and Tony Glover's and
Jon Pankake's commentary in *The Little Sandy Review,* Dylan has sustained one of
the most remarkable levels of critical attention of any contemporary artist. We can't
stop talking (and arguing) about him. We can't stop analyzing his work and trying
to figure out the person who created and performs it. And just when we think he

might be summed up, he adds to the corpus: releases a critically acclaimed album that reaches number one on the charts, writes a remarkable memoir that omits key events and record releases, becomes an archival radio D.J. whose play lists survey the breadth of the American songbook, lends a sour love song and lecherous leer to a Victoria's Secret commercial, and creates a film with himself as "Jack Fate" that can only be read with a Shakespearian lens.

As Haynes explores in his film, Dylan presents riddles, and we can't quite figure out the answer—or answers:

> How many roads must a man walk down?
> How many ears must one man have?
> Are birds free from the chains of the skyway?
> What's the matter with this cruel world today?

AND:

> How did Bobby Zimmerman become Bob Dylan?
> How could Bob Dylan come from Hibbing, Minnesota?
> How could a Jewish boy from northern Minnesota
>   change music around the world?

AND:

> Is he a poet or a songwriter?
> Is he an allusionist or a thief?
> Is his voice horrible or incredible?
> Is he a prophet or a prick?
> Should he receive the Nobel Prize for Literature?

The unsettled and sometimes unsettling nature of Dylan as an artist and of Dylan's artistry make him a compelling subject of study and interpretation. *Highway 61 Revisited: Bob Dylan's Road from Minnesota to the World* offers new perspectives on Dylan's roots and routes, and on his national and worldwide influence. The book diverges from other Dylan anthologies in its geographic and global approach, more fully exploring Dylan's Minnesota Iron Range roots and examining his intersections with broad areas of American culture, while also exploring his links to world cultures, from ancient authors to his impact in Italy, Japan, and other countries.

Over the years, Dylan's work has attracted primarily literary analyses and biographical accounts. It was a photographer, Daniel Kramer, who published the first book publication on Dylan in 1967; it featured documentary photographs taken during pivotal years of change in 1964 and 1965. Kramer captured images of the singer's private life in upstate New York as well as sessions at a Columbia Records recording studio and concert performances. The photographer's own journalistic accounts provided the text, offering a glimpse into the artist's daily routines and Kramer's insights into Dylan's creativity and impact on listeners. In 1971, journalist Anthony Scaduto published a full Dylan biography, the first of what has become an ongoing enterprise in Dylan books: to try to pin down the contours of a life obscured and protected by the subject himself. Scaduto achieved a seriousness of tone and integrity of research that had been lacking in earlier attempts by "Dylanologists," such as A. J. Weberman, who famously rifled through Dylan's garbage to find clues to the artist. That same year, Toby Thompson issued *Positively Main Street: An Unorthodox View of Bob Dylan,* a new journalism approach that presents the author centrally as first-person narrator. Thompson's chief interest was to understand Dylan by exploring his early milieus in Hibbing and Minneapolis. He spent considerable time in both places, where he interviewed members of the singer's family and old friends and acquaintances, most prominently Echo Helstrom, an influential high school girlfriend, whom Thompson also befriended.[3]

Robert Shelton's 1986 *No Direction Home: The Life and Music of Bob Dylan* stands as the magnum opus of Dylan biographies. As a reporter for the *New York Times,* Shelton had followed Dylan from his early days in New York and played a strong role in kick-starting his career through his newspaper coverage of a 1961 performance at Gerdes Folk City, a review that helped Dylan secure a recording contract with Columbia Records. Shelton's unprecedented access to his subject and his astute interpretation of Dylan as a musical figure have kept this work in circulation even as subsequent biographies have followed Dylan into his later life, such as Clinton Heylin's 1991 *Behind the Shades* and Howard Sounes's 2001 *Down the Highway.* Other writers have explored one facet of Dylan's life in considerable depth, as David Hajdu does in his close examination of the intertwined relationships and career moves among Dylan, Joan Baez, Mimi Baez Farina, and Richard Farina in *Positively Fourth Street.*[4]

In 1972, British critic and broadcaster Michael Gray launched the first book-length critical analysis of Dylan's music in relation to folk music traditions, the blues, rock and roll, and literary sources in *Song and Dance Man: The Art of Bob Dylan.* Gray did exhaustive research and close readings of individual songs that treated Dylan's work with the gravitas given a John Keats poem. Gray continued to assess Dylan's new work regularly, issuing an expanded edition of his first book in 1982 and another edition in 2000 that analyzes the singer's work through the 1997 release *Time Out of Mind.* His 2007 *Bob Dylan Encyclopedia,* weighing in at 730 pages (still 200 pages short of *Song and Dance Man III*), compiles information on nearly everyone who played a role in Dylan's life and career as well as providing jewels of information on such topics as "interviews and the myth of their rarity." More than simply a compendium of facts, Gray's opus of Dr. Johnsonian proportions offers spirited comments and analyses along with relevant references.[5]

Though Gray was first on the scene, a growing number of authors have devoted sustained attention to Dylan, generating an expanding critical literature and anthologies. In 1990, Elizabeth Thomson and David Gutman issued *The Dylan Companion,* a valuable collection of short articles and essays published in periodicals ranging from *The Little Sandy Review* to *Rolling Stone, Mademoiselle,* and *The Guardian,* dating from the early 1960s onward. The editors revised and expanded the collection in 2001. In 1991, Canadian poet Stephen Scobie published an idiosyncratic work, *Alias Bob Dylan,* with chapters of historical fiction on Dylan's early life and others devoted to song analyses, looking at the singer's use of ghosts, aliases, and masks.[6]

At the turn of the new millennium, Dylan criticism gained new momentum from several directions. Greil Marcus's 1997 study *The Old, Weird America: The World of Bob Dylan's Basement Tapes* is a tour de force of creative nonfiction, examining Dylan and The Hawks' private sessions in Woodstock and West Saugerties, New York. Marcus redrew the musician's family tree and in the process recovered the imagined historic town of "Smithville," a frontier world conjured by Harry Smith's 1952 *Anthology of American Folk Music.* As in his study of Elvis Presley in *Mystery Train: Images of America in Rock 'n' Roll Music,* Marcus hit bedrock in digging for Dylan's roots and persuasively argued for the deep cultural value of his music and its ties to the foundations of American political philosophies. In 1997, Smith's anthology reached new audiences when Smithsonian's Folkways Records released it as a multidisc CD set, with a reproduction of Smith's original (and often hilarious) notations on the songs. Its liner notes—with an excerpt from Marcus's book and essays by Jon Pankake and other notable authors and musicians—won a Grammy Award in 1998. Soon after, Hal Willner, a concert producer and friend of Harry Smith, teamed up with Nick Cave, who was curator of London's 1999 Meltdown Festival. They decided to use Smith's anthology for a series of concerts in London, New York, and Los Angeles, inviting a huge variety of musicians to cover the songs. Held from 1999 to 2001, each concert ran over five hours. Rani Singh, director of the Harry Smith Archive, reflected:

> By the end of each concert we all felt Smith's wizardry at play in the performances the artists used to transform a specific song and make it their own. The image of Percy Heath playing alongside David Thomas and Van Dyke Parks in "Fishing Blues," Eric Mingus as the preacher under the stained glass of St. Ann's Church, Beth Orton's stripped-down intensity of "Frankie," Beck's reinterpretation of his earliest influences, Robert Johnson in "Last Fair Deal Gone Down," and Elvis Costello rewriting history with his addition to "Omnie Wise"...exemplifies Smith's desire for the Anthology to be a wellspring of inspiration.[7]

The whole endeavor became known as "The Hal Willner Harry Smith Project," and was issued as a box set of CDs in 2006 by The Harry Smith Archives. The attention garnered by the anthology reissues and revivals and Marcus's *Old, Weird America* spurred greater awareness and appreciation of Dylan's ongoing role in keeping the sensibilities of the *Anthology* alive.

Something was stirring as the twentieth century faded into the twenty-first. Dylan turned sixty in May 2001 after a scary stint with a life-threatening heart infection in 1997 ("I really thought I was going to be seeing Elvis soon," he quipped). Dylan sites on the Internet had exploded, from the many fan-generated sites like Expecting Rain to his official Web site, bobdylan.com, with searchable lyrics. In 1997, he released *Time Out of Mind,* which won three Grammys, including Album of the Year. In 2001, *"Love and Theft"* garnered great critical praise. Many argued that the title of the album was a quotation from Eric Lott's 1992 book on minstrelsy—*Love and Theft: Blackface Minstrelsy and the American Working Class*—which fueled more speculation and discussion of Dylan's relationships to African-American music and culture.

Released on the day that has come to be called "9/11," the record seemed to have anticipated and then expressed the raw and wry anxieties that followed. Over the cusp of the new century, Dylan reemerged as a voice to be listened to and reckoned with to a degree that had not been true in the 1980s and early 1990s. Possibly spurred by the singer's new, vital work as well as the premonition—given his age and illness—of a world without Dylan, scholars and critics from many quarters soon issued a new spate of Dylan books. Many of them had grown up listening to Dylan, were close to his age, and had achieved the professional stature that allowed them to speak authoritatively on a popular musician.

At this point, British scholars published key works that put Dylan's music on high literary ground. Neil Corcoran, professor of English at the University of St. Andrews, and author of such books as *English Poetry since 1940* and *Poets of Modern Ireland,* added a volume of commissioned essays on Dylan from prominent literary scholars. The pieces in *Do You Mr. Jones? Dylan with the Poets and Professors* range from Mark Ford's comparison of Dylan to Emerson to Daniel Karlin's fascinating analysis of the significance of names in Dylan's work (including the singer's own).

In 2003, British literary scholar Christopher Ricks published his study *Dylan's Visions of Sin.* Warren Professor of the Humanities at Boston University, Ricks's productive analysis approaches Dylan's work in terms of recurring moral themes based on the seven deadly sins (envy, covetousness, greed, sloth, lust, anger, and pride), the four virtues (justice, prudence, temperance, and fortitude), and the heavenly graces (faith, hope, and charity). In this five-hundred-plus-page study, Ricks groups Dylan's songs by their place in a moral universe, then analyzes them in close lit-crit style, often moving line by line, sometimes word by word. In a dazzling display of erudition, he connects Dylan to deep-seated literary traditions in allusions to Shakespeare, Milton, Tennyson, Keats, and others. To his credit, Ricks also attends to the song as sung and not only as lyrics on the page. *Dylan's Visions of Sin* took Dylan scholarship to a new level—unbound by biography or chronology, Dylan's work was treated as high poetry, a delight to some, an affront to others.

That same year, Mike Marqusee published *Chimes of Freedom: The Politics of Bob Dylan's Art,* a study of Dylan's politics and the context of the 1960s, examining the complicated dance of Dylan's impact on the politics of the era and the impact of the political era on Dylan.[8] As we know, Dylan retreated from direct political speech and action after his early engagement with the civil rights movement, the Beat antibourgeois subculture, and the beginnings of the counterculture. In 1967, refusing to appear at the Woodstock festival in his own backyard, he left the country to play at the Isle of Wight festival in England. As Marqusee effectively argues, although physically absent from the center of the counterculture scene in the late 1960s, Dylan's presence was felt everywhere as a kind of absent presence and sometimes as an antinomian voice. In 1967, he released the austere *John Wesley Harding* while the Beatles released the psychedelic *Sgt. Pepper's Lonely Hearts Club Band.* As often happens with Dylan, Marqusee holds him to a high ethical standard, ultimately disappointed in the singer's rejection of his political role. As cultural critic Mike Davis expresses in a dust jacket blurb, Marqusee "rescues one of the most urgent poetic voices in American history from the condescension of his own later cynicism." Unlike Ricks, who regarded Dylan within a broader moral universe, Marqusee tied Dylan to earth, wishing him to be accountable to real politics.

In 2004, a new Dylan reader was issued, edited by Benjamin Hedin, a professor and writer for *The Nation*. With fifty articles, poems, essays, speeches, and interviews, *Studio A: The Bob Dylan Reader* ranged from early gems like Johnny Cash's 1964 letter to *Broadside* to poems by Allen Ginsberg ("Postcard to D——" and "On Reading Dylan's Writings") and Anne Waldman's "Shaman Hisses You Slide Back into the Night." Bruce Springsteen's Rock and Roll Hall of Fame induction speech sits beside new criticism by Sean Wilentz, Greg Tate, Gary Giddins, Alex Ross, and Robert Polito in a smart collection of writings.[9]

At the same time as major new works added to Dylan's stature in scholarship, other works recognized Dylan's central role in new canons of American literature that brought poetry and popular song into closer affiliation, as in Bryan Garman's *A Race of Singers: Whitman's Working-Class Hero from Guthrie to Springsteen.* Historian Benjamin Filene traced transformations in broad currents of American thought, centered around folk cultures, collectors, and the acoustic guitar in his 2000 study *Romancing the Folk: Public Memory and American Roots Music.* His work examines the concepts of tradition and authenticity, arguing that Dylan was able to brilliantly manipulate the connections between past and present. Filene points to a quality also identified by U2's Bono, who observed that Dylan had shown him that "the best way to serve the age was to betray it."[10] The older singer somehow was able to sound both hip and modern and cranky and ancient, or alternately, cranky and modern and hip and ancient.

Building from this ground of Dylan scholarship, our own book, *Highway 61 Revisited,* argues that "Dylanology" can be said to have moved into what might be called "Dylan studies." While literary readings remain important to this collection, the authors here come to Dylan from many disciplinary and interdisciplinary perspectives: musicology, linguistics, African-American cultural studies and history, feminism, art history, disability studies, Italian and Japanese studies, American studies, poetry, and performance studies. The new scholarship presented here aims for a wide audience of readers, including critics, dedicated Dylan listeners, and students of music and American culture. If the collection addresses some of Dylan's riddles, its aim is not to settle them but to open them up to wider view and analysis. Studying Dylan requires that we look at history, geography, women, mining and labor history, African-American culture, fashion, ancient literature, contemporary Japanese culture, and more.

The authors in this volume take into account Dylan's most recent flurry of new work in multiple disciplines: his *Theme Time Radio Hour,* launched in March 2006 on XM Satellite Radio; his startlingly fresh memoir, *Chronicles, Volume 1* (2004); Martin Scorsese's 2006 documentary *No Direction Home* and accompanying CD with several newly released and live versions of songs; and Dylan's most recent CD, *Modern Times.* These recent efforts have encouraged new readings of Dylan and rereadings of his earlier work.

As we have noted, one of the riddles of Dylan studies is the musician's background in Hibbing, Minnesota. This volume goes deeply into this history. It is as though Dylan had long ago said to everyone on his scent: "Look over there," and that is where people headed, when all the while, the remarkable and relevant history of this Iron Range town was hiding in plain sight. Shelton's 1986 biography is out of print. Other books dealing with Dylan's early life in Minnesota have been produced by small presses in small numbers, such as Dave Engel's *Just Like Bob Zimmerman's Blues: Dylan in Minnesota,* published in 1997 by City River Memories in Rudolph, Wisconsin, also now out of print. Howard Sounes's *Down the Highway* benefits from the author's recent interviews with Dylan's early friends, but many biographies re-tread the same ground and sources.

Dylan wrote a vivid remembrance of—and farewell to—Hibbing in his 1963 prose poem "My Life in a Stolen Moment":

> Hibbing's got the biggest open pit ore mine in the world
> Hibbing's got schools, churches, grocery stores an' a jail
> It's got high school football games an' a movie house
> Hibbing's got souped-up cars runnin' full blast
> On a Friday night
> Hibbing's got corner bars with polka bands
> You can stand at one end of Hibbing on the main drag
> An' see clear past the city limits on the other end
> Hibbing's a good ol' town
> I ran away from it when I was 10, 12, 13, 15, 15½, 17, an' 18
> I got caught an' brought back all but once.[11]

Despite the fact that he got away from Hibbing, key features of that town shaped Dylan and prepared him to head to Minneapolis, then on to New York City, where, within nine months of his arrival, the twenty-year-old had a recording contract with Columbia Records. One influence was the rough-and-ready, frontier quality of Hibbing, a town built on the verge of an abyss: the open pit mine. By the late 1940s, when Bobby Zimmerman was growing up there, the Hull-Rust-Mahoning Mine—located at the very edge of Hibbing—was the largest open pit iron mine in the world: more than three miles long, nearly two miles wide, and five hundred feet deep, a landform dug by human hands and machinery. It lay there as evidence of American ambition and hyperbole, something the singer surely noted and absorbed.

Though a town of only eighteen thousand in a remote part of Minnesota (a four-hour drive north from the Twin Cities), Hibbing is a place of grand ambitions. In addition to its dramatic mining history, the town was the birthplace of Greyhound Bus Lines, an operation that began in the 1910s as a service to take workers to the mining sites. Rudy Perpich, a two-time governor of Minnesota, grew up there, as did food product millionaire Jeno Paulucci, and Kevin McHale, basketball pro and now manager of the Minnesota Timberwolves. The Hibbing mine once contributed 60 percent of the ore needed to make American cars, trains, skyscrapers, refrigerators, and toasters. It also helped build the ships, tanks, bombs, guns, and planes used in World War I and II.

Dylan grew up aware of the grip of iron mining on his town and of the benefits and trade-offs of being linked to a multinational corporation (Hibbing's Oliver Mining was a subsidiary of U.S. Steel). He knew firsthand the close relationship between war and capitalism, seeing its impact on his friends' and neighbors' families as well as his own. His earliest songs, written a couple of years after arriving in New York, demonstrated this knowledge. In Hibbing he also absorbed lessons about people's agency in standing up to powerful interests. When the town moved to allow the mines access to the rich ore lying beneath the settlement, Mayor Victor Power insisted that the company invest millions of dollars in rebuilding fine civic buildings. The section of old Hibbing that was not dug up became a ghost town. Even today, streets, sidewalks, signs, cement steps, and the footings of buildings remain. Beatty Zimmerman, born Beatrice Stone, grew up in North Hibbing, the site of the former community, and her son Bobby grew up with a haunted vision of that part of town, a memory described vividly in his "11 Outlined Epitaphs":

> old north Hibbing . . .
> deserted
> already dead
> with its old stone courthouse
> decayin in the wind
> long abandoned
> windows crashed out . . .
> the old school
> where my mother went to
> rottin shiverin but still livin
> standin cold an lonesome[12]

No wonder his music could so evocatively call up ghosts of the American past.

One of the most valuable "discoveries" of the renewed interest in Hibbing has been the growing recognition of the role B. J. Rolfzen, an English teacher at Hibbing High School, played in Dylan's literary education. Rolfzen taught Robert Zimmerman American literature during his junior year and British literature in his senior year.[13] One realizes the seeds planted in Rolfzen's classroom through such recent finds as Bobby Zimmerman's student essay on John Steinbeck's *Grapes of Wrath*, addressing the question: "Does Steinbeck sympathize with his characters?" The first two pages of Dylan's 1958 essay were displayed in the Experience Music Project exhibition *Bob Dylan's American Journey, 1956–1966*. Reluctant for many years to talk to writers, journalists, and other visitors to Hibbing about his former student, Rolfzen, now eighty-five, more recently has broken his silence. Along with his being featured in the Dylan exhibition, the Martin Scorsese documentary *No Direction Home,* and Mary Feidt and Natalie Goldberg's documentary *Tangled Up in Bob,* this current volume brings Rolfzen more fully into the circle of Dylan studies, particularly in Greil Marcus's opening essay.

In Dylan's 1965 San Francisco press conference, one reporter asked him what he thought of a symposium being held by the University of California, focusing on mimeographs of Dylan's lyrics. The singer replied, "I welcome that with open arms. I'm just kind of sorry that I'm not around to attend."[14] Some forty-two years later, Dylan was present in spirit, image, song, and story at the "Highway 61 Revisited" conference held at the University of Minnesota, March 25–27, 2007. The chapters in this book began their lives as presentations at this international symposium. Organized by the Weisman Art Museum at the university with a large group of advisors, the event coincided with the museum's presentation of the exhibition *Bob Dylan's American Journey, 1956–1966.* The essays in this volume both represent and share in the lively, thoughtful, and artistic insights from those few days in Minneapolis, where we gathered right next to Dinkytown, a few blocks from positively Fourth Street, and a few hours south of that little Minnesota town.

"With Ideas as My Maps"

As we have noted, to chronicle the life and times of Bob Dylan is to engage in the fine art of the travelogue, navigating the distances not only between the Iron Range of Minnesota and the bustling streets of Greenwich Village but also meeting and diverging at the crossroads of past and future, young and old, war and peace, heart and soul, and, perhaps most acutely, the singer and the song.

The essays that frame this present volume are, in many respects, vital signposts from along the way, providing thought-provoking contributions to the study of Dylan's work, as well as evocative readings on Dylan's impact on a wide expanse of disciplines, from literature, philosophy, and history to issues of race, religion, and gender. The volume, as with Dylan's own road to the wider world, begins in a place he called home. Greil Marcus's paean to Hibbing, Minnesota, examines the people and places that inspired a young Robert Zimmerman to first contemplate the magic of poetry and the "mysteries of democracy" within the small American town that first lent a stage to the man who would be Bob Dylan. Marilyn Chiat, who conducted research in the region, and Susan Clayton, who grew up on the Iron Range, provide important historical context for understanding the youthful milieu in Hibbing of the man who once proclaimed, "The country I come from is called the Midwest." Countering many assumptions that the Zimmermans were the lone Jewish family in town, Chiat tells the story of Iron Range Jewish settlement, culture, and religious practices, including the history of the Hibbing synagogue, where the Zimmerman family were members. Though she does not draw direct inferences about the impact of Dylan's Jewish upbringing on his music, Chiat does make use of a rare source: a 1985 interview with Beatty Zimmerman. Though his eventual leave-taking in 1959 signaled the abandoning of the vestiges of his middle-class, Jewish upbringing within ever-expanding and often mercurial fits of fictive biography, Dylan still manages to deftly weave traces of that early home into his songs.

The Dylan of the early sixties became the paragon of both the homeless and the homebound, searching for a home within the music itself, whether it was following the wayward paths trod by Woody Guthrie or following along with the chords of the southern blues and folk balladeers captured by the likes of Alan Lomax and Harry Smith. What began, as Dylan notes in Scorsese's documentary *No Direction Home,* as listening sessions to the late-night radio of his youth soon blossomed into a deep connection with the musical currents of the American South. This connection with the South fostered personal and political allegiances, both with southern-born artists like Johnny Cash and with the burgeoning civil rights movement, which took Dylan, along with mentors like Pete Seeger and Theodore Bikel, to Greenwood, Mississippi, in July 1963. These enduring relationships, explored in essays by Court Carney and Charles Hughes, provide a crucial lens for examining the legacy of Dylan's earliest writing and recording as well as the most recent.

Dylan's return from the South to play the Newport Folk Festival in 1963 coincided with a rapid rise in fame, cementing his reputation among a circle of New York–based recording artists like Joan Baez, with whom Dylan frequently shared a stage, and Peter, Paul and Mary, who scored a hit that summer with Dylan's "Blowin' in the Wind." The following two years not only brought greater identification with the scions of popular culture, like Andy Warhol and Edie Sedgwick, whose relationships Thomas Crow articulates as "Lives of Allegory," but also wedded this fame to a growing international audience, spurring the first of several marked changes of style—from hobo to boho—and substance, culminating in the 1966 tour of the United Kingdom, documented by C. P. Lee and in Scorsese's film. The international reputation secured by Dylan in the years to come would provide a provocative counterpoint to his rapid rise to American icon status. As Alessandro Carrera and Mikiko Tachi note, Dylan's oeuvre would stand as a long-lasting influence on both Italian and Japanese popular songwriting. And as Heather Stur writes, Dylan's move from the somewhat insular world of folk music to the international rock and pop stage provided inspiration to generations on both sides of the Iron Curtain as the cold war continued.

Dylan's seeming timelessness, as Mick Cochrane notes, may have found a correlate in his most recent creative undertaking—as disc jockey. Cochrane points out that Dylan's showcases of both historical and contemporary lyricism in *Theme Time Radio Hour* resonate with earlier historical catalogs, including Samuel Johnson's *Lives of the Poets.* Dylan artfully weaves a persona so entrenched in musical heritage and tradition that he appears to embody the music itself. In similar fashion, Robert Polito explores Dylan's recent musical output, exploring the citational quality of Dylan's past three albums. Polito writes that in *Modern Times, "Love and Theft,"* and *Time Out of Mind,* Dylan is teaching us how to build a memory palace, "'mental structures'—in this instance, songs—that will house past and present, the living and the dead," creating a vast literary and musical tapestry, of which Dylan himself is a significant part. As such, Kevin Dettmar notes, the forty-year legacy of Dylan scholarship in and around popular music and culture often stands separate and distinct from the man and the music.

Dylan's lyricism relies on a collection of accents, from the Okie twang borrowed from Woody Guthrie on the 1962 debut to the gravelly sardonic voice that intones "I used to care / But things have changed" on the Academy Award–winning song from the 2000 film *Wonder Boys*. Taking these as so many costume changes in the Dylanesque drama, Michael Cherlin and Sumanth Gopinath unveil Dylan's vocal mimicry in greater detail. Reading the Dylan corpus from the field of disability studies, Alex Lubet presents a means by which to "corporealize" the music of Dylan, focusing in particular on the function of Dylan's vocals.

Four essays excavate the relationship of race to Dylan's music, including Aldon Lynn Nielsen's "Crow Jane Approximately: Bob Dylan's Black Masque," which delineates the often complex relationship between Dylan's early musical development and the legacy of African-American traditional song. Robert Reginio, focusing on more recent Dylan material, explores how Dylan's "borrowing" from Confederate poet Henry Timrod and the song "Nettie Moore," from Dylan's *Modern Times*, create a tension in which "every moment of border crossing, every moment where the boundaries of race are transcended, is a moment that reinscribes those boundaries," joining (and rejoining) the disparate threads of Dylan's immersion in the traditions of blues, jazz, and gospel music—in various stages of his career—to African-American culture and the influences, from Odetta to Mavis Staples, of the African-American female voice to Dylan's song craft. This concept of femininity within the Dylan song structure is further examined by Daphne Brooks and Gayle Wald, who examine how Dylan's songs are interpreted and reinterpreted by artists such as Staples, Maria Muldaur, and Nina Simone. David Yaffe takes up the concept of covers, too, complicating Dylan's relationship to racial injustice and African-American musicians over many years. Yaffe cleverly explores the implications of the Dylan couplet "There's not even room enough to be anywhere / It's not dark yet but it's gettin' there," from his late and lovely song "Not Dark Yet," as well as other possibly race-related metaphors buried in Dylan's art and artifice. That the word "covers" would be so much more than that is no surprise for Anne Waldman, who, in the essay that closes this volume, quoting Beat poet and Dylan compatriot Allen Ginsberg, describes the phenomenon as "magpie poetics" in which mimicry and mutuality converge.

In one of his current commentaries filmed for *No Direction Home,* Dylan says, "An artist is always in a state of becoming." That statement reveals a good deal about Dylan's metamorphic approach to his art and life. Realizing full well the enigmas and riddles of our subject of study, we have tried to catch some lightning in a bottle in this book.

Notes

1. Television press conference, KQED, San Francisco, December 3, 1965; transcript printed in Jonathan Cott, ed., *Bob Dylan: The Essential Interviews* (New York: Wenner Books, 2006), 65.

2. "Musical expeditionary" is from a recent interview with Dylan in the documentary *No Direction Home,* directed by Martin Scorsese (Hollywood, Calif.: Paramount, 2005); Bob Dylan, *Chronicles, Volume 1* (New York: Simon and Schuster, 2004), 240–41.

3. Toby Thompson, *Positively Main Street: An Unorthodox View of Bob Dylan* (New York: Coward and McCann and Geohagen, 1971). The book was reissued by the University of Minnesota Press in 2007 with a new preface by and interview with Thompson and including previously unpublished photographs.

4. Clinton Heylin, *Behind the Shades: A Biography* (New York: Summit, 1991); revised and updated in a new edition by Heylin, *Behind the Shades Revisited* (New York: W. Morrow, 2001); Howard Sounes, *Down the Highway: The Life of Bob Dylan* (New York: Grove Press, 2001).

5. Michael Gray, *Song and Dance Man: The Art of Bob Dylan* (London: Hart-Davis, MacGibbon, 1972; New York: E. P. Dutton, 1973); revised and updated as *The Art of Bob Dylan: Song and Dance Man* (London: Hamlyn, 1981; New York: St. Martin's Press, 1983). The most recent edition is *Song and Dance Man III: The Art of Bob Dylan* (London and New York: Continuum, 2000). Michael Gray, *The Bob Dylan Encyclopedia* (London: Continuum, 2006; New York: Continuum, 2007), 341.

6. Stephen Scobie, *Alias Bob Dylan* (Red Deer, Alberta: Red Deer College Press, 1991); new edition, *Alias Bob Dylan Revisited* (Calgary: Red Deer Press, 2003).

7. Rani Singh, foreword to liner notes for *The Harry Smith Project: Anthology of American Folk Music Revisited,* audio CDs released by Harry Smith Archives with Shout! Factory LLC and Sony, 2006, 5.

8. Mike Marqusee, *Chimes of Freedom: The Politics of Bob Dylan's Art* (New York: The New Press, 2003); later reissued in paperback, expanded and revised, under the title *Wicked Messenger: Bob Dylan and the 1960s* (New York: Seven Stories Press, 2005).

9. Benjamin Hedin, ed., *Studio A: The Bob Dylan Reader* (New York: W. W. Norton and Co., 2004).

10. Bryan Garman, *A Race of Singers: Whitman's Working-Class Hero from Guthrie to Springsteen* (Chapel Hill: University of North Carolina Press, 2000); Benjamin Filene, *Romancing the Folk: Public Memory and American Roots Music* (Chapel Hill: University of North Carolina Press, 2000); Bono, foreword to Mark Blake, ed., *Dylan: Visions, Portraits, and Back Pages* (London: DK Publishing with Mojo Music Magazine, 2005), 8.

11. "My Life in a Stolen Moment" first appeared in the concert program for Dylan's Town Hall concert in New York on April 12, 1963. It is reprinted in Hedin, *Studio A,* 3–7.

12. "11 Outlined Epitaphs" appeared as liner notes on the back cover of Bob Dylan, *The Times They Are A-Changin',* Columbia Records, 1963.

13. In 1960, B. J. Rolfzen left Hibbing High to teach in the English department at Hibbing Community College, where he remained until retiring in 1987.

14. The quotation included here comes from the video of the live press conference, *Dylan Speaks: The Legendary 1965 Press Conference in San Francisco,* Jazz Casual Productions, 2006. In Jonathan Cott's transcript, the response appears slightly altered; Cott, *Bob Dylan,* 65.

PART I. HIGHWAY 61, FROM NORTH TO SOUTH

1. Hibbing High School and "the Mystery of Democracy"
Greil Marcus

"As I walked out—"

Those are the first words of "Ain't Talkin'," the last song on Bob Dylan's *Modern Times,* released in the fall of 2006. It's a great opening line for anything: a song, a tall tale, a fable, a novel, a soliloquy. The world opens at the feet of that line. How one gets there—to the point where those words can take on their true authority, raise suspense like a curtain, and make anyone want to know what happens next— is what I want to look for.

For me, this road opened in the spring of 2005, upstairs in the once famous, now shut Cody's Books on Telegraph Avenue in Berkeley. I was giving a reading from a book about Bob Dylan's "Like a Rolling Stone." Older guys—people my age— were talking about the Dylan shows they'd seen in 1965: he had played Berkeley on his first tour with a band that December. People were asking questions—or making speeches. The old saw came up: "How does someone like Bob Dylan come out of a place like Hibbing, Minnesota, a worn-out mining town in the middle of nowhere?"

A woman stood up. She was about thirty-five, maybe forty, definitely younger than the people who'd been talking. Her face was dark with indignation. "Have any of you ever *been* to Hibbing?" she said. There was a general shaking of heads and murmuring of noes, from me and everyone else. "You ought to be ashamed of your- selves," the woman said. "You don't know what you're talking about. If you'd been to Hibbing, you'd know why Bob Dylan came from there. There's poetry on the *walls.* Everywhere you look. There are bars where arguments between socialists and the IWW, between Communists and Trotskyites, arguments that started a hundred years ago, are still going on. It's *there*—and it was there when Bob Dylan was there."

"I don't remember the rest of what she said," my wife said when I asked her about that night. "I was already planning our trip."

Along with our younger daughter and her husband, who live in Minneapolis, we arrived in Hibbing a year later, coincidentally during Dylan Days, a now-annual weekend celebration of Bob Dylan's birthday, in this case his sixty-fifth. There was a bus trip, the premiere of a new movie, and a sort of Bob Dylan Idol contest at a restaurant called Zimmy's. But we went straight to the high school. On the bus tour the next day, we went back. And that was the shock: Hibbing High.

In his revelatory 1993 essay "When We Were Good: Class and Culture in the Folk Revival," the historian Robert Cantwell takes you by the hand, guides you back, and reveals the new America that rose up out of World War II. "If you were born between, roughly, 1941 and 1948," he says—"born, that is, into the new postwar middle class"—

> you grew up in a reality perplexingly divided by the intermingling of an emerging mass society and a decaying industrial culture.... Obscurely taking shape around you, of a definite order and texture, was an environment of new neighborhoods, new schools, new businesses, new forms of recreation and entertainment, and new technologies that in the course of the 1950s would virtually abolish the world in which your parents had grown up.

That sentence is typical of Cantwell's style: apparently obvious social changes charted into the realm of familiarity, then a hammer coming down: as you are feeling your way into your own world, your parents' world is *abolished.*

Growing up in the certified postwar suburb towns of Palo Alto and Menlo Park in California, I lived some of this life. Though Bob Dylan did not grow up in the suburbs—despite David Hajdu's dismissal of Dylan, in his book *Positively Fourth Street,* as "a Jewish kid from the suburbs," Hibbing is not close enough to Duluth, or any other city, to be a suburb of anything—he lived some of this life, too. Cantwell moves on to talk about how the new prosperity of the 1950s was likely paradise to your parents, how their aspirations became your seeming inevitabilities: "Very likely, you saw yourself growing up to be a doctor or a lawyer, scientist or engineer, teacher, nurse, or mother—pictures held up to you at school and at home as pictures of your special destiny." And, Cantwell says,

> You probably attended, too, an overcrowded public school, typically a building built shortly before World War I... [you] may have had to share a desk with another student, and in addition to the normal fire and tornado drills had from time to time to crawl under your desk in order to shield yourself from the imagined explosion of an atomic bomb.

So, Cantwell writes, "in this vision of consumer Valhalla there was a lingering note of caution, even of dread"—but let's go back to the schools.

The public schools I attended—Elizabeth Van Auken Elementary School (now Ohlone School) in Palo Alto, and Menlo-Atherton High School in Menlo Park— were not built before World War I. They were built in the early 1950s, part of the world that was already changing. The past was still there: Miss Van Auken, a beloved former teacher, was always present to celebrate the school's birthday. When our third-grade class read the Little House books, we wrote Laura Ingalls Wilder and she wrote back. But the past was fading as new houses went up all around the school. A few miles away, Menlo-Atherton High was a sleek, modern plant: one story, flat roofs, huge banks of windows in every classroom, lawns everywhere, and three parking lots, one reserved strictly for members of the senior class. The school produced Olympic swimmers in the early 1960s; a few years later Lindsey Buckingham and Stevie Nicks would graduate and, a few years after that, make Fleetwood Mac the biggest band in the world. The school sparkled with suburban money, rock-and-roll cool, surfer swagger, and San Francisco ambition—and compared to Hibbing High School it was a shack. "I know Hibbing," Harry Truman said in 1947, when he was introduced to Hibbing's John Galeb, the national commander of Disabled American Veterans. "That's where the high school has gold door knobs."

Outside of Washington, D.C., it's the most impressive public building I've ever seen. In aerial photographs, it's a colossus: four stories, 93 feet high, with wings 180 feet long flying out from a 416-foot front. From the ground it is more than anything a monument to benign authority, a giant hand welcoming the town, all of its generations, into a cave where the treasure is buried, all the knowledge of mankind. It speaks for the community, for its faith in education, not only as a road to success, to wealth and security, reputation and honor, but as a good in itself. This town, the building says, will have the best school in the world.

In the plaza before the building there is a spire, a war memorial. On its four sides, as you turn from one panel to another, are the names of those students from Hibbing who died in World War I, World War II, the Korean and Vietnam Wars— and, on the last panel, with no names, a commemoration of the terrorist attacks of 2001. Past the memorial are steps worthy of a state capitol leading to the entrance of the building. It was late Friday afternoon; there were no students around, but the doors were open.

Hibbing High School was built near the end of the era when Hibbing was known as "the richest village in the world." A crusading mayor, Victor Power, enforced mineral taxes on U.S. Steel, operator of the huge iron-ore pit mines that surrounded the original Hibbing. Elected after a general strike in 1913, he fought off the mine company's allies in the state legislature and the courts in battle after battle. When ore was discovered under Hibbing itself, Power and others forced the company to spend sixteen million dollars to move the whole town—houses, hotels, churches, public buildings—four miles south. The bigger buildings were cut in quarters and reassembled in the new Hibbing like Legos.

Tax revenues had mounted over the years in the old north Hibbing; at one point, the story goes, when a social-improvement society took up donations for poor families, none could be found. But in the new south Hibbing, in a maneuver aimed at building support for lower corporate tax rates in the future, the mining company offered even more money in the form of donations, or bribes: school board members directed most of it to what became Hibbing High, which Mayor Power had demanded as part of the price of moving the town. With prosperity seemingly assured, the town turned out Power in favor of a mayor closer to the mines. Soon, a law was passed limiting public spending to a hundred dollars per capita per year; then the limit was lowered, and lowered again. The tax base of the town began to crumble; with World War II, when the town was not allowed to tax mineral production, and after, when the mines were nearly played out, the tax base all but collapsed. Ultimately, the mines shifted from iron ore to taconite, low-grade pellets that today find a market in China, but Hibbing never recovered. In the 1950s it was a dying town, the school a seventh wonder of a time that had passed, a ziggurat built by a forgotten king. And yet it was still a ziggurat.

When it opened in 1924, Hibbing High School had cost four million dollars, an unimaginable sum for the time. At first it was the ultimate consolidated school, from kindergarten through junior college. There were three gyms, two indoor running tracks, and every kind of shop that in the years to come would be commonplace in American high schools—as well as an electronics shop, an auto shop, and a conservatory. There was a full-time doctor, dentist, and nurse. There were extensive programs in music, art, and theater. But more than eight decades later, you didn't have to know any of this to catch the glow of the place.

Climbing the enclosed stairway that followed the expanse of outdoor steps, we saw not a hint of graffiti, not a sign of deterioration in the intricate colored tile designs on the walls and the ceilings, in the curving woodwork. We gazed up at old-fashioned but still majestic murals depicting the history of Minnesota, with bold trappers surrounded by submissive Indians, huge trees and roaming animals, the

Hibbing High School. Photograph by Colleen Sheehy, 2005.

forest and the emerging towns. It was strange, the pristine condition of the place. It spoke not for emptiness, for Hibbing High as a version of Pompeii High—though the school, with a capacity of over two thousand, was down to six hundred students, up from four hundred only a few years before—and, somehow, you knew the state of the building didn't speak for discipline. You could sense self-respect, passed down over the years.

We followed the empty corridors in search of the legendary auditorium. A custodian let us in and told us the stories. Seating for eighteen hundred; stained glass everywhere, even in the form of blazing candles on the fire box. In large, gilded paintings in the back, the muses waited; they smiled over the proscenium arch, too, over a stage that, in imitation of thousands of years of ancestors, had the weight of immortality hammered into its boards. "No wonder he turned into Bob Dylan," said a visitor the next day, when the bus tour stopped at the school, speaking of the talent show Dylan played here with one of his high-school bands. No matter that the power was cut on the noise they were making. Anybody on that stage could see kingdoms waiting: "no small music box theater," Dylan wrote in 2004 in his memoir *Chronicles, Volume 1,* of his "first appearances in a public spectacle," but "a professional concert hall like Carnegie Hall built with East Coast mining money, with curtains and props, trapdoors and orchestra pit."

There were huge chandeliers, imported from Czechoslovakia, four thousand dollars each when they were shipped across the Atlantic in the 1920s, irreplaceable today. We weren't in Hibbing, a redundant mining town in northern Minnesota; we were in the opera house in Buenos Aires. Yet we were in Hibbing; there were high-school Bob Dylan artifacts in a case just down the hall. There were more in the public library some blocks away, in a small exhibit in the basement, with, scattered among commonplace talismans and oddities, revelations, such as the lyrics to Golden Chords' "Big Black Train," from 1958, a rewrite of Elvis's 1954 "Mystery Train," credited to Monte Edwardson, LeRoy Hoikkala, and Bob Zimmerman:

> Well, big black train, coming down the line
> Well, big black train, coming down the line
> Well, you got my woman, you bring her back to me
>
> Well, that cute little chick is the girl I want to see
> Well, I've been waiting for a long long time
> Well, I've been waiting for a long long time
> Well, I've been looking for my baby
> Searching down the line
>
> Well, here comes the train, yeah it's coming down the line
> Well, here comes the train, yeah it's coming down the line
> Well, you see my baby is finally coming home

The next day, walking up and down Howard Street, the main street of Hibbing, we looked for the poetry on the walls. "A NEW LIFE," read an ad for an insurance

The Golden Chords perform at Hibbing's Little Theater for the Winter Frolic Talent Contest in 1958. From left: Monte Edwardson (guitar), Leroy Hoikkala (drums), Bobby Zimmerman, guitar and vocals. Photographer unknown. Courtesy of Monte Edwardson and Leroy Hoikkala.

company—was that it? Was there anything in that beer sign that could be twisted into a metaphor? What was the woman in Berkeley talking about? Later we found out that the walls with the poetry were in the high school itself.

In the school library there were busts and chiseled words of wisdom. Murals told the story of the mining industry, all in the style of what Daniel Pinkwater, in his young-adult novel *Young Adults,* called "heroic realism." There were sixteen life-size workers, representing the nationalities that formed Hibbing: native-born Americans, Finns, Swedes, Italians, Norwegians, Croatians, Serbs, Slovenians, Austrians, Germans, Jews, French, Poles, Russians, Armenians, Bulgarians, and more. There was a huge mine on the left, a misty steelworks on the right, and, in the middle, to take the fruit of Hibbing to the corners of the earth, Lake Superior. With art-nouveau dots between each word, the inscription over the mine quoted Tennyson's "Oenone"—

LIFTING • THE • HIDDEN • IRON •
THAT • GLIMPSES • IN • LABOURED •
MINES • UNDRAINABLE • OF • ORE

—while over the factory one could read

THEY • FORCE • THE • BURNT •
AND • YET • UNBLOODED • STEEL •
TO • DO • THEIR • WILL

That was the poetry on the walls—but not even this was the real poetry in Hibbing. The real poetry was in the classroom.

After stopping by the auditorium and the library, the tour made its way upstairs to Room 204, where for five years in the 1950s B. J. Rolfzen taught English at Hibbing High—after that, he taught for twenty-five years at Hibbing Community College. Eighty-three in May 2006, and slowed down by a stroke, getting around in a motorized wheelchair, Rolfzen sat on the desk in the small, suddenly steamy room, as forty or more people crowded in. There was a small podium in front of him. Presumably we were there to hear his reminiscences about the former Bob Zimmerman—or, as Rolfzen called him, and never anything else, Robert. Rolfzen held up a slate where he'd chalked lines from "Floater," from Dylan's 2001 *"Love and Theft"*: "Gotta sit up near the teacher / If you want to learn anything." Rolfzen pointed to the tour member who was sitting in the seat directly in front of the desk. "I always stood in front of the desk, never behind it," he said. "And that's where Robert always sat." He talked about Dylan's "Not Dark Yet," from his 1997 *Time Out of Mind:* "'I was born here and I'll die here / Against my will.'" "I'm with him. I'll stay right here. I don't care what's on the other side," Rolfzen said, a teacher thrilled to be learning from a student. With that out of the way, he proceeded to teach a class in poetry.

He handed out a photocopied booklet of poems by Wordsworth, Frost, Carver, the Minneapolis poet Colleen Sheehy, and himself; moving back and forth for more than half an hour, he returned again and again to the eight lines of William Carlos Williams's "The Red Wheelbarrow":

> so much
> depends
> upon
> a red wheel
> barrow
>
> glazed with rain
> water
>
> beside the white
> chickens

He kept reading it, changing inflections, until the words seemed to dance out of order, shifting their meanings. Each time, a different word seemed to take over the poem. "Rain," he would say, opening up the poem one way; "beside," he'd say, and an entirely different drama seemed under way. Finally he came full circle: "so much

B. J. Rolfzen, 1958. Photographer unknown. Courtesy of B. J. and Leona Rolfzen.

depends / upon a red wheel barrow," he said. "*So much depends*. This isn't about *rain*. It's not about *chickens*. So much depends on the decisions we make. My decision to enlist in the Navy in 1941, when I was seventeen. My decision to teach. *So much depends* on the decisions you've made, and will make."

The poem stayed in the air: the loudness of the first lines faded into "beside the white chickens," not because they were unimportant, but because from "so much depends," from the decision with which the poem began, the poem, like a life, could have gone anywhere; it was simply that in this case the poem happened to go toward chickens, before it went off the page, to wherever it went next. Rolfzen made the eight lines particular and universal, unlikely and fated; he made them apply to everyone in the room, or rather led each person to apply them to him or herself. This was not the sort of teacher you encounter every day—or even in a lifetime.

"Bits and pieces of the Great Depression still lie about," Rolfzen wrote in *The Spring of My Life,* a memoir of the 1930s he published himself in 2005—but, he said, "one day of the Great Depression can never be understood or appreciated except by those who have lived it." Nevertheless, he tried to make whoever might read his book understand. He went back to the village of Melrose, Minnesota, where he was born and grew up. He spoke quietly, flatly, sardonically of a family that was poor beyond poverty: "Life during the Great Depression was not a complex life. It was a simple one. No health insurance needed to be paid, no life insurance, no car insurance, no savings for a college education or any education beyond high school, no savings account, no automobile needed to be purchased, no gas was necessary to buy, no utilities beyond the $3.00 a month my dad paid for six 25 watt bulbs." There were eleven children; B. J.—then Boniface—slept in a bed with three brothers.

His father was an electrical worker and a drunk: the "most frightening day," Rolfzen writes, was payday, when his father would stagger home, then and every day until the money ran out. One day he tried to kill himself by grabbing high-voltage lines; instead he lost both arms just below the elbow, and sent the family onto relief. "I never saw my mother with a coin in her hand," Rolfzen writes; everything they bought they bought on credit against fifty dollars a month. There was a family of four that boarded up the windows of its house to keep out the cold, but the Rolfzens would not advertise their misery, even if the windows sometimes broke and before they could be replaced, maybe not until winter passed, maybe not for months after that, snow piled up in the room where Rolfzen slept.

All through the book, through its continual memories of privation and idyll— of catching bullheads, playing marbles, picking berries, working on a farm for three months at the age of sixteen for four cents a day, or the toe of a young Boniface's shoe falling off as he walked to school—one can feel Rolfzen holding his rage in check. His rage against his father, against the cold, against the plague that was on the land, against the alcoholism that followed from his father to his brothers, against the Catholic elementary school he was named for, St. Boniface, run by nuns who "enjoyed causing pain," a place where students were threatened with hell for every errant act—where "religion was a senseless, heartless and unforgiving practice. I still bear its scars."

"In times behind, I too / wished I'd lived / in the hungry Thirties," Bob Dylan wrote in 1964 in "11 Outlined Epitaphs," his notes to *The Times They Are A-Changin'.* "Rode freight trains for kicks / Got beat up for laughs / I was making my own depression," he wrote the year before in "My Life in a Stolen Moment"—speaking of leaving Hibbing, leaving the University of Minnesota, traveling west, trying to learn how to live on his own. "I cannot remember ever having a conversation with my father about anything," Rolfzen writes—but you can imagine him having conversations about the thirties with Robert. Maybe especially about the tramp armies that passed through Melrose, starting every day at ten when the train pulled in, twenty men or more riding on top of the box cars, jumping from the doors, men who had abandoned their families, who broke into abandoned buildings and knocked on the Rolfzens' back door begging for food—"My mother never refused them," Rolfzen writes. With whatever they could scavenge, they headed to a hollow near the tracks, the place called the Bums' Nest or the Jungle. As a boy, Rolfzen was there, watching and listening, but he will not allow a moment of romance, freedom, or escape: "Theirs was a controlled camaraderie with limited laughter. Each man was alone on these tracks that led to nowhere. . . . And so they left. More would arrive the next day. One gentleman in particular I remember. An old bent man dressed in a long shabby coat, a tattered hat on his head and a cane in his hand. The last time I saw him, he was headed west along the railroad tracks, headed for an empty world."

This is not how the song of the open road goes—and while Bob Dylan has sung that song as much as anyone, as the road opened it also forked, even from the start. "At the end of the great English epic *Paradise Lost*," Rolfzen writes, "Milton observes the departure of Adam and Eve from the Garden, and as he observes their leaving by the Eastern Gate, he utters these beautiful words: 'The world was all before them.'" *So much depends*—think of "Bob Dylan's Dream," from *The Freewheelin' Bob Dylan,* in 1963. There he is, twenty-two, "riding on a train going west," dreaming of his true friends, his soul mates—and then suddenly he is an old man. He and his friends have long since vanished to each other. Their roads haven't split so much as crumbled, disappeared—"shattered," he sings. How was it that, in 1963, his voice and guitar calling up a smoky, out-of-focus portrait, Bob Dylan was already looking back, from forty, fifty, sixty years later?

"As I walked out . . ." With those first words for "Ain't Talkin'"—not only the longest song on *Modern Times,* and the strongest, but the only performance on the album where you don't hear calculation—Bob Dylan disappears. Even on "Nettie Moore," with a melody so delicate and yet unbreakable, sooner or later you may hear Dylan's light touch turn heavy; you may hear that the voice that seems to rise out of the melody is in fact dressing it up. But on "Ain't Talkin'," someone other than the singer you think you know seems to be singing the song. He doesn't seem to know what effects to use, what they might even be for. It's the only song on the album, really, without an ending—and with those first four words, a cloud is cast. The singer doesn't know what's going to happen—and it's the way he expects that nothing will happen, the way he communicates an innocence you instantly don't trust, that steels you for the story that he's about to tell, or that's about to sweep him up. He walks out into "the mystic garden." He stares at the flowers on the vines. He passes a fountain. Someone hits him from behind. This is when he finds the world all before him—because he can't go back. There is only one reason to travel this road: revenge.

For the only time on *Modern Times,* the music doesn't orchestrate, doesn't pump, doesn't give itself away with its first note. Led by Tony Garnier's cello and

Donnie Herron's viola, the band curls around the singer's voice even as he curls around the band's quiet, retreating, resolute sound, as if the whole song is the opening and closing of a fist, over and over again, the slow rhythm turning lyrics that are pretentious, even precious on the page into a kind of oracular bar talk, the old drunk who's there every night and never speaks finally telling his story. "I practice a faith that's long abandoned," he says, and that might be the most frightening line Bob Dylan has written in years. "That's been destroyed," Dylan told Doon Arbus in 1997, speaking of "the secret community" of "like-minded people" he found in the early sixties, a fellowship of those who felt themselves "outside and downtrodden," a community that "spread out across America"—"I don't know who destroyed it."

"I know, in my mind, I'm still a member of a secret community. I might be the only one," Dylan said then; in "Ain't Talkin'" the singer moves down his road of patience and blood. You can sense his head turning from side to side as he tells you why his head is bursting: "If I catch my opponents ever sleeping / I'll just slaughter 'em where they lie." He snaps off the line casually, as if it's hardly worth the time it takes to say, as if he's done it before, like William Munny in *Unforgiven* killing children on his way to wherever he went, but that will be nothing to what the singer will do to get wherever it is he's going. God doesn't care: "the gardener," the singer says to a woman he finds in the mystic garden, "is gone."

Now, Bob Dylan didn't need B. J. Rolfzen's tales of the tramp armies that passed through Melrose during the Great Depression to catch a feel for "tracks that led to nowhere." Empathy has always been the genie of his work, of the tones of his voice, his sense of rhythm, his feel for how to fill up a line or leave it half empty, his sense of when to ride a melody and when to bury it, so that it might dissolve all of a listener's defenses—and this is what allowed Dylan, in 1962 at the Gaslight Café in Greenwich Village, at home in that secret community of tradition and mystery, to become not only the pining lover in the old ballad "Handsome Molly," but also Handsome Molly herself.

There's no tracing that quality of empathy to anything—*so much depends*—but if effects like these had causes, then there would be people doing the same on every corner, in any time. On the way to Hibbing, we stopped at an antique store; shoved in among a shelf of children's books was a small, cracked book called *From Lincoln to Coolidge*, published in 1924, a collection of news dispatches, excerpts from congressional hearings, and speeches, among them the speech Woodrow Wilson gave to dedicate Abraham Lincoln's official birthplace in Hodgenville, Kentucky, on September 4, 1916—according to the story a young Bob Dylan was told, just weeks before his one-year-old mother was taken by her parents to see the president campaign in Hibbing from the back of a train. "This is the sacred mystery of democracy," Wilson said that day in Hodgenville, "that its richest fruits spring up out of soils that no man has prepared and in circumstances amidst which they are least expected."

That is the truth, and that is the mystery. In the case of Bob Dylan, as with any person who does things others don't do, the mystery is always there. But from the overwhelming fact of the pure size of Hibbing High School, from the ambition and vision placed in the murals in its entryway, from the poetry on the walls to the poetry in the classroom, perhaps to memories recounted after everyone else had gone— or memories picked up by a student from the way a teacher moved, hesitated over a word, dropped hints he never quite turned into stories—these soils were not unprepared at all.

2. Jewish Homes on the Range, 1890–1960
Marilyn J. Chiat

Robert Allen Zimmerman was born at St. Mary's Hospital in Duluth, Minnesota, on May 24, 1941, to Beatrice and Abraham Zimmerman, children of Yiddish-speaking Orthodox Jewish immigrants who had fled persecution in eastern Europe. Their families were among the nearly two and half million Jews who arrived in the United States between 1881 and 1924, when immigration closed. The vast majority of Jewish immigrants who arrived between 1881 and 1911 settled in ghettoes that were developing in cities along the eastern seaboard; only a relative few ventured farther west, including thirteen thousand who were living in Minnesota in 1910, primarily in Minneapolis and St. Paul. Among the families who arrived at this time were the Solomovich and Zimmerman families, joining relatives already living in Superior, Wisconsin, and Duluth, Minnesota. These families were headed by Robert Zimmerman's great-grandparents, Orthodox Jews who because of their faith, were forced to flee their homes and find refuge in an alien land—a land, however, that offered them for the first time not only the freedom to worship but also the freedom to live and work where they chose. As important as these new freedoms were to these immigrants, it was equally important that they continue to practice their Orthodox form of Judaism. They established synagogues in Superior and Duluth and on the Iron Range along with all the other appurtenances required to maintain their religious traditions and transmit them to the next generation. This is the milieu in which Robert Zimmerman's parents were born and nurtured, and this is the tradition they sought to transmit to their two sons, Robert Allen and David.

The early years of Robert Zimmerman's life have been largely ignored by scholars and biographers or, thanks to Dylan's own mythmaking, been misunderstood or misrepresented. Even members of his own family are at a loss to explain his unwillingness to portray his past in a more factual manner. I hope that this essay based on research conducted on the Iron Range, including interviews with members of Dylan's family, will provide a more thorough understanding of the religious and cultural milieu from which Dylan emerged.[1]

15

Dylan has worn many different masks during his career, each symbolizing a different period in his development as an artist. Each was intended to conceal his true identity, but his roots on Minnesota's Iron Range and, in particular, his Jewish heritage remain visible behind his carefully crafted facade. For those familiar with Jewish culture, Dylan is the continuation of a long line of "Fiddlers on the Roof," itinerant Jewish musicians who have been a part of Jewish life wherever the Jewish people have found a home.[2]

A visitor to Hibbing at about the time that Ben Solomovich, Dylan's maternal grandfather, moved to the Range in 1907 described it as looking "like some doomed Biblical city...situated on the edge of a pit....Scorched stumps...and enormous boulders [were everywhere]....The town was perpetually shaken by the blastings of the mine, and before the mine companies were restrained showers of rock descended often on the streets."[3] Minnesota's Iron Range was obviously no Utopia,

Beatty Stone grew up in Hibbing and moved to Duluth in 1934 when she married Abe Zimmerman. Here she and son Bobby visit friends in Hibbing in 1944: Bobby Zimmerman, age three, with his mother, Beatty Zimmerman *(right)*, and friends Marie Munter with daughter *(left)* and Jean Pryor with son Dennis *(middle)*. Photographer unknown. Courtesy of Marie Munter and Bob and Linda Hocking/Zimmy's Restaurant, Hibbing.

but for thousands of immigrants it held out the promise for a better life—a life that looked increasingly grim in their homelands. Iron ore was discovered in north-eastern Minnesota in the 1840s, but it wasn't until the 1890s that prospecting began in earnest. By the first decade of the twentieth century, one company, U.S. Steel, controlled the vast majority of the industry. Mine owners and operators came from the eastern states, and supervisors were often experienced Scandinavian or Welsh miners from Michigan or Wisconsin, but vast numbers of laborers were needed, and quickly. Recruiters began scouring destitute regions of eastern and southern Europe, seeking cheap labor, no experience needed; they found thousands of willing men. By 1910, the Range had a population of over seventy-seven thousand people with at least twenty-seven different nationalities represented. The Finns were the largest group, numbering over eleven thousand, followed by Slovenes and Italians. Tied for sixteenth place with the Bulgarians were the Jews, numbering just under a thousand each. Finns, Slovenes, Italians, Bulgarians, and Jews—this is not the image people have of Minnesota, particularly those who listen to Garrison Keillor's popular radio show, *Prairie Home Companion,* or have read Sinclair Lewis's *Main Street.* According to these writers, Minnesota is a "white bread" state, populated by stoic Scandinavian Lutherans, long-suffering German Catholics, and a few displaced Yankees. This was true throughout much of the twentieth century; census figures show the state's population was almost evenly divided between folks of Scandinavian or German descent, with about 2 percent being "other." But that was never true in one remote corner of Minnesota, the region known as the Iron Range, where the "other" preferred pumpernickel and rye breads.

It wasn't jobs in the mines that attracted Jews to the Range; it was the goods and services that the mine operators and miners would need. They began to arrive in the late 1880s, settling first on the Vermilion Range, before moving to the larger and more productive Mesabi Range, where they opened shops on the main streets of the area's emerging towns and locations, the latter owned by the mining companies. But the Jewish settlers differed from other immigrant groups on the Range in one other key area besides employment. According to the 1910 census, men on the Range outnumbered women by almost two to one. Many of the miners were putting aside a nest egg so they could return "home" to marry and resume their lives. The situation was quite different for Jewish settlers: the ratio of men to women was nearly even. The Jewish immigrant had no homeland to return to; most had fled from religious persecution, and America was their "Golden Medina," a golden land of opportunity. Thus, many of the Range's Jewish settlers were married couples, their immediate families, and often elderly parents and siblings. This was the case for the Solomovich family as well as the Edelstein family, which included Dylan's maternal grandmother, Florence.

The Edelstein family was already established in Hibbing when Ben Solomovich moved there and met Florence. By this time Ben had changed the family name to Stone (ironically the name of one of the major mine operators on the Range) and opened a small store in Stevenson's Location about seven miles from Hibbing. Ben and Florence married in 1911 and moved into rooms above the store. The family soon included two children, Vernon, born in 1912, and Beatrice, born in 1915, followed by Louis and Irene, who was born in 1927, the year the store burned down and the family moved to another location, Leetonia, only three miles from Hibbing. Florence operated the small store at that location, while Ben opened another shop in Hibbing. Like so many other Jewish merchants at this time, the family continued to live in crowded conditions above the store in Leetonia.

Regardless of their financial situation, it was important to the Jewish settlers that they maintain and practice their faith. By 1910, forty Jewish families living in the Hibbing area had formed a congregation, Agudath Achim (Fellowship of Brothers), which until the 1920s held services in members' homes or rented halls. Dylan's maternal grandfather, Ben Stone, was one of the congregation's first presidents. Although Orthodox, the congregation rarely had a rabbi and was led primarily by laity, who also prepared young boys like Vernon Stone for their bar mitzvahs.[4] Living outside the Jewish mainstream, however, required accommodations to be made to how they practiced their faith. Miners were paid on Friday, so Friday and Saturday were the major shopping days. Traditionally Orthodox Jews would observe the Sabbath by avoiding all types of labor and attending morning, afternoon, and evening services in the synagogue. This was not possible, however, for the merchants on the Iron Range if they wanted to maintain their livelihood. Instead the merchants would attend the synagogue early on Saturday morning and then open their shops for business, and then return to the synagogue in the evening after their shops closed and the sun had set for the Havdalah service that signals the end of the Sabbath. At home, however, their wives were able to observe kashruth, the separation of meat and milk and the eating of ritually slaughtered meat and poultry, thanks in part to a ritual slaughterer in Chisholm who kept them supplied with kosher chickens.

By the 1920s, thanks to the growth of the mining industry, Jewish merchants like the Stones were entering the middle class. The entire family moved to Hibbing in 1932, where they were able to buy a home. In the 1920s, the town of Hibbing was forced to move because of the discovery of iron ore beneath it. This move provided the Hibbing congregation with the opportunity to purchase the now-displaced white clapboard Gothic Revival Swedish Lutheran church, move it to a new location, and transform it into a synagogue by first removing its steeple and then placing a large Star of David in an oculus window on its front facade. The interior was also reconfigured to have a bimah (platform), upon which stood the Holy Ark that held the Torah scrolls. The synagogue became the focal point for Hibbing Jews and gave them increased visibility in the larger community. Although the economic success of the Jewish merchants placed their families solidly in the middle class, they were still seen by others as an "in group closed to outsiders," but certainly not as isolated or marginalized, as many of the Jewish people were in larger cities such as Minneapolis (then called "the anti-Semitic capital of the United States").[5]

During the first decades of the past century, religion, class, and ethnicity were all highly politicized on the Range and the source of division within Range life. The Protestant elite claimed that southern and eastern Europeans were "black" (the term used by the elite); only "true Americans" (Yankees) and those of northern European descent were to be considered "white."[6] Hibbing had a large "black" population, (meaning "miners"), more so than the town of Virginia, which was described in contemporary literature as the only "white" city on the Range.[7] The miners' ongoing attempts to unionize (especially Finnish miners) and the sixty saloons on Hibbing's Main Street, which were allegedly contributing to immoral behavior, led the "good" Protestants to call in the Ku Klux Klan, which held cross burnings and parades to instill fear in the miners' hearts. The miners' efforts to unionize placed the Jewish community in an awkward position. Coming primarily from eastern Europe, Jews could be considered "black," but their position firmly in the middle class placed them in the "white" category. Adding to their dilemma was their traditional support for workers' rights, which could be seen elsewhere in the nation but was not evident on the Range. Here they kept their leftist sympathies to themselves because of their status as retailers selling to both mining company interests and the workers. A Jewish man whose family had a small cigar-making factory on the Range is quoted as saying, "What was good enough for U.S. Steel, was good enough for me." Or as one merchant put it more bluntly, "We kept our mouths shut!"

From its earliest days, the Range had an incredibly vibrant cultural life, at first limited to the ruling white-collar class, which brought in celebrities including, according to one informant, Oscar Wilde, although this cannot be verified. In the prosperous twenties, the growing middle class began to hunger for more programs, ranging from classical music to vaudeville acts, the latter often appearing in Dylan's uncles' (the Edelsteins') theaters. A Range Community Concert Series was established, which brought in major artists including Mischa Elman, John Charles Thomas, Todd Duncan, an African-American singer, and Judith Anderson and Raymond Massey, who performed in the play *John Brown's Body*. Harland Sapero of Hollywood, California, was hired to give an exhibition of dances popular on the West Coast, including the Charleston. Children were offered free music lessons in the schools, and almost every middle-class home had a piano, even if no one could actually play it. Each ethnic group had its own musical tradition, so children were exposed to an amazing variety of musical styles. Hibbing High School even had a jazz group, whose pianist was a talented young Jewish woman who was a good friend of Beatrice Stone.

All children on the Range, regardless of class, had access to an excellent education, thanks to the mining companies' largess. It wasn't just out of the goodness of their hearts that these schools were built. The companies had a specific purpose: education was intended to acculturate the immigrants' children as a means of lessening their attachment to what were described as "leftist" and "subversive" ideas. It is impressive how many young people in the 1920s were accepted into elite colleges and universities, including Jewish children, who attended, among other schools,

Pennsylvania's Wharton School of Finance, the University of Chicago, Smith, and Vassar. Some chose to return to the Range following graduation. Hibbing in 1940 had two Jewish lawyers, a doctor, and three dentists.

The Depression hit the mining companies hard; the Range population declined, and stores on Main Street began to close. The number of Jews on the Range dipped from a high of 1,112 in 1920 to about 775 in the 1930s. However, Agudath Achim still had 78 members and 60 children in its religious school, including several of the Stone children. Beatrice graduated from high school in 1932 and attended Hibbing Junior College for two years before going to work in her father's store—cheap help during a difficult period. Jewish teenagers were discouraged from dating non-Jews, so when they reached marriageable age, they were often sent elsewhere to meet other young Jews. Some traveled to Minneapolis and St. Paul, others to Chicago, but most ended up in Duluth and Superior. This is where Beatrice, now known as Beatty, met a quiet, handsome young man, Abe Zimmerman, who was fortunate to have a steady job as a bookkeeper for Standard Oil in Duluth. Beatty and Abe married on June 10, 1934, in her family's home in Hibbing and then moved to Duluth, where their two children were born, Robert Allen in 1941, and David in 1946. After living in Duluth for fourteen years, the Zimmermans decided to move back to Hibbing, where Abe accepted a job as a bookkeeper in his brothers' appliance store. It was a smart move, as the Range was booming in the 1940s as a result of the war and its aftermath.

World War II brought the Range's diverse population together. The people, regardless of religion or ethnic origin, were united in an effort to defeat a common enemy. According to one historian, this resulted in the people "developing into a new ethnic group based on the regional social experience rather than Old World ties and the experience of immigration."[8] Ethnic ties still remained vital, but they were now being balanced with the larger group identity: Iron Ranger.

In the years following World War II, the Iron Range Jewish population remained stable at about 750 to 800; in 1951 there were 280 Jews living in Hibbing, including the Stone, Edelstein, and Zimmerman families. It was during this period of increased openness and acceptance that the Jewish people began to have more social interaction with their non-Jewish neighbors. Jewish men began to join and become officers in various fraternal organizations, and women became active in the League of Women Voters and the Business Women's Club. Annual brotherhood programs became popular, as the Hibbing newspaper noted: "We have learned to co-operate in war. Protestant, Catholic, and Jew have planned and worked and fought together. Let us resolve to work together in peace."[9]

The Agudath Achim Sisterhood took the initiative in forming the Volunteer Council consisting of women from various church auxiliaries and clubs that offered assistance to the needy regardless of their faith. The new sense of tolerance among groups could be seen in the guest lists for bar mitzvahs and weddings held in Hibbing. When their son Robert Allen was to become a bar mitzvah in 1954, invitations for the dinner held at the Androy Hotel in Hibbing were sent out to over four hundred people. According to Beatty, the guest list included not only their Jewish friends and relatives, but many of their Christian friends and neighbors as well. Family and friends who attended Bob's bar mitzvah recall how well he read from the Torah and chanted the traditional melodies. When Etheldoris Stein, Beatty's friend the jazz pianist and daughter of the local pharmacist, was to be married, her gown was custom made in New York City, and over five hundred people attended the ceremony, which because of the numbers, was held in the Odd Fellows Hall above her father's drugstore. As an aside, Etheldoris's husband, also a pharmacist, owned Gray's Drug Store in Dinkytown, where Robert Zimmerman had a room for a short time prior to his departure for New York. Etheldoris recalls going with the Zimmermans to Bob's apartment and finding it empty; he had left without telling anyone.

Beatty, in an oral interview conducted in 1985, recalled what it was like for a Jewish family in Hibbing in the 1940s and 1950s.[10] After Ben Stone died, Florence, Beatty's mother, moved in with the Zimmermans and lived there for fifteen years until she died. Because of the size of their home, Abe and Beatty were able to have the entire family for the Jewish holidays, including the Passover seder. When the number got too large, they would have the seder in the synagogue, inviting fifty or sixty guests. Their Christian neighbors would always be invited to their home for potato pancakes on Hanukkah, and in turn, the Zimmermans would attend midnight mass at the Catholic church on Christmas Eve. Beatty remarked that "living in a town like Hibbing made us all the more conscious of living in the outside world, also." But the "outside" world also held out the possibility of intermarriage, still an anathema to Range Jewry. (Beatty's two brothers had married non-Jews.) So although she expressed pleasure that her sons were "very close" to Catholic children, it was still important that they have Jewish friends as well. Bob and David were sent every summer to Herzl Camp, a Jewish Zionist camp in Webster, Wisconsin, where they were able to meet other Jewish children from the Upper Midwest. Former campers' most vivid memory of Bob was his constantly hugging his guitar. None mentioned his actually playing it.

Beatty joined all the Jewish women's organizations on the Range and was president of Hadassah, a Zionist women's group. She was invited to join several non-Jewish women's groups but chose not to, claiming she "didn't feel like an 'outcast,' but had enough to do without belonging to their organizations." Beatty believed she was never looked upon as a "Jewish" person: "I was looked upon as an American . . . [who] went to school, [and] enjoyed every one of my Christian friends." Beatty also worked outside of the home, selling handkerchiefs at Feldman's Department Store. She recalled the effort made to unionize the store's employees, noting that she and her family were very sympathetic to the miners' efforts in the "early days" to form unions because it provided the miners with more money to support their children. However, she felt it was more difficult for shopkeepers to pay union scale, so they were forced to lay people off. She said, "I am not really a great firm believer of unions today. . . . In my time it put Herbergers out of business."

While Jews and Christians may have shared memberships in various organizations and would even meet at times in each other's homes, members of the two faiths

AUG • 57

Rosanne Tenenbaum and Bobby Zimmerman at Herzl Camp near Webster, Wisconsin, 1957. Photographer unknown. Courtesy of Jewish Historical Society of the Upper Midwest.

would socialize separately on a more personal level. The Jewish women, although busy with their various philanthropic efforts or outside work, still found time for bridge and mah-jongg parties. Beatty had many of these gatherings at her home, and those who attended have shared their memories of them. Most vivid is little Bobby Zimmerman, a quiet and polite boy, sitting on the couch during their games, writing poems that his mother would later find scattered throughout the house. His aunt Irene often wondered what happened to those scraps of paper. She said that her sister always believed Bobby would become a writer, but never a musician! The family had a piano in the parlor, which Abe would occasionally pick out a tune on, but it was David who was the family musician. While Bobby refused to take piano les-sons, David happily did and later majored in music at the University of Minnesota.

By the late 1950s the demand for iron ore began to diminish once again. Several violent strikes had taken place, and it was becoming increasingly apparent to Iron Rangers that their children would have find their livelihood elsewhere. Once again, education was going to be their ticket to success. Jewish students who graduated from Range high schools in the late 1950s and early 1960s recall how their parents urged them to go to college, to get a profession, and, if need be, move elsewhere. Many said it was not just Jewish parents who foresaw the decline of the region; their other classmates experienced similar pressure. It is understandable in this context why the Zimmermans insisted that Bob attend the University of Minnesota, as Abe hopefully suggested, to study architecture. Abe and Beatty were married during the Great Depression, and they shared memories of the sacrifices their parents had made to succeed and become part of the Range's middle class. They also remem-bered the times when Jews were not readily accepted as part of the larger commu-nity. As a result, like so many other Jewish parents, they instilled in their children the need for a higher education, arguing, as mine did, that while all else could be taken away from you, that which is between your ears will always be yours.

Bob Zimmerman, a product of a generation that did not want for anything and who was not viewed because of his faith as an "outsider," could not understand his parents' concern. Lacking, as we all do, foresight, Abe and Beatty did not recognize the talent their son would later exhibit. But I would argue that the Jewish home he was brought up in and his exposure to the multicultural Range community con-tributed to his artistry. The Jewish people on the Range learned how to live dual lives: they were able to maintain their Jewish identity and still be "Iron Rangers." This need to integrate a dual identity is one that many artists confront: to live both as an artist with universal appeal and as an individual with a unique heritage. The conflict that often ensues can result in genius—maybe even a Bob Dylan.

Notes

1. Research on Iron Range Jewry was part of the Project to Document Jewish Settlers in Minnesota, which I directed. Information on Iron Range Jewry in this essay is based on research and oral interviews that I and students at the University of Minnesota conducted for the project. The majority of that material is stored in the archives of the Jewish Historical Society of the Upper Midwest located at the Andersen Library, University of Minnesota. The interview with Beatrice Zimmerman Rutman is not available to researchers.

2. Folk musicians such as the *klezmerim* have been described as "wanderers between two worlds." See Marc Chagall's famed paintings "The Fiddler" (1913–14) and "The Violinist" (1911–14) for images of the strolling Jewish fiddler in a rural scene.

3. Chester Jay Proshan, "Eastern European Jewish Immigrants and Their Children on the Minnesota Iron Range, 1890s–1980s," (Ph.D. diss., University of Minnesota, 1998), 36. Proshan was the project's research assistant and used the project's data in his dissertation.

4. A bar mitzvah is celebrated on a Jewish boy's thirteenth birthday. He is called up before the congregation for the first time to read from the Torah (the Five Books of Moses), indicat-ing that he is prepared to become a full-fledged member of the congregation.

5. Carey McWilliams, "Minneapolis: The Curious Twin," *Common Ground* 8, no. 1 (Autumn 1946): 61–65.

6. Paul B. Landis, *Three Iron Mining Towns: A Study in Cultural Change* (New York: Arno Press, 1970), 24. For another reference to "white" immigrants on the Range, see U.S. Congress, Senate, "Immigrants in Industries: Iron Ore Mining," 61st Cong., 2d sess., 1909–10, Senate Documents, vol. 78, 348–49.

7. Ibid.

8. Proshan, "Eastern European Jewish Immigrants," 298.

9. Ibid., 306.

10. The interview with Beatrice Zimmerman Rutman was conducted on July 12, 1985, for the Project to Document Jewish Settlers in Minnesota. It is in the author's private collection and not available to researchers.

3. Not from Nowhere:
Identity and Aspiration in Bob Dylan's Hometown
Susan Clayton

In his Bob Dylan biography *No Direction Home*, Robert Shelton ponders the similarities between the storefronts of downtown Hibbing, Minnesota, and Sinclair Lewis's fictional Gopher Prairie.[1] As a native of Hibbing myself, I have always thought that if Carol Kennicott had stepped off the train there in the early twentieth century, she would have found plenty of willing participants in her cosmopolitan undertakings. As documented in the archives of the Hibbing Historical Society and the Minnesota Historical Society, the stories of the first settlers of Hibbing tell the tale of a town's good fortune. Despite the distance from a larger city, the movers and shakers of Hibbing's formative years seemed to have had no qualms about the feasibility of establishing a sophisticated town in a relative wilderness. Although the scene would shift a bit by the time Bob Dylan was a boy, this was the atmosphere his mother, Beatty Stone Zimmerman, knew as a Hibbing girl.

When speaking about his hometown in Martin Scorsese's *No Direction Home*, Dylan says, "There really wasn't any philosophy, any idiom, any ideology."[2] However, a study of the building and cultural initiatives that took place at the edge of the iron ore pits that sustained the town illustrates that there certainly was an abiding belief in progressive ideals that developed as various ethnic groups settled and began to assimilate. Due to a convergence of natural resources, strong personalities, and a prevailing faith in American progress, Hibbing in the twentieth century was a place of genuine interest. Ambition and achievement were encouraged and supported. As they say in Minnesota, "it could'a been worse" for young Bob.

The Hibbing story began in 1892 when speculator Frank Hibbing discovered a rich lode of iron ore at his Minnesota camp in the northern woods. For years, similar strikes had been made in the region, but Frank Hibbing had dibs on developing this particular stretch of land, which was incorporated under his surname and platted almost immediately.[3] Trees not yet felled by the lumber industry were quickly cleared. Job seekers of diverse nationalities, coming from dozens of European countries, found their way to the remote locale.

MAHONING HULL RUST IRON MINE, HIBBING, MINNESOTA, THE LARGEST OPEN PIT IRON MINE IN THE WORLD

Hull Rust Mine, 1920. Courtesy of the Minnesota Historical Society.

Prospecting is a gamble, but the situation in Hibbing was definitely boom, not bust. A first population count was 325.[4] By the time of the 1900 census, the figure was 2,481, and that more than tripled by the next census in 1910.[5] Paul Henry Landis's 1933 thesis, *Cultural Change in a Mining Town,* confirms that many boomtown stereotypes applied to Hibbing in the early twentieth century. It had crowding, filth, and plenty of saloons. It was a land of opportunity for miners, gamblers, and prostitutes.[6]

Because the vast ore deposits could support ongoing mining, workers began to settle with their families. For convenience, little communities, referred to as "locations," sprang up near the open-pit mines scattered throughout the region. The town of Hibbing—neighboring the expansive Hull-Rust mine—would dominate, given its proximity to the richest and most accessible ore veins. Frank Hibbing was the first benefactor of his namesake settlement, securing funds for water and power plants and building the first hotel, sawmill, and bank.[7] With the new economy supported and governance in place, residents made efforts to provide for education, entertainment, and fraternity.

Perhaps the convergence of Hibbing's polyglot immigrant population and their aspirations for what life would hold in the new town are best reflected in the development of the town's school system. Soon after incorporation, a teacher—Miss Murphy—was recruited from Wisconsin and offered a very competitive sum for the day. This first hire set the bar high for an emphasis on education and on the town's ability to attract top-quality teachers, aspects that defined Hibbing schools for the twentieth century. Miss Murphy's first task was to start an early version of an English-as-a-second-language program at a school full of children who spoke several tongues. Americanization and citizenship courses were part of the curriculum, with parents and children alike attending.

Outside of the school system, other organizations began to form. The first newspaper, *The Sentinel,* was published in 1894. An 1897 headline proclaimed, "Hibbing has a band!" announcing the formation of a new group of Finnish musicians, complete with matching uniforms.[8] An array of fraternal lodges began: the Odd Fellows, Masons, Elks, Moose, Swedish Vasa Lodge, and an especially strong Sons of Italy

Colonial Hotel being moved from North to South Hibbing. Courtesy of the Minnesota Historical Society.

and Finnish Workers Hall. In the ensuing decades, a chapter of almost every national organization of the day was launched in Hibbing, including an Izaak Walton League, Knights of Columbus, American Legion, Lions, Rotary, YWCA, Boy and Girl Scouts of America, and 4-H, among others. These groups acted as cultural bridges, offering gathering places where familiar customs could be practiced, while also providing lessons on how to navigate life in America.

A women's Saturday Club, designed along the lines of the organizations then in vogue in larger cities, began meeting in 1903, with committees for education, civic service, and the arts. The Saturday Club backed the emerging library system, begun when Captain Walter McCormack, a railroad watchman, started loaning materials from his private library of more than one hundred books, all stored in his shack. By 1907, thanks to the efforts of the Saturday Club, the town had been granted a Carnegie library.[9]

In addition to initiatives that grew organically in the new settlement, outside influences had their impact. Traveling circuses, complete with elephants, made the trek to the far north as early as the 1890s. From Hibbing's early days, civic space was devoted to live performances. An "opera house" on the second floor of the Village Hall hosted homegrown productions as well as popular touring performers. Various live theaters came and went around town. Motion pictures arrived in 1906. Soon after, one of Dylan's maternal families, the Edelsteins, established a circuit of movie theaters, which endured into the 1980s.[10]

Moving a church from North to South Hibbing. This church was later converted into a synagogue, Agudath Achim (Fellowship of Brothers), where the Zimmerman family were members. Courtesy of the Minnesota Historical Society.

In 1900, the Hibbing Speedway Association formed, and members soon built a track and grandstand for horse racing and, later, for auto racing. By 1905, the site was ripe to become the new location for the St. Louis County Fair, when the city of Duluth deemed the event no longer profitable. The fair at Hibbing became a much-anticipated highlight of the year for generations. The annual event provided a chance to gather with folks from surrounding towns and the big city of Duluth and an opportunity to exhibit farm, forest, culinary, and craft skills.[11]

Ore was abundant, and business was good. Revenues from the mining industry were plentiful. As sociologist Paul Landis framed it, the feeling was " 'We might as well spend the money: if we don't it'll go to the damn capitalists down east.' Hibbing people asked not 'Where can we save?' but rather, 'Is that all we can levy?' "[12]

Full coffers spurred ambitious building developments. Hotels and retail were especially thriving, prompting a Chamber of Commerce to form in 1905. The town boasted a three-story, stone and brick Village Hall and an equally fine St. Louis County District Courthouse. Oliver Mining Company, the local subsidiary of U.S. Steel, built an opulent club for employees with a reading room, gym, billiard tables,

Street scene, Hibbing, circa 1930. Courtesy of the Minnesota Historical Society.

and a bowling alley. When Lincoln School opened in 1907, complete with one of the first public school swimming pools in the nation, it became the largest structure in town.

The tale of Iver Lind helps to set the tone of the times. Around 1900, Lind was injured by a mule that was spooked by a mine blast. He sued the mine for damages and won. Lind's was one of many similar suits that illustrate the early willingness of the mining companies to make expenditures that would ensure cooperation from Iron Range settlers.[13]

Enter the charismatic mayor Victor Power, a former blacksmith turned lawyer, who would fully exploit this willingness on Hibbing's behalf during his tenure from 1913 to 1923. As reported in *American Mercury* magazine, he was "a Huey Long to the mine owners, an Abraham Lincoln to the miners, and a Santa Claus to building and equipment salesmen."[14] Power found his constituency among Hibbing's working class. A self-appointed watchdog of the mining companies, he was shrewd at extracting the maximum tax revenues out of them. Power's idea of service was to build a modern village for the townspeople, and he was hard on those who didn't agree with his goals or methods. He famously checked catalog orders at the post office to identify those who opted not to buy locally.[15] Power ran a tax-and-spend administration and was often at war with the mining companies being levied and in

Village Hall, 1937. Photograph by Al Heitman. Courtesy of the Minnesota Historical Society.

court defending himself against charges of graft. In an emblematic scenario, when one firm enacted a sizable layoff as a message to the mayor, Power promptly put the unemployed on the city payroll, increasing the tax load to the mines.[16]

Worth mentioning is a fight that Power did not win. In 1915, temperance proponents successfully won enforcement of an 1855 Indian treaty prohibiting the sale of liquor in the region. From a one-time high of almost sixty saloons, Hibbing was pronounced officially dry until the national repeal of Prohibition in 1934. Bar business had been falling off, and one of the newspapers speculated that with other, more wholesome entertainments increasingly available in town, there was a waning need for legal liquor. A song was written to mark the occasion: "Farewell then oh ye lager, Farewell rock and rye, It's a long way to Old Virginia [Minnesota], when Hibbing goes dry."[17]

During Power's administration, Hibbing's streets were paved and finished with curbing. Streetlights created "white ways" in the downtown. Bennett Park, located on fifty-six acres south of town, was enhanced with bridges, pools, a conservatory, and a zoo. A rare amenity for a small northern town, the zoo became home to bears, buffalo, antelope, elks, monkeys, and lions.[18]

These developments were similar in some respects to those in other growing American towns. The Hibbing school system, for example, was inspired by a successful model from Gary, Indiana.[19] Yet, in Hibbing, the scale of investment, the breadth of growth, the quality of civic design, and the speed at which new buildings and programs were enacted made this small town in a northern wilderness truly remarkable. Longtime Superintendent of Schools John Slattery, who spent his childhood in Hibbing and returned with his college diploma, posited that immigrant miners arrived with a strong belief in the American dream and felt that Hibbing was a place that offered the best benefits for their offspring.[20] Slattery's view resonates with language in the press at the time. The town was often referred to by hyperbolic monikers: "The Razzle-Dazzle Village," "The Richest Little Village in Nation," "The Wonder Village of the World."

The progressive reforms in Hibbing were, to some extent, also an effort to acculturate immigrant workers, who, *Western Magazine* noted in 1916, "brought with them all of their old time habits, their uncleanliness and their ignorance."[21] The author of the piece is pleased to find that in a photo of Hibbing's graduating class, "few traces remain of the original foreign characteristics."[22] A name check of board members overseeing Hibbing schools, library, and hospital administration discloses a distinct group of players, for the most part lawyers and businessmen rather than miners.[23] Ambitious building and programs certainly reflected *their* values, put into play on behalf of the town.

Hibbing was not the only Iron Range town in lucrative circumstances. With mining company headquarters far away in the East, the whole Range was on a spending spree, with an element of competition between the villages. Victor Power's efforts gave Hibbing the edge. In his 1921 history of St. Louis County, Walker Van Brunt declared, "Hibbing is no longer a mining camp; it is a metropolitan, cosmopolitan city, in which the [immigrant] miner may, and does, hold his head high and provide for his family a typical American home."[24]

Local transportation enterprises gave working people mobility and increased communication. From 1912 to 1927, an electric railway connected Hibbing with other Iron Range towns of Chisholm, Eveleth, and Virginia, before autos and improved roadways made the system obsolete. The Hibbing Transportation Company, incorporated in 1915, began primarily to bus workers between mining locations. It eventually grew into the Greyhound Bus Company.[25] In 1919, a library bus that took books in Croatian, Serbian, Slovenian, Finnish, Italian, Norwegian, and Swedish to the small mining locations was touted as the first bookmobile in the nation. "Here is a fulfillment of America's promise to many foreigners," declared the pamphlet announcing the launch of this new service.[26]

Hibbing residents lived with the prospect that ore reserves would run out sooner or later. Nonetheless, public opinion was mixed when in the 1910s the news came that the town might have to move to allow the mining company to get at a rich vein of ore. Relocating a town was not without local precedent. Eveleth, Hibbing's neighbor to the east, had experienced a move on a smaller scale. Between 1896 and 1900, one hundred Eveleth buildings were moved one-quarter mile. Hibbing's move would be double that size and would take decades.[27] Many of its buildings, including the Village Hall and Carnegie Library, had been built to last but would have to be demolished.

Planning for the town's move coincided with American involvement in World War I, which caused some delays but also provided more justification for the action. Public interest in providing steel for the war effort should be primary, some thought, over private interest in preserving one's home. In other words, it was patriotic to move your house or business almost two miles south. Some structures were slated for demolition. Others were loaded onto trailers, pulled by horses or locomotives. A few dramatically collapsed en route. Although most buildings were moved in the 1920s and 1930s, a few remained in service into the 1950s.

Construction commenced on the new site, sponsored to varying degrees by the mining companies. As North Hibbing (the name adopted for the original settlement area) sputtered from boomtown to ghost town, a new town hall, school building, and entire business district were rising to the south. Storefronts were offered at attractive terms to retailers. Howard Street, the main thoroughfare, was built as a unified business district with two-story brick buildings attracting several national chain stores. Soon, South Hibbing was home to a Woolworth's, J. C. Penney, and Montgomery Ward in addition to established local concerns such as Feldman's Department Store, where Dylan's mother worked in the 1950s. Part of Dylan's family theater chain, the State Theater, with its can't-miss-it marquee, opened in 1925. These modern structures served as incentives to propel private homeowners to move nearby. New housing clustered just off the main drag. A fresh start meant that central heating in these homes was a given.

Completed in 1921, Village Hall was built in the heart of the new business district on land donated by the Warren Mining Company. With a tall clock tower, columns, and commissioned murals, its design was inspired by Independence Hall in Philadelphia. A tree planted on its grounds came from the spot where George Washington received command of the Revolutionary army.[28] Next to the civic buildings, the 160-room Androy Hotel, with its plush Crystal Lounge and expansive porch facing Howard Street, opened for business. In its prime, the Androy was *the* place for special occasions as well as for visitors. WMFG, the first radio station on the Range, hit the airwaves in 1935, broadcasting from the Androy.[29] In 1944, Robert Zimmerman celebrated his bar mitzvah dinner there.

The most splendid structure built at this time was the Hibbing High School, dedicated in 1924. Commissioned murals installed along the main staircase summarize the mission of the project. Painter David Ericson used loaded symbolism in images of Columbus arriving in the New World, pioneers moving west in covered wagons, and immigrants swearing allegiance to the United States. Intended to be

Hibbing High School and Junior College from the Air, and Assumption Hall School in Background

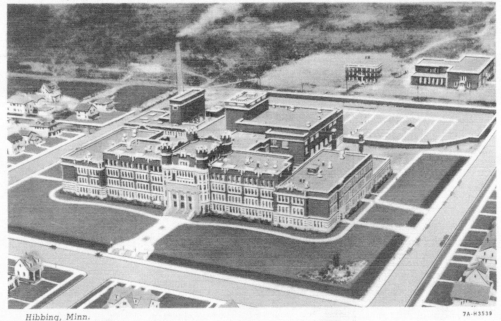

Hibbing, Minn.   7A-H3539

Hibbing High School and Junior College, circa 1940.
Courtesy of the Minnesota Historical Society.

instructive as well as uplifting, the murals linked local events to the greater American story and reinforced the process of assimilation to all who came through the doorways.[30]

The palatial high school auditorium, its design based on a full-scale Broadway venue, resulted in decades of well-attended performances and concert series that drew audiences from across the Range. Hibbingites gathered there to hear national acts, personalities, and leaders. Early on, John Philip Sousa and his band played there, and Will Rogers performed "Great Men I Have Met at the Stage Door" and "All I Know Is What I Read in the Papers."[31] Concerts were offered by such performers as the Mills Brothers, the Boston Pops, and the Vienna Boys Choir, and public figures, such as Eleanor Roosevelt, offered inspirational speeches. Hibbing had become a showplace. In 1928, when President Calvin Coolidge scheduled a stop at the Hull-Rust on the edge of town, the mine was renowned as the largest of its kind in the world. An observation platform was built for the occasion. Maintained as a tourist amenity ever since, the observation area made strip mining a spectator sport.[32]

In Hibbing, the Depression of the 1930s was fairly well weathered.[33] Sewer and water lines were maintained in part with Works Projects Administration funds, which also provided for a sixty-block paving program and the construction of an airport for training civilian pilots. When the recreation building burned to the ground, a Public Works Administration grant ensured that a new Memorial Arena—larger

David Ericson, *Swearing Allegiance to the United States, 1922–23.* Oil on canvas, 68 x 77 inches. Installed on interior wall at entrance to Hibbing High School, Hibbing, Minnesota. Collection of Hibbing High School. Courtesy Tweed Museum of Art, University of Minnesota–Duluth. Photograph by Tom Lindstrom.

than Duluth's—quickly replaced it.[34] This building hosted legendary games between hockey rivals and appearances by popular performers and politicians, including the flamboyant wrestler Gorgeous George. The local economy boomed again with the advent of World War II, as iron ore again played a crucial role in the war effort.

By midcentury, there were many ways of belonging in Hibbing, colored by overt hints about greater possibilities waiting outside of town. Ironically, perhaps, the town fathers and mothers had built a place that empowered young people to leave. Hibbingites were especially proud of those who went out into the world, made a name for themselves, and then gave something back to the town, as exemplified by entrepreneur Jeno Paulucci, author and Charles Manson family prosecutor Vincent Bugliosi, and basketball great Kevin McHale. (Perhaps its history of high expectations for high achievement explains why Hibbing has been reluctant to embrace its own "poet of a generation.") Hibbing's record of enterprises and firsts, along with the success of multiple civic endeavors and organizations, signifies how

Hibbing High School Auditorium, 1924. Courtesy of the Minnesota Historical Society.

townspeople strove for more than mere sustenance. The rich veins of ore had provided the means for many to fully realize an American dream in a land of opportunity.

Abe and Beatty Zimmerman, Bob Dylan's parents, were patrons of much of the cultural activity at the time. Beatty belonged to the Saturday Club, which continued to meet into the 1960s. The family appliance store donated a refrigerator when the Range Artists Association formed.[35] To commemorate the Minnesota Centennial in 1958, Hibbing mounted an original stage production of *Growin' Pains*, penned by a hometown composer who had studied at the Oberlin Conservatory. *Growin' Pains* tells the Hibbing story in song, part Broadway, part operetta. The Zimmermans were sponsors of the original production. Certainly their sons, Robert and David, saw the performance at the Hibbing High School Auditorium. David would produce and serve as musical director of a 1976 revival of the piece that traveled to Washington, D.C., during that bicentennial year.[36] The synopsis of the work is telling:

> A young girl is engaged in conversation by a stranger. The stranger learns that she is dissatisfied with her environment and bored by a "here" that she seems to want no part of, since "nothing ever happens." By means of a magic guitar, the stranger recreates, for her eyes and ears, many "happenings." She is witness to the growing pains and other experiences shared by a past of sixty-five years— a past that lends itself richly to her environment, and uniquely so. It is said that

**Album cover design for *Growin' Pains*. Hibbing's
history told through a musical was created for the
Minnesota State Centennial in 1958 and was
performed on the Hibbing High School Auditorium
stage. Cover art by Austin S. Hanson.**

distance lends enchantment, and so it does for this young girl; for the "long
range" peek at the past excites her hopes for her future, and perhaps your
growth and future run parallel to hers.[37]

In the 1960s, innovations in mining technology revived the Hull-Rust operations. New processes meant that taconite, a low-grade ore, could be transformed
into pellets for steel production. The mining industry resurged for a few decades,
but eventually the ore ran low again. In the 1980s, while empty storefronts multi-
plied in downtown, the Village Hall was named to the National Register of Historic
Places, and funds were successfully raised to restore murals from the lost Carnegie
Library. These, along with the high school and other monuments, outlasted the ore
to give visible testimony to the boom times. Today, Hibbing is well past its economic

heyday. But the community remains vital for those who choose it as home, and there are glimmers of tourism to bring new income to town.

Since 1991, local entrepreneurs, in partnership with the Chamber of Commerce, have successfully promoted the annual "Dylan Days." Held in May around the singer's birthday, the event celebrates Dylan and his work. Reminiscent of earlier municipal efforts, the weeklong event is also designed to encourage the growth of an arts community in the region. Still, geography is hard to conquer, as the old dichotomy between staying and leaving remains for many young people. Hibbing punk band "Post Boredom" recently posted a YouTube video shot in town, featuring the lyrics: "gotta get away from here, we're in the middle of nowhere."[38]

The history of Hibbing demonstrates how from its earliest days the town benefited from a connection to the greater nation. Mining took resources to the nation as a whole; the immigrants brought their own cultures from northern, eastern, and southern Europe, and Ukraine and Russia. The town attracted regional and national cultural fare despite its remote, northern location. Hibbing is a place that bred ambition and the impetus to achieve—often by moving away. The ideologies of Americanization and the American dream may not have been everyone's ideal, but they were prominent in the place where Robert Zimmerman grew up in the 1950s.

Notes

1. Robert Shelton, *No Direction Home: The Life and Music of Bob Dylan* (New York: William Morrow, 1986), 22.

2. *No Direction Home: Bob Dylan*, directed by Martin Scorsese (Hollywood, Calif.: Paramount, 2005).

3. Sam Guello, *Hibbing: The Man and the Village* (Hibbing, Minn.: Hibbing Historical Society, 1983), 9.

4. Ibid., 14.

5. Paul Henry Landis, "Cultural Change in the Mining Town: A Sociological Study of Three Mesabi Iron Range Towns: Eveleth, Hibbing and Virginia" (Ph.D. diss., University of Minnesota, 1933), 54.

6. Ibid., 247.

7. Guello, *Hibbing*, 9.

8. "Hibbing Has a Band!" *The Sentinel* (Hibbing, Minn.), February 6, 1897.

9. "Library Established in Hibbing While Community Still Was in Its Infancy," *Hibbing Daily Tribune*, Diamond Jubilee Edition, August 10, 1968.

10. "Hibbing Has Colorful History in Theatrical Field," *Hibbing Daily Tribune*, Diamond Jubilee Edition, August 10, 1968.

11. "Hibbing Fair Started in 1905, Now One of State's Best," *Hibbing Daily Tribune*, Diamond Jubilee Edition, August 10, 1968.

12. Landis, "Cultural Change in the Mining Town," 55.

13. Seventy-fifth Anniversary Committee, *Hibbing Minnesota, 1893–1968; Diamond Jubilee Days Souvenir Book* (Hibbing, Minn., August 11–18, 1968), 54.

14. Nathan Cohen, "Razzle-Dazzle Village," *American Mercury*, May 1944.

15. Ibid.

16. Guello, *Hibbing*, 77.

17. "'Indian Territory' Ruling in 1915 Closes Hibbing Saloons," *Hibbing Daily Tribune,* Diamond Jubilee Edition, August 10, 1968.

18. "Bennett Park Top Recreation Center," *Hibbing Daily Tribune,* Diamond Jubilee Edition, August 10, 1968.

19. Edmond DeLestry, "Out-Garying Gary," *Western Magazine* (St. Paul), May 1916, 270.

20. John Slattery, interview by author, Hibbing, Minn., March 22, 1981.

21. Edmond DeLestry, "Romance of a Town," *Western Magazine* (St. Paul), May 1916, 262.

22. DeLestry, "Out-Garying Gary," 278.

23. Guello, *Hibbing,* 36–49.

24. Walter Van Brunt, *Duluth and St. Louis County: Their Story and People* (New York: American Historical Society, 1921), 262.

25. Marvin Lamppa, *Minnesota's Iron Country: Rich Ore, Rich Lives* (Duluth, Minn.: Lake Superior Port Cities, 2004), 198–201.

26. Hibbing Public Library Service Pamphlet, ca. 1919.

27. Lamppa, *Minnesota's Iron Country,* 165.

28. "National Historic Landmark: Hibbing City Hall," *Hibbing Daily Tribune,* May 13, 1981.

29. "WMFG Was First on Range," *Hibbing Daily Tribune,* Diamond Jubilee Edition, August 10, 1968.

30. Thomas O'Sullivan, "David Ericson's Hibbing Murals: A Painted Pageant for Students and Immigrants," in *David Ericson, Always Returning: The Life and Work of a Duluth Cultural Icon* (Duluth, Minn.: Tweed Museum of Art, 2005), 83–90.

31. Contract detailing Will Rogers's 1925 Hibbing appearance, sponsored by the Hibbing YWCA.

32. "Coolidge Visit Made Mine Observation Easy," *Hibbing Daily Tribune,* Diamond Jubilee Edition, August 10, 1968.

33. Lamppa, *Minnesota's Iron Country,* 219.

34. "New and Old," *Hibbing Daily Tribune,* Diamond Jubilee Edition, August 10, 1968.

35. Range Artists Association, *History of the Range Artists Association Inc.,* www.rangeartcenter.org/history.htm (accessed January 21, 2007).

36. Al Reller, interview by author, January 8, 2008. Reller was the stage director of the 1976 production of *Growin' Pains.*

37. Program, *Growin' Pains,* Range Centennial Production (Hibbing, Minn., July 30–31, 1958).

38. Post Boredom, 2007, "middle of nowhere," www.youtube.com/watch?v=RVbjTRIYBb0&mode=related&search (accessed September 1, 2007).

4. "A Lamp Is Burning in All Our Dark": Bob Dylan and Johnny Cash

Court Carney

In the spring of 1969, in the midst of the loud, psychedelic rejection of tradition and convention, Bob Dylan and Johnny Cash joined forces at the establishmentarian epicenter of country music: Ryman Auditorium. The two singers stepped onto the stage with the seemingly obvious agenda of rehearsing a few songs for Cash's new television program. The mainstream country appeal of the show forced Dylan (and his fans) to confront the embedded tradition of the entire endeavor. Neither country nor folk, the music produced by Dylan in the late 1960s exploded arbitrary labels and connected instead to the totality of American music as represented by Highway 61. Forever connected to Dylan and southern blues culture, Highway 61 binds the incorrupt mythic to the hardscrabble realities of life in America. As the Ryman performance signified the melding of two musical genres, Highway 61 geographically and symbolically joined Minnesota to Louisiana, lashing together the Iron Range with the Deep South. Separated by a thousand miles but sutured together by Highway 61, Hibbing, Minnesota, and Dyess, Arkansas (the boyhood home of Cash), provide geographic resonance to a cultural moment that culminated on stage in Nashville, Tennessee.

The connection between Dylan and Cash dated back a half decade before the Ryman show to when Cash publicly acknowledged his appreciation of Dylan's music in the pages of *Broadside*. A brief flurry of letters between the two men followed, culminating with a well-noted meeting at the 1964 Newport Folk Festival. As shocking in its own way as Dylan's electric performance the next year, Cash's praise of Dylan helped break down the invented boundary between country music and folk music. Despite a career-defining catalog of singles released on Sun Records in the late 1950s, the 1960s witnessed Johnny Cash's career apogee. "The 1960s were probably my most productive time," Cash asserts in his autobiography, "I ventured out."[1] Cash, much more than Dylan, revealed his influences early on, with a spate of folk-themed albums in the early 1960s. These records showcased Cash's most popular-oriented mainstream country work, but at the same time they were undercut with a strong folk identity. "I was deeply into folk music in the early 1960s," Cash noted, and he adopted both a folk music repertoire as well as a folk music mentality.[2] The folk muse led Cash both to "authentic" folk songs as well as to a general political outlook centered on the idea that a song could effect social change. This focus found its most direct expression in *Bitter Tears* (released in 1964) with Cash producing a song cycle deeply rooted in the American Indian experience.

As Cash adopted a folk persona, Dylan quietly moved away from the strict parameters of the folk genre. Throughout 1964 and 1965, Dylan began to pursue a new style of songwriting, at once more experimental in language and more centered on the ambiguities involved with crafting an identity.[3] As Cash became increasingly comfortable with a folk image, Dylan became increasingly dismayed by it. And though the 1969 *Nashville Skyline* would sound almost audacious in its overt country rhythms and rhymes, the seeds of that record permeate *Highway 61 Revisited* and *Blonde on Blonde*.

Throughout this period, Dylan and Cash forged a relationship musically manifested in a series of songs recorded by Dylan during the 1960s. Two songs in particular—"Belshazzar" and "Girl from the North Country"—illustrate the ways in which Dylan challenged, redefined, and absorbed the career of Cash. These songs define in many ways Dylan's connection to the musical legacy of "Highway 61" and its associations with travel, myth, musical synthesis, and American promise. Connecting Duluth to New Orleans, via Memphis and St. Louis, Highway 61 tangibly incorporated the landscape of the blues, jazz, and rock and roll to Dylan's childhood existence on the Iron Range. The road traversed through the heart of the meaning of America and inspired Dylan in its symbolic vastness. A Sun Records single turned hidden soul track and a folk song at once ancient and modern, Dylan's recordings of "Belshazzar" and "Girl from the North Country" underscore his search for meaning in American music.

Hidden away in Woodstock in 1967, Dylan and The Band ran through a series of songs that would later coalesce as "The Basement Tapes."[4] In the course of these sessions, Dylan introduced a rather obscure Johnny Cash song, "Belshazzar." One of Cash's first attempts at songwriting, "Belshazzar" was the last single released by Sun Records after Cash had left for Columbia Records. Cut from the same cloth as recordings by his more famous Sun Records label mates, Cash's recording relies on lightly syncopated verses surrounding a biblical chorus warning: "he was weighed in the balance and found wanting."[5] Borrowing the basic structure of the song but replacing Cash's Sun Studio vibe with an organ straight out of Stax Records, Dylan's version conjures up something far more mysterious. The syncopated rhythm disappears, and the chorus skips past as a mumbled half croon. At first listen, "Belshazzar" is a likeable throwaway, a song with a number of "Basement Tape" peers. But in this song lay the seeds to Dylan's most important late-1960s record, *John Wesley Harding*, in which Dylan uses biblical parables not as messengers of truth but as damning examples of unresolvable mystery. Using one of the more confounding stories of the

Old Testament as inspiration, Dylan's "Belshazzar" is an ancient story refashioned as a garage-soul single.[6]

The most obvious interaction between Dylan and Cash came in 1969 with their duet on "Girl from the North Country." Before this public interaction, however, there was an earlier collaboration on one of Cash's own songs, "I Still Miss Someone." This Cash song had a particular pull on Dylan, as he performed it several times throughout this period and revisited it again in the 1980s. The song was also the center of the infamous pairing of Dylan and Cash in the ill-fated documentary *Eat the Document*. Despite its rather inauspicious beginning, this version paved the way for a series of informal recordings between the two singers a few years later. The 1969 sessions featured a much stronger version of "I Still Miss Someone" as well as a hodgepodge of Cash's earlier singles, Jimmy Rogers's tunes, and even a version of "You Are My Sunshine." Although routinely dismissed, these recordings contain something to recommend them. "Careless Love," in particular, retains a gleeful ad hoc charm (Dylan: "You can pass my hive"; Cash: "Your what?") that stands in stark contrast to the fleeting gallows humor of *John Wesley Harding* or some of the forced Nashville-styled rhymes on *Nashville Skyline*.[7] As Cash himself wrote, these recordings were "very informal, kind of loose things. Some of them don't have a real beginning or a real ending."[8] These sessions also begat "Girl from the North Country," a song that reached back to Dylan's folk music past. If "I Still Miss Someone" connected to Cash's Sun Records career, "Girl from the North Country" dated back to the ancient ballad tradition, via Dylan's early Columbia recordings.

In this version of "Girl from the North Country," one hears the convergence of tradition and innovation, modern popular music and traditional roots, Cash's iconographic voice and Dylan's newly found idiosyncratic croon. Reflecting on this duet for a piece in *Vogue*, Richard Goldstein writes that listening to the song is "an eerie experience for any long-ago folkie, because here's that song you once thought exclusively yours, opened wide again by a low-slung easy voice, with Dylan just tagging along in there."[9] In a more pointed critique of the endeavor, Tom Dearmore, writing for the *New York Times*, rejects as outmoded the central conceit of country music as an idiom connected inextricably to tradition and the past. "Cash's most serious shortcoming," Dearmore argues, "is that he leans excessively on the Depression, which is fast becoming ancient history." Dearmore strips Cash of any "folk" authority by noting that he "sings about the poor of yesterday, but not about the poor of today (with the exception of convicts and Indians, who are a tiny fragment of the whole)."[10] Though clocking in at a breezy thirty minutes, Dylan's *Nashville Skyline*, generally, and his duet with Cash, specifically, remain a potent reminder of the culture wars embedded in words such as *folk, country*, and *the people*.

Twenty-five years after *Nashville Skyline* and the Ryman performances, Dylan and Cash crossed paths again, albeit in a more indirect fashion. In 1993, Dylan released *World Gone Wrong*, a critically acclaimed collection of modern-tinged Appalachian music. The next year, 1994, Johnny Cash produced his own late-career-defining record, *American Recordings,* a set of sparse, lonely sounding songs. For both musicians, these albums awakened a critical resurgence, as Dylan and Cash delivered their most vital recordings in years. Consumers as well as music writers responded to the "authenticity" (or at least the marketable authenticity) resonating from these records. Both *World Gone Wrong* and *American Recordings* exploded chronological and musical boundaries. These records also underscore the way that Cash and Dylan, long after their public work together, produced, apparently completely by accident, one final conversation. This time the dialogue centered on an unfortunate woman named Delia.

On *World Gone Wrong,* accompanied only by his guitar, Dylan sings "Delia" with the emphasis on himself: "All the friends I ever had were gone." According to Dylan, "Delia" was a song about "counterfeit loyalty"—the misplaced loyalty of the "gambling girl," perhaps, but also of those absent friends as one faces the solitude of prison.[11] On *American Recordings,* Cash records "Delia's Gone," a song that shared roots with Dylan's "Delia." Cash's version emphasizes the blood and brutality as a larger part of the action. He makes sure to mention, for example, that he had to shoot her twice before she died. And yet, Cash's lyrics are much lighter, with the violence intended for laughs (his "submachine") and with remorse almost nonexistent. Delia's ghost—a significant but barely mentioned image in Dylan's song—is a main character in Cash's version, where it plays as more of a nuisance than a tragic reminder of a blood-soaked night gone wrong. In their separate recordings, Dylan and Cash explored the two basic sources of the song, with Dylan referencing Blind Willie McTell's "Little Delia" from the 1940s, and Cash echoing Blind Blake's "Delia's Gone" from the late 1920s.

Fusing the folk tradition to late-twentieth-century recordings, Dylan and Cash produced songs that testified to the determination of both men to translate the past for a contemporary audience. In 1964, in his famous public letter of support of Dylan, Cash makes the enigmatic comment that "a Lamp is Burning in All our Dark."[12] Perhaps proof of the progressive hope that so many people placed in Dylan and perhaps, too, a comment on the murky definitions of country and folk music, Cash's reference speaks to the shadow and light that so defined their conjoined careers. In a moment of symmetry, Dylan responded in kind in 2003 when *Rolling Stone* asked him to reflect on Cash's death. "Johnny was and is the North Star; you could guide your ship by him," Dylan wrote. Recalling an image of light once more, Dylan concludes: "I think we can have recollections of him, but we can't define him any more than we can define a fountain of truth, light and beauty."[13] Throughout their careers, Dylan and Cash sought to understand these lights and shadows—the ambiguity and complications within modern life—as they attempted to navigate the promise of American music.

Notes

1. Johnny Cash (with Patrick Carr), *Cash: The Autobiography* (San Francisco: HarperSanFrancisco, 2003), 268.

2. Ibid., 266.

3. As Benjamin Filene notes, Dylan began to see that the protest-song "movement" had crested. Benjamin Filene, *Romancing the Folk: Public Memory and American Roots Music* (Chapel Hill: University of North Carolina Press, 2000), 212, 213–15.

4. The most important book on these sessions remains Greil Marcus, *The Old, Weird America: The World of Bob Dylan's Basement Tapes* (New York: Picador, 2001).

5. Although several spelling variations exist for this song, in the interest of clarity, this paper will use the title "Belshazzar" for the recordings produced by both Johnny Cash and Bob Dylan. Cash's version first appeared as the B-side to "Wide Open Road" and can be found on Johnny Cash and the Tennessee Two, *The Complete Original Sun Singles* (Varese Records, 1999).

6. The story of King Belshazzar of Babylon and the "writing on the wall" is found in the Book of Daniel 5:1–31. Furthering the connection between the basement tapes and *John Wesley Harding*, Dylan drawls the word *Paradise* in "Belshazzar" with the exact intonation as in a later song with similar allegorical ambiguity: "The Ballad of Frankie Lee and Judas Priest."

7. Unreleased commercially, "Careless Love" can be found on various bootlegs of the Johnny Cash and Bob Dylan sessions.

8. Cash, *Cash*, 169.

9. Richard Goldstein, "Johnny Cash, 'Something Rude Showing,'" *Vogue*, August 15, 1969, reprinted in Michael Streissguth, *Ring of Fire: The Johnny Cash Reader* (Cambridge, Mass.: De Capo Press, 2002), 90.

10. Thomas Dearmore, "First Angry Man of Country Singers," *New York Times Magazine*, September 21, 1969, reprinted in Streissguth, *Ring of Fire*, 107.

11. Bob Dylan, liner notes to *World Gone Wrong* (Sony, 1993).

12. Johnny Cash, "Letter," *Broadside*, March 10, 1964, reprinted in Benjamin Hedin, ed., *Studio A: The Bob Dylan Reader* (New York: W. W. Norton and Company, 2004), 20–21.

13. Bob Dylan, "Remembering Johnny," *Rolling Stone*, October 16, 2003.

5. Allowed to Be Free:
Bob Dylan and the Civil Rights Movement
Charles Hughes

On October 16, 1992, three weeks before election day, Stevie Wonder took the stage at the Bob Dylan Thirtieth Anniversary Celebration to revisit the song that in 1966 gave him a number one rhythm-and-blues hit. His fingers striking stately gospel chords, Wonder introduced "Blowin' in the Wind" with personal, historical testimony: "The significance of this song to me," Wonder testified, "is that this is a song that will last unfortunately for a long, long time. And when I say unfortunately, I'm talking about the fact that it will always be relevant to something that is going on in this world of ours." He mentioned the civil rights movement, Vietnam, Watergate, Steven Biko and antiapartheid, and the fight to end starvation. "Today in the '90s, the song is still very relevant." With the gospel-based musical conversation building between singer, band, and audience, Wonder turned from his well-received history lesson to a direct call to the congregation, challenging the Madison Square Garden crowd to remember *their* obligations in the continuing freedom struggle: "And as you think about who you should vote for, I want you to vote for that person who is going to commit to bringing unity to all people, not only throughout the world but in this country." With the invocation concluded, and nearly three minutes into his performance, Wonder performed "Blowin' in the Wind" with an intensity that transcended even his own previous version. Wonder punctuated his soaring take on the song's crucial question—"How many years can some people exist before they're allowed to be free?"—with a cry of "Let my people go!" directly invoking the tradition of African-American resistance. On a night that sometimes felt like a memorial service, Stevie Wonder's living, breathing performance provided a clear reminder of Dylan's continuing relevance to ongoing struggles for justice and equality.

Understanding Bob Dylan's relationship to the black freedom struggle of the 1960s and beyond is not limited to an appreciation of his direct involvement with movement causes, nor even the role that he and his music played for activists and fellow artists. Indeed, while those factors are crucial, there is more to be learned by placing Dylan and his music in conversation with the ideological, strategic, and spiritual foundations from which the movement took its multiple shapes. Dylan's vision combined gospel redemption with scathing critiques of American society, an ideological combination exhibited by nearly every important strain of the civil rights movement, and most firmly linked by the Student Nonviolent Coordinating Committee (SNCC). It is little surprise that SNCC became Dylan's strongest movement connection. Even when Dylan "abandoned" protest music, his songs yet reflected deep questions of freedom, equality, and identity that spoke to similar concerns within SNCC, the movement, and—indeed—America. Dylan was by no means a central figure in the black freedom movement, but understanding his work in this way offers important perspectives. Recent writing has greatly complicated the previous narrative, particularly the work of Mike Marqusee, who explores Dylan's relationship to 1960s political moments and movements in unmatched detail.[1] Still, Marqusee's precedent should provoke further efforts to situate all facets of Dylan's connection to civil rights politics within larger contexts of African-American political and musical traditions, as well as within a fuller understanding of Dylan's personal ideology and worldview.

Although this political consciousness dates from his earliest Minnesota days, Dylan's direct involvement with civil rights activism began in his earliest New York days. His girlfriend Suze Rotolo was a volunteer for CORE, the Congress of Racial Equality, which in 1960 launched the tumultuous "Freedom Ride" campaigns. Rotolo suggests that although Dylan's love of Woody Guthrie and Pete Seeger had politicized him to a certain degree, civil rights "was new to him."[2] Dylan himself recalled that he "checked out" his early protest material with Rotolo's mother, a union activist who—according to Dylan—"was into this equality-freedom thing long before I was."[3] The influence of the Rotolo women (including Suze's sister Carla, also a CORE activist) inspired Dylan to perform at a CORE benefit in New York and to write a series of songs based around questions of racism and racial oppression. Even at this earliest stage, Dylan—who had listened to gospel and blues for years—engaged both the transcendent energies of the growing movement and its horrifying challenges. He performed "The Death of Emmett Till" at the CORE show, having lifted the melody from his friend, black songwriter Len Chandler (who is partially credited with popularizing "Eyes on the Prize" as movement anthem), and the lyrics from the news of Till's murder, which helped galvanize the movement of the 1950s.[4] "The Ballad of Donald White" was similarly inspired, although Rotolo suggests that "'Donald White' was only partly a journalistic approach. [Dylan] *felt*... it was more poetical."[5] In 1962, Dylan described the song's perspective: "When are some people gonna wake up and see that sometimes people aren't really their enemies but their victims?"[6]

Next to these narratives, which he often called "finger-pointing songs," Dylan also composed what Clinton Heylin describes as "rallying cries for the civil rights cause," assertive anthems of hope and perseverance that could perhaps be understood as "freedom songs," reflecting both their roots in gospel (such as "Ain't A-Gonna Grieve" or "Train A-Travelin," from these early years) and their ability to give voice to communities "in struggle."[7] "Paths of Victory," written in 1962 but not released until 1991, is perhaps the strongest example of the young Dylan keenly manipulating the sounds, themes, and spirit of the "freedom song" movement into his own writing. "Paths" bears striking resemblance, for example, to "Woke Up This Morning with My Mind on Freedom," particularly in the use of "walking" as insistent central action. As Marqusee argues, the "freedom songs, more even than . . . Guthrie, inspired Dylan to adapt traditional material to new ends," and Dylan's early "freedom songs"—most of which he recorded for *Broadside* magazine—were spiritual in musical foundation and just barely secular in metaphor and imagery.[8] His early covers also reflected both sides: in early shows, he occasionally performed versions of the spiritual "No More Auction Block," as well as "Black Cross," a Lord Buckley song concerning the murder of a literate black farmer by an ignorant white mob. On his debut album in 1961, Dylan includes a fierce take on "Gospel Plow," the church-based antecedent to "Eyes on the Prize."

Dylan's breakthrough second album, *The Freewheelin' Bob Dylan,* includes "Oxford Town," a deceptively playful ode to the home of the University of Mississippi, where federal troops clashed with the Mississippi National Guard over the right of James Meredith to attend classes at the segregated institution. Dylan's near-comic imagery is laced with recognition of the incident's near-tragic consequences: "Somebody better investigate soon," Dylan implores, echoing years of similar entreaties to the federal government by freedom fighters. Also included on *Freewheelin',* of course, is "Blowin' in the Wind," which Dylan readily admitted had black roots: "'Blowin' in the Wind' has always been a spiritual. I took it off a song called 'No More Auction Block'—that's a spiritual, and 'Blowin' in the Wind' sorta follows the same feeling."[9] The song deserves special mention for several reasons. First, it provided Dylan with his first hit, thanks to the decidedly *non-gospel* cover by Peter, Paul and Mary. Second, the lyrics reflect Dylan's dual conceptions of human struggle as, on one hand, the ongoing pursuit of the real meanings of freedom and equality, and, on the other, a series of specifically addressable issues, here in the form of provocative questions. Third, "Blowin' in the Wind" made a great impact on his black musical contemporaries, who received the song as both a powerful artistic call and a surprising source of inspiration. Mavis Staples, who met Dylan in 1962, remembered thinking "This is what my *father* went through. . . . So, where is he coming from?"[10] The Staple Singers later recorded the song, marking the first time the family released a single that was not explicitly gospel. Of course, as Mavis Staples understood, "[Dylan's] were inspirational songs . . . the same as gospel."[11] (Dylan later remembered being a regular attendee at weekly gospel shows at Madison Square Garden.)[12] Most famously, the song inspired Sam Cooke—excited and slightly angered by the fact that a white man had a hit with such unmasked politics—to write "A Change Is

Gonna Come," his majestically soulful anthem to the pain and promise of the constant struggle.[13] Over the years, many African-American artists have recorded "Blowin' in the Wind," with Cooke, Etta James, the Caravans, Duke Ellington, and the Edwin Hawkins Singers (among others) joining Stevie Wonder and the Staple Singers.

SNCC activist Sam Block was one of the many who heard "Blowin' in the Wind," and Block later suggested that Dylan was inspired to write the song after his visit to Greenwood, Mississippi, in 1963.[14] While this chronology is, frankly, impossible, it is not hard to imagine that Dylan's visit to one of the most turbulent battlegrounds of the freedom struggle and long-term exposure to SNCC's grassroots campaigns spoke to the same impulses that inspired both the transcendent and confrontational sides of Dylan's larger vision. SNCC began in 1960 as a reaction to attempts by both the Kennedy administration and the Martin Luther King–led Southern Christian Leadership Conference (SCLC) to influence—or perhaps co-opt—the activities of the southern college students (mostly, though not exclusively, black) whose actions and ideas had driven the pivotal sit-ins of 1960.[15] Guided by Ella Baker, the veteran activist whose broad swath of influence renders her one of the most influential figures of the twentieth century, SNCC organized itself around the principle of radical, nonviolent confrontations with white supremacy.[16] These ground-level struggles would be led and developed principally by local activists, rather than through the top-down leadership structure that Baker and others grew to resent in the NAACP and SCLC. "Strong people don't need strong leaders," Baker famously remarked, and—despite the presence of powerful and effective figures like Bob Moses, Diane Nash, and Julian Bond—SNCC built its "beloved community" of activists around local people already struggling for, in this case, voting rights in Mississippi.

For Dylan, who later remarked that "I wasn't going to fall for any kind of being a leader"—not to mention "don't follow leaders, watch your parking meters"— SNCC's youth, enthusiasm, decidedly nonconformist attitude, and radical blend of redemption and reckoning made for a near-perfect fit.[17] The appreciation seems to have been mutual. SNCC secretary James Forman, who oversaw many of the organization's early campaigns, consciously recruited Dylan.[18] In addition, original SNCC member Bob Zellner remembers the young Dylan performing at a variety of SNCC events in New York as his fame grew through 1962 and early 1963, helped into the fold by the stalwart Pete Seeger. The importance of having "stars," who could raise money and awareness, connected with the movement was crucial to its success, but Zellner also suggests that Dylan expressed notable enthusiasm at the chance to perform in collaboration with SNCC: Dylan "wanted to sing at all our events in Mississippi," he recalls.[19] (Zellner also remembers James Forman explaining how the celebrities "wanted to hang out with the movement 'stars.'")[20]

Despite Dylan's growing reputation as one of SNCC's most avid "star" allies, he had yet to get what Theodore Bikel called a "first-hand impression" of the front lines; Bikel thus urged Dylan to appear in Greenwood. Apparently, this immersion worked, since Bikel recalls Dylan's stunned reaction to "Jim Crow" society.[21] The previous months in Greenwood had been especially difficult, even in the soul-shaking contexts of SNCC's larger campaign.[22] In February, SNCC worker Jimmie Travis was nearly killed in a drive-by shooting perpetrated by white terrorists. In June, Mrs. Fannie Lou Hamer—one of the group's most important "local people"—and two companions were viciously beaten and sexually assaulted in the nearby Winona jail.[23] Beyond extreme violence, the ongoing repression of white supremacist forces and the active refusal of the Kennedy administration to follow through on a promised lawsuit against Greenwood's government made for very trying times for the "beloved community."

Into this came Dylan and company, performing at a small rally in the hazy Mississippi countryside, joining Pete Seeger, Len Chandler, and the SNCC Freedom Singers, the Georgia-based ensemble who performed at meetings across the South, had became folk-revival favorites, and had often shared bills with Dylan at previous SNCC fund-raisers.[24] In front of about three hundred black farmers, Dylan performed some of his newest material, including "Only a Pawn in Their Game," his striking examination of race and class in which he dared to argue for the relative insignificance of the man who assassinated Mississippi NAACP head Medgar Evers only weeks earlier, suggesting instead that the true guilt rested with those powerful men whose socioeconomic status helped them control not only blacks but poor whites.[25] Activist Dorothy Zellner recalls that day: "[Dylan] was extremely young. A very small guy, not very social. . . . He sang 'With God on Our Side,'" which Zellner considered "a very odd choice, [since] it was probably the black church, and the comfort that the black church provided, that had gotten people through hundreds of years of suffering."[26] Whether or not Dylan misread his audience—and judging by many accounts (including Zellner's), he was warmly received—it quickly became clear that his experience in Mississippi, most of which he spent traveling with the always endangered activists, gave him an even greater sense of connection to the group. "I know a lot of the people in SNCC," he explained, ". . . That's the only organization I feel a part of *spiritually*" [emphasis added].[27] The appreciation, again, was mutual: Zellner says that Dylan's appearance in Greenwood was "very important to us," and Gloria Clark—who worked for SNCC in Holly Springs, Mississippi, in 1964–65—remembers that at the SNCC freedom house was "when I first heard Dylan. Someone was always putting his album on the turntable. It was very compatible with what we were doing at the time."[28]

Dylan's visit to Greenwood helped him develop two important relationships with SNCC activists that he had begun forging in New York in 1962. Dylan met Cordell and Bernice Johnson Reagon, whose work for desegregation in Albany, Georgia, coincided with their formation of the SNCC Freedom Singers. Dylan loved the Freedom Singers and suggested they might be singing more relevant material than that printed in *Broadside:* "They're singing about themselves and the kind of lives they're living," Dylan remarked.[29] The Reagons proved lasting friends and influences for Dylan in the coming years, even after his exit from active politics. The

Freedom Singers ensemble sang with Dylan many times, including the famous finale at the 1963 Newport Folk Festival, where Dylan, the Freedom Singers, Joan Baez, Seeger, and Peter, Paul and Mary linked arms in versions of "Blowin' in the Wind" and "We Shall Overcome" in a powerful representation of the "black-and-white-together" idealism of the moment.[30] The community of artists and allies symbolized by the Freedom Singers captured Dylan's attentions both musically and ideologically.[31]

Dylan developed particular attachment to Bernice Johnson Reagon, whose profound mix of intellectual fervor, political passion, and musical genius led her from SNCC to Sweet Honey in the Rock, the black women's musical collective she founded nearly four decades ago, to her acclaimed work as author, teacher, and archivist. "He was fascinated with Bernice Reagon," Dorothy Zellner remembers of Greenwood, "and the two of them sat there and sang."[32] Dylan's long-rumored crush on Reagon is supposed to have led him to write "To Ramona," which certainly fuels suspicion with its images of the entrancing woman whose work in the South is keeping her from Dylan's desperate affections. (Marquee offers a particularly eloquent analysis of this theory in *Chimes of Freedom,* his towering examination of Dylan's relationship to the politics of the 1960s.)[33] Reagon, who impressed Dylan in New York in 1962 with her ability to sing the many lyrics to Dylan's millennial ballad "A Hard Rain's A-Gonna Fall," has long expressed (platonic) admiration for her counterpart: "We all thought," she later attested, "those of us in the movement and those of us in the Freedom Singers, that Dylan was fantastic as a songwriter and as a person."[34]

Dylan's experiences with SNCC were proving as important a touchstone as the Beat poets and folk revival. While my sense differs from Dorothy Zellner's of the distance between the critical vision of "With God on Our Side" and the revolutionary tenets of Afro-Christianity, of which black Mississippians like those in Greenwood would certainly have been aware, the song most definitely interrogates the notion of basing political ideology in religious terms: in 1966, while being questioned about his exit from politics, Dylan fumed that "people that use God as a weapon should be amputated upon. . . . People that march with slogans and things tend to take themselves a little too holy. It would be a drag if they, too, started using God as a weapon."[35] (SNCC activists, who used to poke fun at Martin Luther King by referring to him as "De Lawd," might not disagree.) There is also the recorded version of "Only a Pawn in Their Game." Much as Dylan echoes, among others, Frederick Douglass, who perceived economic and racial relationships as inherently linked, Dylan's conception stood in concert with increasing articulations of these issues within the movement, issues that—though ageless in African-American political thought—did not always have political traction.[36] Even though Ella Baker, as early as 1960, had warned that the cause was far greater than access—"more than a hamburger," she put it, in reference to lunch counters—it was in the second half of the decade when nearly all sectors of the movement—from Martin Luther King to Fannie Lou Hamer to the Nation of Islam—began to more forcefully argue for the significance of class in understanding racism and racial oppression. Nonetheless, the "pawn," Byron De La Beckwith, remained unconvicted of Evers's murder for thirty years, so Dylan's argument for the greater complicity of the system than the person remains notable. Howard Romaine, with a long record of involvement with SNCC, the NAACP, and other organizations, remembered the song vividly forty years later: "it was an awakening prophetic cry which penetrated to the core," he described, suggesting that "the SONG CAME THRU" [emphasis in original] where other writing on racial justice did not. "[The song] led me and others from the Memphis NAACP to Mississippi Freedom Summer, where we heard [activist] Margaret Burnham singing the words as we came in," Romaine remembered.[37]

In "The Lonesome Death of Hattie Carroll," Dylan is unafraid to condemn both William Zanzinger and the unjust system that freed him. As Dylan warns against the desire to abstractly "philosophize disgrace," his rhetorical approach to describing this atrocity recalls the anti-lynching campaigns of Ida B. Wells-Barnett, who accompanied heart-wrenchingly specific stories of injustice with forceful admonitions to enact concrete changes.[38]

Accompanying angry condemnation, once again, is a vision of gospel transcendence, this time in the form of "When the Ship Comes In." (Dylan later remarked that Patti LaBelle should cover the song, signaling his recognition of its gospel-soul roots.)[39] Here, even more strongly than in previous biblical visions, Dylan combines the movement's dual revolutionary ideologies: the vision is millennial, but the desired response is immediate change, just as James Baldwin (who frequented some of the same Greenwich Village clubs as Dylan) warned of in *The Fire Next Time*.[40] The ship shares its triumphant power with the train of—among literally countless others—the Impressions' "People Get Ready," later covered by Dylan, in which Curtis Mayfield drew on gospel tradition to craft a similar vision of the new day dawning. Dylan's ship also possesses the power to defeat the "foes" who would hold back the tide of justice. He suggests that the "whole wide world is watchin'" as the apocalyptic upheavals take place: "like Pharaoh's tribe, they'll be drowned in the tide / And like Goliath, they'll be conquered." At the March on Washington on August 28, 1963, Dylan, introduced by actor Ossie Davis, played "When the Ship Comes In," the righteous voice of gospel vindication, and "Only a Pawn in Their Game," the bluesy voice of anger.[41] Martin Luther King's speech itself demonstrated this duality: while "I Have a Dream" is more famous and ultimately more compelling, the "dream" section of the speech was essentially improvised, with gospel singer Mahalia Jackson urging King (on the platform) to include that section, which King had delivered as part of a previous sermon. King's original speech consisted of an extended meditation on the unpaid debt—King's metaphor was the "cancelled check"—yet owed to black Americans. In addition, although SNCC leader John Lewis's radical comments were famously censored by skittish march organizers—who feared exploding the fragile alliance between the movement and the Kennedy White House—Lewis was still able to present a blunted version of his attack on disconnected politicians who failed to sufficiently support activists daily bleeding for their rights. Despite the infighting and SNCC's ultimate ambivalence toward the event, the march gained a reputation as a peak of the struggle's early energy.[42]

However, like many of his SNCC friends, Dylan expressed skepticism. According to William McKeen, "Dylan wondered aloud to a friend what effect it would have on America, on the millions watching the event on television. 'Think they're listening?' he asked, nodding towards the dome of the capitol in the distance. 'No, they ain't listening at all.'"[43] Whether or not the "whole wide world" was watching that August day, getting a fair hearing on the true meanings of freedom and justice proved a hard road to travel in the coming years. The civil rights movement never possessed ideological unity or even strategic consensus, and Dylan's work never fit into his much-disdained categories of "topical" or "protest" categories, but the March on Washington yet remains a symbolic hinge point.

Dylan articulated some of these transitions on *Another Side of Bob Dylan*, released in the summer of 1964. Alongside "Chimes of Freedom" (the richly textured chronicle of human struggle and survival that Dylan composed on travels with SNCC to southern schools Emory University and Tougaloo College) sits "My Back Pages," usually pointed to as Dylan's most direct commentary on his increasing political detachment. What Dylan seems to be attacking most strongly in "My Back Pages" is *pride,* or at least unquestioned self-assurance. "I've never been able to understand . . . the seriousness of pride," he once observed. "People talk, act, live as if they're never going to die. And what do they leave behind? Nothing. Nothing but a mask."[44] Even SNCC fell under Dylan's sharpening eye: "I tell you, I'm never going to have anything to do with any political organization again in my life."[45]

Dylan's shift in perspectives aligns well with similar moments of transition throughout the freedom movement and make this material as "relevant" as earlier, more explicitly "political" songs. The disillusionment of "My Back Pages" and other songs of this period has less to do with an abandonment of the *idea* of freedom or equality, and more with his refusal to commit to the limitations of specific *causes.* The difference may seem hairsplitting, but—in 1966—he made it plain, again responding to charges that he had abandoned the struggle: "[It's] not pointless to dedicate yourself to peace and racial equality, but rather, it's pointless to dedicate yourself to the *cause.* . . . They're all afraid to admit that they don't really know each other."[46] Here, again, Dylan echoes the writing of Douglass, Baldwin, Ralph Ellison, Richard Wright, and others who—in quite explicit terms—all undertook to explore the negative effects on personal freedom of strict adherence to political doctrine.[47] As Marqusee points out, Dylan here also echoes women in SNCC and elsewhere who too criticized that the movement did not "practice what it preached" when it came to gender roles and chauvinism.[48]

Throughout his heady musings in this period, Dylan also gestured to growing questions over interracialism in the civil rights movement. SNCC expelled its white members in 1966, and an entirely new breed of white opposition emerged once the freedom movement moved north, to Chicago or Milwaukee. Dylan addressed this issue with an honesty that many blacks found lacking in other white allies: "I do be-lieve in equality, but I also believe in distance," he remarked. When asked, "Do you mean people keeping their racial distance?" Dylan replied, "I believe in people keeping everything they've got."[49] Dylan's words here seem as close to black nation-alism as they do to political apostasy or segregationism, recalling his similarity to Malcolm X when speaking of friends in Harlem—"some of them junkies, all of them poor"—who need freedom as much as anybody else. "What's anybody doing for *them*?" Dylan implores.[50]

Earlier, Dylan admitted: "[It's] not that I'm pessimistic about Negroes' rights, but the word Negro sounds foolish coming from my mouth. What's a Negro? I don't know what a Negro is."[51] In these remarks, Dylan was referencing his infamous acceptance speech at the 1963 awards dinner of the Emergency Civil Liberties Committee (ECLC). On that night, Dylan—at the height of his status as the Left's darling spokesman—challenged the previous generation's activists to not only "get out of the new [world] if you can't lend a hand," but also to recognize the hypocrisy of their lavish affair. At one point, Dylan even criticized his fellow March on Wash-ington participants: "I looked around at all the negroes there and I didn't see any negroes that looked like none of my friends. My friends don't wear suits. My friends don't have to wear any kind of thing to prove they're respectable negroes."[52] Dylan oversimplifies the issue, particularly in terms of the complicated role of "respectabil-ity" within black political history, but he is certainly hinting at the rejection of "white-ness" that defined "Black Power." Accepting the award in part on behalf of James Forman, Dylan left the audience in a state of stunned discomfort, which would revisit him when he blasted into "Maggie's Farm," his electrified work song, at the Newport Folk Festival in 1965.

Dave Marsh recently examined Dylan's apology letter to the ECLC, and finds this document more revealing than the actual speech. As Marsh points out, Dylan speaks again directly to the growing, pivotal issue over the role of white participa-tion in the black freedom movement. "It showed Dylan acting out," writes Marsh, "...the principle over which SNCC 'broke'—that white people needed to be ad-dressing the problems of white people in their communities, not trying to solve problems for black people in black communities."[53] (Perhaps, as Dylan put it earlier, people "keeping everything they've got.") This was, Marsh finds, not the only pre-scient part of Dylan's remarks: he mentions the struggle in Selma, Alabama, over a year before the country's attention turned there.[54]

Just as "civil rights" and "black power" do not divide neatly into two separate periods or ideologies, so too does Dylan's work challenge simplified narratives. "Ballad of a Thin Man" is probably the most famously political of his 1965–66 cre-ative burst, although the biblical metaphors of "Gates of Eden" and lynching imagery of "Desolation Row," for example, suggest other continuities. Over minor-key piano blues, Dylan lambastes the foolish "Mr. Jones" for his inability to grasp the changing nature of the game. While the song was taken up by any number of young radicals, perhaps the most surprising—and telling—use of the song was by the Black Panther Party. Huey Newton was inspired to write his first position paper after he and Bobby Seale listened to the song repeatedly. "The song is hell," Seale described. "You've got to understand that this song is saying a hell of a lot about society."[55] Scholar Lary May, a UCLA graduate student in the late 1960s, remembers attending a speech by influential Panther Eldridge Cleaver where "Ballad of a Thin Man" was played over the loudspeaker both directly preceding and following Cleaver's comments.[56]

Other black activists, too, recognized that Dylan still had a "hell of a lot" to say about American life. (After all, Gloria Clark remembers hearing Dylan in Mississippi in 1965.) In a most telling comment, Bernice Johnson Reagon hints at the reason: "Some whites moved with us out of some special sort of love for blacks, while others were just loaded with guilt. Dylan wasn't the same. When he simply drifted away from the movement, it was the whites in [SNCC] who were resentful. The blacks in [SNCC] didn't think that, or say that. We only heard the phrase 'sellout' from the whites, not from the blacks."[57] Reagon's words second Marsh's observation about the similar questions facing Dylan and SNCC over white participation in the movement, and also point to potentially even deeper links between Dylan's understanding of the struggle for justice and those of his African-American allies; once again, Dylan combines the specific contexts with the overarching questions. These complications are simply missing in any study of Dylan that does not foreground his relationship with SNCC, the movement, and African-American traditions of resistance, which—of course—include black music.

Black musical responses to Dylan in this period are perhaps even more striking than Reagon's words. The Staple Singers—active supporters of movement causes—continued to cover their old friend's work, including a startling version of "A Hard Rain's A-Gonna Fall" in which the Staples transform the song's balladry and unearth the call-and-response seemingly inherent in the lyric's Revelations-esque litany. (It is also noteworthy, though unsurprising, that the Staples change "blue-eyed son" to "wandering son," thus deracinating—or at least "de-whitening"—the song's protagonist.) Their version of "Hard Rain" is a rare cut sung by Pervis, the group's only male child, who—according to his little sister Mavis—became "really tight buddies" with Dylan in these years.[58] Dylan had long loved the group's sound, telling one interviewer that his three favorite performers were the Staple Singers, Rasputin, and Charles de Gaulle, and grew to have a special fondness for Mavis.[59] "We actually courted back in the sixties," Staples later revealed. "Bobby was a cutie and I was a cutie too."[60] (Many accounts have Dylan asking Pops Staples for Mavis's hand in marriage; Pops responded that Dylan would have to check with her.) Beyond being "cuties," Mavis understood the deeper link: "We kind of bonded, in a way, music-wise, you know. . . . What we were singing and what he was writing."[61] This bond led to a clear exchange of influences: the Stapleses' signature "folk-soul" sound (and mind-set) owed much to Dylan's example, and Dylan—who has worked with Mavis on occasion—was clearly affected by her voice but also by Pops's distinctive guitar, a bluesy and reverb-drenched sound that Dylan echoed on many of his recent recordings. (Pops Staples also long believed that Dylan wrote his early antiwar song "John Brown" for him to record.)[62]

The Staples were not alone in admiring Dylan. A few notable examples include Stevie Wonder, who took his gospel-soul cover of "Blowin' in the Wind" to the top of the rhythm-and-blues charts in 1966; Jimi Hendrix, who legendarily recorded a blazing take on the apocalyptic "All along the Watchtower"; and Nina Simone, whose musical and political development in many ways paralleled that of Dylan and who recorded a variety of his songs throughout her career. By the time Simone recorded her Dylan covers, she was—like the Staples—intimately associated with the radical end of the black freedom struggle. Simone selected covers from across Dylan's catalog, recording compelling takes on "Ballad of Hollis Brown," "The Times They Are A-Changin'," "Just Like a Woman," "Just Like Tom Thumb's Blues," and "I Shall Be Released." Simone finds common interpretive opportunity in these songs, despite their differing lyrical and musical textures, and often—as on the aching, gospel-jazz version of "The Times They Are A-Changin'"—imbues them with a distinctly *black* sound. Like Hendrix's "Watchtower," Simone's recording of "I Shall Be Released" demonstrates that—even after his motorcycle accident— black artists responded to Dylan's growing catalog. Dylan later returned to the gospel sounds and sentiments of "I Shall Be Released" at a 1986 tribute show for Martin Luther King, for whom Dylan continues to express admiration. At the show, he added a new lyric, asserting the urgency of immediate redemption and signifying on Wilson Pickett's legendary soul hit: "You're laughing now, you should be praying / This being the midnight hour of your life."[63]

Ironically, when Dylan returned to explicitly "civil rights"–linked discussions of freedom and justice in the next decades, he did so with the kind of "finger-pointing" songs that gave him such early inspiration. Just as "Emmett Till," "Donald White," "Hattie Carroll," and even "Only a Pawn in Their Game" examined larger wrong through the details of a specific atrocity, Dylan took a similarly narrative approach in "George Jackson" and "Hurricane." Dylan was now writing in a much different context: many movement leaders, activists, and symbolic heroes were dead or in jail, including "Soledad Brother" Jackson and boxer Rubin Carter, who sent Dylan his autobiography because of Dylan's reputation as a defender of civil rights. Oddly, as critical as Dylan became of journalistic songwriting, his elegy to Jackson and especially his Carter broadside sound quite like the "protest music" he earlier sought to escape. ("Hurricane" was even used as an anthem for the "Free Rubin Carter" campaign.) Rock critic Lester Bangs, for one, was not convinced:

> Look at it this way: every four years Dylan writes a "new" protest song and it's always about a martyred nigger and he always throws in a dirty word to make it more street-authentic. . . . Dylan doesn't give a damn about Rubin Carter. . . . Dylan merely used Civil Rights and the rest of the movement to advance himself in the first place.[64]

Bangs dug deeper:

> "Hurricane," like many Dylan songs of his distant past, purports to be a diatribe expressing abhorrence of racism, but there are many forms of inverted, benevolent prejudice known to the liberal mentality.... Maybe that's what enables Rubin Carter to sit like Buddha in a ten-foot cell.[65]

In light of Bangs's criticism, this is a convenient place to stress the danger in idealizing Dylan's relationship to black politics. First of all, other "folk revival" artists did far more to consistently and actively support movement issues and activists. Besides Seeger, Baez, Odetta (whose acoustic gospel, blues, and folk proved crucial for Dylan's artistic development), and Len Chandler, there is Harry Belafonte, who—though often set up on the inauthentic "pop" side of the musical equation—may well have contributed more time and money to the movement than any other entertainer. Second, even the most popular artists of the "folk revival"—or later "folk-rock"—had only limited importance for most black audiences, who drew far greater inspiration from rhythm and blues, soul, and gospel music. Third, there is the issue of gender, which—with important exceptions—bears little of the nuance of Dylan's portrayals of race and identity. While a full examination of this issue requires far more space than can be afforded here, one significant entry point has been provided by Daphne Brooks and Gayle Wald, who posit the covering of Dylan songs by female artists (mostly black) as not merely a sign of his ongoing resonance with some of music's most gifted women, but also as the assertive reinterpretation of the meanings of the songs and the subjectivity of their black female performers.[66] Finally, there is no doubt that Dylan sometimes expressed the idealization of blackness, black people, and black culture that befell many sympathetic whites during this period, a flaw that is certainly not unique to Dylan but—with Bangs's words as provocative reminder—nonetheless deserves to be restated.

In many ways, Dylan's most important later contributions to the musical and ideological mix that he brought to his movement songs are found in his Christian period. Here, explicitly playing gospel (in both word and sound), Dylan returned to the dual themes of redemption and reckoning. "Gotta Serve Somebody" foregrounds themes of personal choice and responsibility that remained common within movement rhetoric. On "When He Returns," Dylan explicitly asks, "How long can I listen to the lies of prejudice?" Most of all, the insistent "Pressing On," in every important respect, directly recalls the "freedom songs" of earlier eras. The revelatory *Gotta Serve Somebody* project of 2005, in which talented gospel artists (as well as soul survivors Mavis Staples and Aaron Neville) recorded selections from Dylan's "Christian era" material, contains a powerful recording of "Pressing On" by the Chicago Mass Choir and Regina McCrary, which—complete with the "keep pushing" echo of Curtis Mayfield—makes the connections between Dylan's songs and "Negro spirituals" drawn by choirmaster Louvinia Pointer in the accompanying documentary even more abundantly clear.[67]

Putting Dylan in conversation with "Negro spirituals," movement-era "freedom songs," and the fertile artistic landscapes of contemporary African-American artists offers an important, multifaceted opportunity to contextualize his work within longer, larger traditions of African-American struggle, traditions that reached one of their highest historical peaks during the years when the young singer-songwriter from Minnesota received much of his musical and political education.[68] Although he remains unpredictable, Dylan himself seems interested in maintaining these connections. He appeared at the Apollo Theater in 2004, on the seventieth anniversary of the famed venue. Once again, he was introduced by Ossie Davis, who began by speaking of Dylan's influence on Sam Cooke and the importance of both "Blowin' in the Wind" and "A Change Is Gonna Come" as movement anthems. Davis then recounted the story of the March on Washington, before telling the Apollo audience that he was "pleased—nay, happy—to reintroduce this artist again tonight."[69] Dylan, who early in his career said he was afraid to play at the Apollo due to its famously critical denizens, then played "A Change Is Gonna Come."[70] In his autobiography Dylan says of the song: "Sometimes you know things have to change, are going to change, but only you can feel it—like in that song of Sam Cooke's, 'Change Is Gonna Come'—but you don't know it in a purposeful way."[71] By responding to Cooke's call, itself a response to "Blowin' in the Wind," Dylan was—in his typically unpredictable way—once again placing himself in conversation with the music and politics of the civil rights era, a deep river containing—as Dylan suggests—both thought and feeling. The timeless lessons can be applied to razor-sharp specifics of the moment, in the finest tradition of his SNCC friends and allies. Redemptive visions of justice remain intermingled with unflinching sociopolitical reckoning. People are still not free. Goliath waits to be conquered.

Notes

1. See Mike Marqusee, *Chimes of Freedom: The Politics of Bob Dylan's Art* (London: New Press, 2003).

2. David Hajdu, *Positively Fourth Street: The Lives and Times of Joan Baez, Bob Dylan, Mimi Baez Farina, and Richard Farina* (New York: North Point Press, 2002), 108. For more information, see Rotolo's autobiography: Suze Rotolo, *A Freewheelin' Time: A Memoir of Greenwich Village in the Sixties* (New York: Broadway Press, 2008).

3. Hajdu, *Positively Fourth Street,* 107.

4. Ibid.

5. Anthony Scaduto, *Bob Dylan: An Intimate Biography* (New York: Gossett and Dunlap, 1971), 116.

6. Quoted in Hajdu, *Positively Fourth Street,* 118.

7. Clinton Heylin, *Bob Dylan: Behind the Shades Revisited* (New York: Harper, 2003), 114.

8. Marqusee, *Chimes of Freedom,* 46.

9. Interview quoted in Todd Harvey, *The Formative Dylan: Transmission and Stylistic Influences, 1961–1963* (New York: Scarecrow Press, 2001), 15.

10. From interview with Mavis Staples, *No Direction Home,* directed by Martin Scorsese (Hollywood, Calif.: Paramount Pictures, 2005).

11. Ibid.

12. Jonathan Cott, interview, *Rolling Stone,* November 16, 1978, in Jonathan Cott, *Bob Dylan: The Essential Interviews* (New York: Wenner Books, 2006).

13. See Daniel J. Wolff, *You Send Me: The Life of Sam Cooke* (New York: Quill Press, 1996), 281.

14. Quoted in Pete Seeger and Bob Reiser, *Everybody Says Freedom* (New York: Norton, 1989), 166–67.

15. For the sit-ins, see William Chafe, *Civilities and Civil Rights: Greensboro, North Carolina, and the Black Struggle for Freedom* (New York: Oxford University, 1981). For a larger examination of SNCC, see Clayborne Carson, *In Struggle: SNCC and the Black Awakening of the 1960s* (Cambridge, Mass.: Harvard University Press, 1995). For specific discussions of SNCC's work in Mississippi, see John Dittmer, *Local People: The Struggle for Civil Rights in Mississippi* (Champaign: University of Illinois Press, 1995); and Charles Payne, *I've Got the Light of Freedom: The Organizing Tradition and the Mississippi Freedom Struggle* (Berkeley: University of California Press, 2007).

16. Unquestionably, the best extended work on Ella Baker is Barbara Ransby, *Ella Baker and the Black Freedom Struggle: A Radical Democratic Vision* (Chapel Hill: University of North Carolina Press, 2005).

17. Quoted in Scaduto, *Bob Dylan,* 269.

18. See Dave Marsh, "Message from Bob Dylan: A Direction Home," CounterPunch.org, October 1, 2005.

19. Bob Zellner, with Constance Curry, *The Wrong Side of Murder Creek: A White Southerner in the Freedom Movement* (Montgomery, Ala.: New South Books, 2008), 272–73.

20. Ibid.

21. Quoted in Marqusee, *Chimes of Freedom,* 74.

22. See Payne, *I've Got the Light of Freedom,* 132–80; and Carson, *In Struggle,* 111–33.

23. For more on Mrs. Hamer, see Chana Kai Lee, *For Freedom's Sake: The Life of Fannie Lou Hamer* (Champaign: University of Illinois Press, 2000).

24. See "Northern Folk Singers Help Out at Negro Festival in Mississippi," *New York Times,* July 6, 1963, reprinted in Craig McGregor, *Bob Dylan: The Early Years (A Retrospective)* (New York: Da Capo, 1990), 85.

25. Footage of this performance appears in *Dont Look Back,* directed by D. A. Pennebaker (Pennebaker Films, 1967); and in *No Direction Home,* directed by Scorsese.

26. Dorothy Zellner, interview by author, March 15, 2007.

27. Nat Hentoff, "The Crackin', Shakin', Breakin' Sounds," *The New Yorker,* October 24, 1964, in Benjamin Hedin, *Studio A: The Bob Dylan Reader* (New York: Norton, 2004), 26.

28. Zellner, interview. Gloria Clark, e-mail in possession of author, March 14, 2007.

29. Robert Shelton, *No Direction Home: The Life and Music of Bob Dylan* (New York: Da Capo, 2003), 149.

30. Footage from this performance appears in *No Direction Home,* directed by Scorsese.

31. Cott, interview, *Rolling Stone,* November 16, 1978, in Cott, *Essential Interviews,* 267.

32. Zellner, interview. A photo of Dylan in Greenwood shows Dylan and Reagon sitting next to, and presumably singing or speaking with, each other. See Danny Lyon, *Memories of the Southern Civil Rights Movement* (Chapel Hill: University of North Carolina Press, 1992), 10.

33. See Marqusee, *Chimes of Freedom,* 107–9.

34. Quoted in Shelton, *No Direction Home,* 149–50.

35. Bob Dylan, interview, in Ron Rosenbaum, "Playboy Interview: Bob Dylan," *Playboy,* February 1966, http://www.interferenza.com/bcs/interw/play78.htm.

36. See Frederick Douglass, *My Bondage and My Freedom* (Ann Arbor: University of Michigan Press, 2006).

37. Howard Romaine, e-mail in possession of author, March 30, 2007. Romaine begins this e-mail by perfectly transcribing—supposedly from memory—the song's first three verses.

38. See Ida B. Wells, *Southern Horrors and Other Writings: The Anti-Lynching Campaign of Ida B. Wells, 1892–1900,* ed. Jacqueline Jones Royster (New York: Bedford/St. Martin's Press, 1996).

39. Quoted in Paul Zollo, "The Songtalk Interview," 1991, reprinted in Jim Ellison, *Younger Than That Now: The Collected Interviews with Bob Dylan* (New York: Thunder's Mouth Press, 2004), 262.

40. See James Baldwin, *The Fire Next Time* (New York: Modern Library, 1996).

41. Dylan returned to "When the Ship Comes In" two decades later, at the Live Aid concert for African starvation relief, where he famously—and controversially—remarked that some of the fund-raising should go to help the desperate straits of American family farmers.

42. For a Dylan-specific analysis of the March on Washington, see Marqusee, *Chimes of Freedom,* 1–10.

43. William McKeen, *Bob Dylan: A Bio-Bibliography* (New York: Greenwood Press, 1993), 25.

44. Scott Cohen, "Bob Dylan Not Like a Rolling Stone Interview," *Spin,* December 1985, reprinted in Ellison, *Younger Than That Now,* 231.

45. Hentoff, "The Crackin', Shakin', Breakin' Sounds," in Hedin, *Studio A,* 37.

46. Rosenbaum, "Playboy Interview."

47. Ralph Ellison engages this issue throughout his groundbreaking *Invisible Man,* and Richard Wright makes it a central element to the later sections of his novel *The Outsider.*

48. Marqusee, *Chimes of Freedom,* 111. For a view of women in SNCC, see Constance Curry et al., *Deep in Our Hearts: Nine White Women in the Civil Rights Movement* (Athens: University of Georgia Press, 2000).

49. Rosenbaum, "Playboy Interview."

50. Hentoff, "The Crackin', Shakin', Breakin' Sounds," in Hedin, *Studio A,* 38.

51. Shelton, quoted in Marqusee, *Chimes of Freedom,* 110.

52. Speech quoted in Marqusee, *Chimes of Freedom,* 88.

53. Marsh, "Message from Bob Dylan."

54. Ibid.

55. Bobby Seale, *Seize the Time: The Story of the Black Panther Party and Huey P. Newton* (New York: Black Classic Press), 90.

56. Lary May shared this recollection with the author on March 27, 2007.

57. Quoted in Shelton, *No Direction Home,* 350.

58. David Cantwell, "Mavis Staples: The Circle and the Moan," www.livinginstereo.com.

59. Bob Dylan quoted in "Austin Interview," 1965, in McGregor, *Bob Dylan,* 163.

60. Cantwell, "Mavis Staples."

61. Mavis Staples, interview, in *No Direction Home,* directed by Scorsese.

62. Shelton, *No Direction Home,* 151.

63. Heylin, *Bob Dylan,* 589. Greil Marcus's foundational work on this period of Dylan's career explores this material and its deeper roots in great and eloquent detail. See Greil Marcus, *The Old Weird America: The World of Bob Dylan's Basement Tapes* (New York: Picador Press, 2001).

64. Lester Bangs, "Bob Dylan's Alliance with Mafia Chic," *Creem,* April 1976, in *The Dylan Companion,* ed. Elizabeth Thompson and David Gutman (New York: Da Capo, 2005), 210–11.

65. Ibid., 212–13.

66. See Daphne Brooks and Gayle Wald, "Women Do Dylan: The Aesthetics and Politics of Dylan Covers," chapter 14, this volume.

67. Louvinia Pointer, interview, in *Gotta Serve Somebody,* directed by Jeffrey Gatskill (Image Entertainment, 2006).

68. Writer Greg Tate recently offered another aspect of these discussions, framing Dylan's recent work in the context of the West African trickster figure "elegba eshu." See Tate, "Intelligence Data," in Hedin, *Studio A,* 276–77.

69. Greil Marcus, *Like a Rolling Stone: Bob Dylan at the Crossroads* (New York: PublicAffairs, 2006), 41–42.

70. Ibid.

71. Bob Dylan, *Chronicles, Volume 1* (New York: Simon and Schuster, 2004), 61–62.

PART II. **PLANET WAVES**

6. Lives of Allegory:
Bob Dylan and Andy Warhol
Thomas Crow

Bob Dylan's British tour in May 1965 had given him his first real taste of pop-star adulation, both in terms of ecstatically adoring crowds and record sales that thrust his older albums simultaneously into the UK top twenty—a phenomenon that reverberated back to America but without the same degree of chart success.[1] He certainly took notice of the spectacular inroads into the American mass market by the top British bands, making one abortive attempt during his London stay to record with an all-star group of blues rockers (which included Eric Clapton).[2] But he groped for new musical ideas of his own, and it was unclear how he could match the popularity of hit cover versions of his old songs by the Animals and the Byrds. Friendship with the Beatles redoubled his envious astonishment at their ability to combine aesthetic experimentation with mass success, while the all-acoustic concerts that he was playing in Britain—essentially greatest-hits packages—felt to him repetitive and stale.[3]

Just at that juncture, Dylan's orbit was crashed by another set of emerging international celebrities branded as Pop. Just as his British tour was concluding with two concerts at the Royal Albert Hall, Andy Warhol and Edie Sedgwick turned up in London (accompanied by helpmates Gerard Malanga and Chuck Wein).[4] The group had been flown to Paris by the dealer Ileana Sonnabend, who was staging an exhibition of Warhol's flower paintings; while there, they had been greeted by excited crowds and delirious responses in the French press—never known for sympathy to anything branded as American. After making a public announcement that he was renouncing painting in favor of movie making, Warhol took his excited group on to London, where they were anything but invisible. They joined the audience at a reading by Allen Ginsberg, who was then spending most of his time in the Dylan entourage. They spent time with Warhol's London dealer of the time, Robert Fraser, who derived a large measure of cachet from his public friendships with the Beatles, Rolling Stones, Marianne Faithfull (all present at the Albert Hall concerts), and others of Dylan's peers in the music elite. The same can be said of photographers David Bailey and Michael Cooper, both of whom photographed the Warhol group during their time in London.

Bob Neuwirth, famously along for the ride during the British tour, recalls no encounters with the Warhol party in London.[5] But he and Dylan had known Sedgwick well since December of the previous year.[6] In a larger sense, Dylan's attention—never less than alert to the slightest shifts in his surroundings—had to have been drawn in some measure to the wave of international enthusiasm over Pop Art. Fraser had become a celebrity in his own right via his simultaneous prominence in the realms of Pop Art and pop music. At just that moment, The Who were undergoing a publicity makeover whereby their canny manager was seeking to distinguish his powerful emerging group by identifying them with the visual markers of Pop Art. Drummer Keith Moon appears in contemporary publicity photographs wearing T-shirts emblazoned with Jasper Johns–style targets. Pete Townshend, for his part, adopted a jacket tailored from the Union Jack as trademark and indirect homage to Johns's famous paintings of the American national symbol.[7] "The Who are linking their image with pop art," reported the music weekly *Melody Maker* just after

Photograph of The Who, later used as cover of the single "Substitute/Instant Party." Michael Ochs Archives/Stringer. Copyright 2007 Getty Images.

Dylan's departure, "They describe their current chart success, 'Anyway, Anyhow, Anywhere', as 'the first pop art single.'"[8] The campaign took hold: A photograph of Dylan on his next trip to London captured him beneath the iconic Pop Art image of the band.

Looking back on the seismic change that "Like a Rolling Stone" had effected in his old Greenwich Village scene, Dylan later reflected that folk music had "got swept away by fashionable things.... British invasions and pop art and medium-is-the-message type of things."[9] And while he offered this observation with a note of regret, he returned to America at the beginning of June 1965 immersed in precisely these currents, and they fortified him as he faced down the entrenched folk-revival subculture. Alongside the provocation of electric instrumentation and drum kit, his style of dress left behind all traces of working-man's authenticity in favor of Carnaby Street plumage in striking colors and patterns.

As he returned from England at the beginning of June, he began to fill some six to perhaps twenty pages with barely connected verse, prose, and song lyrics, from which a musical, singable core only latterly emerged—and with it a fresh and urgent sense, so he tells it, of how to go on: "I knew I had to sing it with a band. I always sing when I write, even prose, and I heard it like that."[10]

What he heard in his head he appears to have found at those legendary mid-June sessions that produced "Like a Rolling Stone." There then intervened some six weeks of frenzied new songwriting to generate the remainder of the tracks on the album *Highway 61 Revisited*.[11] "'Like a Rolling Stone' changed it all," he later reflected, "I didn't care anymore after that about writing books or poems or whatever."[12] But a restless preoccupation with the claims of other creative pursuits—not just his frustrations with the promised novel *Tarantula* but visual art in particular—stayed with him. In an interview conducted that August, he manifests a seemingly gratuitous hostility to the precious status enjoyed by painting:[13] "Have you ever been in a museum? Museums are cemeteries. Paintings should be on the walls of restaurants, in dime stores, in gas stations, in men's rooms. Great paintings should be where people hang out.... It's not the bomb that has to go, man, it's the museums." The vehemence of this judgment suggests he had been brooding on the subject, in particular, disputing the claim that painting could ever be truly Pop: "The only thing where it's happening is on the radio and records," he insists by way of contrast, "Music is the only thing that's in tune with what's happening."

Dylan soon found the opportunity to manifest that disdain and sense of aggrieved rivalry with pictorial art in the person of Warhol himself. An invitation in late July to sit for a Factory *Screen Test* turned into something of a ceremonial visit in the company of a large entourage.[14] Photographer Nat Finkelstein's pictures of the event record a scene of wary confrontation: In one particularly resonant shot, Warhol and Dylan appraise one another under the gaze of a doubled gun-slinging Elvis on canvas, as if enacting a showdown's moment of truth. Dylan reluctantly did his duty, silently sitting in front of the stationary camera as many others among

Barry Feinstein, *Bob Dylan in Carnaby Street,* **1966.**
Copyright Barry Feinstein.

Nat Finkelstein, *Warhol, Dylan, and Elvis,* 1965.
Copyright Nat Finkelstein.

Warhol's designated Superstars and celebrity visitors had done. The sitting concluded, he commanded in return a gesture of tribute from the artist, who let him take that same silver Elvis canvas away as a gift. Dylan's companions summarily strapped it to the roof of their station wagon and drove it off to his Catskills retreat in Woodstock (where he ultimately traded the painting to his manager Albert Grossman in return for a couch).[15]

But Warhol had Dylan locked in a film can, one more celebrity trophy of his determined enterprise as a cinema impresario. While this ritual dance and exchange of portraits counts as Dylan's only documented visit to the Factory, Warhol testified to more contacts and a much longer acquaintance between them, a pattern of less fraught encounters "through the MacDougal Street/Kettle of Fish/Café Rienzi/ Hip Bagel/Café Figaro scene."[16] He describes Sedgwick's bringing Dylan to a party thrown by another Factory regular, the young curator Sam Green, his apartment strewn with borrowed furs: "He was already slightly flashy when I met him, definitely not folksy anymore—I mean he was wearing satin, polka-dot shirts. He'd released *Bringing It All Back Home,* so he'd already started his rock sound at this point." Warhol adds blandly, "I even gave him one of my silver Elvis paintings in the days when he was first around."[17] Neuwirth would not long after embark on a lengthy and intense personal relationship with Sedgwick, while she simultaneously embraced her new role as Warhol's social alter ego and the reigning beauty among the Factory Superstars.

"They're selling postcards of the hanging," Dylan wrote in the opening line of "Desolation Row":

> They're painting the passports brown. The beauty parlor's filled with sailors.
> The circus is in town.

The style is all Dylan, down to the spots of awkward scansion on the page that resolve themselves in the way he delivers the song. The first line evokes old photographs of lynchings, the nightmare confronting the civil rights movement (all part of Dylan's left-populist inheritance), as well as a locally famous act of vigilante racial murder in Duluth, Minnesota, one witnessed by members of his own family.[18] At the same time, for any acute listener, the line just as inescapably calls to mind Warhol's *Race Riot* and *Electric Chair* paintings. Where else in American culture but in the circle of Warhol and his Superstars would transformations of gruesome and mundane photography naturally connect with a spectacle of gender crossing, homosexual desire, and outlandish performance? And Dylan flirts in a later verse of the same song with an explicit citation of the source, where "the superhuman crew" rounds up victims at midnight to "bring them to the factory."

The late Robert Shelton, Dylan's long-serving Boswell, wrote tellingly of the singer's "own poetic otherworld, into whose dreams we enter half-fearfully... a host of unsettling demons, spirits, devils, and malignant muses. Rilke saw his angels, Blake met his prophets Isaiah and Ezekial. Dylan painted freaks and geeks."[19] On his return from England, the Warhol spectacle lay before Dylan as an amalgam of Pop Art's glamour and the dark carnival of allegory toward which his own art was setting its course. Warhol's turn toward film had provided the necessary magnet drawing together his cast of Superstars, most of whom acquired some new name that designated their assigned part in the ongoing School for Scandal: Baby Jane, Viva, Ultra Violet, Ondine, Ingrid Superstar, International Velvet, Sugar Plum Fairy, Billy Name, Candy Darling, Rotten Rita, Holly Woodlawn, Paul America, et al. He could then sit with seeming impassivity in the center of a cast of obsessives and exhibitionists, each of whom could act out some aspect of his divided self-perception and inner life. Heiress Edie Sedgwick reigned over the ensemble as the Woman, who embodied, in her studied persona and uncannily androgynous beauty, both the subject's displaced object of desire and its cherished ego ideal.

In that light, consider these familiar lines:

> You said you'd never compromise
> With the mystery tramp, but now you realize
> That he's not selling any alibis
> As you stare into the vacuum of his eyes
> And ask him, do you want to make a deal?

**Gerard Malanga, *Warhol Factory Group Shot,* 1968.
Copyright Archives Malanga.**

Or these:

> You used to be so amused
> With Napoleon in rags and the language that he used.
> Go to him now, you can't refuse.
> When you've got nothing, you got nothing to lose.
> You're invisible now, you got no secrets to conceal.

Warhol figures in these lyrics under various thin disguises: he is the Mystery Tramp and Napoleon in rags (remembering that kinder, gentler nickname of Raggedy Andy); he also appears as the Diplomat, who rides a chrome horse—here Dylan gestures toward the famous silver iconography of the Factory—and "took from you everything he could steal." It follows that the "you" and "your" addressed in this relentless second-person rant can only be Edie Sedgwick, who had "gone to the finest school" (St. Timothy's boarding school in Maryland), the "Princess on the steeple" among "all the pretty people," and so on. In his memoir of the 1960s, Warhol recounts being told by intermediaries that Dylan "feels you destroyed Edie...you're 'the diplomat on the chrome horse'"[20]

Bob Adelman/Magnum Photos, *Andy Warhol and
Edie Sedgwick, New York,* 1965.

While it has been a commonplace in the extensive Dylan literature that the later (and lesser) songs of 1966, "Leopard-Skin Pill-Box Hat" and "Just Like a Woman," take Sedgwick as their subject, similar recognition has largely been withheld from "Like a Rolling Stone."[21] The narrative embedded in the song, it must be said, represents no simple piece of reportage dressed up in allusive imagery. During that spring and summer, Warhol and Sedgwick seemed the golden couple of an international avant-garde; her precipitous decline and disaffection of the coming winter could only have been guessed at. Thus the riches-to-rags theme of "Like a Rolling Stone" represents less a feat of insight or prescience than a projection of Dylan's own needs and frustrations onto an actually existing scenario, one already cast in terms of striking and slightly unreal personae. The scenario of Warhol and Sedgwick gave him a story to tell, one that channeled his artistic and personal frustrations into a work capable of overcoming them.

That August Dylan told young interviewers Nora Ephron and Susan Edmiston (in the course of the same conversation where he attacks museums of painting) that the whole idea of folk music had been betrayed by the assumption of its simplicity, a protocol enforced by "all the authorities who write about what it is and what it should be, when they say keep things simple, they should be easily understood."[22] In the first of several such outbursts, he protests that "folk music is the only music that isn't simple. It's never been simple." While revivalist musicians were certainly permitted to sing the true old ballads, there was a prohibition in place, Dylan is asserting, against anyone creating new music in their true, nonsimplifying spirit— in that such creation entailed for him both the layered electric sound and the kaleidoscopic profusion of allegorical characters that he had hit upon the previous June.

It is standard allegorical practice that the unresolved components and experiences of the authorial self distribute themselves over an array of external substitutes, none of which needs represent its complete or permanent state. Warhol, fudged and indistinct as a personality even while standing in the full glare of modern publicity, had of course his own company of players—and no account of him is complete without them.[23] Indeed, these inhabitants of his artistic project brought to life a panoply of emblematic characters already present within the body of painting that first made him famous.

Much of the effort invested in the vast literature devoted to interpreting those works has been wasted in the attempt to situate their meaning in an attitude toward each individual referent—each film star, product label, or newspaper photograph. But the flat, emblematic character of these images drains from them most of the semblance of life, even that retained in the mediated surrogates that provided Warhol with his original templates. His consistent manner of transforming these sources makes them resemble one another much more than they resemble any particular person or thing in the world.

Few, however, have asked just how Warhol's choices of image correspond to one another, what sort of world they might be taken to constitute by means of their interrelationships. The emblematic position occupied within the Factory by Sedg-wick, with both her magnetic attraction and strikingly wide and open gaze, had as its typological precedent Warhol's reiterated renderings of Marilyn Monroe. Present like a hovering mirage but distant as an unapproachable divinity, the face of Marilyn functions like the Lady in the Tower ("the Princess on the steeple") who commands the fealty of the flawed protagonist in an old romance. The nightmare landscape conjured by Warhol's "death and disaster" cycle—the horrific automobile accidents, the fatally tainted food, marauding police, thugs and gangsters—stands in for the outlandish obstacles and dangers that protagonist must confront if he is to fulfill the imperious wishes of his lady. Blandishments for cheap goods and services map his own adequacy and consequent need for a redeeming recognition from on high.

The heraldic note struck by Warhol's use of crudely flattening silk screens under-scores the plausibility of some such quasi-medieval scenario, which arises from the entire body of painting and most likely lies behind its undiminished popularity; that is, the appeal of romance enduring as the currency of its real-world referents continues to fade. In keeping with the many cultural archaisms that persist in popular culture, that romance continues in overt form via each new book or film or fashion spread that reconstitutes the legend of the Factory.

Nat Finkelstein, *Dark Edie,* 1966. Copyright Nat Finkelstein.

Andy Warhol, *Red Shot Marilyn*, 1964. Synthetic
polymer paint and silkscreen ink on canvas,
40 x 40 inches. Copyright Andy Warhol Foundation
for the Visual Arts/Artists Rights Society, New
York. Trademark 2007 Marilyn Monroe, LLC by
CMG Worldwide, Inc. www.MarilynMonroe.com.

Much the same could be said of the agelessness of Dylan's enigmatic songscapes. While his personal affect seemed all the more edgy and aggressive by comparison to Warhol's studiously passive demeanor, his growing entourage inevitably invited comparison with the Factory's "superhuman crew."[24] And he had an even larger, more emblematic company in his mind's eye. In 1993, bristling at the American-roots pretensions of latecomers like Bruce Springsteen, he snapped to an interviewer: "They weren't there to see the end of the traditional people. But I was."[25] In the early 1960s, many of the Appalachian and Mississippi Delta musicians recorded in the late 1920s and early 1930s had lately become fixtures in clubs, festivals, and college concerts, living bearers of memory conjured from the hollers and plantations of the rural American South. The memories carried by many of them reached back to the British popular ballads of the seventeenth century, carried to the new world by the rough Scots-Irish immigrants who had bypassed the coastal cities for isolated inland settlements.[26] While his younger self had assiduously mastered these forms, the Dylan of 1965 embarked on an inspired mission to insure their continuity. As he told the *New York Times* as recently as 1997: "Those old songs are my lexicon and my prayer book.... My songs, what makes them different, is that there's a foundation to them. That's why they're still around.... It's not because they're such great songs. They don't fall into the commercial category. They're not written to be performed by other people. But they're standing on a strong foundation, and subliminally that's what people are hearing."[27]

Subliminally, then, those people would be hearing echoes from the courtly verse romances of the Middle Ages, the primary source material selected and adapted in the folk traditions of both Old and New Worlds, hence, as Clinton Heylin observes, "the preponderance of ladies in their bowers and reckless knights in these 'new' popular ballads."[28] In America, "Lady Isabel and the Elphin Knight" might have been decanted into a "Pretty Polly," but Dylan took it upon himself to repopulate the American song world with a plethora of reinvented heraldic characters to make good the loss.

Warhol, to the extent that the above redescription of his early paintings holds good, was himself reaching back to a well of romance that persisted in mid-twentieth-century culture, though in more diffuse channels than the Appalachian popular ballad. The apparent paradox involved is that such recourse to an extremely old artistic genre occurred as part and parcel of two artists enjoying a degree of public attention that only the modern mass media could deliver. Greil Marcus has memorably written that the Dylan of 1965 "seemed less to occupy a turning point in cultural space and time than to be that turning point, as if the culture would turn according to his wishes or even his whim; the fact was, for a long moment it did."[29] While hyperbolic in tone, this judgment comes close to the mark, with the single proviso that one could substitute the name Andy Warhol—who laid down the single claim for visual art that could stand up to the juggernaut of the post-Dylan rock industry—and it would be just as true.

Allegory once flourished as an art of courts and feudal conflict, and each of these artists commanded a court of his own, accompanied by a following beyond the reckoning of passing consumer choices—and one that plainly carried the shadow of palpable danger as well, driving Dylan into seclusion and Warhol into the path of an assassin. By any objective measure, gallery prices or record sales, neither

Warhol nor Dylan was the most "popular" artist in his field, but both had in common an unreachable kind of sovereignty, an exceptional reckoning with the power of fame and how it could be figured in an aesthetic practice. Archaic form laid a common ground for what the world took to be the most up-to-date reports on its condition.

Notes

1. See Derek Barker, "So You Want to Be a Rock and Roll Star," in *Bob Dylan: Anthology Volume 2: Twenty Years of Isis*, ed. Derek Barker (New Malden, UK: Chrome Dreams, 2005), 91. Columbia Records took out advertisements in music trade publications at the end of May headlined "NOW BOB IS BIGGER THAN BIG BEN!"

2. See Clinton Heylin, *Bob Dylan: A Life in Stolen Moments: Day by Day, 1941–1995* (New York: Schirmer, 1996), 74.

3. See the 1966 *Ramparts* interview with Ralph J. Gleason, "The Children's Crusade," reprinted in *Bob Dylan: The Early Years: A Retrospective*, ed. Craig McGregor (New York: Da Capo, 1990), 186: "That was the end of my older program. I knew what was going to happen all the time, y'know. I knew how many encores there was, which songs they were going to clap loudest at and all this kind of thing." According to Barker, "So You Want to Be a Rock and Roll Star," 102, the interview was conducted in December 1965.

4. See Andy Warhol and Pat Hackett, *Popism: The Warhol '60s* (New York and London: Harcourt Brace Jovanovich, 1980), 113–14: also Victor Bockris, *The Life and Death of Andy Warhol* (New York: Bantam, 1989), 167–68.

5. Bob Neuwirth, personal communication, April 2005.

6. Quoted in Jean Stein and George Plimpton, *Edie: An American Biography* (New York: Knopf, 1982), 166: "Dylan and I occasionally ventured out into the poppy nightlife world," he has recalled, "I think somebody who had met Edie said, 'You have to meet this terrific girl.' Dylan called her, and she chartered a limousine and came to see us. . . . I think we met in the bar upstairs at the Kettle of Fish on McDougal Street, which was one of the great places of the Sixties. It was just before the Christmas holidays." On Sedgwick's joining the Factory entourage, see Bockris, *The Life and Death of Andy Warhol*, 162.

7. On the transformations of this motif, see David Mellor, *The London Art Scene in the 1960s* (London: Phaidon, 1992), 119–26.

8. "They Think the Mod Thing Is Dying . . . But They Don't Intend to Go Down with It," *Melody Maker*, June 5, 1965, 7. Townshend was quoted the next month declaring: "We stand for pop art clothes, pop art music and pop art behaviour. This is what everybody seems to forget—we don't change offstage. We live pop art." See Nick Jones, "Well, What Is Pop Art?" *Melody Maker*, July 3, 1965, 11.

9. Quoted in Clinton Heylin, *Bob Dylan: Behind the Shades* (New York: Harper Collins, 2003), 215.

10. Gleason, "The Children's Crusade," 187.

11. See Clinton Heylin, *Bob Dylan: The Recording Sessions* (New York: St. Martin's Press, 1995), 39–44.

12. Interview with Nat Hentoff, *Playboy*, March 1966, reprinted in Jonathan Cott, *Bob Dylan: The Essential Interviews* (New York: Wenner Books, 2006), 98.

13. See 1965 interview (conducted shortly after August 28) with Nora Ephron and Susan Edmiston, reprinted in Cott, *Essential Interviews*, 54.

14. For images and a verbal account, see Nat Finkelstein, *Andy Warhol: The Factory Years 1964–1967* (Edinburgh: Canongate, 1999), unpaginated. Also Bockris, *Life and Death,* 172. Billy Name (Linich) also took photographs of the visit and Dylan sitting for the *Screen Test,* dated July 1965; see Debra Miller, *Billy Name: Stills from the Warhol Films* (Munich: Prestel, 1994), 16, 20. The visit had been arranged by filmmaker Barbara Rubin, on whom, see Daniel Belasco, "The Vanished Prodigy," *Art in America,* December 2005, 61–65, 67. On the *Screen Tests,* see Callie Angell, *Andy Warhol Screen Tests: The Films of Andy Warhol Catalogue Raisonné* (New York: Whitney Museum of American Art and Harry Abrams, 2005). The entry for the Dylan *Screen Test* appears on page 66, mistakenly dated to 1966.

15. Eventually sold by Sally Grossman, widow of Albert Grossman, the painting is now in the collection of the Museum of Modern Art, New York.

16. Warhol and Hackett, *Popism,* 107–8.

17. Ibid.

18. Greil Marcus, personal communication, March 2007.

19. Robert Shelton, *No Direction Home: The Life and Music of Bob Dylan* (New York: Da Capo, 1986), 267–68. Gleason, a similarly seasoned commentator, wrote in 1966 ("Children's Crusade," 177): "Dylan's world is a nightmare world. . . . In his world are all sorts of carnival freak show figures"; "Einstein disguised as Robin Hood . . . with his friend a jealous monk"; "the motorcycle black madonna two wheel gypsy queen"; "Dr. Filth . . . his nurse, some local loser, she's in charge of the cyanide hole"; "Mack the Finger," etc. "Recurrent figures in the Dylan poetry include the monk, the hunchback, the sideshow geek and clown, and Napoleon. It's a gaudy, depressing grotesquerie. . . ."

20. Warhol and Hackett, *Popism,* 108.

21. One guarded exception can be found in the valuable study by C. P. Lee, *Like the Night (Revisited): Bob Dylan and the Road to the Manchester Free Trade Hall* (London: Helter Skelter Publishing, 2004), 162, in which he describes his younger self at Dylan's 1966 Manchester performance: "Now, this may or not be another song about Edie Sedgwick. . . . We didn't know the ins and outs of the New York Glitterati's love affairs. We knew little of contemporary Popular Culture, except for the dribs and drabs that were fed to us via the medium of the Sunday broadsheet colour supplements. Suddenly, here was Dylan, offering us a view of the Socialite life of the Big Apple, that we wouldn't have known much about anyway, but still, thank you Bob for offering it."

22. Interview with Ephron and Edmiston, in Cott, *Essential Interviews,* 50.

23. See, most prominently, Stephen Koch, *Star-gazer: Andy Warhol's World and His Films* (New York: Praeger, 1973); and Steven Watson, *Factory Made: Warhol and the Sixties* (New York: Pantheon, 2003).

24. See Finkelstein, *Andy Warhol,* n.p., who refers—with some hyperbole—to the two groups as "the Guelphs and Ghibellines of the New York underground scene engaged in a fraternal rumble deep in that insulated New York culture womb."

25. Quoted in Greil Marcus, *Invisible Republic: Bob Dylan's Basement Tapes* (New York: Henry Holt, 1997), 195.

26. The literature on this pattern of settlement is vast: for the most comprehensive account, see David Hackett Fischer, *Albion's Seed* (Oxford: Oxford University Press, 1989). Heylin, in his invaluable *Dylan's Daemon Lover: The Tangled Tale of a 450-Year-Old Pop Ballad* (London: Helter Skelter, 1999), 104–15 and passim, provides a capsule description of the phenomenon as it bears on the passage of the ballad "The House Carpenter" to the New World.

27. Interview with John Pareles, *New York Times*, September 1997, reprinted in Cott, *Essential Interviews*, 396. In these later remarks on this theme, Dylan understandably expands his range of examples to include African-American blues and sacred music, as well as early commercial country-and-western songs. In that light, it makes the restriction of his examples in the interviews of 1965 to the British ballad tradition all the more striking, as he was conversant with all of these genres at the earliest stages of his career.

28. Heylin, *Daemon Lover*, 132.

29. Marcus, *Invisible Republic*, ix.

7. Like the Night:
Reception and Reaction Dylan UK 1966

C. P. Lee

In 1956 film director John Huston wanted the sea shanties for his epic movie *Moby Dick* to be as authentic as possible. To create that authenticity, he selected a former whaling man, singer, and political activist called A. L. "Bert" Lloyd to be his adviser. He was so taken with Lloyd's efforts that he gave him a role in the film, and he can be seen leading the crew of the *Pequod* in a rousing version of "Blood Red Roses" as they haul on the bowline and the ship sails out of Nantucket harbor in quest of Captain Ahab's great White Whale. In 1965 in "Bob Dylan's 115th Dream," Bob Dylan and Captain "Arab" *[sic]* sang "Haul on the bowline" as they harpooned another White Whale by using electric guitars on what was supposed to be a "folk" album.

One year later, on Tuesday, May 17, 1966, I was sixteen years old and fired up with youthful excitement at the thought of attending a Bob Dylan concert at the Free Trade Hall in my hometown of Manchester, England—the time and place where the most famous heckle in rock history took place . . . an incident in popular culture on a par with the booing of Diaghilev and Stravinsky's *The Rite of Spring* in 1913. It wasn't until thirty-two years after leaving the Dylan concert that evening in 1966, bewildered and perplexed in trying to make sense of what I had just witnessed, that I thought I'd reached enough conclusions to write my book *Like the Night: Bob Dylan and the Road to the Manchester Free Trade Hall.*[1]

Yet it didn't end there. My continuing research into the reception and reaction of that night specifically and the position of "Tradition" in popular culture in general has brought me to another point in my work where I find myself still asking the question, why did Bob Dylan and his "new" music raise such animosity? And to answer it, we have to go back to 1951 and the beginning of what was known as the "Second British Folk Revival."

In 1951 the National Cultural Committee of the CPGB (Communist Party of Great Britain) published a pamphlet titled *The American Threat to British Culture.* This was essentially a polemic bewailing the lack of opportunities for homegrown singers and songwriters, who, the party claimed, were in danger of being swamped by mass-produced popular culture forced onto the UK market by "American Big Business." It ended with a call to arms to revitalize the indigenous traditional musical culture of the British Isles. To this end two members of the CPGB were given the task of initiating a revival. The first member was Bert Lloyd. The second was Ewan MacColl.

Further information regarding Lloyd's credentials include the following. He was born in London in 1908 and emigrated to Australia when a teenager. There he worked a variety of jobs—stockman, sheep shearer, and factory laborer. In the mid-1930s he worked on board a whaling ship of the Atlantic fleet and then found himself back in the UK. In London he combined party work with research into folk songs in the reading room of the British Museum. This resulted in his first and highly influential publication *The Singing Englishman*.[2] It was a publication that would position him as the leading expert in the country on folk songs, but as Mike Brocken in his book *The British Folk Revival* points out, Lloyd's approach to folk music and the resulting book are filtered through a strict Marxist viewpoint.[3] Despite his unswerving adherence to party policy, Lloyd is remembered as mischievous and fun loving. In contrast, his partner in the revival, Ewan MacColl, is more often portrayed as a rather dour, puritanical figure. MacColl, author of two international hit songs, "Dirty Old Town" and "The First Time Ever I Saw Your Face," was born Jimmy Miller in Salford, England, not Auchtermerdy, Scotland, as is often cited. Before World War II he was heavily involved in radical theater with his first wife, Joan Littlewood. After deserting from the army during the conflict, he reappeared as Ewan MacColl in 1945.

In 1951 MacColl was inspired to switch from drama to folk after meeting legendary American folklorist and song collector Alan Lomax. There followed an intense period of conceptualization about the dialectics of the revival, while Lloyd and MacColl began performing as well as collecting. Things began to formalize with the opening of the Ballads and Blues Club in London in 1953. It's important to note the cross-cultural titling—"Blues" and "Ballads." At this stage the rigid nationalism of the revival wasn't in place. With a physical base from which to theorize and experiment (within strict Marxist lines), the revival began to gather pace. The Ballads and Blues Club soon gave way to the Singers' Club, which became a kind of franchise with clubs of that name springing up across the country. MacColl claimed that by 1957 there were fifteen hundred Singers' Clubs in the UK with a membership of over eleven thousand—figures that Brocken claims are open to some scrutiny.

What isn't in doubt is the success of Lloyd and MacColl's campaign to promote folk as a viable musical alternative to the banalities of the pop charts. Lloyd's book *The Penguin Book of English Folk Songs* became a best seller.[4] With its out-and-out promotion of traditional British music, it was a perfect companion to MacColl and Lloyd's efforts to promote contemporary songwriting (always of a political nature). This in turn impressed Pete Seeger, so much that after seeing firsthand the burgeoning new song scene in the UK, he decided to do as much as possible to promote new songwriting in America. This in turn would have a profound influence on the young Bob Dylan.

The revival also found a home on BBC Radio in a series of eight groundbreaking documentaries from 1957 to 1964 known as *The Radio Ballad* series. These used location recordings, real voices, and especially composed songs to tell the stories of ordinary people. They were not simply a broadcasting success but became highly influential on the structure of documentaries for the next four decades and beyond. Folk also found its way into the nation's school curriculum. In the early 1960s schoolchildren in Britain were issued with a copy of *Something to Sing,* a handbook for schools.[5] In his introduction, the compiler, Geoffrey Brace, thanks Lloyd and MacColl for their help in choosing the songs for the volume. At my school we had one hour a week of "folk" and then another hour of "musical appreciation," which usually involved listening to folk recordings. An attempt to introduce English country dancing met with less enthusiasm. It was far preferable to simply sit and listen.

By the early 1960s the folk revival in the UK was highly successful but with very specific ground rules. For example, two folk fanzines from the time, *Folk Review,* volume 1, number 3, and *Folk Music,* volume 1, number 11, circa 1963, show quite clearly the debate that had been going on since the late 1950s as MacColl, and to a lesser extent Lloyd, had struggled to impose party theories on the newly emerging folk scene.

Singers' Club "policy rules" to a degree were influenced by Theodor Adorno and the Frankfurt School's critique of mass culture and the so-called purity of workers' culture, from which it is believed traditional songs had emanated. At the insistence of Pete Seeger's sister Peggy, who was now living with MacColl, a debate was started that was to lead to a policy rule that stated

> If the singer was from England then the song had to be English. If the singer was
> from America the song had to be American and so on.[6]

The issue of *Folk Music* mentioned above features more of MacColl's thoughts on folk music. On pages 10 and 11 there appears a précis of just a few of the distilled rules and definitions. For example, in statements on what is meant by "Folk Music" and "Traditional" and "Commercial" and "Professional" and "Amateur" and "Ethnic," all of the definitions fit perfectly into the concepts of the policy rules prevalent in the British folk scene at the time.

British traditional singer Shirley Collins remembers MacColl's instructions on how she was to dress for singing: no nail varnish, and a hairstyle appropriate for a traditional singer![7] This is a good example of the debates that raged in the early 1960s. To ignore the policy rules was to risk being considered "commercial" and being accused of having "sold out" to the "Money Men," whoever they might be. Dylan up until circa 1965 was deemed all right as long as he was singing protest or topical songs, though, as we will see, MacColl loathed him from the first time he met him. The moment Dylan's music became more personal, he opened himself up for attacks by the traditionalists. Irwin Silber, editor of *Sing Out!* castigated Dylan for his introspective material in an open letter as early as 1964. Approximately a year later, the British folk music scene became divided between the traditionalists and the modernists—for Dylan or against him. The confrontation that had been brewing as far back as Dylan's first visit to Britain in 1962 now had its battle lines established.

In 1962, Dylan had been invited to the UK to appear in a BBC television play, *Madhouse on Castle Street,* and was taking time out to check out and perform in some folk clubs. On December 22, he arrived at the Pindar of Wakefield public house in London, and, according to Anthea Joseph in Clinton Heylin's *Behind the Shades,* he was reluctantly allowed in by Bruce Dunnett,[8] a Communist Party member, who said, "No, I don't want to let that shit in . . . but (Peggy) said I had to let him in."[9] A brilliantly telling photograph by Brian Shuel captures the moment Dylan took the floor that evening at the Singers' Club. The young American was allowed to sing three numbers, which according to contemporary accounts included "The Ballad of Hollis Brown" and "Masters of War." Lloyd, as can be seen in the photograph, appeared happy, but MacColl and his wife, Peggy Seeger, sat stony-faced throughout his performance. It is unknown quite why their reaction was so vehemently anti-Dylan, especially as at that time he was virtually unknown in the UK, but I would like to suggest as one possibility the following reason.

MacColl's mentor and friend Alan Lomax had a worker in his office called Carla Rotolo. She was the sister of Dylan's ex-girlfriend Suze. It is well documented that Carla had fallen out with Dylan over his relationship with her sister. This would have been known to Lomax, who likely then reported it to the MacColls. Hence Dylan's reception from them at the Singers' Club was frosty and distant. Throughout the rest of his life MacColl never changed his opinion of Dylan. In 1965 he wrote to *Sing Out!*

> The present crop of contemporary American songs has been made by writers who are either (a) unaware of these disciplines, (b) or incapable of working inside the disciplines [of Traditional music], or are at pains to destroy them. "But what of Bobby Dylan?" scream the outraged teenagers of all ages . . . a youth of mediocre talent. Only a completely non-critical audience, nourished on the watery pap of pop music, could have fallen for such tenth rate drivel. . . .[10]

A couple of years before he died, MacColl told writer Robin Denselow that

> I was shaken when Dylan began to make it, when I found people treated him as a serious poet. That's how I felt then and that's how I feel now.[11]

So it was that between 1962 and 1966 the whole world changed—from music to fashion, from literature to film, from the politics of the cold war to the politics of ecstasy. The London that Dylan came back to in 1966 was now swinging and culturally almost unrecognizable from the drab, gray landscape of only a few years before. Some things, though, hadn't changed, and if anything, they had become more entrenched: folk rules! The showdown between traditionalists and modernists was about to take place, and the catalyst was Bob Dylan.

Reaction in 1966 to Dylan's appearance orbits around the traditionalists' concepts of "commercialization" and "authenticity." At the University of Manchester (UK) the members of the Folk Music Society had a meeting where they voted to boycott the concert because of Dylan's having "sold out." In Edinburgh members of the Young Communist League decided after much debate to attend, but if Dylan insisted on playing electric guitar, they would stage a walkout. By the time the Dylan circus hit Manchester, his audience was on edge with anticipation. Remember, there was no Internet then, no instant MP3 downloads minutes after Dylan and the Hawks had gone offstage, and only a scattering of reports from Dublin and Bristol had been printed in the music press, all of which made for disturbing reading. For example, *Melody Maker*'s headline of May 14, 1966, was "The Night of the Big Boo."

So it was that on the May 17, in the foyer of the Free Trade Hall, people stated their positions with partisan fervor, and if you'll pardon the expression, the atmosphere was "electric." After the first half's acoustic set, there was a virtual sigh of relief that soothed and progressed through and among the crowd of two thousand, and it seemed to me that not many people moved about during the intermission. I never left my seat, such was the level of anticipation and awe I experienced as I sat in front of the stack of amplifiers the likes of which I had never seen.

The second half opened with a crash of Mickey Jones's drum kit and a blistering "Tell Me Mamma." It was, as many that night reported afterwards, like being blasted back in your seat—the volume was that loud. By three numbers into the second half, the audience's shock had worn off and was replaced by anger. Dylan was beginning to get heckled! Slow handclapping began, and a young woman moved to the front and handed Dylan a note. He read it, confidently bowed, and blew her a kiss. Thirty-seven years later when I was researching my book, I found out what the note had said. It read, "Tell the band to go home."[12] Finally, after the group's forty-minute electric firestorm came the most infamous heckle in rock music history—"Judas!"—following which Dylan and the band smashed their way into an apocalyptic version of "Like a Rolling Stone." Then, at the end of the grinding juggernaut of sound, Dylan waved and said thank you and left. His audience sat stunned, and then slowly we moved out, not all of us able to comprehend what we'd just witnessed. My position certainly didn't match that of the traditionalists I could hear on the way out, and we can now witness in Martin Scorsese's TV documentary *No Direction Home* (2006) such outbursts as "Pop groups play better rubbish than that," "It was a disgrace—he wants shooting!" and "He's a traitor!"

This fracas was a drama that was reenacted across the UK on each tour night. Mickey Jones told me that he and the rest of the group would go back to their hotels and listen to recordings of that night's particular gig and wonder what it was exactly that they were doing wrong—why weren't the audiences getting it? In fact a lot of them were. It's just that the traditionalists were a lot louder in their protestations. The "Judas" shout was meek and mild in comparison to an incident at Dylan's Glasgow hotel room when an embittered "fan" tried to get in with a knife. There were threats, seemingly stupid at the time but frightening now with later assassinations in mind, of shooting Dylan if he came on stage with his Fender guitar. But it passed by, and Dylan left it all behind at the end of the tour; he simply went away, fell off his motorbike, and invented country rock, while in Britain the furor continued.

"We're Only in It for the Money" was a 1973 working paper on the dilemmas facing folk music in a world of popular culture that was published by the Birmingham Centre for Cultural Studies.[13] It's interesting to note that many of the traditionalist arguments about folk music were still being paraded in its pages so long after the events of 1966. In 1986, I attended a folk club in the Lake District of England, and a heated argument ensued because one of the performers playing that night wanted to use an amplifier. They weren't allowed to because, as the organizer said, "This is a traditional club." As recently as February 2007, the *Guardian* newspaper reported that the BBC Folk Awards were in uproar over the winning entry by young musician Seth Lakeman.[14] His song "The White Hare" had been entered into the category of "Best Traditional Recording," and some of the more traditionalist listeners and judges were arguing that his song wasn't traditional and that it was a personal composition, not one handed down through the folk tradition despite Lakeman's protestations about its authenticity. There appears to be no end to the argument, as though the argument itself has established itself as a tradition. Certainly there is evidence aplenty that the controversy over what is "traditional" folk music rages on.

Notes

1. C. P. Lee, *Like the Night: Bob Dylan and the Road to the Manchester Free Trade Hall* (London: Helter Skelter Publishing, 1998).

2. A. L. Lloyd, *The Singing Englishman* (London: Workers' Music Association, 1944).

3. Michael Brocken, *The British Folk Revival 1944–2002* (Aldershot, UK: Ashgate Publishing Limited, 2003).

4. Ralph Vaughan Williams and A. L. Lloyd, eds., *The Penguin Book of English Folk Songs* (London: Penguin Books, 1959).

5. Geoffrey Brace, ed., *Something to Sing* (Cambridge: Cambridge University Press, 1963).

6. Robin Denselow, *When the Music's Over: The Story of Political Pop* (London: Faber and Faber, 1989), 28.

7. Brian Hinton and Geoff Wall, *Ashley Hutchings: The Guv'nor and the Rise of Folk Rock* (London: Helter Skelter Publishing, 2002).

8. Clinton Heylin, *Behind the Shades* (London: Summit Books, 1991).

9. Colin Harper, *Dazzling Stranger: Bert Jansch and the British Folk and Blues Revival* (London: Bloomsbury Publishing, 2000), 111.

10. *Sing Out!* 15, 4 (September 1965).

11. Denselow, *When the Music's Over,* 29.

12. Lee, *Like the Night,* 145.

13. Trevor Fisher, "We're Only in It for the Money: A Discussion of Folk Song and Popular Culture" (Birmingham: Centre for Cultural Studies, Birmingham University, 1973).

14. Colin Irwin, "Nowt So Queer as Folk," *Guardian,* February 16, 2007.

8. Oh, the Streets of Rome: Dylan in Italy
Alessandro Carrera

> So, is this the way it ended up? New York is still a sublime city....
> And yet, compared to three years ago, everything seems on hold,
> almost dead. Where has Ginsberg disappeared to? And Bob Dylan?
>
> —*Pier Paolo Pasolini, 1969*

A Postcard from Rome

My purpose in this essay is to illustrate the impact Dylan had on Italy and the impact Italy had on Dylan. I begin with an assessment of Dylan's trip(s) to Rome at the start of 1963. In January, while he was in Rome, he performed at the Folkstudio Club and traveled to Perugia in search of his girlfriend Suze Rotolo. He also discovered William Burroughs's experimental prose in European underground magazines. Yet, as is suggested by a recently surfaced postcard dated February 1963, Dylan may have returned to Rome one month later. Since the Folkstudio Club was managed in 1963 by an American painter, it is hardly a coincidence that in his 1971 song "When I Paint My Masterpiece," Dylan attributes the song's narrating voice to an expatriate American artist. On the other hand, there is much more to that song than pure reminiscence. A comparison between Dylan's song and a poem by Anthony Hecht shows that "When I Paint My Masterpiece" might be considered a short but worthy meditation on the American sublime.

Dylan was not to return to Italy until 1984, when he began the Italian part of his tour on the Arena di Verona's operatic stage. Since then, he has been a regular presence in Italy, and in 1997 he played for Pope John Paul II at the Eucharistic Conference in Bologna. An analysis of Dylan's cultural impact in Italy must consider how politically and religiously charged the Italian public debate is. While his brief conversion to evangelical Christianity in the late 1970s puzzled Catholics and non-Catholics alike, his Italian audiences have always expressed a strong tendency (indeed, a desire) to find political messages in Dylan and judge him according to his distance or proximity from political commitment. In the second part of this essay, I examine therefore the papal concert and its cultural relevance.

Dylan has been an obvious influence on generations of Italian songwriters. In the 1960s, music and myth preceded the words, but the first Italian translation of his songs was published in 1971, even before *Writings and Drawings* was available in the United States. Other translations have appeared since then, and each one has been a significant step in Dylan's growing status in Italy. In the third part of this essay, I address the role of Dylan's Italian translators as mediators in their effort to make Dylan's linguistic uniqueness understandable to Italian readers. Precisely because of that uniqueness, I have found translating *Chronicles, Volume 1* to be a difficult task (even more than the translation of the complete lyrics). Some remarks about Dylan as an "oral" writer bring the essay to its conclusion.

The most accurate biographies maintain that Dylan's first trip to Rome took him a few days in January 1963. According to Clinton Heylin's meticulous account of Dylan's life day by day, he flew from London on January 5, 1963, to join Odetta, who was scheduled to appear on an Italian TV program (his manager, Albert Grossman, who was also Odetta's manager, was in Rome, too). As Heylin has it, "During his brief stay he performs at the Folkstudio Club, as well as composing 'Girl from the North Country' and 'Boots of Spanish Leather,' both of which take a large part of their melodies from Martin Carthy's arrangement of 'Scarborough Fair.'"[1] Again according to Heylin, Dylan returned to London by January 10 to attend another Odetta show at the Prince Charles Theatre. On January 16, Dylan and Eric von Schmidt flew back to New York. By February 1963, Dylan was busy recording demos for "Broadside," appearing on Skip Weshner's New York radio show, and being photographed with Suze Rotolo in Greenwich Village for the cover of *The Freewheelin' Bob Dylan*.

Recently, however, a document has surfaced that may challenge this chronology. In 2006, Christie's auctioned a postcard of Piazza Navona sent from Rome to "Sue Rotolo c/o Bob Dylan 161 West 4th Street New York City, N.Y. U.S.A." The postcard was mailed from "Poste Roma Centro" (the main post office), and the postal seal reads "22-2-1963." Even conceding that in 1963 the Italian mail system may not have been the fastest in the world, a postcard would hardly have waited almost two months in Poste Roma Centro before being sent off. It is possible that Dylan gave the postcard to someone who forgot to mail it until February 22. Even in this case, however, other questions arise. Anthony Scaduto and other biographers have assumed that while in Italy, Dylan went looking for Suze in Perugia, where she was enrolled in an art course. He did not know that she had sailed from Naples on December 13, 1962, and was already back in New York.[2] From this postcard, however, we realize Dylan knew very well where Suze was. And we learn other things as well: that if he didn't open his mouth, everybody assumed he was Italian; that he was leaving for Turin; that he was learning a song called "Se Dio vorrà"; that his initial assumption, namely, that all Italian women were like Mama Rosa and Anna Magnani, now had to be corrected since they all looked like Sophia Loren; and that he planned to meet the pope and have a conversation with him about all the colored people coming to Italy.[3] And what was the purpose of his planned trip to Turin, an elegant but severe northern industrial town whose residents did not share Rome's penchant for *la dolce vita*? Besides, he could hardly have traveled to Perugia and Turin, strolled around Rome, spent time with Odetta, performed at the Folkstudio, and composed "Girl of the North Country" and "Boots of Spanish Leather" all in five days (trips to London included). Dylan could do magic in his early years, but the whole list of activities sounds too daunting to be accomplished in such a short time. On the other hand, wouldn't it be foolish to speculate that, for reasons unknown, Dylan went back to Rome for a few days in the second half of February, while Suze was safely waiting for him at home?

Maybe Dylan had already made up his mind at the beginning of February. We get our clue from "Going Back to Rome," an improvised and unfinished song he performed at Gerde's Folk City on February 8, 1963, which is part of what collectors call "The Banjo Tape": "Well you know I'm lying / But don't look at me with scorn," sings Dylan, "I'm going back to Rome / That's where I was born." In the third stanza, Dylan even says to his American audience that they can keep Madison Square Garden if they give him the Coliseum as an exchange.

Our revisionist chronology forces us to assume that, struck by Rome, Dylan went back and rushed to see the Coliseum for the second time. However, something funny happened to him on his way to the Roman past *grandeur*. Now he has been in Rome twice, has seen things twice, and has had the opportunity to think twice about the impact the city was having on him. The postcard to Suze shows no trace of second thoughts, but two years later, in the fall of 1965, a different idea of Rome emerges in the first of the two *Playboy* interviews with Nat Hentoff (the one that remained unpublished). When Hentoff asks Dylan where he gets his kicks today, this is Dylan's answer:

> B.D.: "Well, the kicks, you know... Like the first time, you say, I was in Rome, I saw... I was standing there and digging that, you know, whaddya call it? Big Stadium..." Nat Hentoff: "Coliseum." B.D.: "Coliseum. Yeah, you know, it was a kick, you know. Just being... Just the whole thing, you know. The whole feeling of being around there and whatever happened, whatever else happened. The second time I was there, you know, it just distracted me, you know. Like this Coliseum and how beautiful it was—it was distracting, man, you know."[4]

Why wasn't it possible for Dylan to enjoy the Coliseum a second time? What was the Coliseum distracting him from? While reading the unpublished *Playboy* interview, I was reminded of the well-known passage in Ralph Waldo Emerson's "Self-Reliance" about the futility of traveling:

> Traveling is a fool's paradise. Our first journeys discover to us the indifference of places. At home I dream that at Naples, at Rome, I can be intoxicated with beauty, and lose my sadness. I pack my trunk, embrace my friends, embark on the sea, and at last wake up in Naples, and there beside me is the stern fact, the sad self, unrelenting, identical, that I fled from. I seek the Vatican, and the palaces. I affect to be intoxicated with sights and suggestions, but I am not intoxicated. My giant goes with me wherever I go.[5]

The Coliseum represents sublimity of history. Its magnitude is without compare, not because it is immeasurable, but because its spatial presence is charged with a long stretch of historical time. In his *Critique of Judgment,* Immanuel Kant chose the Egyptian pyramids as examples of the "mathematical sublime" because nothing in their surroundings suggested their real dimensions to the traveler who saw them from afar. Without being infinite, the pyramids insinuated the idea of infinitude in the traveler's mind. As the largest architectural remnant of its era, with nothing nearby approaching its magnitude (modern monuments such as the Altare della Patria may be bigger but do not carry the same historical aura), the Coliseum similarly suggests infinity even though its ruinous state speaks for decay more than eternity. But the American artist, the way Emerson envisions him, is not searching for the Roman decayed sublime. The Emersonian artist *has no time* for that kind of historical time. The new American sublime that the American artist will have to embrace, suggests Emerson, will be more geographical than historical, more dynamical than mathematical. American art will not be concerned with static infinitude mired in the past but with an imaginative power that must be great enough to match the American landscape's boundlessness. When Dylan came to Rome, he had already composed "Let Me Die in My Footsteps," which was his early Guthrian exploration of America. He had not yet composed "Lay Down Your Weary Tune," his most Emersonian song, in which the river's water (serenely running like a hymn and humming like a harp) reminds the reader of Emerson's "I yielded myself to the perfect whole" (from "Each and All"). And he could not have written "Chimes of Freedom" (his most Whitmanian song) if he had not felt the need to take heed of the distracting ruins of the Coliseum.

The giant that walks with the poet carries the poet's landscape with him. But the giant per se is the poet's language. Between 2006 and 2007, when I was working on the critical apparatus for the new Italian edition of *Tarantula,* I looked for evidence of William Burroughs's influence in the occasional cut-ups interspersing the prose parts of that interestingly failed work. I was intrigued by this passage from another 1965 interview, which probably took place shortly before the Hentoff one I have already mentioned. Asked by Nora Ephron and Susan Edmiston if he knew Burroughs, Dylan said, "I haven't read *Naked Lunch* but I have read some of his shorter things in little magazines, foreign magazines. I read one in Rome."[6]

From 1959 to 1969, Burroughs indeed contributed to a great number of obscure and not so obscure art, literature, and even medical European journals.[7] If Dylan discovered Burroughs in Rome, he may have felt that the unbounded possibilities of American English, as they were laid out in Burroughs's experiments, were calling him home. The same feeling of urgency that was driving Dylan to his imaginary meeting with the pope reappears, and with the same words used in the postcard to Suze, in two passages from *Tarantula.* In the final poem of "Ballad in Plain Be Flat," for example, we find, "gotta go. there's a / fire engine chasing me," and again in the final poem of "Prelude to the Flatpick" we also read, "gotta go. someone's /coming to tame my shrew." Dylan "had to go" and meet the pope (and thirty-four years later he did), but he also wanted to go home to meet his language, while in fact he was running away from it, heading for an uncharted destination, halfway between a language that can be shared and an extremely private idiolect. Dylan's best cut-ups are not to be found in *Tarantula* but in the cubist blocks of the *Blonde on Blonde* lyrics, where written language is reduced to rubble by the sheer power of musical build-up and performance.

Still, one biographical question remains: where in Rome could Dylan read the journals Burroughs contributed to? Again, we can speculate that it was at the Folkstudio, the club where he performed one night between January 5 and 9, 1963. Located on Via Garibaldi, in the heart of Trastevere working-class-cum-bohemian neighborhood (Rome's equivalent of Greenwich Village), the Folkstudio was the creation of Harold Bradley. Born in Chicago in 1931, Bradley was an African-American painter and gospel singer with a degree in art from the University of Iowa. Having enrolled in the art classes at the University of Perugia with a student visa that seemed never to expire, he turned his Roman apartment and studio into a place where painters, artists, and musicians from all over the world came to meet, play, and sing until late at night. Since the neighbors were complaining about the noise, Bradley and his associate, Giancarlo Cesaroni, a chemist with a passion for music, asked for permission and renamed the place a "non-political private cultural club."

It was 1961, and there was nothing like it in Rome. It was *la dolce vita* at an affordable price. Two years later, at the start of 1963, the Folkstudio was in its heyday, a Greenwich Village–type club with three or four performers every night and a generous open-stage policy. Bradley, who didn't want trouble with the authorities, tried to keep his club as far from politics as possible, but when he was not around the new breed of politically committed folksingers and singer-songwriters of the early 1960s used his place as a nonstop workshop for their topical songs and political discussions. Bradley was too busy to notice. He had created his own gospel group, the Folk Studio Singers, with Italian and American performers, and he was often touring with them in Italy and Europe.

This was the place where some fellow musicians brought Dylan on January 1963. He played no more than three or four songs, and Cesaroni, who was there, later said that there were no more than fifteen people in the audience. In retrospect, however, Dylan's appearance at the Folkstudio acquired such a mythical status that there are hundreds of people in Rome who, without knowing that the Folkstudio was moved years later from its original location in Via Garibaldi to the neighboring Via Sacchi, are ready to swear they went to Via Sacchi to listen to Dylan. The Folkstudio's fame reached the United States too, becoming the subject of a 1964 *Time* magazine article:

> "There ain't no place around this holy town where a fella can get all them devils out of his throat," the expatriate folk singer complained—and he was right: for all its glories, Rome had no nightclub for folk singers. Such a cultural omission might have been easily endurable, but when an American Negro painter named Harold Bradley opened his II Folk Studio two years ago, Rome greeted it like springtime....

Bradley, a 33-year-old former fullback for the Cleveland Browns, offers his audience as few comforts as possible.... To pure folk singers, though, the problems are minor, and the Studio has become a shrine that wins the affectionate services of such stars as Odetta, Bob Dylan and Pete Seeger when they pass through town.[8]

A rare witness of Dylan's performance at the Folkstudio was Natalie Darbeloff, sister-in-law of Italian screenwriter and assistant director Gerardo Guerrieri, who wrote in her blog:

One night a skinny kid in a baseball cap sat at the back and listened attentively and eventually, like almost everyone else who came to the Folkstudio, sloped up to the front and sang a couple of songs. To my eternal shame I cannot remember what he sang or whether I liked it. What I do know is that he (accompanied by his manager, Al Grossman) came out with us to a corner bar and was hilariously, articulately drunk, probably stoned too, and that I haven't laughed so much in all my life. Unfortunately I can't recall a single word of what Bob Dylan said that made me laugh.[9]

Harold Bradley and his German wife, Hannelore, left Rome in 1967. Back in Chicago, Bradley became a successful radio and TV producer, whereas in Rome Cesaroni turned the Folkstudio into a temple of the new Italian song until his death in 1999.[10] In 1971, when Dylan wrote "When I Paint My Masterpiece," assuming the persona of an American painter in Rome, was he thinking of Bradley? "Oh, the streets of Rome are filled with rubble / Ancient footprints are everywhere," sings Dylan, "Got to hurry on back to my hotel room / Where I've got me a date with Botticelli's niece." As happens with many of his songs, Dylan has never performed "When I Paint My Masterpiece" exactly the way it is printed in the three editions of his lyrics. Neither did The Band in their 1973 cover included in *Cahoots.* "Botticelli's niece" is almost constantly replaced by "a pretty little girl from Greece" or, in some performances by Dylan in 2000, by "somebody [who] says her name's Denise." But the Coliseum in the second stanza has always been there ("Oh, the hours I've spent inside the Coliseum / Dodging lions and wastin' time"), as an allegory of the music business arena, where the artist must learn how to dodge lions and not to waste time, and the European wasteland, where the American artist cannot but waste his time.

The way out of the Coliseum is the "long, hard climb" that takes the singer on the train running "through the back of [his] memory" (a nice turn on the more common phrase, "the back of my mind") up to the hilltop where the wild geese take their flight. We may have not strayed very far from Rome. The sacred geese on the top of Capitol Hill saved Rome from the Gauls with their shrieks, and Dylan, who was in the Latin Club at Hibbing High, knows his ancient history. But wild geese and hilltops are also essential to Duluth, the vertical city on Lake Superior where Dylan was born, with its straight roads from the shores of the lake to the top of the surrounding hills. Dylan has mentioned Hibbing only indirectly, as "that little Minnesota town" in "Went to See the Gypsy," but he did mention "the hills of old Duluth" and the Great Lakes in "Something There Is about You." What makes "When I Paint My Masterpiece" a meditation on the American sublime is precisely its shift from the crowded splendor of Imperial Rome to the silent majesty of the "rainy days on the Great Lakes," the same unique landscape that Dylan would sparingly evoke thirty-four years later in *Chronicles, Volume 1.*

There is some point in comparing Dylan's shift with a similar vision that affected another expatriate American artist, the poet Anthony Hecht, in a poem aptly called "A Hill": "In Italy, where this sort of thing can occur, / I had a vision once—though you understand / It was nothing at all like Dante's, or the visions of saints, / And perhaps not a vision at all..." Then the noises stopped, and the people dissolved. "And even the great Farnese Palace itself / Was gone, for all its marble." In its place there was a mole-colored, bare hill. Suddenly it is cold, almost freezing. Then the voices of the Italian vendors come through, and the poet is restored to the sunlight and his friends. But for many days he remains scared by the "plain bitterness" of what he has seen. Then, one year later, the poet remembers that hill: "it lies just to the left / Of the road north of Poughkeepsie; and as a boy / I stood before it for hours in wintertime."[11]

The scene takes place in Campo de' Fiori, as far from the American giant as he thinks he can be, when the sudden presence of a barren Poughkeepsie hill tears apart the crowded Italian landscape. The American sublime has overwritten the entire scenery with the haunting feeling of an alien nature, hostile to mankind, and yet a nature that can*not* and must *not* be humanized as the Italian landscape has been. The poet recognizes in the Poughkeepsie hill the giant that walks with him, and this insight allows him to grasp, at least for an instant, a Dantesque tinge, a pre-Renaissance, pre-humanistic feeling of nature in which man does not lavish praises on himself as the *axis mundi*. It *was* a vision like Dante's, after all, revealing that the architecture of the world will remain alien to us forever, and the human microcosm will never grow to be as large as the macrocosm. After Dante, this feeling that nature (or God's sublime) will always be immensely stronger than history (history's sublime, the Coliseum's or Palazzo Farnese's) resurfaces only in a few poets and thinkers of the Italian canon (Giordano Bruno and Giacomo Leopardi, to name two of them). For an American poet, however, the same feeling is often a given, an assumption, an operating device—not a conclusion but a starting point.

It took a long time before Dylan, who gradually came to feel the weight of history on his shoulders as very few artists feel it in our time, could make his peace, so to speak, with the Coliseum and everything the Coliseum stands for. Again, it happened in Rome, July 23, 2001, at a press conference before his concert, when Dylan gave his own take on the *querelle des anciens et des modernes:*

> This is the Iron Age, you know. We are living in the Iron Age. When was the last Age? The age of Bronze, or something? We can still feel that Age. I mean, if you

walk around in this city.... People today can't build what you see out there. When you walk around in a town like this, you know that people were here before you, and they were probably on a much higher grander level than any of us are. I mean, they just have to be, we couldn't conceive a building.... These kind of things.... America doesn't really have stuff like this.

Then the conference was over, and while everybody was leaving, Dylan said his last words, captured by the microphone just one moment before it was turned off: "Now, I am going to see the Coliseum."[12]

Meeting with the Pope

September 27, 1997. At the Twenty-third Eucharistic Congress in Bologna, an outdoor concert attended by 300,000 people and 200 cardinals celebrates John Paul II's pastoral visit to the city that once was the northern outpost of the papal state. A roster of Italian pop stars is scheduled, and English and American covers alternate with Italian songs. Gianni Morandi and Barbara Cola sing John Lennon's *Imagine* in translation (no problem with "Imagine no religion"; in Gino Paoli's version it becomes "a world without gods"—Roman gods to an Italian ear, that is). Adriano Celentano sings "Pregherò" (I will pray), his translation of "Stand by Me." More ambiguously, Lucio Dalla and jazz pianist Michel Petrucciani perform a jazzy version of Carole King's "You've Got a Friend." Andrea Bocelli gets away easily with "Panis angelicus" and "Nessun dorma," and the Harlem Gospel Singers welcome Karol Wojtyla with a rousing rendition of "Oh Happy Day." Then a young actor reads the text of "Blowin' in the Wind" in Italian, with a discreet guitar accompaniment in the background. John Paul II follows the text on a handout and then proceeds to give a speech that will make history in the annals of Dylanology:

> A representative of yours has just said on your behalf that the answer to the questions of your life "is blowing in the wind." It is true! But not in the wind which blows everything away in empty whirls, but the wind which is the breath and voice of the Spirit, a voice that calls and says: "come!" (cf. Jn 3:8; Rv 22:17). You asked me: *How many roads* must a man walk down before you call him a man? I answer you: *one!* There is only one road for man and it is Christ, who said: "I am the way" (Jn 14:6). He is the road of truth, the way of life. I therefore say to you: at the crossroads where the many paths of your days intersect, question yourselves about the truth value of every choice you make. It can sometimes happen that the decision is difficult or hard, and that there is an insistent temptation to give in. This had happened to Jesus' disciples, for the world is full of easy and inviting ways, downhill roads that plunge into the shadow of the valley where the horizon becomes more and more limited and stifling. Jesus offers you an uphill road, which is heavy going but lets the eye of the heart sweep over ever broader horizons.[13]

John Paul II didn't know that in 1980 Dylan had written: "There's only one road and it leads to Calvary / It gets discouraging at times, but I know I'll make it / By the saving grace that's over me." The bishops who organized the conference didn't know about Dylan's Christian period. Being young priests in the 1960s, they only remembered "Blowin' in the Wind" as a perennial hit in Catholic meetings. When Dylan appeared on stage, they were probably expecting him to sing that old song, but he didn't. John Paul II had already done his cover, and nobody, not even Dylan, could top that.

Four years later, May 24, 2001, I was in Alba, a northern Italian small town, invited to the first Italian Dylan festival, on the occasion of his sixtieth birthday. There was a guitar player, a seasoned session man, who strolled the streets of Alba obsessively playing "Blowin' in the Wind"—the only Dylan song he knew and the only one he wanted to play. He wandered around as if he were there by mistake, a night-club jazz musician among rockers, and there was something mysterious about his casual demeanor and fixation with "Blowin' in the Wind." He looked a little like the magician in Fellini's *8½*, who whispers to Marcello Mastroianni, "Everything is ready," and then disappears behind a circus tent. His name was Jimmy Villotti. He had been at the Eucharistic Congress in Bologna and had played "Blowin' in the Wind" in the background while the text was being read to John Paul II. And he told me, "When the Pope said, 'It is true! Not in the wind which blows everything away, but the wind which is the breath of the Spirit!' his voice changed, it became a cry that gave me the goose pimples, me, who don't care a bit about religion, but if I think about it now it still gives me the chill! Let me tell you, that day the only rock star was the Pope!"

For his appearance in Bologna, Dylan had scheduled five songs. Then he was told by the organizers that the pope was tired and was leaving after the second song. Dylan dropped two numbers (one of them was rumored to be "With God on Our Side," of all choices), and performed "A Hard Rain's A-Gonna Fall" and "Knockin' on Heaven's Door," possibly the highlight of the entire concert. Then he climbed the steps to the pope's chair to shake hands with John Paul II, stumbling a little and taking off his cowboy hat *at the very last moment before meeting eye to eye with the pope*— which left everybody breathless for a few seconds—either because he was too nervous or because of his always impeccable Chaplinesque timing. After John Paul II left, a relieved Dylan performed "Forever Young."[14]

A few hours later, a friend of mine caught this piece of conversation among teenagers on a train leaving Bologna: "Who was that old guy with a cowboy hat? He was *terrible*, he was *atrocious*." "They told me he's a Jew." "Oh, maybe they invited him for political correctness."

It might have been the beginning of a new anti-Dylan backlash. The media were happy with their picture of Dylan and the pope, and Dylan's Catholic fans were satisfied enough, but Dylan's Italian audience, Catholic campfires aside, comes mostly from the Left. And the Left has always had some reason to feel betrayed by Dylan. The dewy-eyed leftists, lulled in their fixation that Dylan was *the* spokesperson for the sixties movement, *the* most vocal critic of the Vietnam War, and *the* fearless champion of the "Other America," did not digest very well his bowing to anti-Liberation theology Karol Wojtyla.[15] The more militant or extreme Left, besides, had always felt strongly that Dylan was a fraud (they bought his records, they cherished his songs, they learned his lyrics by heart, still feeling he was a fraud).[16]

Dylan elicits impossible expectations, and is therefore destined to frustrate everybody at least once. Still, he is like Coca-Cola. You may hate the brand, but you love the product ("Oh, to be back in the land of Coca-Cola!" he sings in "When I Paint My Masterpiece"). By May 28, 1984, when his first Italian tour began at the Arena di Verona, everything was forgotten and forgiven (even his tragically underrehearsed band of that night). Then came the mid-1980s, and Dylan had his long stretch of wandering inspiration. People who were not obsessed about him were blessed into forgetting him, at least until the 1997 Eucharistic Congress, when he returned on prime-time TV as a supporter of the biggest rock star the planet has ever seen. Looking at him singing "A Hard Rain's A-Gonna Fall" while the camera was framing John Paul II in the distance, I could not help being reminded of what prominent Americanist and oral historian Alessandro Portelli had said about the Christian Dylan. In a transcribed conversation, Portelli pointed out the structural affinity between *The Times They Are A-Changin'* and *Slow Train Coming,* and between the beginning of "I Believe in You" and the first bars of "Smoke Gets in Your Eyes," arguing that Dylan never strayed from his musical, even pre-folk, roots. And he also said:

> I was also struck by that song about the snake, "Man Gave Names to All the Animals," that stops exactly when the snake comes in. Something scary has broken into the idyllic order of creation, and silence follows. I had a daring insight, that the snake's scary intrusion was the Sixties and therefore Dylan himself, with all of the Sixties Dylan was a symbol for. And now he was looking at the Sixties as if they were the snake, and it was a little like he was exorcising himself. Therefore I would say that Dylan is coherent with his past, but not so much in terms of politics or cultural direction, but at the deepest linguistic level.[17]

Had Dylan really exorcised himself? Was he, or were the 1960s, exorcised enough in 1997? Maybe not. Definitely not enough for the next pope, Benedict XVI, who was never a supporter of John Paul II's *theatrum catholicum.* In the spring of 2007, when his memoir on John Paul II hit the bookstores, Joseph Ratzinger's dismissal of the pop parade at the Eucharistic Congress in Bologna made the news around the world. Apparently, Benedict XVI said he had reasons to doubt whether it was a good idea to allow the performance of "that kind of 'prophet,'" namely, Dylan, who had a totally different message from what the pope had.

A curse, it was a curse. No matter how hard Dylan had prayed the cup of prophecy be taken away from him, the "prophet" definition was still around, as much as it was in this example of insane devotional prose, a review of *Before the Flood* that appeared in the Italian press in 1974:

> Our Prophet is back. You need to know, all of you need to know. *Before the Flood* is one of the pinnacles of rock music. If you want to experience it the way you

are supposed to, get as stoned as you can, turn up the volume of your stereo, and begin to fly. . . . And then the last song, welcomed by an impassioned roar: "Blowin' in the Wind," the parable of a little, great man, a Jew, like That Other Jew, who was brought by the wind. Let's pray, now that we have found him again, that the wind will never take him away from us. Never, never again.[18]

However, before we turn Benedict XVI's suspicion of Dylan as a "false prophet" into an updated version of the Grand Inquisitor parable from the *Brothers Karamazov* (it would be even too easy, considering that Joseph Ratzinger *was* the Grand Inquisitor), we need some linguistic assessment. Indeed, Benedict XVI was misquoted. This is my translation of the original Italian passage:

> The Pope appeared tired, exhausted. At that very moment the stars of young people arrived, Bob Dylan and others whose names I do not remember. They had a completely different message from the one which the Pope had. There was reason to be skeptical—I was, and in some ways I still am—over whether it was really right to allow these types of "prophets" to appear.[19]

"Prophets," said Benedict XVI, not "prophet." Although he was kind enough to extend everybody a definition originally crafted for Dylan, we cannot help but wonder whether there were actually other prophets on stage that night. Maybe there were. What about Adriano Celentano, a flamboyant conservative Catholic rock and roller, the closest thing to Jerry Lee Lewis Italy has ever produced? Did John Paul II know that in 1985 Celentano directed a film in which he played a rock-and-roll Jesus Christ (absurdly named "Joan Lui") coming down to Earth to save mankind from Communism, drug dealers, abortion, organ trade, and a Japanese Satan, and that the film was a smash hit in the Soviet Union?

And what about Lucio Dalla, a gay rock and pop singer with a great "soul" voice and deep roots in jazz? In 1990, one year after the fall of the Berlin Wall, Dalla defiantly released a song called "Comunista" whose lyrics, penned by poet Roberto Roversi, began with "I sing the man who is dead, not the God who is risen."[20] Did John Paul II know about that? Did he care?

Maybe not, or not too much. Relentlessly anti-Communist as he was, he had lived in Italy long enough to understand that "cattocomunismo" (Catholic Communism, or Communist Catholicism) has been the unique Italian response to the cold war madness. And Dalla didn't sing "Comunista" to the pope, of course not. He sang "You've Got a Friend." Who was the friend he was suggesting was around? John Paul II himself? Bob Dylan? Jesus Christ? Well, if you listen long enough to *Canzoni*, Dalla's 1996 album (his most successful), you'll find a hidden track called "Vieni, spirito di Cristo" (Come, Spirit of Christ). It is also quite remarkable that the usual watchdogs of Dylan's revolutionary purity were outraged at his singing for the pope but found nothing objectionable in Dalla's presence on the same stage. "Cattocomunismo" indeed.

Dylan did not belong to this peculiar Italian drama of religion and ideology. Neither did Wojtyla.[21] But they have both waded in the waters to stop the flood of postmodernity, and what they have in common goes well beyond ideology. Possibly, it is their "visions of sin," to quote from Christopher Ricks.[22] More likely, their vision of Hell opening up beneath everybody's feet. And they have shared the impulse to stage that vision, to face its burden the only way they knew: by turning it into a theater, a song, a speech, a Eucharistic Congress, a never-ending tour, knowing all too well that nothing is never-ending in this mortal world, and what for a singer and a pope is blowin' in the wind may turn into an idiot wind for the next singer or the next pope.

Translating Dylan's Voice

The history of Dylan's translation into Italian is a tale of linguistic illusions, hazardous insights, unpoetic distortions, felicitous moments, and a general feeling of inadequacy at the uniqueness of Dylan's language. Dylan is not untranslatable, because he is a "great poet." With some exceptions, great poets are (more or less) translatable. They write, and some features of what they write—given the loss of their particular sound and the genius of a specific language—can be transferred into another language. Dylan, however, is not a writer. He may be presumed to write in English, but in fact he writes in a language he has largely fashioned for himself, where the rules of grammar, syntax, and logic are in constant probation. Dylan's writing is a supplement to his voice and does not have full autonomy unless it manages to incorporate the voice of his author in the writing process—as it happens, rather miraculously, in *Chronicles, Volume 1*. Translating Dylan means translating his voice, so much so that every Dylan translation sounds like the by-product of the (impossible) translation of his voice.

The poems and poetic prose of his early years, including *Tarantula,* are a warehouse of embryonic utterances waiting for their master's voice to turn them into an aural performance. "Last Thoughts on Woody Guthrie" may or may not be a great poem, but it is great material for Dylan's voice performing it at the New York Town Hall in 1963. Even *Chronicles,* which was supposed to be Dylan's access to pure writing, is a totally oral book. As a matter of fact, *Chronicles* may very well be the real "mouthbook" Dylan wanted to compose when he jotted down *Tarantula* ("The Falcon's Mouthbook" is the title of *Tarantula*'s first chapter). On the other hand, Dylan's voice is many voices as well, an anthology of American voices forcing the singer who carries them to adopt constantly new approaches and new styles. Dylan is always singing. He never strays from singing, no matter if he speaks or writes. He sings when he speaks, as can be heard in many of his most inspired interviews and especially in the unending melody of his commentary during the *Theme Time Radio Hour,* which he hosts. And his writing is at its best when you can hear him singing between the lines.

It wasn't just the poor knowledge of American idioms that created problems for the first Italian translators of Dylan's songs, but also their failure in understanding Dylan's subtle, and sometimes not so subtle, revolt against writing (the *Basement Tapes* are a case in point, yet the same could be said for several songs in the *Blonde on Blonde* period).

The first translation *(Blues, ballate e canzoni)* appeared in 1971, with an introduction by Fernanda Pivano, whom Allen Ginsberg used to call "a very distinguished Italian literary lady."[23] How the Roman-based Newton Compton publishing house managed to obtain or circumvent copyrights two years before the first official publication *(Writings and Drawings,* Knopf, 1973) is still a mystery. Young translator Stefano Rizzo deserves credit for the heroic task he faced. Equipped with just a basic knowledge of blues and folk jargons, despite awkward moments and unavoidable mistakes, he managed to put together a serviceable translation that has remained, for many, the first and maybe only access to the classic Dylan of the 1960s. In 1972 Rizzo published a second volume *(Canzoni d'amore e di protesta),* which included several songs available only on bootlegs. Without access to copyrighted transcriptions, it is very likely that he transcribed directly from the recordings or relied on transcriptions that tried, not always successfully, to penetrate Dylan's arcane pronunciation. His most famous mistake, as was debated for months by the readers of *Linus* (an intellectual comic book magazine that brought *Peanuts* to Italy, and hosted music reviews and discussions), was his interpretation of "Don't think twice, it's all right." Rizzo translated it as "non credere che vada bene" (don't think that's all right, or don't think it's all right that way). To his puzzled readers, Rizzo explained that Dylan never used commas; therefore, the line had to be read as one sentence. Indeed there are no commas in Rizzo's transcription, but they are definitely there in *Writings and Drawings.* The point is, however, that it makes no difference whether Dylan used them or not. Punctuation belongs to writing, and not to the voice. It is the pause in Dylan's voice that suggests what the line is about.[24]

In 1973, Mondadori, the largest Italian publisher, put out *Tarantula.* The translator, Andrea D'Anna, strove against the impossible. No one at the time knew the intricacies of American pop culture enough to get *Tarantula* approximately right. In D'Anna's translation the innocuous pop singer Fabian, a minor idol of the late 1950s, becomes "un fabiano," while the translator's note dutifully explains that Dylan was referring to the Fabian Society, a vaguely socialist British association that for a few years counted H. G. Wells among its members. "Maria needs a shot" becomes "Maria ha bisogno di una chiavata" (Maria needs some f——ing). A list of the translator's mistakes in the first chapter of *Tarantula* would take several pages. The point, again, is not the translator's insufficient training, but his assumption of dealing with a "written" text, so much so that "broad save the clean" (which is obviously a phonetic pun on "God save the Queen") is translated adventurously as "con magnanimità salva gli innocenti" (with generosity, he saves the innocent).[25]

In 1978 Newton Compton published a third collection, *Folk, canzoni e poesie.* The translator, Alessandro Roffeni, was a young scholar of American literature with a good knowledge of folk and blues tradition. His translations are a major step ahead in terms of understanding and accuracy. In his introduction, Roffeni is also at pains to distance himself from dylanolatry. His admiration for Dylan notwithstanding, Roffeni is not particularly impressed by Dylan's borrowings from Symbolist poetry. He does not think that Dylan deserves to be considered a "great poet" or, even less, "the greatest American poet of the 20th century," as Pivano was championing him (when she was not championing Ginsberg). Yet, Roffeni sincerely appreciates Dylan's poetical output, such as "11 Outlined Epitaphs" and "Some Other Kind of Songs…" not as great poetry, but because it shows that the time for great poetry is over, and a nervous, impure, erotic language is all that is left to the present-day poet.

An equally competent, if less elegant, translation appeared two years later (*Tutte le canzoni 1973–1980,* by Marina Morbiducci and Massimo Scarafoni), covering the period from *Planet Waves* to *Saved* (again, copyright issues were mysteriously resolved or ignored by another Roman publisher, Lato-Side).

Between 1990 and 1993 the then Milan-based Arcana Edizioni published *Mr. Tambourine. Tutte le canzoni e le poesie,* in three volumes. It was the first official translation of Dylan songs, entirely based on *Lyrics 1962–1985* (Knopf, 1985). The translator was Tito Schipa Jr., son of one of the finest lyric tenors of the twentieth century (1888–1965). Tito Jr. has had an undeservedly obscure career as a rock innovator and songwriter. In 1967 he composed *Then an Alley (E poi una strada),* a one-act "musical situation" based on eighteen Dylan melodies, and staged it at the Sistina Theater in Rome. In January 1970 he followed up with *Orfeo 9,* a "rock opera" that became a double album and a film (Academy Award winner Bill Conti was the musical conductor). In the early 1970s, Schipa seemed bound to become a powerful singer-songwriter, but in fact his success rarely went beyond the Roman clubs where he often performed. I counted myself among his fans, and I could not but feel severely disappointed when I read his Dylan translations.

Schipa was obsessed with rhyme scheme, to the point of sacrificing the economy of the verse, metric consistency, wit, and the power of Dylan specific imagery, not to mention the Italian language's elegance, for the sake of rhymes that often were unnatural, farfetched, or just unnecessary. His ignorance of American idioms was sometimes puzzling: to quote a couple of examples out of hundreds, in "Highway 61 Revisited" he translated "a promoter who nearly fell off the floor" as if the promoter had actually fallen through the floor. In "Yeah! Heavy and a Bottle of Bread," he translated "me and the comic book" as "il libro allegro e io," as if the comic book were actually a "merry" book. He even tried to Italianize Dylan, with results that verged on the grotesque. Again in "Highway 61 Revisited," which could be a case study for a very bad translation, he rendered "Georgia Sam" with "Bingo-Bongo" in order to make the reference more understandable to Italian readers. The name "Bingo-Bongo" comes from a song performed by Sophia Loren in *Too Bad She's Bad* (*Peccato che sia una canaglia,* directed by Alessandro Blasetti, 1954), and refers to an African black man who is scared of Western civilization. It is not even an Italian reference. The source is "Civilization" by Bob Hilliard and Carl Sigman, a hit for Danny Kaye and the Andrews Sisters in 1947 ("Bongo, Bongo, Bongo, I don't want to leave the Congo…"). To make it worse, the name "Bingo-Bongo" has assumed very unpleasant tones in current Italian language (the racist Northern League party uses it to address African immigrants), and it did not sound very good in 1990 either. Dylan's "Georgia Sam" is a made-up name, but it reminds the blues-alerted Dylan listener of Blind Willie McTell and Thomas A. Dorsey, who sometimes adopted the record-ing names of "Georgia Bill" and "Georgia Tom." The proof of translation is in its reversal, and if we retranslate "Bingo-Bongo" into English, we are forced to come up with words that sound worse than "Uncle Tom" and whose presence in Dylan's lexicon is unthinkable.

Dylan can and must be freely adapted in a musical cover version needing to keep the rhythmic pattern of the original, but not on the translator's page, which is too dependent on the facing English text. Schipa, on his part, has resisted all criticism raised against him, arguing that his creative approach was much more Dylanesque in spirit than any mere service translation. His work has been influential to the extent that for many years no other comprehensive collection of Dylan lyrics and poems was available.

Beginning in June 1999, however, the Internet began playing a role. Created by Michele Murino, a comic-book seller based in Aosta, in northern Italy, www.maggiesfarm.it is now one of the most comprehensive Dylan Web sites in any lan-guage, if not *the* most comprehensive. With slow pace and determination, Murino has been posting and translating every bit and piece ever written, sung, spoken, or mumbled by Dylan. His Web site includes alternate lyrics, additional stanzas, live performance variations, and every cover that Dylan has performed, not to mention poems, interviews, letters, postcards, liner notes, and laundry lists. His translations are firmly grounded in the service department, but Murino has reserved a more creative space for himself with a few translations in *romanesco,* and he has also in-cluded Neapolitan translations volunteered by contributors to his Web site.

I was working on my translation of *Lyrics 1962–2001* when I read Murino's *ro-manesco* rendition of "Like a Rolling Stone" in which "Miss Lonely" becomes "Miss puzza-ar-naso." An English equivalent would be "Miss Snotty" or "Miss Stiff-Upper-Lip." Neither translation, however, does justice to the slangy quality of "puzza-ar-naso," which describes a young lady who goes around as if smelling a bad odor under her nose. Although Murino's solution is obviously stronger than "Miss Lonely," it is a good approximation of Dylan *singing* "Miss Lonely" the way he does. Dutifully impressed, I immediately revised my translation of "Like a Rolling Stone," trying to lower the style, to make it sound more like Dylan's voice rather than Dylan's words. However, there was a problem.

In American English, the colloquial or slangy level does not necessarily sound like low style (I am referring here to the classical distinction of styles in "high," "medium," and "low" as it is discussed in ancient rhetoric, which largely identifies style with lexical choices). Italian lost its slangy side when it became standardized and had to leave it to regional dialects. "Miss-puzza-ar-naso" (even in the correct spelling, "Miss-puzza-*al*-naso") would be perfect in a theater, with an actor per-forming the song as a monologue, but as a standard translation of "Miss Lonely," it is simply too low. Rewriting the whole Dylan corpus in streetwise Italian would not be impossible. But then we would have a truly monotone Dylan, deprived of his high style — the style of "Lay Down Your Weary Tune," "Chimes of Freedom," "Mr. Tambourine Man," "Every Grain of Sand," "Angelina," "Jokerman," and "I and I," not to mention "Not Dark Yet" or "Ain't Talkin'." Dylan's output is an oeuvre meant to prove that, as in the Emerald Tablet, "that which is below is like that which is above" (Isaac Newton's translation), and no style must be allowed to take over at the expense of the others. Therefore, instead of my style I lowered my pride and translated "Miss Lonely" with "Miss Malinconia." I wanted the alliteration "mi-ma-li" as an equivalent of the English "mi-lo-ly," and I also remembered a song of the 1930s that began with "Buongiorno tristezza, amica della mia malinconia" (Good morning loneliness, friend of my melancholy). It was one of those songs supposed to make young ladies cry, and it could be a good ironic commentary on the young upper-class lady who didn't know that her destiny was to become a rolling stone.

Faced with 355 songs to translate, I realized I could not confine myself to a specific style or defend my idiosyncrasies as a translator. I had to embrace all stylistic choices: versified prose ("Hurricane"), free verse ("A Hard Rain's A-Gonna Fall"), blank verse ("Motorpsycho Nightmare"), limited and strategic use of rhyme ("Desolation Row"), and full rhyme and metric ("Love Minus Zero/No Limit"). In the case of "Mozambique," a song that I have always disliked, I am sure I spent more time translating it than Dylan and Jacques Levy spent writing it, because without the rhyme pattern it looked like it was written by a travel agent.[26]

A real challenge (one of the most revealing of the "unwritten" quality of Dylan's output) was the first stanza of "My Back Pages." Its elliptical syntax eludes both writing and orality. It was Robert Christgau who observed that "Crimson flames tied through my ears" was one of the ugliest lines ever written by Dylan.[27] On the other hand, my colleague David Mikics of the University of Houston has admitted to me his enduring fascination with the same line. I had thoroughly analyzed the personal and political implications of "My Back Pages" in my Dylan book, or so I thought, but it was only during the translation process that I understood why the song could elicit such different reactions.[28] Its strangeness may go unnoticed when we hear it sung, or if we read it without paying too much attention, but the translator cannot afford such luxury. I had to come up with three syntactic interpretations of the song's first stanza before I could decide which one I was going to translate:

> Hypothesis 1 (the "crimson flames" are the only grammatical subject and "pounced" is a past perfect): "*Crimson flames* tied through my ears / Rolling high and mighty traps / *Pounced* with fire on flaming roads / Using ideas as my maps."
>
> Hypothesis 2 (first the crimson flames tie their rolling traps, and then they pounce roads and use ideas): "Crimson flames tied [were tying] through my ears / [Their] *rolling* (high and mighty) *traps*. / [The crimson flames] pounced with fire on flaming roads, / Using ideas as my maps."
>
> Hypothesis 3 (the one I adopted, after discussing it with David Mikics): "Crimson flames tied through my ears / [Were] rolling high and mighty traps. / Pounced with fire on flaming roads, / [I was] using ideas as my maps."[29]

Chronicles, Volume 1 (2005) was the greatest challenge, though. Sometimes awkwardly, sometimes wonderfully, *Chronicles* takes writing by the hand and brings it back into the realm of voice. In chapter 5, Dylan observes that with folk songs "You could exhaust all the combinations of your vocabulary without having to learn any vocabulary."[30] The same could be said about Dylan's writing. Dylan cannot write in the conventional sense, yet he writes as no one else writes. It is also true that he cannot sing, and yet he sings as no one else could.

Before receiving the proofs of *Chronicles,* I had a xeroxed copy of the copyist's manuscript to work with. Not Dylan's original manuscript, but a fair approximation of Dylan's writing process. Dylan typed the whole book in first draft and as fast as he could, Kerouac style, keeping the capital case key always pressed so that he did not have to lose time alternating between capital case and lower case. The copyist was ordered to reproduce the manuscript without changes, except reinserting the lower case in the text. The result that I had in my hands was a nightmare of typos, errors, misspellings, and the constant use of "it's" instead of "its." The recognizable mistakes, however, were easy to deal with. The real problem was the unpredictability of paragraphs that crossed different stylistic levels in the space of a few lines. I had to find a way to re-create the strangeness of Dylan's prose in Italian, at the risk of looking like a translator who cannot write. For example, in his last paragraph on the American Civil War (chapter 2), Dylan creates an impervious linguistic wall when he writes:

> The age that I was living in didn't resemble this age, but yet it did in some
> mysterious and traditional way. Not just a little bit, but a lot. There was a broad
> spectrum and commonwealth that I was living upon, and the basic psychology of
> that life was every bit a part of it. If you turned the lights towards it, you could
> see the full complexity of human nature. Back there, America was put on the
> cross, died and was resurrected. There was nothing synthetic about it. The god-
> awful truth of that would be the all-encompassing template behind everything
> that I would write.[31]

It is a beautiful passage. Even more remarkably, it falls miraculously short of stylistic chaos. Of course you are not supposed to say "but yet," but I didn't feel compelled to reproduce that oddness in Italian. "There was nothing synthetic about it," however, was another matter. Did Dylan mean there was nothing chemical, nothing prefabricated or artificial in the way America ran to its crucifixion? Or did he mean there was nothing, in the whole process of the Civil War, pointing toward a synthesis? I opted for an Italian expression that was as ambiguous as it was in English: "Non c'era sentore di sintetico in ciò," meaning "one could feel (or smell) nothing synthetic in it." And what about "broad spectrum and commonwealth," which takes an unexpected turn toward high style? And "was resurrected"? My good editor at Feltrinelli's at the last moment changed my translation "fu risorta" into the most common "risorse." But Dylan was quoting Paul, 1 Corinthians 15:4 ("he was raised on the third day" in the King James version), and I wanted to preserve the old biblical sound of "fu risorta" (was raised) the way I used to hear it during Mass when I was a boy, and not the plain "risorse" or "resuscitò" (raised) found in more recent translations.

Too bad, but not too bad. There was worse ahead. I remember that one night, coming across a specific page in chapter 3, I felt suddenly relieved, as if I had been given a moment of reprieve from the idiomatic tornado I was weathering. As it happened, I was translating Dylan's quote from Archibald MacLeish's *Scratch,* and MacLeish writes *in English,* just plain average English, standard English, *New York Times* English.[32] On the other hand, and after reading *Scratch* and *Conquistador* (MacLeish's long poem also quoted by Dylan), I daresay that Dylan, with all his knockin' on the language's doors, is a greater poet than MacLeish.

Because he is an inventor. He invents unheard-of linguistic combinations. At the end of chapter 4, Dylan gives his definition of the future artist: "Someone with a chopped topped head and a power in the community."[33] A "chopped head car" is a car with a flat front. A "chopped top car," however, is a modified race car, its hood removed to give more air to the engine. An insanely literal translation would require the artist of the future to be someone with a squarely cut head and the hood removed (mind that Dylan manages to say all of the above in three syllables). My final version was: "Qualcuno a cui era saltata la calotta del cranio ma che era anche radicato nella sua comunità" (someone whose head top had been blown off but was also rooted in his community). Definitely not three syllables, but it was three o'clock in the morning when I decided that I could do no better.

Dylan might have written *Chronicles* like Kerouac, but he did not write it in the style of Kerouac. He also took care in keeping his distance from Kerouac, for example, when he observed that in the end characters like Moriarty inspire only idiocy. It was not only anxiety of influence on his part. Very little in Dylan's prose reminds us of Kerouac. Hemingway's Nick Adams is a closer reference. I was alerted to the Hemingway trail when I came across this sentence in chapter 4: "Long time ago, good; now, no good." I thought it sounded like a quote, and a quick Google search proved that it came from "Fathers and Sons," one of the Nick Adams stories. Here is another one from "The Last Good Country": "There's only one day at a time here, then it's tonight and then tomorrow will be today again" (the "then it's tonight and then tomorrow will be today again" part is quoted verbatim by Dylan, again in chapter 4).[34]

I don't want to start another Henry Timrod case. I have just said that Dylan is an inventor. He is also a *bricoleur,* and he may be an inventor precisely to the extent he is a *bricoleur.* Much more significant than all this love and theft is the way Dylan channels some great characters of American literature into his writings. That was my real discovery as a translator. Dylan never imitates Hemingway, Kerouac, Salinger, or Bellow. Rather, he adopts the language and idiosyncrasies of their characters. In a word: their *voices.* When he tries to explain the metaphysical implications of the guitar accompaniment style he learned from Lonnie Johnson, he sounds like Dean Moriarty explaining Schopenhauer to Sal Paradise. When he is supposed to be busy with a Columbia manager and instead allows his thoughts to wander outside the manager's office window, he is not writing like Salinger, but Salinger could have put in Holden Caulfield's mouth the same words Dylan uses. When he describes the people he met in Minneapolis or the newspapers of the Civil War with the most unexpected turn of phrase, he is not writing like Saul Bellow, yet he speaks with the same bizarre language of Augie March.[35]

Dylan does not write just because he is a writer. But who is a writer? Dylan writes because he is possessed by voices that go through him and that he lets through. He does not write the way he speaks (anybody could do that). He writes the way he sings.

Notes

1. Clinton Heylin, *Bob Dylan: My Life in Stolen Moments: Day by Day, 1941–1995* (New York: Schirmer Books, 1996), 38–39. "Boots of Spanish Leather" owes something to "Barbara Allen" as well.

2. "Bob went to Italy after the first of the year. He rushed to Perugia, but Suze had left for New York just a couple of days before. Dylan later told me: 'I was in Italy with Odetta. Suze had gone back to the States and that's when I worked up the melodies of 'Boots of Spanish Leather' and 'Girl from the North Country.'" Anthony Scaduto, *Bob Dylan* (London: Helter Skelter, 1996), 129. Scaduto's chronology, however, may not be accurate. It is very likely that Bob and Suze missed each other in New York. According to Heylin, Suze Rotolo sailed from Naples on the *Leonardo Da Vinci* on December 13, arriving in New York "five days later" (on December 18), while Dylan flew to London on December 17 or 18.

3. Dylan may refer to *Mama Rosa,* an ABC sitcom of the 1950s with Anna Demetrio and Vito Scotti. Mama Rosa's, however, was also a favorite student restaurant in Dinkytown in Minneapolis. My thanks to Colleen Sheehy for this bit of information.

4. The quote from the unpublished *Playboy* interview is taken from "Every Mind Polluting Word: Assorted Bob Dylan Utterances: A Collection of Speeches, Interviews, Press Conferences, etc." updated to August 28, 2006, PDF file of 1,391 pages assembled by "artur, the xxxx" (http://hisbobness.info/download/empw060911.pdf).

5. Ralph Waldo Emerson, "Self-Reliance," in *Emerson's Essays,* with an introduction by Irwin Edman (New York: Harper and Row, 1951), 59–60.

6. The interview took place in Forest Hills, New York, late summer 1965. It first appeared in Craig McGregor, ed., *Bob Dylan: The Early Years: A Retrospective* (New York: Morrow, 1972; New York: Da Capo, 1990), 84. Now also in Jonathan Cott, ed., *Bob Dylan: The Essential Interviews* (New York: Wenner Books, 2006), 49.

7. Between 1959 and the beginning of 1963, Burroughs's bibliographers list *Jabberwock* (Edinburgh, 1959), *La nouvelle Revue Française* (1960), *Haute Societé* (1960), *Sidewalk* (Edinburgh, 1960), *British Journal of Addiction* (1960), *Locus solus* (Isére, 1960), *Olympia* (Paris, 1961), *Rhinozeros* (Hamburg, 1961), *Nul* (Belgium, 1962), *Transatlantic Review* (London, 1962), and *Randstad* (Amsterdam, January 1963). See Joe Maynard and Barry Miles, *William S. Burroughs: A Bibliography 1953–73* (Charlottesville: University Press of Virginia, 1978), 32–50.

8. "For the Love of It," *Time,* Friday, April 10, 1964. Pete Seeger performed at the Folkstudio in November 1962.

9. http://www.nataliedarbeloff.com/autobio15.html; thanks to John Hinchey for the reference.

10. For information on the Folkstudio, see Matteo Guarnaccia and Antonio Tettamanti, *Bob Dylan. Le risposte nel vento in formato poster* (Rome: Ottaviano, 1980); Dario Salvatori, *Folkstudio Story* (Turin: Studio Forma, 1981); and Ignazio Macchiarella, *Il canto necessario. Giovanna Marini compositrice, didatta e interprete* (Udine: Nota, 2005).

11. *A Hill* was originally included in Anthony Hecht, *The Hard Hours* (New York: Atheneum, 1967). Here it is taken from *La luce migliore. Poeti americani in Italia*, ed. Alessandro Carrera and Thomas Simpson (Milan: Medusa, 2006), 94–97.

12. July 23, 2001, press conference, De La Ville Intercontinental Roma Hotel, Rome, Italy. Our transcription comes from an audio recording. A rather accurate account is in *Isis* 99 (October-November 2001): 46–50. It does not include, however, Dylan's last mention of the Coliseum.

13. Libreria Editrice Vaticana's official translation, http://www.vatican.va/holy_father/john_paul_ii/speeches/1997/september/documents/hf_jp-ii_spe_19970927_youth-bologna_en.html.

14. Dylan *was* tense. In the epic of Dylan-besotted guys from all over the world, there is room for Alessandro Allemandi, an art publisher from Turin, who stalked Dylan during the whole papal concert. Dylan and his band were waiting for their access to the stage. As Mr. Allemandi later told me, Dylan was standing still, his liquid eyes moving quickly in every direction, caring for nothing except the cue he was waiting for, like a track-and-field runner one moment before the pistol shot. After he left the stage, Dylan was so relaxed that he even shook hands with Allemandi (which made him, for all eternity, the first person Dylan shook hands with after he shook them with the pope).

15. In the summer of 2005 I was invited to attend a Dylan night in a Roman folk club. After a brief sermon on Dylan the pacifist and anti-Vietnam war hero, the lead singer of the cover band looked at me (as the resident expert) for a confirmation of what he had just said. Not wishing to spoil the party, I mumbled something about Dylan being definitely on the side of the angels, even though he never said anything specific about Vietnam. The lead singer (who was approximately my age) looked at me again and very loudly said, "Are you telling me that for forty years I have believed just a bunch of bullshit?"

16. When *Modern Times* came out, however, while the "rock critics" who do not understand musical references prior to "Love Me Do" dismissed it, more politically inclined journalists were beside themselves. *L'Unità*, newspaper of the former Communist Party, ran an article about *Modern Times* being the most political album Dylan had ever released (which may be the truth, for all we know). Even *Il Sole 24 ore*, the Italian equivalent of the *Wall Street Journal*, claimed that the whole album was a portrait of America from the point of view of the impoverished working class (which may also be the truth). It is hard not to sympathize with people who have waited forty-four years for Dylan to say the word "proletariat." Their patience outdoes Griselda's, the faithful woman who in the last tale of Boccaccio's *Decameron* waits twenty years, amid horrible humiliations, for her husband to say, "You deserve to be my wife."

17. "Conversazione con Alessandro Portelli," in Bob Dylan, *Tutte le canzoni (1973–1980)*, ed. and trans. Massimo Morbiducci and Marina Scarafoni (Rome: Lato-Side, 1980), 249–50; my translation.

18. Manuel Insolera, "Feroce e tagliente: Bob Dylan è tornato," *Ciao 2001*, July 28, 1974, 30; my translation.

19. "Il Papa appariva stanco, affaticato. Proprio in quel momento arrivarono le *star* dei giovani, Bob Dylan e altri di cui non ricordo il nome. Avevano un messaggio completamente diverso da quello per cui il Papa si impegna. C'era ragione di essere scettici—io lo ero e, in

un certo senso, lo sono ancora—di dubitare se davvero fosse giusto far intervenire questo genere di 'profeti'"; Joseph Ratzinger Benedetto XVI, *Giovanni Paolo II. Il mio amato predecessore*, ed. Elio Guerriero (Cinisello Balsamo: Edizioni San Paolo, 2007), 25–26.

20. "Canto l'uomo che è morto, non il Dio che è risorto," Dalla-Roversi, "Comunista," in *Cambio* (Pressing, 1990).

21. Or did he? Poland can be as strange as Italy. In the summer of 1978 I was studying German (sort of) at the Maria Laach Benedictine Abbey in West Germany. There I met Pater Cyrill von Korvin Krasinski (1905–92), director of the abbey's school and a well-known scholar of Asian religions and Tibetan medicine. In the following years, Pater Krasinski would have often been called to Rome to perform Tibetan massages on his old friend Karol Wojtyla. On December 13, 1981, when Communist General Wojciech Jaruzelski, apparently to prevent a Russian invasion, imposed martial law against the Solidarnosc revolution, a friend of mine who was in Maria Laach heard Pater Krasinski mutter, "My cousin has always been a little impulsive in his judgment." His cousin was General Jaruzelski.

22. Christopher Ricks, *Dylan's Visions of Sin* (New York: Viking, 2003; New York: Ecco Press, 2004).

23. Fernanda Pivano (b. 1917), a *legendary* translator—she was even incarcerated in the 1940s by the Fascist regime for translating American literature—had actually met Bob Dylan, together with Allen Ginsberg (she would later become Ginsberg's translator), Lawrence Ferlinghetti, and Michael McClure, in San Francisco on December 2, 1965, the day before the famous televised press conference of December 3. It was the beginning of an enduring fascination on her part, as well as a long string of articles in which she has always adopted the Old West notion of journalism ("When the fact becomes a legend, print the legend"). They met again in Rome on July 5, 1998, when she went backstage after his concert. Dylan looked at her and said: "Nanda? That's not possible." He hugged her, and as Pivano told later (she has never been known for playing it cool), in that moment she felt she had received her Nobel Prize.

24. Rizzo's translations are still in print today, proudly uncorrected, unedited, and untouched. On the back cover of *Blues, ballate e canzoni*'s latest reprint (2005), it is possible to learn that Dylan grew up in a little town called Higging.

25. To be honest, when Santo Pettinato and I retranslated *Tarantula* for our annotated edition, we had to work nights and days without even being sure if the book deserved all the effort we were putting in it. "Broad save the clean," however, was relatively easy to wrestle with. We began with "Dio salvi la regina" (God save the Queen) with the idea of modifying it gradually until we were as close as possible to an Italian equivalent of the original pun. First we came up with "la zoccola salvi la fregola" (the broad save the heat—the sexual heat, that is), then with "zio salvi la cugina" (uncle save the cousin—"zio" being a common substitute for "Dio" in mild blasphemous speech), and finally with "zio salvi la sgualdrina" (uncle save the broad), which can be understood, if one wants to, as "God save the broad." But we were not always that lucky.

26. So far, I have translated *Chronicles, Volume 1*—"1"instead of "One" being the only difference in the title (Milan: Feltrinelli, 2005), *Lyrics 1962–2001* (Milan: Feltrinelli, 2006), and *Tarantula*, with Santo Pettinato (Milan: Feltrinelli, 2007). For copyright reasons, our new translation of *Tarantula* is still credited to Andrea D'Anna, translator of the first Italian edition (Milan: Mondadori, 1973), while Pettinato and I appear as the book's editors. *Lyrics* and *Tarantula* include extensive notes and indexes.

27. Robert Christgau, "Rock Lyrics Are Poetry (Maybe)," in *The Age of Rock: Sounds of the American Cultural Revolution—A Reader*, ed. Jonathan Eisen (New York: Vintage, 1969), 233.

28. Alessandro Carrera, *La voce di Bob Dylan. Una spiegazione dell'America* (Milan: Feltrinelli, 2001), 169–79.

29. Fiamme cremisi strette fra le orecchie / tendevano le più arroganti trappole. / Tempestato dal fuoco su vie in fiamme, / mi servivo di idee come mie bussole. It goes without saying that my translation of *Lyrics 1962–2001* did not come out without some embarrassing oversights. In "Subterranean Homesick Blues" I got it right about Maggie and the heat putting plants in her bed, but I forgot that "Keep a clean nose" does not mean that one has to keep his nose clean.

30. Bob Dylan, *Chronicles, Volume 1* (New York: Simon and Schuster, 2004), 240.

31. Ibid., 86.

32. Dylan's quote does not fully correspond to MacLeish's *Scratch* as it was published by Houghton Mifflin in 1971 (94–95). Dylan may have quoted from a draft in his possession.

33. Dylan, *Chronicles*, 219.

34. The two Hemingway quotes are at pages 131 and 181. In his blog, a very puzzled Edward M. Cook has listed five borrowings found in *Chronicles:* Here's one from *Huckleberry Finn:* "Every night we passed towns, some of them away up on black hillsides, nothing but just a shiny bed of lights. . . . There wasn't a sound there; everybody was asleep." Dylan's reworking: "One night when everyone was asleep and I was sitting at the kitchen table, nothing on the hillside but a shiny bed of lights . . ." (165). In chapter 2, the description of Chloe Kiel as "cool as pie," "a Maltese kitten, a solid viper" owes something to a passage from *Really the Blues,* by Mezz Mezzrow and Bernard Wolfe (New York: Random House, 1946): "Baby this that powerful man with that good grass that'll make you tip through the highways and byways like a Maltese kitten. Mezz, this is my new dinner and she's a solid viper." And later on in the same book, we read of a black man "talking to a woman cool as pie." Jack London is subjected to some borrowings as well: "casting an embracing glance over the primordial landscape" in *Children of the Frost* becomes "I cast an embracing glance over the primordial landscape" (167). From *Tales of the Klondyke,* "Another tremendous section of the glacier rumbled earthward. The wind whipped in at the open doorway" is turned by Dylan into "Wind whipped in the open doorway and another kicking storm was rumbling earthward" (217). From Proust's *Within a Budding Grove,* "I caught a glimpse of the sea through the leafy boughs of trees. . . . But on the other hand I was no longer near enough to the sea. . . . I no longer felt any power beneath its colours." And here is Dylan in chapter 4, giving an impression of his home garden in Malibu: "Walking back to the main house, I caught a glimpse of the sea through the leafy boughs of the pines. I wasn't near it, but could feel the power beneath its colors" (162). The boughs of the pines are not exactly "leafy," but never mind. All quotes can be found at ralphriver.blogspot.com/2006/09/more-dylan-thefts.html.

35. Again, it was my colleague David Mikics who pointed out to me that the way Augie March speaks of Ira Einhorn could easily come out of *Chronicles.* This is a random sample: "Thus, without risking a cent, Einhorn made more than four hundred dollars in this particular deal. He was proud, gleeful with me; this was what he really dug. It was a specimen triumph of the kind—only bigger and bigger—he wanted his whole history to consist of." The last sentence sounds distinctively Dylanesque.

9. Bob Dylan's Reception in Japan in the 1960s and 1970s

Mikiko Tachi

Since the mid-1960s, Bob Dylan has enjoyed a strong presence in Japan, and today he has followers among people of different ages. Many musicians and artists credit Dylan for inspiration. On October 9, 2006, for example, Japanese rock musician Koji Wakui organized a concert and talk show in tribute to Dylan to celebrate the release of *Modern Times*. Artists and critics gathered to discuss Dylan's influence on them: they performed Dylan's pieces as well as their own compositions as the audience packed a live music club in Daikanyama, Tokyo. Given Dylan's popularity and the high regard for his work among Japanese artists, it is surprising to find that when he came to Japan for his first concert tour in 1978, many in the media portrayed him in a negative manner, some even resorting to anti-Semitism. In this essay, I examine newspaper and magazine articles on Dylan between 1965 and 1978 and demonstrate changes in his reception in this country. Placing Dylan in the historical montage of folk music in Japan, I argue that he was partially criticized because Japanese folk music had already been established before his arrival, with Japanese folksingers as the figures of authority.

Bob Dylan as the Protest Singer-Songwriter and "God of Folk"

Bob Dylan first came to be known in Japan as the writer of folk songs popularized by such well-known folksingers and groups as Peter, Paul and Mary and Joan Baez. *Heibon Punch*, a weekly magazine for youth, was the first popular magazine to speak about Dylan. An article in the April 26, 1965, issue introduced him to the Japanese audience:

> The readers may not be familiar with the name Bob Dylan. He is a 23-year-old young man, a singer and a guitarist who also plays the harmonica, who has written numerous masterpieces of contemporary folk songs known to the public as hit songs by Peter, Paul and Mary.[1]

This article, titled "Odetta, Whom Harry Belafonte Admires, Comes to Japan," was written to announce the upcoming visit of Odetta. The name of Belafonte, who had already gained popularity in Japan through his 1960 visit, was used to suggest the importance of Odetta. However, a significant portion of the article ended up describing how popular Dylan was in Great Britain at that time. Although by the time this article appeared, Dylan had already released songs where he used electric instruments, he was still perceived as a "folk" singer in contrast to rock-and-roll musicians such as the Beatles. The article reported that the Beatles would appear at Dylan's upcoming concert and that it would be an "on-stage battle" between Dylan's folk music and the Beatles' "rhythm and blues."

Japanese youth were first exposed to folk music through radio, records, and singers' visits to Japan, starting with Harry Belafonte in 1960, the Kingston Trio in 1961, the Brothers Four in 1962 and 1964, Pete Seeger in 1963, and Peter, Paul and Mary in 1964.[2] It was especially after the 1962 Brothers Four concert that Japanese folk fans took up guitars themselves and performed American folk songs on their own, modeled on American folksingers. Joan Baez's rendition of "Donna Donna," in particular, was a popular introductory piece for the young enthusiasts of folk songs and guitar.[3] Baez was dubbed the "queen of folk," and many Japanese admired her angelic soprano singing voice along with her physical appearance and pacifist activities.

The media showcased Dylan as a protest singer and songwriter. An article in *Heibon Punch* in February 1966, for example, portrayed Dylan as a socially conscious, anti-commercial troubadour who traveled freely around the country, stopping by college campuses to sing songs and rejecting lucrative offers for television shows. The article reported that Pete Seeger, Bob Dylan, and Joan Baez were the three protest singers that taunted the White House by gaining the support of young college students through antiwar songs. It explained that while popular media censored or blacklisted them, serious college students preferred these "outcasts of the pop music world" to the more commercial folk-singing groups such as the Kingston Trio, the Limeliters, and the Brothers Four. The article also suggested that the popularity of Seeger, Dylan, and Baez far exceeded that of Elvis Presley and the Beatles. The writer of the article explained that the trio appealed to students because their songs "voiced the frank feelings of young Americans who hate the war and do not want to be drafted."[4]

Dylan came to be labeled the "god of folk" *(foku no kamisama)*. Japanese singer-songwriters and protest folksingers looked up to Dylan as a model and source of inspiration. Goro Nakagawa, one of the pioneers of political folk songs in Japan, translated and sang Dylan's songs, including "Masters of War," in Japanese. In addition, his protest song titled "Jukensei Blues" (1967), which addressed the problem of the education system in Japan by depicting the miserable life of a student preparing for college entrance examinations, was based on the tune of Dylan's "North Country Blues." Singer-songwriter Takuro Yoshida emulated Dylan with his guitar and harmonica style and came to be known as the "Japanese-made" *(wasei)* Bob Dylan. Folksinger Kenji Endo heard "Like a Rolling Stone" on the Far East Network (FEN) as a college student and started to play the guitar in 1967. Tetsuo Saito was also inspired by Dylan to become a folksinger.[5] Nobuyasu Okabayashi led the protest folksong movement in Japan from the mid- to late 1960s and was compared to Dylan. He was dubbed Japan's *(nihon no)* Bob Dylan, even inheriting Dylan's title as the "god of folk."[6] By acknowledging Dylan's influence on them, these Japanese folksingers claimed their legitimacy as folksingers.

Dylan's change in direction was reported in detail in April 1967 in Japanese *Playboy* magazine in an article titled "LSD-like Life of Bob Dylan, Former Lover of Joan Baez – Can the 'King of Folk-Rock' Revive?":

> Bob Dylan's name is well known in Japan as "the hero of protest songs" and "Joan Baez's former lover." But two years ago, he suddenly turned his back on politics and became the idol of teenagers all over the world as "the king of folk-rock." His former comrades now call him "traitor," and Joan Baez left him as well. Since his motorcycle accident last year, he leads a tumultuous and chaotic life, which evokes the world of LSD.[7]

The article summarized Dylan's life by describing the key moments in it: his running away from home on several occasions as a young boy, his relocation to New York in search of freedom and his encounter with his idol Woody Guthrie, his romance with Joan Baez and his ascendancy to stardom in the folk scene, the 1965 Newport Festival incident, and the motorcycle accident, which left him "seriously injured." The article reported that Dylan had once been the superstar among protest folksingers and had come close to marrying the queen of folk; however, having forsaken both, he was reduced to writing LSD-inspired songs and songs with homosexual themes, which might jeopardize his career. The article quoted an anonymous music critic who expressed his doubt as to whether Dylan would be able to appear on stage again.[8] Dylan's life had already assumed legendary status within the set narrative of the rise and fall of a folk star.

The Mystery of Bob Dylan: Negotiating the Implications of Bob Dylan's Songs

After his motorcycle accident in July 1966, Japanese popular media did not have much to report about Dylan until he began his concert tour with The Band in 1974. During this period, *New Music Magazine,* the first rock music magazine in Japan, periodically published essays on Dylan written by music critics. In fact, the magazine was founded by the music critic Toyo Nakamura precisely for the purpose of analyzing the new direction in music adopted by Dylan; Nakamura thought that both Dylan and the Beatles had paved the way for a new type of music. While the popular media focused on the personal life of Dylan in the mid-1960s, music critics focused on the lyrics (mostly through translation) and the "philosophy" behind Dylan's works; they rarely analyzed their musical aspects.

There were three major themes in the articles pertaining to Dylan written by Japanese music critics during this period, and these themes set the tone for the following periods as well. First, Japanese critics agreed that Dylan was a cryptic artist who defied understanding. They attributed this incomprehensibility partially to language and cultural differences that made accurate interpretations difficult. Despite the difficulty in understanding (or perhaps because of that), music critics assumed that Dylan's work was important and took him rather seriously. For example, music critic Kazuo Mihashi wrote that he had even suffered from insomnia and acute gastritis in his attempt to comprehend Dylan; Mihashi concluded that it was not necessary to understand every word of Dylan's songs and it was sufficient to *feel* something and take it back home.[9] Second, critics continued to look for signs indicating that Dylan remained a protest singer who conveyed messages through his songs. Third, critics and folksingers identified Dylan as the direct progenitor of Japanese folksingers, thereby occasionally relegating him to the past or suggesting that particular Japanese folksingers had surpassed him.

The assumption that Dylan was an important, mysterious artist who was beyond the comprehension of the Japanese was apparent in the essay "Incomprehensible Yet Beautiful: An Approach to Bob Dylan the Poet," by music critic and lyricist Reiko Yukawa. In the opening passage, Yukawa revealed her uneasiness with regard to claiming to comprehend Dylan:

> It was not until I learned that Bob Dylan was not necessarily a difficult poet to understand that I got interested in Bob Dylan. That does not mean, however, that he is easy to understand. . . . According to native speakers of English, Bob Dylan's songs are beautiful. . . . They say that it is sometimes not clear what he means but his words are beautiful.[10]

Although it was unclear who exactly the "native speakers" were, or where she obtained the information, Yukawa reasoned that Dylan's songs must be worth examining if native speakers had a liking for them. She proceeded to examine the manner in which Dylan's songs were actually "difficult to understand but beautiful" by analyzing "Rainy Day Women #12 & 35," a song that she did not find beautiful when she first heard it in 1966. Yukawa wrote that she had come to understand the song better after her visit to the Haight-Ashbury district, where she witnessed hippies who had "got stoned." She then comprehended other songs, including "Mr. Tambourine Man," as "drug songs" and wrote that Dylan's drug-inspired songs were more beautiful than his earlier pieces, as Dylan's imagination was more active in such songs. Thus, the concept that Dylan was on drugs enabled Yukawa to comprehend Dylan's songs; however, she conceded in the end that since she was Japanese, her opinion would not be of much importance.

The belief that there was probably some deep meaning in Dylan's songs and that it would ultimately be impossible to understand him completely was a common thread among articles in *New Music Magazine*. For example, at the beginning of his essay on Dylan's newly released album *Self Portrait*, Yosuke Kawamura wrote, "Everyone has been talking about what Dylan was thinking, and I'm fully aware that I am not capable of answering such a question."[11] Similarly, Satoru Hamano and Shinzo Ishiura agreed, after having written six-page essays on the subject of Dylan's *Self Portrait,* that it was extremely difficult to understand Dylan. Ishiura concluded that Dylan was a "code" that did not want to be deciphered but "invited the audience to be codes themselves."[12]

Although Japanese critics believed that they were unable to sufficiently understand Dylan because of language differences, American critic Paul Williams argued that the fact that the Japanese appreciated Dylan implied that Dylan's lyrics were not his strongest appeal. In "Aquarelle with Words and Sound: Maturing Bob Dylan," Williams wrote that it was intriguing for Americans like him to learn that Dylan, whose lyrics were puzzling even to Americans, was a hero greatly admired in Japan. Williams reasoned that contrary to popular belief in the United States, Dylan's emotional appeal lay not in his lyrics but in his singing voice; it was the manner in which he attempted to communicate with the audience that was most appealing.[13]

In addition to Dylan's incomprehensibility and the uncertainty with which music critics attempted to analyze him, the concept that Dylan was a protest singer persisted. Poet Yuzuru Katagiri, who translated Dylan's lyrics, argued that Dylan protested against the establishment through his love songs. According to Katagiri, Dylan's "It Ain't Me, Babe" was a strong anti-romance protest song, claiming the right of men to be "effeminate." He claimed that conventional manhood manifested through heterosexual monogamy served the interest of rulers who enforced capitalism and Christianity, akin to the Japanese military leaders during World War II who imposed ideal manhood on the Japanese in order to secure their blind loyalty to the country. Katagiri asserted that challenging the dominant notion of masculinity and the institution of marriage was a greater threat to the establishment than political activism; therefore, Dylan's anti-love songs like "It Ain't Me, Babe" were, in fact, powerful and subversive.

Despite their uneasiness with claiming to be able to comprehend Dylan, Japanese critics and folksingers assumed that Dylan was the direct progenitor of Japanese folksingers. In the September 1969 issue of *New Music Magazine,* folksinger and music critic Tadasu Tagawa wrote what appeared to be a parody song or poem titled "Hey Mr. Dylan," and claimed that Japanese folksingers had already caught up with and surpassed Dylan. While the song title was reminiscent of "Mr. Tambourine Man," the content of the poem resembled "Like a Rolling Stone" in the sense that the narrator of the song addressed Dylan in a nagging, unkindly manner. In the song, Tagawa indicated that though it had been less than a decade since "Blowin' in the Wind" and "Masters of War" were released, Dylan was already on the threshold of being surpassed in Japan by powerful Japanese folksingers, including Nobuyasu Okabayashi; this was also exemplified by hit songs such as "Kaze" (wind) (1969), created by a Japanese folk group called Hashida Norihiko to Shuuberutsu. Further, Tagawa called Dylan "fertile" with numerous offspring, listing the first names of

American and Japanese musicians: Al (Cooper), Mike (Bloomfield), Johnny (Cash), Joan (Baez), Tomoya (Takaishi), Nobuyasu (Okabayashi), Haruomi (Hosono), Goro (Nakagawa), and Kenji (Endo). The narrator anticipated that although currently people were examining Dylan's every move in detail, someday they would be indifferent to Dylan. Tagawa's song may be better perceived as a playful tribute to Dylan in the form of a song rather than a serious vocal attack on him. However, through this song, Tagawa succeeded in asserting his viewpoint—that Japanese folksingers were direct descendants of Dylan—thereby authenticating the Japanese folk scene, while at the same time claiming that the Japanese folk scene had matured to such an extent that Japanese folksingers had already surpassed (or would soon surpass) Dylan.

With the release of *Planet Waves* in 1974, *Blood on the Tracks* in 1975, *Desire* in 1976, the Rolling Thunder Reviews in 1975 and 1976, and a brief reunion with Joan Baez, Dylan began to be featured in popular magazines again. *Desire* sold two hundred thousand copies in Japan.[14] In particular, "Hurricane," a song that supported a former middleweight boxer charged with murder, which the boxer claimed he never committed, caught the attention of popular magazines, beginning with the report of Japanese *Playboy* magazine in December 1975.[15] Among the eleven magazine articles on Dylan in 1976, four of them noted this song. *Shukan Post* reported that the song "revealed the aspect of American society that the Americans are most embarrassed about," and that Dylan had reaffirmed the same point when he sang "Blowin' in the Wind" with Baez.[16] *Playboy* magazine sent a reporter to Rubin "Hurricane" Carter in his New York office for an interview. The article concluded, "Together with Baez, Dylan used to be in the forefront of folk protest. He still is."[17] It was evident that the media felt more comfortable with the idea of Dylan creating protest songs.

The mid-1970s was a turning point in the Japanese folk music scene as well. In the late 1960s, folk music was political and anti-commercial, but from 1970 onward, folk music in Japan became commercial and the lyrics introspective; by the mid-1970s, it had turned into a genre of refined popular songs with middle-class taste. This new type of folk music was termed "New Music."[18] The establishment of the Japanese folk scene was marked by the historic outdoor concert in Tsumatoi, Gumma Prefecture, from August 2–3, 1975, where Takuro Yoshida and a folk group called Kaguyahime sang nonstop for twelve hours to an audience of thirty thousand people. Although, on the surface, this event was symbolic of Japanese independence in folk music, the concept for the concert was based on an American one. In the July 1975 issue of *Young Guitar* magazine, Yoshida explained that it was Dylan who had inspired him with the idea of planning an outdoor concert on a large scale: "In short, [the Tsumagoi concert] is a Bob Dylan concert. When Dylan gives a concert in Los Angeles, for example, people get together from all over the country, not just from Los Angeles. Since Japan is a smaller country, I thought it would be possible to do the same thing. I asked [the staff] to find a large place."[19]

Bob Dylan in Japan, 1978

Popular media hyped Dylan's Japan tour scheduled for February 1978 as soon as it was announced in December 1977. In the period between December 1977 and April 1978, twenty national magazines carried thirty-nine articles and ten roto-gravures regarding Dylan's visit to Japan. Numerous pages were expended on reviewing Dylan's life and the myths surrounding him; in addition, articles speculating about the reason for his decision to visit Japan and what his visit would be like, accompanied by sensational headlines and a plethora of pictures, were also published. The press described Dylan as the only superstar who had not visited Japan; Elvis Presley and Bing Crosby had died, and the Rolling Stones had been denied entry into the country in 1973 because of Mick Jagger's use of drugs. Further, Dylan was portrayed as a mysterious, mythical figure, whom the magazine articles claimed to unveil and demystify.

The portrayals of Dylan by popular media were like those from the past. Calling Dylan the "god of folk," the magazines emphasized the notion of Dylan as the progenitor of Japanese folksingers and cited the names of the leading figures in the Japanese folk scene, including Takuro Yoshida and Nobuyasu Okabayashi, calling them "Dylan's children." *Josei Jishin,* the weekly magazine for women, published an illustrated guide to Dylan that portrayed a figure of Dylan holding ropes that connected him to the names of groups of people who were of some importance in Dylan's life. Among these groups were "the women Dylan loved" (including Echo Star Helstrom, Suze Rotolo, Joan Baez, Sara Lownds, and Ronnie Blakely), "the people who influenced Dylan the most" (Woody Guthrie, Pete Seeger, Elvis Presley, Hank Williams, and Charlie Chaplin), and "Japanese who [had] been influenced by him," which listed seven people including Okabayashi and Yoshida.[20] The influence that Dylan had on Japanese folksingers was presented as an important element of his life.

The media speculated about the reason for Dylan's sudden decision to visit Japan after allegedly having declined the invitation from Japanese promoters multiple times for over a decade; the explanation provided by the media was that Dylan was in need of money after his recent divorce. *Bisho,* a women's magazine, quoted Toshiyuki Sugano (who later anglicized his name to Heckel Sugano), director of CBS Sony, as saying that Dylan was liable to pay alimony since the divorce was a result of his extramarital affair, which included his taking his mistress home, to the disbelief and anger of his wife.[21] Other magazines also emphasized the unusually expensive performance fee of 350,000,000 yen ($1,750,000 in 1977–78)—over double the amount that had been paid to Frank Sinatra—and reported that this amount would help Dylan to pay alimony to his estranged wife, Sara; moreover, the Japan tour would be lucrative for him because of the increase in the value of the yen.

According to biographer Howard Sounes, the motive behind the world tour was indeed an economic one. In Dylan's own words: "I've got a few debts to pay off. . . . I had a couple of bad years. I put a lot of money into the movie, built a big house . . . and there's the divorce." Dylan "agreed to sell his soul" and "embarked on a lucrative world tour."[22] The Japanese media exploited this fact in their narrative, which was designed to create a flattering image of Japan. An author of an article in the weekly magazine *Shukan Shincho* wrote: "If the reason [for his decision to visit Japan] was to save the economic crisis caused by the divorce litigation, it could be said that Japan was looked down upon by Dylan; on the other hand, it could mean that Japan has become an economic power."[23]

Further, the Japanese media made its best attempt to seek additional information related to Dylan's tour that would boost the ethnic and national pride of the Japanese. The magazines reported that Dylan wished to visit Japan because he appreciated Zen and Eastern philosophy. *Josei Seven* quoted Toshiyuki Sugano as saying, "Dylan is very pleased to be visiting Japan because he himself is very interested in Eastern philosophy."[24] Sugano also testified in another magazine that "the reason why Dylan decided to start his world tour with Japan is probably because he came to be interested in Eastern philosophy through Alan Ginsburg and Leonard Cohen."[25] In addition, Japanese *Playboy* magazine reported that Hisashi Miura, a college professor who translated works on Dylan, stated that the philosophy behind Dylan's songs was similar to Zen Buddhism, and that "Like a Rolling Stone" expressed the same ideas as those written in the Record of Linji *(rinzai roku)*.[26] *Shukan Post* reported that Dylan had an expensive Japanese garden in his Malibu mansion, which was more expensive than the swimming pool on the same property.[27] It is evident that the media were seeking clues that would indicate that Dylan was interested in Japanese culture.

Certain magazines, however, exhibited anti-Semitism and attributed Dylan's "commercialism" and "greed" to his Jewish background. *Shukan Post* criticized Dylan in an article titled "The Jewish Business Practice of B. Dylan Who Demanded an Extraordinarily Expensive Performance Fee." In the article, a "music critic Mr. M." was quoted as saying, "Bob Dylan's real name is Robert Zimmerman, a Jewish American, and he is therefore very greedy for money." He continued, "When he was still singing protest songs in 1966, he demonstrated his tough negotiation skills by demanding a royalty of 10 percent and contract money of 1,500,000. That was when Andy Williams, who was the top super-star, only got a royalty of 5 percent and contract money of 5,000,000 dollars. He was selling himself expensively while pretending to be an anti-establishment singer."[28] The article reported that there was an agreement between Dylan and the Japanese promoters that the performance fee would be paid half in dollars and half in yen, "a contract that shows the Jew's keenness in taking into account international monetary uncertainty."[29]

Shukan Post strongly emphasized the concept of Dylan's "Jewish characteristics" with two additional articles, one of them in the issue of February 17, 1978, where the magazine repeated the same story; in addition, it also quoted an anonymous music critic who had allegedly said that Dylan's decision to perform overseas and be interviewed could be attributed to his "impatience over becoming outdated and his attachment to money which is peculiar to the Jews."[30] *Shukan Post* presented another outrageous claim: that Dylan's life might be in danger during his stay in

Japan, as he was a target of a left-wing extremist group, which allegedly claimed that Dylan was a "Zionist" and "a rock star produced by the Jewish capital."[31] The article went on to cite dubious anonymous sources to explain that Dylan was indeed a "Zionist" who supported Israel, and that his lyrics reflected his Jewish roots; however, no example or analysis was provided. One source allegedly claimed without any evidence that "Clive Davis, former President of CBS Columbia, [was] a known Zionist" (Davis was vice president of Columbia), and that "he could be planning to spread pro-Israeli sentiment among Americans through music."[32]

According to David Goodman and Masanori Miyazawa, authors of *Jews in the Japanese Mind,* Japanese images of Jews became increasingly negative in the 1970s as anti-Zionism became widespread. The left-wing extremist groups in Japan, who were disillusioned with their own causes, identified with the Palestinian Liberation Organization and denounced Israel. The anti-Zionist ideology "was domesticated and legitimized by prominent Japanese academics and intellectuals" and "popularized by the mass media."[33] Further, Goodman and Miyazawa argue that the Japanese had traditionally used foreigners as a guise to deal with their anxiety and define their ethnic identity, and anti-Semitism as well as philo-Semitism stemmed from this tradition. While the essentialist, racist assumption of *Shukan Post* and the dubious conspiracy theory were conspicuous, other magazines also pointed out Dylan's Jewish background when describing him.

An expert on Dylan also suggested that Dylan was already past his prime. In the February 1978 issue of *New Music Magazine,* music critic Toyo Nakamura, who had written the earliest liner notes for Dylan's recordings in Japan and served as an expert who introduced him to the Japanese public, become critical of Dylan. Nakamura recalled that he first became aware of Dylan merely as a protest singer-songwriter; however, he was bewildered when Dylan turned electric. Nakamura said he

> came to the conclusion that Dylan and the Beatles were moving toward the same direction. The phrase "new music" seemed to be most appropriate in expressing their new types of popular music, hence I named this magazine the *New Music Magazine* in order to follow them in this new direction.
>
> However, by the mid-1970s, as new music and new lifestyle and new thought of young people ceased to challenge society, Dylan went along with the trend and started to lose his edge.[34]

Nakamura lamented that Dylan, who once challenged the older generation with the phrase "The Times They Are A-Changin'," was now silent regarding the changes occurring among the younger generation.[35]

In light of Tagawa's "Hey Mr. Dylan," a song written nine years earlier, it is evident that Dylan was portrayed as an outdated star who had now been surpassed by his "children" in Japan. An article in the weekly magazine *Shukan Myojo* reported that neither Takuro Yoshida nor Nobuyasu Okabayashi would attend the upcoming Dylan concert. According to the article, there were approximately twelve million Japanese folk fans, half of them followers of Bob Dylan; however, Yoshida's closest source told the reporter of the magazine that Yoshida had no interest in attending the Dylan concert, and that "after seeing Dylan's come-back concert [in 1974] in the U.S., Takuro suddenly stopped talking about Dylan." The article also claimed that Okabayashi, another of "Dylan's Children," was focused on his own concert tours and therefore would not be interested in attending Dylan's concert.[36] The article criticized Dylan for being outdated and out of touch with young people, but contrary to the prediction in the article, Okabayashi did attend the Dylan concert. In a similar vein, *Shukan Bunshun* reported in January 1978 that tickets for the Dylan concert were not selling well. As it turned out, however, as the same magazine reported in March, tickets sold well; more than a dozen young rock fans even began to line up in front of the ticket center the night before the advance sale of the tickets.[37]

Despite a large number of negative articles, a majority of magazines continued to treat Dylan as a mysterious and mythical figure. With few exceptions, magazines did not seek new information directly from Dylan but repeated the same stories that had been previously circulated. The magazine articles revealed less about Dylan himself than about the Japanese perception of him. Before Dylan even appeared in Japan, the magazines molded Dylan into a set narrative and image that was not flattering to him: a mysterious, mythical "god of folk" who belonged to the past, a "fallen idol," and a "greedy Jew" who was after Japanese yen. This negative portrayal was accompanied by a flattering self-image of the Japanese: boasting a strong economy, traditional culture, and folksingers who surpassed Dylan.

However, an article based on a direct source revealed a different picture of Dylan. *Heibon Punch* sent a reporter to Santa Monica, California, to interview Dylan in person shortly before his visit to Japan. Dylan revealed that he possessed only a limited knowledge and interest in Buddhism or Eastern philosophy. The reporter mentioned the picture of the Great Buddha at Kamakura on the jacket of *Desire* and asked whether Dylan was interested in Buddhism and Eastern philosophy. Dylan answered that he used to be interested in "Buddha before he became Buddha," because before Buddha was deified, he was simply another human being. Dylan said that he had studied Zen at one time but had forgotten most of the teachings; the only memory he had of it was learning about nothingness.[38]

Further, Dylan did not display any particular interest in Japan; he reportedly said that the reason why he had decided to visit Japan was simply that he had a large number of fans there. In addition, contrary to what the Japanese media continued to emphasize in their articles, Japan would not be the first non-English-speaking country where he would perform, as he had already been on a tour to Europe. When asked whether he had any advice to give to "Dylan's children" in Japan, he answered that they (Japanese musicians) would need to work hard and go to the United States if they wanted to study this kind of music; this suggested Dylan's disinterest in his Japanese followers and low expectations for the abilities of the musicians in Japan. The reporter said that after the interview, he was left with the feeling that he was unable to comprehend Dylan at all, thus reinforcing the image of Dylan as a mysterious artist.[39]

When Dylan arrived in Tokyo on February 17, 1978, he faced a few of the same questions at a press conference, which he attended immediately after his arrival from the airport. Magazines portrayed him as unfriendly and difficult to comprehend. One magazine described the interview as a "Zen dialogue," where Dylan offered single-sentence answers to each question he was asked.[40] According to the magazines, only a few music critics who had been nominated in advance were permitted to ask questions. A large number of questions were regarding Dylan's opinion of Japan. Dylan responded, through an interpreter, that he was "just a person." When asked the reason for his decision to visit Japan, Dylan offered no explanation. The reporters also asked Dylan to define the age that they lived in, to which Dylan replied, after some hesitation, that it was the "Zen age." When he was asked to elaborate, he conceded that he did not know much about Zen, except that he had once read about it in a book.[41] Instead of asking questions that would have elicited new information about Dylan, the reporters asked the same questions based on old assumptions.

During the recording of his live album *Bob Dylan at Budokan,* Dylan sang his hit songs with unusual arrangements done with a big band. Dylan also dressed himself in a lavish white suit and wore pale makeup, while his female backup singers were dressed in costumes that made them look, in the words of one participant, "like hookers."[42] Dylan performed at eleven concerts in two cities: February 20, 21, and 23 in Tokyo; February 24, 25 and 26 in Osaka; and February 28 and March 1, 2, 3, and 4 in Tokyo, with a different mix of audiences and varied reactions.[43] He rounded off each concert with "Forever Young" and "The Times They Are A-Changin'." Overall, Dylan connected better with the audiences in Osaka than with those in Tokyo.[44]

According to Eiji Ogura, who attended all eleven concerts and wrote a comprehensive account that was published in the *New Music Magazine,* the dominant reaction of the audience in the first Tokyo concert was one of mixed feelings; they were glad to watch Dylan live and taken aback by how much he had changed. Dylan performed one song after another without speaking much. Ogura observed that by the third concert in Tokyo, Dylan had started to connect with the audience. Nonetheless, it was in Osaka that the audience responded with great enthusiasm. Ogura attributed this to the fact that the majority of the audience in Osaka comprised young people, in contrast to the Tokyo concerts, where members of the audience were divided into youth and older adults.[45] Similarly, *Heibon Punch* reported that approximately 80 percent of the audience in Osaka appeared to be of college age or younger and that they were responsive to Dylan, who, in turn, complimented the audience and talked a lot between songs.[46] When Dylan returned to Tokyo, the audience reaction was lukewarm, making him seem bitter and aggressive.[47]

Heibon Punch reported Dylan's activities at the concerts and on city streets in detail. A reporter followed Dylan around for ten days and observed him exploring the city of Tokyo, including shopping for clothes and drinking orange juice at a fruit parlor in Shinjuku. Unlike many other magazine articles that depicted Dylan as mysterious and unfriendly, this article portrayed Dylan as an affable and personable man who did not mind giving autographs to fans passing by and was curious enough to try new food from vendors on the street. The article concluded with a description of Dylan's interest in Japanese culture. Dylan showed interest in the game of *go* and bought a set. He also visited the traditional city of Kyoto after his successful concert in Osaka, where he "gazed at the Kamo-gawa River and the completely Japanese stone garden of the Ryuan-ji Temple and was deeply satisfied." Despite the fact that Dylan had revealed his lack of knowledge or interest in Zen Buddhism, the writer of the article mentioned that Dylan "had wanted to see Zen, Mount Fuji, and a river that flows."[48]

Ogura's comprehensive reports on Dylan's concerts that appeared in *New Music Magazine* and the *Heibon Punch* article detailing his activities on- and offstage were two rare exceptions to most other reports in magazines. Many popular magazines portrayed Dylan as an unfriendly, incomprehensible former "god of folk" who confused the audience with weird arrangements of his otherwise familiar songs. Japanese *Playboy* reported that at the February 20 concert in Budokan, Dylan started singing immediately after he appeared on stage and simply performed one piece after another without any communication with the audience. The only words he spoke apart from the songs he sang were the title of each song and "thank you" at the end of each performance.[49] In contrast, William McKeen, author of *Bob Dylan: A Bio-Bibliography*, wrote that "Dylan, who was often taciturn during concerts (he barely spoke from the stage during the tour with The Band) was verbose while talking to his Japanese fans."[50] *Shukan Bunshun* relegated Dylan to the past by portraying his concerts on that tour as nostalgic events for Japanese fans who were young in the 1960s. According to the article, the audience "put their hands on their laps and listened to the music quietly, as if they had been listening to Mozart."[51]

Shukan Myojo dismissed Dylan by reporting on a celebrity in the audience. Hibari Misora, a singer who was considered the "queen" of Japanese popular music at the time, was reported to have left the concert hall during the intermission. She was quoted as saying, "I didn't come here to listen to the Beatles. I was expecting something that sounded more like folk music, but the sound was rather.... I had meant to stay until the end of the concert, but I decided to leave because I thought I had figured it out already." Further, as described in the article, while getting inside her white Cadillac, she added, "Okabayashi-kun is much better than Dylan. You should support the Japanese folk scene more."[52]

Dylan's reception in Japan should be considered not in isolation but in the context of Japanese folk music history. Japanese folksingers domesticated American folk songs and established themselves as creative singer-songwriters who sang on Japanese issues and attracted large Japanese audiences. Dylan served to authenticate them. This study of Dylan's reception in Japan revealed that the Japanese were not passive audiences for the American icon but actively used him to serve their own interests.

Coda: Dylan in Japan after Budokan

Dylan hysteria came to an end after he left Japan. Articles about Dylan in popular magazines decreased significantly in the early 1980s. However, some media maintained an interest in Dylan and continued to report his career developments. Some newspapers and magazines reported Dylan's conversion to born-again Christianity, and music critics reviewed his new albums when they were released. During the next few decades, Dylan returned to Japan several times. In April 1985, he secretly visited Tokyo for a week to shoot a music video for his new song "Tight Connection to My Heart." The writer who reported his visit in the photographic weekly *Focus*—a copy of which also appeared in Dylan's video—wrote that the Japanese should be proud that Dylan picked Tokyo as the location for his video.[53] The following year, Dylan returned to Japan for a concert tour with Tom Petty and the Heartbreakers. Reviewers observed that Dylan was more relaxed than he had been in 1978 and that he connected well with mature audiences. Dylan even greeted them in Japanese ("domo, domo, domo").[54] According to the reviewer from the national newspaper *Asahi Shimbun,* Dylan had transformed himself "from the god of folk to one musician."[55]

Dylan visited Japan on three occasions in the 1990s: for a concert tour in February 1994; for the Great Music Experience concert *(Aoiyoshi)* backed by UNESCO at Todai-ji Temple, Nara, in May 1994; and for another concert tour in February 1997. Eiji Ogura, who had written a comprehensive review of the concerts in 1978, wrote a short review for *Asahi Shimbun* of Dylan's February 1994 concert. While Ogura claimed to have found Dylan's performance rather dull and less dynamic than in previous concerts, he wrote that he liked the way Dylan seemed to enjoy himself on stage while playing the lead guitar.[56] At the Great Music Experience concert, Dylan performed "A Hard Rain's A-Gonna Fall," backed up by a full orchestra. After the 1997 concert, Toyo Nakamura, who had criticized Dylan for having lost his edge in 1978, praised Dylan as a performer while maintaining that Dylan's heyday as a songwriter was long past.[57]

Japanese folksingers, who some critics claimed surpassed Dylan in the 1970s, came to have a weaker presence in the Japanese music scene, as folk music merged with popular music by the late 1970s. Today, the word *folk* reminds the Japanese more of Japanese folksingers of the 1970s than of American folksingers of the 1960s. For example, in its August 16 and 23, 2007, issues, *Shukan Bunshun* published a nostalgic look back on the 1970s; the article contained interviews of Japanese folksingers who were popular in the 1970s, and their pictures from back then and today were contrasted.[58] The magazine did not have to point out that by "folk," they meant Japanese folksingers and not Dylan or Baez.

Dylan is still discussed with reverence and awe by some. At the "Dylan Summit" in Tokyo in October 2006, where Japanese musicians and critics discussed Dylan and performed his pieces, rock musician Koji Wakui, the organizer of the event, insisted that since Dylan was one of the most important and influential figures of the twentieth century, many Japanese popular cultural products of today could trace their lineage back to Dylan. The young audience and band members present at the event also testified to Dylan's continued appeal to youth. The idea of Dylan as both guru and role model for artists persists to this day in Japan.

Notes

1. Ichiro Fukuda, "Kaigai no wadai: Berafonte betabore no Odetta rainichi su" [What's happening outside Japan: Odetta, whom Belafonte admires, comes to Japan], *Heibon Punch,* April 26, 1965, 110.

2. Yoshitake Maeda and Koji Hirahara, *60-nendai foku no jidai* [The Age of Sixties Folk] (Tokyo: Shinko Music, 1993), 238–39.

3. Ibid., 25.

4. "Howaito hausu o nayamasu san-nin no hansen kashu" [Three antiwar singers who taunt the White House], *Heibon Punch,* February 14, 1966, 25.

5. Ken-ichi Nagira, *Nihon foku shiteki taizen* [My Personal Accounts of the Japanese Folk Scene] (Tokyo: Chikuma, 1999), 102, 147.

6. Nagira, *Nihon foku shiteki taizen,* 35; Maeda and Hirahara, *60-nendai foku no jidai,* 223.

7. "Jon Baezu no koibito datta Bobu Diran no LSD-teki seikatsu" [LSD-like life of Bob Dylan, former lover of Joan Baez], *Playboy,* April 11, 1967, 42–43.

8. Ibid., 44–45.

9. Kazuo Mihashi, *60 nendai no Bobu Diran* [Bob Dylan in the Sixties] (Tokyo: Shinko Music, 1991), 42–44.

10. Reiko Yukawa, "Wakaranai dakedo—utsukushii: shijin Bobu Diran e no apurochi" [Incomprehensible yet beautiful: An approach to Bob Dylan the poet], *Music Magazine,* July 1969, 13.

11. Yosuke Kawamura, "Amerika ongaku ni kaiki shita? Bobu Diran" [Has he returned to American Music? Bob Dylan], *New Music Magazine,* September 1970, 24.

12. Satoru Hamano and Shinzo Ishiura, "Bobu Diran o kangaeru: danpenteki oboegaki" [Thinking about Bob Dylan: Memos], *New Music Magazine,* April 1972, 67, 71.

13. Paul Williams, "Kotoba to oto ni yoru suisai-ga: enjuku ni mukau Bobu Diran" [Aquarelle with words and sound: Maturing Bob Dylan], trans. Yoshihiro Masaki, *New Music Magazine,* June 1975, 25. Williams's article was available only in Japanese translation.

14. Heckel Sugano, interview with Masayoshi Koshiya, March 25, 2002, in *Sotokushu Bobu Diran* (Tokyo: Kawade shobo, 2002), 105.

15. "Amerika kenkoku 200nen ni mukatte ugokidashita Bobu Diran: hyotto suruto rainen wa rainichi no kanousei mo" [Bob Dylan has started to work toward the bicentennial: Perhaps he may visit Japan next year], *Playboy,* December 23, 1975, 79.

16. "Beikokujin no chibu o uta ni takusu Bobu Diran no shinban kaibo" [Analyzing Bob Dylan's new album that puts to music what Americans are ashamed of], *Shukan Post,* March 5, 1976, 144.

17. "Bobu Diran no shi ga ore o ningen ni kaeshite kureta! hariken kata no kokoro no sakebi" [Bob Dylan has turned me back into a human being: The heartfelt cry of Hurricane Carter], *Playboy,* July 20, 1976, 47.

18. Tadasu Tagawa, *Nihon no foku & rokku shi: kokorozashi wa doko e* [The History of Japanese Folk and Rock: Where Have the Aspirations Gone] (Tokyo: Ongaku no tomo sha, 1982), 103–5, 119.

19. "Dokyumento Tsumagoi no 12 jikan Takuro Kaguyahime ga moeta atsui yoru" [Twelve hours in Tsumagoi: The night when Takuro and Kaguyahime passionately sang],

Young Guitar, July 1975, reprinted in *Foku ogon jidai* [The Golden Age of Folk] (Tokyo: Shinko Music, 1992), 179.

20. "2 gatsu 20 nichi rainichi hatsu koen Bobu Diran" [Bob Dylan, who visits Japan on February 20 and gives his first performance], *Josei Jishin,* March 2, 1978, 182–83.

21. "Rikon no isharyo kasegi! Foku no kamisama Bobu Diran 2 gatsu rainichi no ura niwa!" [God of folk comes to Japan in February to earn money for alimony], *Bisho,* January 14, 1978, 244.

22. Howard Sounes, *Down the Highway: The Life of Bob Dylan* (New York: Grove Press, 2001), 314.

23. "Foku no kamisama no rainichi: jitsu wa rikon isharyo kasegi" [The upcoming Japan visit of god of folk: The real purpose is to earn alimony], *Shukan Shincho,* December 22 and 29, 1977, 127.

24. "Foku rokku no teio Bobu Diran karei na ai to hangeki no zen shinwa" [The emperor of folk and rock, Bob Dylan: His myth of romance and rebellion], *Josei Seven,* February 9, 1978, 44.

25. "'Ochita guzo' 'kako no hito' to akuhyo punpun no rainichi zenya Diran-kun 'kami-gakari' dake wa yamete hoshii no yo" ["Fallen idol," "person of the past"—filled with bad reputations: Mr. Dylan, we can't stand your theomania], *Playboy,* February 14, 1978, 70.

26. Ibid., 70.

27. "Kata daitouryo kara Ari made habahiroi yujin o motsu Bobu Diran sono shinwa to jitsuzo" [Bob Dylan, who is friends even with President Carter and Ali: His myth and the real image], *Shukan Post,* February 17, 1978.

28. "Ijo na kogaku gyara o yokyu shita B. Diran no yudaya shoho" [The Jewish business practice of B. Dylan who demanded an extraordinary amount of performance fee], *Shukan Post,* January 27, 1978, 58.

29. Ibid., 59.

30. "B. Diran rainichi wa 'shirake dori': hansen imeji kisetsu hazure [Lukewarm reaction to B. Dylan's visit to Japan: The image of antiwar is outdated]," *Shukan Post,* February 24, 1978, 42.

31. "B. Diran wa kagekiha ni nerawarete iru [B. Dylan is a target of the extremists]," *Shukan Post,* March 10, 1978, 30.

32. Ibid., 32.

33. David Goodman and Masanori Miyazawa, *Jews in the Japanese Mind: The History and Uses of a Cultural Stereotype* (Lanham, Md.: Lexington Books, 2000), 211.

34. Toyo Nakamura, "Toyo's Talk," *New Music Magazine,* February 1978, 162–63.

35. Ibid., 163.

36. "2-gatsu 20-nichi Bobu Diran rainichi: sono toki Takuro Okabayashi wa . . ." [February 20th Bob Dylan's Japan visit: Where will Takuro and Okabayashi be then], *Shukan Myojo,* January 1, 1978, 205.

37. "Rokku fu no Bobu Diran 'kamisama henshin' ni tomadotta orudo fan" [Rocklike Bob Dylan: Old fans were bewildered by the transformation of the god of folk], *Shukan Bunshun,* March 9, 1978, rotogravure pages.

38. "Bobu Diran tono atsui 50 fun" [Fifty hot minutes with Bob Dylan], *Heibon Punch,* February 13, 1978, 37.

39. Ibid., 36–39.

40. "Sonoyo Bobu Diran ni sogu shita suta-tachi no fukuzatsu na hanno" [Various reactions of stars who saw Bob Dylan that night], *Shukan Myojo,* March 5, 1978, 28.

41. "Ore no uta de yononaka ga kawatta" [My songs have changed the world], *Shukan Josei*, March 7, 1978, 177.

42. Sounes, *Down the Highway*, 315.

43. Eiji Ogura, "Diran zen konsato no kiroku" [The record of all the Dylan concerts], *New Music Magazine*, April 1978, 50–60.

44. "Bobu Diran in Japan 240 jikan kamisama wa chotto kimagurena haikai yaro datta" [Bob Dylan in Japan 240 hours: The god of folk was a whimsical rambling guy], *Heibon Punch*, March 13, 1978, 42.

45. Ogura, "Diran zen konsato no kiroku," 52–53, 57.

46. "Bobu Diran in Japan," 42.

47. Ogura, "Diran zen konsato no kiroku," 58–59.

48. "Bobu Diran in Japan," 42–43, 43, 43.

49. "Bobu Diran 'Kami dewa nai tada no otoko' no zessan to genmetsu no suteji" [Some glorify Dylan's performance while others were disenchanted by it; Dylan is "a man and not a god"], *Playboy*, March 14, 1978, 64–65.

50. William McKeen, *Bob Dylan: A Bio-Bibliography* (Westport, Conn.: Greenwood, 1993), 110–11.

51. "Okurete kita Bobu Diran" [Bob Dylan came late], *Shukan Bunshun*, March 2, 1978, 22.

52. "Sonoyo Bobu Diran ni sogu shita suta-tachi no fukuzatsu na hanno," 30.

53. "'Kamisama' gokuhi Nippon taizai ki" [The record of god's stay in Japan], *Focus*, June 7, 1985, 52–53.

54. Masakazu Kitamura, "Hageshiku myaku utsu rizumu: senretsu henshin Bobu Diran [Hard beating rhythm: Bob Dylan's drastic change]," *Asahi Shimbun*, March 12, 1986, 13; Tadasu Tagawa, "'Karisuma' kara 'tabi geinin' ni kawatta Bobu Diran no budokan konsato [From a charismatic artist to an itinerant entertainer: Bob Dylan Budokan concert]," *Shukan Asahi*, March 21, 1986, 140–41.

55. Kitamura, "Hageshiku myaku utsu rizumu," 13.

56. Eiji Ogura, "Suteeji Bobu Diran soboku de honpo rafu na saundo" [Bob Dylan's stage: Unsophisticated, uninhibited, and rough sound], *Asahi Shimbun*, February 15, 1994, 13.

57. "Jidai o tsukkiru 55 sai no 'kamisama'" [Fifty-five-year-old "god" who keeps up with the times], *Asahi Shimbun*, February 15, 1997, 19.

58. "Seishun! 70 nendai foku kashu taizen" [When we were young: A collection of folk-singers of the 1970s], *Shukan Bunshun*, August 16 and 23, 2007, rotogravure pages.

10. Borderless Troubadour:
Bob Dylan's Influence on International Protest during the Cold War
Heather Stur

Alone onstage, the singer strummed his guitar and sang a song about a woman's reaction to war: "I have two hands free / I have two lips free / All the men have died / And I forget the human language."[1] In the audience, composed primarily of college students, several young women wept. The singer's music expressed the sorrows of war and told stories of mothers grieving for their lost children, brothers killing brothers, and the absurdity of combat. The songs were his attempt to make sense of the war that devastated his country.

The year was 1967, and the singer's name was Trinh Cong Son. The twenty-eight-year-old musician from South Vietnam had developed a following among students at the University of Saigon, and he had emerged as a musician the *New York Times* called "the most popular college singer and composer in Saigon." When asked to name his musical influences, Son named Bob Dylan. "His voice is a cry, a lament," Son said. "I sing what is on the minds of my listeners," he continued. "I'm describing their sadness, their grief at the war.[2] He believed Dylan did the same thing for his own fans. Legend has it that Joan Baez called Son the Bob Dylan of Vietnam.

Trinh Cong Son was just one example of a musician who drew inspiration from Dylan during the cold war. This is the story of musicians trying to make sense of the cold war as it affected them and their parts of the world. At the heart of the tale is Dylan. In a time when decolonization and wars for independence rocked the planet, and the specter of nuclear annihilation haunted citizens of nations all around the globe, Dylan's music expressed the uncertainty, fear, and hope of an insecure world. American popular culture has claimed Dylan as a distinctly American icon—the voice of a generation, a master of reinvention, a rugged individual who went his own way. But Dylan's influence transcended the borders of the United States, and his music helped singers and songwriters in other countries come to terms with the ways in which the events of the cold war affected their homelands. His songs about personal freedom, alienation, exile, and social justice resonated throughout the world. Some musicians specifically named Dylan as their inspiration. Others exhibited Dylan's spirit in their music and their mission. Dylan may not have intended to be a spokesman for a world in transition, but his ability to comprehend and give voice to the deepest of human emotions spoke loudly above the din of cold war–era conflict.

Some of Dylan's cold war songs expressed a specifically American experience, such as the "duck and cover" culture of civil defense in the atomic age. Others articulated broader global concerns about war, corruption, and social change. Dylan was writing in an era in which wars for independence in Africa and Asia tore down colonial empires that in some cases had controlled regions for a century or more. In 1954, Vietnamese nationalists defeated French military forces at Dien Bien Phu, ending nearly one hundred years of colonialism. But combat in Vietnam continued as American political advisers and troops replaced the French. That same year, French imperialism suffered another blow when the Algerian National Liberation Front launched a war for Algeria's independence. Algeria achieved freedom in 1962 after nearly eight years of fighting. In 1955, newly independent nations in Africa and Asia formed the Conference of Nonaligned States and met at Bandung, Indonesia, to take a stand against neoimperialism. Representatives at the conference announced that their nations would not take sides in the ongoing conflict between the United States and the Soviet Union. In 1960 alone, seventeen African nations gained independence. It was in this context that Dylan's music resonated with musicians whose physical worlds were far from his but whose minds grappled with the same concerns. Some critics have argued that Dylan abandoned social criticism in 1964 with the album *Another Side of Bob Dylan*, but themes of struggle, alienation, loss, and hope continued to run through his music, and the sentiments are at the heart of politics. The international response to Dylan illustrates that his music remained political and topical throughout the cold war.

South Vietnam's Trinh Cong Son admired Dylan as a singer and a songwriter. By day, Son supported his mother, two brothers, and five sisters, writing love songs for Vietnamese television shows. He lived with his family in Hue, Vietnam's former imperial capital, about 450 miles north of Saigon. But as fighting erupted around him, he decided to use his music to express his opposition to war—a sentiment he soon learned many young Vietnamese shared. He began writing antiwar music in 1958 during the oppressive regime of Ngo Dinh Diem, and by 1970, he had written 150 protest songs. "Wars, any wars, bring about death and destruction, and I am against war generally," he said. Son had the look of a rock-star poet. He sported a wispy goatee and black glasses, and when he performed, he usually wore a white shirt, tight black pants, and pointy black shoes. He was quiet and unassuming when he took the stage at concerts, but as soon as he began to play and sing, the audience always joined him in loud choruses. In interviews, Son often named Dylan and Joan Baez as his main musical inspirations.[3]

Just as Dylan used the themes of love and loss as political metaphors, Son used love stories to convey the pain that war inflicts on those left at home. "Love Song of a Madwoman" tells the tale of a woman who has lost all her lovers to war.[4] But even though Son's music called for social change, he did not have a strategy for enacting change. "I am only an artist," he said. "I only speak of what I dream, but I do not know how to achieve the dream. This social revolution I speak of is just a way of saying something. It sounds so big. Call it a revolution with bare hands."[5] Like Dylan, Son was interested in salvation, but he didn't necessarily have the tools for saving souls.

Because of Son's antiwar stance, the government of South Vietnam banned his music in 1969 and forbade him from performing protest songs. Officials confiscated sheet music and tape recordings that Son had sold in Saigon before and after his shows. The move was part of a wave of suppression by President Nguyen Van Thieu to crack down on political dissidents. Before enacting the ban, representatives of Thieu's regime had invited Son to discuss the meanings behind his songs, but he refused. Then officials asked him to write explanations of his songs to be distributed to radio and television stations. Again, Son refused. "I said that explaining songs is not my job," he told a reporter. "Even the most intelligent of them are imbeciles," Son said of politicians. "I call them inspired murderers."[6]

Years later, Son abandoned protest music for love songs, children's music, and painting. After Vietnam was reunified in 1975, Son spent time in a reeducation camp and on a government-owned farm. In 1978, police took him to a television station and told him to state a "self-criticism" for broadcast. Rather than obeying the command, "I sang a song about a woman going to market," Son said. Authorities then tried to make him write a self-critical article. The clever musician "did it in the form of a letter to an unknown person, in which I expressed my joy at the unification of the country."[7] Son held on to his rock-star spirit even when faced with prison or worse. It seemed that Dylan had inspired more than just Son's music. Son was released from prison in 1980, and he settled into a quiet life of songwriting and painting in Ho Chi Minh City, the former Saigon.

While Son was writing Dylan-inspired music protesting the war in Vietnam in the mid-1960s, a Russian teenager named Boris Grebenshchikov was combing the backstreets of Leningrad, his hometown, for Dylan bootlegs. Western music was banned in the Soviet Union at the time, but Grebenshchikov, a budding rock star, imitated Dylan as he learned to play guitar, hoping to achieve the sound he called "poetic rock." In 1972, he formed a band called Aquarium, and he tried to incorporate Dylan's style of electric blues into Russian folk music. He also spent some time translating Dylan's lyrics into Russian.[8] Because the Soviet government had banned Western music, playing Dylan was a dangerous thing in the Soviet Union circa the 1970s. Grebenshchikov and his musician friends would gather in apartments or warehouses to jam, and when police would show up to bust the sessions, they would take their instruments and jump out windows to escape.

But they refused to let the law prevent them from making music. They recorded tracks on crude equipment in a makeshift studio and spread their music illegally by handing out cassettes and encouraging listeners to pass them along to their friends.

It was a form of samizdat, the printing and distribution of banned literature, often performed by the dissident poets and authors themselves.[9] Grebenshchikov eventually earned a reputation as the "Russian Bob Dylan."[10] He became the ultimate rock-and-roll rebel and incorporated government-prohibited Western styles of music into the Russian folk songs he performed. He defied the cultural repression of Soviet society and refused to allow authorities to silence him.

Mikhail Gorbachev's policy of glasnost, a term meaning "openness," allowed Grebenshchikov to travel to the United States and record an album with Dave Stewart of Eurythmics. It was called *Radio Silence,* and Annie Lennox and Chrissie Hynde guest-starred on it.[11] A review of the album notes that Grebenshchikov's "husky voice recalls Bob Dylan."[12] More than that, though, Grebenshchikov's act of recording rock and roll in a time when much of it remained banned demonstrated Dylan's influence. A *New York Times* discussion of rock and roll leaking from the Soviet Union called it true "rebel music" and noted that American "punk bands usually don't have to worry about being shut down, fired from their jobs, or arrested."[13] Grebenshchikov's outlaw spirit spoke for those people Dylan called out to in songs such as "Chimes of Freedom"—"the abandoned and foresaked," the exiles and the oppressed.[14]

Speaking for the oppressed had its price, and for some musicians, the cost was life. It is what Victor Jara paid for writing music that called for social justice in his homeland of Chile. Jara was a teacher, poet, folksinger, activist, and one of the founders of La Nueva Canción Chilena, or New Chilean Song. In the 1960s, Jara wrote songs condemning corruption among Chile's ruling elite, and he supported the left-wing Popular Unity movement and its presidential candidate, Salvador Allende. In the 1970 presidential campaign, Chileans chose Allende in a democratic election.[15]

But the victory was short-lived, and on September 11, 1973, a military coup led by Augusto Pinochet overthrew the Allende government. Jara, who at the time was teaching at the University of Santiago, was arrested and taken to Chile Stadium, a large sports arena in Santiago, with other prisoners. For four days, he was beaten and tortured. His wrists and hands were broken, and survivors of the stadium captivity have said that captors mocked Jara, placing a guitar in front of him and demanding that he play it with his broken hands. Refusing to let torture silence him, Jara allegedly sang a song praising Popular Unity and Allende. On September 15, he was shot to death, and his body was left on a road just outside Santiago. He was thirty-eight years old.[16]

The Pinochet regime destroyed most of Jara's recordings, but his wife, Joan Jara, had managed to smuggle some of them out of Chile when she fled after her husband's murder. The music has since been made available on CD. *Manifesto,* which was released worldwide in 1998, includes a reading of the last poem Jara wrote, while imprisoned in Chile Stadium. The poem includes the line "Silence and screams are the end of my song," and it stops midsentence, apparently just as executors arrived and shot Jara repeatedly with machine guns. Joan Jara considered the posthumous release of her husband's music a testament to his resilience. "They could kill him, but they couldn't kill his songs," she said.[17]

Although Jara's music was classified as protest music, he denounced what he called the commercialization of protest music and the creation of "protest music idols." To him, commercial music was an example of U.S. imperialism. He believed that mass-produced protest music deadened its rebel spirit and bred cynicism in the young people true protest music aimed to inspire. Rejecting the term *protest songs* altogether, he referred to his music as "revolutionary."[18] Jara embodied the spirit of justice that Dylan expressed in his own songs.

The same was true of Wolf Biermann, an East German poet, folksinger, and playwright. Biermann performed music that spoke of social justice and freedom and denounced political corruption. He was a socialist and believed in the virtues of true democratic socialism, but he criticized the East German government in his art and music. He attracted the attention of authorities in 1963 when he wrote a satirical play about the Berlin Wall, and as a result, he was expelled from the East German Communist Party.[19] By 1966, Biermann was on the list of examples of a cultural crisis in East Germany. Critics of Biermann accused him of creating a "cult of doubt" about the ways the East German government employed socialism. Because of Biermann's skepticism about East Germany's use of socialism, Hermann Claudius, vice president of the East Berlin Academy of Fine Arts, called Biermann "an anarchist individualist." In response to accusations of state censorship, Claudius argued that East Germany supported literary freedom, but the country banned books discussing fascism, racism, militarism, and pornography.[20] When a group of writers gathered in Berlin in November 1966 and pledged their support to the government of East Germany, Biermann was conspicuously absent.[21]

Biermann's music and poetry expressed the alienation and disillusionment young East Germans felt about their government. In a 1965 poem called "Reckless Bitching," he proclaims, "I am the individual. / The collective has isolated itself / from me."[22] At the end of World War II, Biermann had had high hopes for a socialist East Germany. He believed socialism would bring equality and freedom to East Germans, but government corruption, censorship, and strict laws seemed to quash freedom rather than facilitate it. The collective that was supposed to draw all East Germans to it in a sense of social and political unity began to exhibit symptoms of totalitarianism rather than democratic socialism.

The years that followed ushered in a period of censorship and widespread repression of playwrights, authors, musicians, and other artists.[23] In 1967, the government of East Germany tried to silence "We Shall Overcome," a song that young East Germans, taking a cue from the American civil rights movement, had adopted as their theme song. In the newspaper *Neues Deutschland*, authorities stated that East German musicians should compose their own songs, songs that glorified the nation of East Germany. It was in this climate of censorship that East German officials stripped Biermann of his citizenship as punishment for condemning the government. When he tried to return to his homeland after a concert tour of West Germany, border patrol denied him entry. In 1976, Joan Baez and others wrote letters to East Germany's Ministry of Culture, petitioning for Biermann's reentry to the country.[24]

Near the end of the cold war, in 1989, Chinese students protesting government oppression adopted a song called "Nothing to My Name" by Cui Jian, a classically trained trumpet player turned rock star. He had performed for years with the Beijing Philharmonic but left classical music and formed a rock band in the early 1980s when reforms opened China to Western commerce and culture. He devoured rock and roll, especially that of Dylan and other musicians who had made names for themselves in the 1960s. Cui Jian earned the nickname the "father of Chinese rock and roll" because of his influence on the 1989 Tiananmen Square movement, where students, workers, and intellectuals demanded reforms and an end to corruption in the Chinese government. Cui Jian sang about liberation and individual freedom, but because of government censorship, he often hid his messages in metaphors and symbols. He found inspiration in American rock and roll and is referred to today as "China's Bob Dylan."[25]

Cui Jian grew up during China's Cultural Revolution, and the repression of the era shaped the way Jian thought about freedom and liberty. When Deng Xiaoping began instituting economic reforms and opened China to Western contact in the 1980s, Cui Jian fused rock and roll with traditional Chinese music to create his own sound. He found rock and roll to be a more personal form of expression than playing the trumpet as part of an orchestra.[26] He performed in cafés and college dormitories to try to build a reputation, but he achieved widespread popularity with Chinese youth after the students organizing the Tiananmen Square protest rallies adopted "Nothing to My Name" as their battle cry. Cui Jian performed in Tiananmen Square, wearing a red bandana over his eyes to symbolize the sense of emptiness the students felt as China attempted to balance its past with its future. After the Tiananmen Square performance, Chinese officials banned Cui Jian's music, but it thrived underground as fans worked to spread it to new listeners.

In some cases, the link between Dylan and international musicians was long-lasting. When Trinh Cong Son died in 2001 from complications due to diabetes, his obituary in the *New York Times* stated that "he became known internationally as the Bob Dylan of Vietnam, singing of the sorrow of war and the longing for peace in a divided country."[27] The BBC announced that "Vietnam mourns its 'Dylan.'" In a subtle way, Dylan's influence on Son was not a one-way street. Yusef Komunyakaa, a Vietnam veteran and Pulitzer Prize–winning poet, mentions Son in his poem "After the Fall," about a Vietnamese woman roaming through Saigon after all the Americans had left: "Hoping for a hard rain / she moves through broken colors / flung to the ground / mixing up the words to Trinh's 'Mad Girl's Love Song' / & 'Stars Fell on Alabama.'"[28] Through music or through symbol, Son had an impact on an African-American soldier-poet stationed in the middle of the Vietnam War. It was as though Dylan's messages had come full circle, reaching an American through a

Vietnamese songwriter, "A Hard Rain's A-Gonna Fall" and "Love Song of a Mad-woman" speaking the same language.

Tom Wilson, Dylan's producer at Columbia Records in the early 1960s, summed up well why Dylan resonated with so many listeners. "He's not a singer of protest so much as he is a singer of concern about people," Wilson told *The New Yorker* music critic Nat Hentoff in 1964.[29] Empathy for human experience connected Dylan with musicians from Vietnam, the Soviet Union, East Germany, and China as artists attempted to come to terms with the effects of the cold war. American culture may have crowned Dylan a national prophet, but his influence is not confined by nationalism.

Notes

1. Bernard Weintraub, "A Vietnamese Guitarist Sings of Sadness of War," *New York Times,* January 1, 1968.

2. Ibid.

3. Joseph B. Treaster, "Saigon Bans the Antiwar Songs of Vietnamese Singer-Composer, *New York Times,* February 12, 1969.

4. Gloria Emerson, "Hero of Youth in Vietnam Assails War," *New York Times,* October 6, 1970.

5. Ibid.

6. Ibid.

7. Henry Kamm, "Vietnam Poet Sings a Song of Endurance," *New York Times,* April 4, 1993.

8. Dean Schabner, "Playing with God: Russian Rocker Gives Fans What They Want," *Rock Paper Scissors,* January 24, 2002, http://www.rockpaperscissors.biz/index.cfm/fuseaction/current.articles_detail/project_id/65/article_id/234.cfm.

9. Ibid.

10. Julia Barton, "Back in the USSR," *Salon.com,* June 10, 1998.

11. Stephen Holden, "The Pop Life," *New York Times,* April 12, 1989.

12. Jon Pareles, "Soviet Singer Far from His Roots," *New York Times,* April 17, 1989.

13. Jon Pareles, "Rock from Underground," *New York Times,* July 16, 1989.

14. Wayne Hampton, *Guerrilla Minstrels: John Wayne, Joe Hill, Woody Guthrie, and Bob Dylan* (Knoxville: University of Tennessee Press, 1986), 170.

15. "They Couldn't Kill His Songs," BBC, September 5, 1998, http://news.bbc.co.uk/2/hi/americas/165363.stm.

16. Ibid.

17. Ibid.

18. Victor Perera, "Law and Order in Chile," *New York Times,* April 13, 1975.

19. Leslie R. Colitt, "East German Poet Is Called Betrayer," *New York Times,* January 23, 1966.

20. Philip Shabecoff, "Beatles Winning in East Germany," *New York Times,* April 17, 1966.

21. "East German Authors Pledge Loyalty," *New York Times,* November 6, 1966.

22. David Binder, "Two Literatures in Germany Seen," *New York Times,* April 7, 1967.

23. "Popularity of U.S. Rights Hymn Irks German Reds," *New York Times,* March 5, 1967.

24. "Montand and Joan Baez Plead for East German," *New York Times,* December 28, 1976.

25. Sheryl WuDunn, "A 6-Foot-3, Blue-Eyed Taiwanese-American Is China's Top Rocker," *New York Times,* October 24, 1989. See also "Cui Jian, Chinese Father of Rock and Roll," Asia Arts: UCLA Asia Institute, http://www.asiaarts.ucla.edu/article.asp?parentid=11612.

26. Ibid.

27. Seth Mydans, "Trinh Cong Son, 62; Stirred Vietnam with War Protest Songs," *New York Times,* April 5, 2001.

28. Yusef Komunyakaa, "After the Fall," in *Unaccustomed Mercy: Soldier-Poets of the Vietnam War,* ed. W. D. Ehrhart (Lubbock: Texas Tech University Press, 1989), 84–85.

29. Nat Hentoff, "The Crackin', Shakin', Breakin' Sounds," in *Studio A: The Bob Dylan Reader,* ed. Benjamin Hedin (New York: W. W. Norton, 2004), 27.

PART III. THE ANCIENTS, WHOM ALL MODERNS PRIZE

11. Bob Dylan's Lives of the Poets:
Theme Time Radio Hour as Buried Autobiography
Mick Cochrane

In 1777, Samuel Johnson was approached by a committee of booksellers to write biographical prefaces to the works of forty-seven poets whose writing they hoped to present to readers in a new popular edition.[1] At the time, by the acknowledgment of his contemporaries, Johnson, in his sixties, possessed an unmatched command of English literature. The author of the *Dictionary of the English Language* and editor of Shakespeare, according to Adam Smith, Johnson "knew more books than any man alive." His erudition was monumental, legendary, and memorably mythologized by his biographer James Boswell, who tells how young Sam Johnson, as a boy searching for apples his brother may have hidden in their father's bookshop, discovered on a high shelf not apples but a folio volume of Petrarch, a book he then and there read "a great part of" with "avidity," thus embarking on a lifetime's ravenous reading.[2] Such was the power of Johnson's reputation at the time that the booksellers permitted Johnson to name his own terms—and were relieved when he requested a very modest two hundred guineas.[3] What Johnson wrote was a labor of love: rather than the short prefaces the booksellers would have been content with—what they wanted most was Johnson's name on the project—he, with a congenial subject and in a relaxed mood, gave them 370,000 words, the equivalent, it has been pointed out, of about five modern novels: anecdote, critical commentary, appreciation, literary theory, observations on life, and, in particular, the life of writing—the distilled wisdom of a lifetime. Many of the poets Johnson wrote about are obscure, of little interest today—how many people still read William Garth or William Shenstone or Mark Akenside or Edmund Smith? What remains of enduring fascination is what Paul Fussell calls "buried autobiography," glimpses of Johnson's mind at work and of the man himself.[4]

In 2006, Bob Dylan, likewise in his sixties, was approached by XM Satellite Radio about the possibility of hosting a weekly program. One imagines that what XM may have initially most desired was Dylan's name, a worthy competitor to Howard Stern, who had recently signed on with Sirius Satellite Radio; one also imagines Dylan requested more than two hundred guineas. If Johnson was, as the novelist Tobias Smollett called him, the "great cham" of English literature in the eighteenth century, Dylan is the great cham of twentieth-century music. His encyclopedic knowledge of American song has been frequently noted, described, and admired. Martin Scorsese—Dylan's Boswell—gives us the mythic anecdote of Dylan's finding in his father's house not a book of poetry but a record player and the 78 recording of "Drifting Too Far from Shore," a song, Dylan says, that made him feel like someone else.

Theme Time Radio Hour stands in nearly the same relation to Dylan's career as the *Lives of the Poets* does to Johnson's. We hear Dylan late in his life, for the moment no longer combative, in a generous mood and working within a capacious form, the one-man repository of a great tradition now playing the role of gregarious old codger, speaking to a popular audience in an accessible format, willing now to share his astonishing knowledge and record collection with the next generation. He reveals his Johnsonian love of biographical detail, his sometimes dark sense of humor, his love of corny jokes, and his desire to rescue from oblivion art he clearly loves and treasures.

Some may have expected Dylan's radio program to be a straightforward autobiographical exercise of some kind: he would play a song—something from Woody Guthrie, say, or from old pals like George Harrison or Johnny Cash—and then reminisce. Such expectations were quickly disappointed: you could read the complaints on the Internet. Again and again, Dylan does play and mention musicians whose careers have intersected his own—Mike Bloomfield, Augie Myers, T-Bone Burnett, among others—though for the most part, he steers clear of direct personal commentary. (There are some memorable exceptions: on the "Cars" program, Dylan claimed he once rode in a Lincoln with Joni Mitchell and noted she "was a good driver," who made him "feel *safe*."[5] On the Texas episode, Dylan remarked that Willie Nelson, his former touring partner, runs his bus on cooking oil: "Sometimes late at night, you can see us," Dylan said, "I'm filling up my tank at the gas station; he's filling up his at Denny's.")[6] But when Dylan introduces the Staple Singers, he doesn't mention his long personal association with Mavis Staples, whom he may have in fact proposed marriage to at one time; instead, he comments on the guitar technique of Pops Staples, how beautifully he controls the tremolo.

However much some fans may have wished for the kind of nostalgic song-and-story show Roger McGuinn loves to present these days, what Dylan delivers is far more complex and far more interesting. Of course it is not straightforward. Greil Marcus quite rightly asserts that "few performers have made their way onto the stage of the twentieth century with a greater collection of masks."[7] As Johnson, who wrote essays under the names "The Rambler" and "The Idler," well understood, the mask allows both protection and liberation.

"Where would radio be without a disc jockey?" Dylan asked on the "Radio" episode by way of introduction to Boyd Bennett and His Rockets' "Cool Disc Jockey," a 1959 rockabilly song Dylan may well have heard for the first time over the radio.[8] The mask of the deejay is one that Dylan seems to wear with considerable pleasure and even pride. It aligns him with Sonny Boy Williamson II, well known both as the king of blues harmonica and as the longtime host of *King Biscuit Time* from KFFA in Helena, Arkansas, whose "Don't Start Me to Talkin'" Dylan covered so memorably on *Late Night with David Letterman* in 1984 and who is a *Theme Time* favorite, played five times during the first season.

A deejay's task is to introduce music, and even though inevitably formulaic to some extent, Dylan the deejay's introductions are often revealing. Robert Zimmerman, the boy from Hibbing, Minnesota, who wanted variously to become James Dean, Little Richard, and Woody Guthrie, whose life changed when he signed with Columbia Records, not surprisingly typically tells us where an artist comes from, the label he recorded on, the name he was born with and the names he may have assumed. He seems especially attuned to musical identity. "We forget how much Elvis wanted to be Dean," Dylan remarked after playing Dean Martin's "I Don't Care If the Sun Don't Shine."[9] There are moments of what can only be described as a kind of artistic projection: Randy Newman, for example, Dylan introduced as "obstinately self-willed," known for refusing to conform to popular trends.[10] Dylan, who thinks of singers and songwriters as coming from somewhere in particular—Irma Thomas and Fats Domino from New Orleans, Bruce Springsteen from New Jersey, They Might Be Giants from Massachusetts—notes with apparent pleasure the Minnesota roots he shares with Judy Garland, Eddie Cochran, and Prince. And on the "School" episode, Dylan played the Minneapolis–St. Paul version of Tommy Facenda's "High School USA," released in 1959, when Dylan was a student at Hibbing High School. The song was released in thirty versions nationwide, each one naming local schools: "Central, North, and Edison / Harding, Henry, Bloomington," Facenda sings, "Johnson, Murray, Fergus Falls, Roosevelt High was having a ball."[11]

The relationship between a radio deejay and listener is built around the illusion of a certain kind of intimacy. In his fine new book *Something in the Air: Rock, Radio, and the Revolution That Shaped a Generation,* Mark Fisher describes how radio, "for all its artifice, its deejays with fake names, its sameness and phony familiarity," nevertheless can succeed in creating a real sense of community and in forging deep and abiding bonds with its listeners.[12] Unlike a rock performer, say, who comes to us amplified, at a distance, in a huge public place like a hockey arena, who appears as a speck onstage or as an image on a screen, the deejay enters our lives, our cars, our kitchens, even our bedrooms. Put your radio under your pillow, Dylan advised an e-mail correspondent on the "Baseball" show; that's what he says he used to do. Dylan's deejay persona is built around his voice, his greatest instrument, sounding absolutely ancient now, like the voice of someone who may have traveled or played with the likes of Charlie Patton or Son House.

What a deejay needs to do is choose and play music. Today, in the age of personal play lists and customized Internet radio and interactive and open-ended and

choose-your-own art of all kinds, it is probably worth noting how old-fashioned—
and typically Dylanesque—this approach is. He doesn't give us what we want; he
gives us what he thinks we need. Jakob Dylan told an interviewer once he remembered driving with his dad on vacation: they were headed to northern Minnesota,
and his dad played a single tape the whole way, Hank Williams, over and over and
over again. Jakob says he didn't object; he figured his dad was trying to teach him
something. Since then, Dylan has varied his list and developed a line of patter, but
still, to listen to *Theme Time Radio Hour,* you have to get in the car.

Further evidence, perhaps, that the country of *Theme Time Radio Hour* is ruled by
a benevolent dictator is the fact that though each program includes an e-mail from
a listener, all of them appear more or less cooked. One wonders who might be the
real author of this one, read on the "Mothers" show, used to introduce Ernie K. Doe's
"Mother-in-Law": "Dear Bob: I've got a hammerhead of a mother-in-law, an ugly,
evil-lookin' old woman, so pitiful. She's careworn, drawn and pinched—gaunt and
lank. I bought her a new chair, but she won't let me plug it in. She belittles me, de-
preciates me, disparages me. She downgrades me, berates me, censures me and
condemns me, libels me and raps me, dismisses me and rejects me. Could you
please play a song for her?" Another comes from a certain George Clooney: "Dear
Bob, My auntie used to sing. Do you think you could play one of her songs?"[13]

In his first show devoted to trains, Dylan expressed impatience with those who
make requests, which, he noted, usually involve someone asking to hear a record
they already own and presumably love and want someone else to play so they can
hear it again. If you want to hear your own records, Dylan says, play them yourself.
What he is trying to do, he says, is to "shine the light" on music that otherwise
might not be known.[14] Johnson demonstrated a similar urge in the *Lives of the Poets:*
"an instinctive desire to rescue them, if only briefly, from extinction in the sludge
of time," Walter Jackson Bate says, "to see them as part of the general drama of
human effort, experience, risk, hope, and disappointment."[15] Dylan's *Theme Time
Radio Hour* is preoccupied with mortality. He seems to take an almost perverse delight in reciting accounts of early deaths, boating and car accidents, plane crashes,
alcoholism and cirrhosis, drug overdoses. He takes the roll of all those gone before
their time: Otis Redding, Hawkshaw Hawkins, Cowboy Copas, Patsy Cline, Shorty
Long, Lefty Frizzell, Leroy Carr. On the other hand, in the face of time and mortality, our deejay is trying to save something. Especially revealing in this regard are
Dylan's remarks on Tiny Tim: before playing "Tiptoe through the Tulips with Me,"
he praised Tiny Tim for his knowledge of obscure music: "A lot of people think he
was a joke," Dylan said, "but no one knew more about old music than Tiny Tim did.
He studied it and he loved it. He knew all the songs that only existed as sheet music.
When he passed away, we lost a national treasure."[16]

The first show opened with Dylan playing Muddy Waters's "Blow Wind Blow."
Many journalists were quick to notice that this is an interesting choice by the author
of "Blowin' in the Wind." It has also been noted that the lyrics are a clear precur-

sor to Dylan's "It Takes a Lot to Laugh, It Takes a Train to Cry." Even more interesting may be that 2006 is the year Dylan was recording a Muddy Waters song for *Modern Times*, his version of "Rollin' and Tumblin'," a song that so resembled the original, that it inspired disgusted charges of plagiarism and likewise passionate defenses with references to the rich folk tradition of artistic appropriation.

Just as revealing as the artist and song Dylan chose to begin his show was his manner of introducing Muddy Waters: "One of the ancients by now," Dylan called him, "whom all moderns prize." This is a classic eighteenth-century distinction, Ancients versus Moderns, embodied memorably in Jonathan Swift's *Battle of the Books*, and in Johnson's own magisterial preface to Shakespeare, when in 1765, he acknowledges that Shakespeare "may now begin to assume the dignity of an ancient, and claim the privilege of established fame and prescriptive veneration."

"I think I shall be among the English poets after my death," John Keats famously said near the end of his life, and there was no doubt who it was he aspired to be among: Dryden, Milton, and Shakespeare. One way to think about Dylan's *Theme Time* enterprise, then, is this: it is his own roll call of the artists he would aspire to be among. Dylan is week by week constructing a canon of his own. T. S. Eliot in his famous essay "Tradition and the Individual Talent" asserts that when a new work of art comes into being, all existing works rearrange themselves around it: the new reconfigures the old. Dylan's radio show is his own oblique contribution to the ongoing debate regarding how to place his work, the question of where he belongs: Is it with Allen Ginsberg and Williams Carlos Williams in the pages of the *Norton Anthology of Poetry*? Or is it, as Christopher Ricks has suggested, among the English poets—Keats, Tennyson, and Hardy?[17] Or as Gordon Ball and others have suggested, is it among the Nobel laureates—Faulkner, Toni Morrison, Seamus Heaney?

Dylan's response, as I said, is oblique: it is characteristically sly. He seems to be saying once again that he is a song-and-dance man, kin to the Carter family and Slim Harpo, with his harp on a rack, or to bluesmen like Lonnie Johnson, to the cowboy bands, to the Spaniels, whom he claims again to have seen as part of the doomed Winter Dance Party. Dylan's gift for eclectic appreciation, one of the great surprises of his *Chronicles, Volume 1* perhaps, his penchant for weirdly suggestive, metaphoric epigrams of praise, these are perfectly suited for a deejay's commentary before and after a song.[18] Tommy Duncan's "Daddy Loves Mommyo," Dylan says, is "all hydrogen and sulfide." Warren Storm's "Prisoner's Song" is a "hard-boiled hayburner," and Hank Williams's "My Son Calls Another Man Daddy" is "the Battle of the Bulge of all songs."

On the other hand, Dylan again and again brings in poets in juxtaposition with his beloved blues and country singers. He recites Lawrence Ferlinghetti on baseball, Gregory Corso on weddings. He began the show devoted to the Devil by reciting a passage from the first book of Milton's *Paradise Lost*, the magnificent description of Satan's fall, while in the background, Reverend Gary Davis is heard strumming "The Devil's Dream":

Him the Almighty Power
Hurled headlong flaming from th' ethereal sky
With hideous ruin and combustion down
To bottomless perdition, there to dwell
In adamantine chains and penal fire,
Who durst defy th' Omnipotent to arms.[19]

The combined effect of Dylan's voice, Milton's verse, and Davis's guitar work is deliciously spooky, and just the sort of juxtaposition Dylan incorporates into the show again and again. He followed Milton and *Paradise Lost* with Robert Johnson, "Me and the Devil Blues," and the Louvin Brothers, "Satan Is Real." "That's how Christopher Marlowe said it," Dylan announced after reading from "The Passionate Shepherd to His Love"; "Kim Shattuck and her band the Muffs have another way of putting it," he said, and let them launch into their own grungy, punkish "Laying on a Bed of Roses." In some of Dylan's best-known songs, figures from literature and popular culture coexist—Ma Raney and Beethoven, Ophelia, the Good Samaritan, the Hunchback of Notre Dame, Ezra Pound, and T. S. Eliot. They issue from the same imagination and live in the same songs. In *Chronicles,* Dylan acknowledges his admiration of Thucydides, Edgar Allan Poe, Bertolt Brecht, Frank Sinatra, Gorgeous George, Dave Van Ronk, and Ricky Nelson. Behind the more recent albums are both literary influences—F. Scott Fitzgerald, Virgil, Shakespeare, Henry Timrod—and blues and country singers—Memphis Minnie, Merle Haggard. Clearly, in Dylan's imagination there are no distinctions, no categories. The radio show permits jug bands and lyric poets to bump up against each other, to engage in an open-ended conversation. When Dylan in the "Coffee" episode of the show asserted that another name for manic depression or bipolar disorder was "The Blues," I don't think he was taking a Tom Cruise–like swipe at modern psychiatry; instead he was making an argument for the continuity of human experience, of human nature: our terminology may change; human nature does not. This is a bedrock assumption of Samuel Johnson's literary criticism. The ones who speak to it with enduring insight—Shakespeare and Lightnin' Hopkins, Lefty Frizzell and Emily Dickinson, Dylan Thomas and Skip James, and, of course, Dylan himself—they are the Ancients. "The great songs live outside their moment of inception," Dylan says about Jimmie Rodgers.

One obstacle for satellite radio, one that Marc Fisher points out in his book on radio, is that because its signal goes everywhere, it seems to come from nowhere: "Most channels are voice-tracked well in advance of broadcast, so there are few references to anything happening right now, and obviously nothing about what's going on in your hometown."[20] For someone like Dylan, for whom the Civil War seems more immediate than the Iraq war, who recently expressed his preference for Ted Mack's *The Original Amateur Hour* over *American Idol,* timeliness is not a worry. But Dylan does manage to draw upon the deeply imaginative power of radio to evoke a sense of place. Like his fellow Minnesotan's *A Prairie Home Companion, Theme Time Radio Hour* emanates from a fictional place, not so fully realized as Garrison Keillor's

Lake Wobegon, but still vivid. The show is recorded, we are told, in the Abernathy Building, Studio B. Dylan tells us at various times he is planning to head off after the show to Samson's Diner or Elmo's Bar. He mentions Carl the barber, whose shop is located in the Abernathy Building. But ultimately, *Theme Time Radio Hour* emanates not from any studio, but from the vast, still unexplored teeming landscape of Dylan's imagination, a country as large and inclusive as Walt Whitman's America, full of heartbreak and jokes, stories and crazy characters, recipes, and songs, songs that so long as we love and grieve and laugh and shed tears will celebrate our flawed and glorious humanity.

Notes

1. Johnson later suggested four poets (James Thomson, Isaac Watts, John Pomfret, and Thomas Yalden) be added. In choosing artists for inclusion, he was acting even more in the manner of a modern disc jockey. For this idea, and for the one known literary connection between Johnson and Dylan ("They say that patriotism is the last refuge / To which a scoundrel clings," from "Sweetheart Like You," an echo of Johnson's famous pronouncement), I am indebted to Christopher Ricks.

2. James Boswell, *The Life of Samuel Johnson, L.L.D., with a Journal of a Tour to the Hebrides,* 6 vols., ed. George Birkbeck Hill and rev. L. F. Powell (Oxford: Clarendon Press, 1934–64).

3. Walter Jackson Bate, *Samuel Johnson* (New York: Harcourt Brace Jovanovich, 1977), 526.

4. Paul Fussell, *Samuel Johnson and the Life of Writing* (New York: Harcourt Brace Jovanovich, 1971).

5. "Cars," *Theme Time Radio Hour,* XM Satellite Radio, July 2006.

6. Ibid.

7. Greil Marcus, *The Old, Weird America: The World of Bob Dylan's Basement Tapes* (New York: Picador, 1997), 220.

8. "Radio," *Theme Time Radio Hour,* XM Satellite Radio, August 2006.

9. "Weather," *Theme Time Radio Hour,* XM Satellite Radio, May 2006.

10. "Mothers," *Theme Time Radio Hour,* XM Satellite Radio, May 2006.

11. "School," *Theme Time Radio Hour,* XM Satellite Radio, September 2006.

12. Marc Fisher, *Something in the Air: Radio, Rock, and the Revolution That Shaped a Generation* (New York: Random House, 2007), xviii.

13. "Mothers."

14. "Trains," *Theme Time Radio Hour,* XM Satellite Radio, March 2006.

15. Bate, *Samuel Johnson,* 531.

16. "Flowers," *Theme Time Radio Hour,* XM Satellite Radio, June 2006.

17. Christopher Ricks, *Dylan's Vision of Sin* (New York: Ecco, 2004).

18. Bob Dylan, *Chronicles, Volume 1* (New York: Simon and Schuster, 2004).

19. "Devil," *Theme Time Radio Hour,* XM Satellite Radio, August 2006.

20. Fisher, *Something in the Air,* 301.

12. Bob Dylan's Memory Palace
Robert Polito

You could call them "covers," these invocations of poems and novels that Dylan slips into his songs on recent recordings, and the collections are effortlessly retitled: *Bob Dylan Sings the Exile Poems of Publius Ovividius Naso, Henry Timrod Revisited, Ovid on Ovid, Live from the Black Sea,* and *From Twain to Fitzgerald: Nobody Sings Studies in Classic American Literature Better Than Dylan.*

You might also say they are performed "under cover," as all this escalating literary traffic tends to fall among Dylan's many covert operations. Poems and novels infiltrate his songs mostly through the camouflage of more flagrant smuggling. In "Rollin' and Tumblin'," or "Nettie Moore," or "Summer Days," it is Muddy Waters, "Gentle Nettie Moore," and Charlie Patton you register first, and then only later, if at all, Ovid, Timrod, and *The Great Gatsby.* Dylan's literary stealth tilts toward the second story: a bygone Timrod rather than a celebrated Poe, Whitman, or Dickinson; Ovid's obscurer *Tristia* over his *Metamorphoses.* So that when during "Thunder on the Mountain," the lead-in track to *Modern Times,* Dylan sings, "I've been sitting down studying *The Art of Love* / I think it will fit me like a glove," that glove is calculated to point at Ovid while also covering up the significant fingerprints here. Of the perhaps twenty nods to the Roman poet across the songs that follow, none (as far as I can tell) will touch *The Art of Love,* the Ovidian sleight of hand inside *Modern Times* emanating instead from *Tristia, Black Sea Letters,* the *Amores,* and his "Cures for Love."

Poems, novels, films, and songs, whatever else they do, direct a conversation with the great dead, and Dylan's ghostwriting on his last three CDs, *Time Out of Mind, "Love and Theft,"* and *Modern Times,* is the most far-reaching of his career. Late in the sixteenth century, historian Jonathan Spence recounts, the Jesuit missionary Matteo Ricci "taught the Chinese how to build a memory palace. He told them that the size of the palace would depend on how much they wanted to remember. . . . One could create modest palaces, or one could build less dramatic structures such as a temple compound, a cluster of government offices, a public hostel, or a merchants' meeting lodge. If one wished to begin on a still smaller scale, then one could erect a simple reception hall, a pavilion, or a studio. . . . In summarizing this memory system, he explained that these palaces, pavilions, divans were mental structures to be kept in one's head, not solid objects to be literally constructed out of 'real' materials. . . . To everything we wish to remember, wrote Ricci, we should give an image; and to every one of these images we should assign a position where it can repose peacefully until we are ready to reclaim it by an act of memory."[1]

With *Modern Times*, *"Love and Theft,"* and *Time Out of Mind*, Dylan is teaching us how to build a memory palace, "mental structures"—in this instance, songs—that will lodge the past and the present, the living and the dead. In *Chronicles, Volume 1*, his prose investigation of artistic self-invention and reinvention, he concluded his account of going inside the New York Public Library to read contemporary news- paper reportage on the Civil War with a spatial image for his memory that shrinks Ricci's elite palace to a roadside storage unit. "I crammed my head full of as much of this stuff as I could stand and locked it away in my mind out of sight, left it alone," Dylan writes. "Figured I could send a truck back for it later."[2] Echoing Aquinas, Augustine, and Ignatius of Loyola, Ricci stressed that the memory palace must not be envisioned as a passive repository, but by "incorporate[ing] these 'memories' of an unlived past into the spiritual present," his mnemonic system was an instrument for spiritual practice with ancient links to alchemy, magic, and writ- ing.[3] "As for those worthy figures who lived a hundred generations ago," Ricci argued, "although they too are gone, yet thanks to the books they left behind we who come after can hear their modes of discourse, observe their grand demeanor, and understand both the good order and the chaos of their times, exactly as if we were living among them."[4] Or, as Dylan sings in "Rollin' and Tumblin'":

> Well, the night's filled with shadows, the years are filled with early doom
> The night is filled with shadows, the years are filled with early doom
> I've been conjuring up all these long dead souls from their crumblin'
>   tombs.

Making the dead available to the living, the memory palace proposes a mecha- nism for rendering all time—past, present, future—modern times. Since in this little verse of "Rollin' and Tumblin'" the opening repeated phrases derive from "Our Willie," an 1865 poem by Timrod, and the final line comes from Ovid's poem of circa 16 BCE the *Amores*, and both are cut inside a blues out of Hambone Willie Newbern and Muddy Waters, Dylan manages at once here to describe and embody that mechanism.

As a culture we appear to have forgotten how to experience works of art, or at least how to talk about them plausibly or smartly. A latest instance was the "controversy" in fall 2006 shadowing Dylan's recurrent adaptation for *Modern Times* of phrases from poems by Henry Timrod, a nearly vanished nineteenth-century American poet, essayist, and Civil War newspaper correspondent. That our most gifted and ambitious songwriter would revive Timrod on a No. 1 best-selling CD across America,

Europe, and Australia might prompt a lively concatenation of responses ranging from "Huh? Henry Timrod? Isn't that interesting..." to "Why?" But narrowing the Dylan/Timrod phenomenon (see the *New York Times* article "Who's This Guy Dylan Who's Borrowing Lines from Henry Timrod?" and a subsequent op-ed piece "The Ballad of Henry Timrod" by singer-songwriter Suzanne Vega) into possible plagiarism is to confuse, well, art with a term paper.[5]

Timrod was born in Charleston, South Carolina, in 1828, his arrival in this world falling two years after Stephen Foster and two years before Emily Dickinson. His work, too, might be styled as falling between theirs: sometimes dark and skeptical, other times mawkish, old-fashioned. Following are passages from five Timrod poems Dylan recast for "When the Deal Goes Down":

From "Retirement":

> There is a wisdom that grows up in strife,
> And one—I like it best—that sits at home
> And learns its lessons of a thoughtful ease.

From a sonnet, "I thank you, kind and best beloved friend":

> If I, indeed, divine their meaning truly,
> And not unto myself ascribe, unduly,
> Things which you neither meant nor wished to say,
> Oh! Tell me, is the hope then all misplaced?

From "Two Portraits":

> Still stealing on with pace so slow
> Yourself will scarcely feel the glow...

From "A Rhapsody of a Southern Winter Night":

> These happy stars, and yonder setting moon,
> Have seen me speed, unreckoned and untasked,
> A round of precious hours.
> Oh! here, where in that summer noon I basked,
> And strove, with logic frailer than the flowers,
> To justify a life of sensuous rest,
> A question dear as home or heaven was asked,
> And without language answered. I was blest!

From "A Vision of Poesy":

> ...and at times
>
> A strange far look would come into his eyes,
> As if he saw a vision in the skies.[6]

Dylan, I am guessing, is fascinated by both aspects of Timrod, the antique alongside the brooding. Often tagged the "laureate of the Confederacy"—a title apparently conferred upon him by none other than Tennyson—he still shows up in anthologies because of poems he wrote celebrating and then mourning the new southern nation, particularly "Ethnogenesis" and "Ode Sung on the Occasion of Decorating the Graves of the Confederate Dead at Magnolia Cemetery." Early on, Whittier and Longfellow admired Timrod, and his "Ode" stands behind Allen Tate's "Ode to the Confederate Dead" (and thus in turn behind Robert Lowell's "For the Union Dead").

On *Modern Times* Dylan shuns anthology favorites, but his album focuses at least thirteen instances of phrases spread across five songs—"Spirit on the Water," "Workingman's Blues #2," "Beyond the Horizon," "Rollin' and Tumblin'," and "When the Deal Goes Down"—culled from as many as eight Timrod poems (from "Katie" and "To Thee," besides the six Timrod poems already noted), mostly poems about love, friendship, loss, death, and poetry. Dylan quoted Timrod's "Charleston" in "'Cross the Green Mountain," a song he contributed to the soundtrack of the 2003 Civil War film *Gods and Generals.* Two years earlier he glanced at "Vision of Poesy" for "Tweedle Dee and Tweedle Dum" on *"Love and Theft."*

For "Tweedle Dee and Tweedle Dum," Dylan cribbed those "stately trees" and "secrets of the breeze" from Timrod's "A Vision of Poesy," as well as the epigrammatic "A childish dream is a deathless need," and the ensuing rhyme of "need" and "creed." On *Modern Times* Timrod accents texture, tone, and atmosphere. For "Spirit on the Water," Dylan found "explain / The sources of this hidden pain" in "Two Portraits." For "Workingman's Blues #2," he located "to feed my soul with thought" in "To Thee," and that rhyming "lover's breath" and "a temporary death" also in "Two Portraits." "Beyond the Horizon" teases out at least four Timrod poems: "In the long hours of twilight" arriving via "A Vision of Poesy"; "mortal bliss" from "Our Willie"; "an angel's kiss" from "A Rhapsody of a Southern Winter Night"; and those chiming "bells of St. Mary" from "Katie." Dylan often absorbs Timrod by reversing or otherwise varying the original sense: "But *not* to feed my soul with thought," Timrod wrote, and sleeping "virtues" rather than sleep itself intersected "a temporary death."[7] "I always try to turn a song on its head," Dylan told Robert Hilburn in a 2004 interview about songwriting. "Otherwise, I figure I'm wasting the listener's time."[8]

The pining strains of Timrod's inflections notably complement the 1920s, 1930s, and 1940s popular singers Dylan steadily evokes on *Modern Times,* such as Bing Crosby, who presumably too is acknowledged here, also via that reference to *The Bells of St. Mary's.* Perhaps more surprisingly, Timrod does not (as far as I can tell) grace "Nettie Moore," Dylan's revisiting of "Gentle Nettie Moore" (aka "The Little White Cottage"), a minstrelsy song about a young girl sold into slavery published by Marshall S. Pike and James S. Pierpont in 1857.

But Henry Timrod, I want to suggest, might only inscribe another deep-cover Dylan covert operation, a deflective gesture intended to divert our scrutiny from the actual priority of Ovid on *Modern Times.* During his sophomore year at Hibbing High School, Robert Zimmerman joined the Latin Club, and once recognized, Ovid is everywhere, *Tristia, Black Sea Letters,* "Cures for Love," and the *Amores,* all in translations by Peter Green: the early love poems, certainly, but especially the poems

Ovid wrote after he was exiled by Augustus to Tomis, on the shores of the Black Sea, perhaps because of his scandalous verses, perhaps because of still-enigmatic offenses against the Empire.[9] From "Spirit on the Water," "Rollin' and Tumblin'," and "Someday Baby" through "Workingman's Blues #2," "Nettie Moore," "The Levee's Gonna Break," and "Ain't Talkin'," at least seven of the ten songs refocus language, often entire lines from Green's Ovid, and the Ovidian netting emerges as more ubiquitous than any of the Dylan Web sites have so far indicated.[10] Amid variations for his own metrical designs, Dylan pirates locutions no songwriter would need to steal from a Latin poet, since they sound like they already spring from old blues, country, and rockabilly lyrics—"a face that begs for love," "am I wrong in thinking / That you have forgotten me," "I swear I ain't gonna touch another one for years," "dearer to me than myself, as you yourself can see," "you got me so hooked," and "I want to be with you any way I can."[11]

During the anatomy of his reading in *Chronicles,* Dylan recalls that on the shelves of Ray Gooch's New York library, "Ovid's *Metamorphoses,* the scary horror tale, was next to the autobiography of Davy Crockett."[12] Here, classical mythology jostles American legend. Publius Ovidius Naso was born into a landed-gentry family at Sulmo (now Sulmona) in central Italy in 43 BC. As Green observes in his introduction to *The Poems of Exile,* this was "the year after Caesar's assassination," and Ovid "grew up during the violent death throes of the Roman Republic."[13] Ovid published a version of the *Amores* as early as 15 BC, soon followed by *Heroides, The Art of Love, Remedia Amoris, Metamorphoses,* and *Fasti.* Augustus exiled him to Tomis (now Constanta) in AD 8. "It was two offenses undid me," Ovid alleged in *Tristia,* "a poem and an error: / on the second, my lips are sealed."[14] One genealogical angle on the Dylan-Ovid connection is that in *Chronicles* Dylan traces his own family back to the cities and towns along the Black Sea. "My grandmother's voice possessed a haunting accent," he reports, "face always set in a half-despairing expression. . . . Originally, she'd come from Turkey, sailed from Trabzon, a port town across the Black Sea." He links Odessa—the city his grandmother traveled from to America—to Duluth: "the same kind of temperament, climate and landscape and right on the edge of a big body of water."[15]

I am guessing that Green's translations appeal to Dylan because Green himself is so mercurial a verbal trickster, and there are moments when Ovid even appears to be channeling early Dylan. "You better think twice," Green has Ovid advising on the same page of the *Amores* where Dylan would have discovered, "Catch your opponents sleeping / And unarmed. Just slaughter them where they lie."[16]

Ovid is talking about lovers and bedroom maneuvers here, and much as Timrod, he insinuates ambiance, timber, and character across *Modern Times.* Along with those "crumbling tombs" for "Rollin' and Tumblin'" (or as Green blues-ily translates Ovid: "She conjures up long-dead souls from their crumbling sepulchres / And has incantations to split the solid earth"), Dylan plucked that "house-boy" and "well-trained maid" from the *Amores,* albeit in a neat inversion. Whereas now it is the singer who's "nobody's houseboy," and "nobody's well-trained maid," Ovid originally advised a Roman gentleman intent on seduction, "You must get yourself a houseboy / And a well-trained maid, who can hint / What gifts will be welcome." An ostensibly Katrina-esque detail from "The Levee's Gonna Break"—"Some people got barely enough skin to cover their bones"—first appeared in *Tristia* amid Ovid's description of his own harsh life in Tomis, after his exile from Rome. For "Someday Baby," Dylan gleaned "I'm gonna drive you from your home just like I was driven from mine" from a contrast Ovid posed between his own fate on the Black Sea and the journey of Odysseus: "He was making for his homeland / A cheerful victor: I was driven from mine,/ fugitive, exile, victim."[17]

Yet Ovid, unlike Timrod, also furnished essential structural scaffolding for songs on *Modern Times,* yielding transitions and key images. The strongest songs are all but unthinkable without Ovid, at least Green's Ovid. The devastating final tag of the chorus for "Nettie Moore"—"The world has gone black before my eyes"—issues from a dream vision in the *Amores.* Beyond the bluesy phrases already noted, a partial inventory for "Workingman's Blues #2" tracks "My cruel weapons have been put on the shelf," "No one can ever claim / That I took up arms against you," and "I'm all alone and I'm expecting you / To lead me off in a cheerful dance" back to *Tristia.*[18] Ovid loops through "Ain't Talking" as insistently as the "Heart's burning, still yearning" refrain Dylan imported from the Stanley Brothers:

> If I catch my opponents ever sleeping,
> I'll just slaughter them where they lie.
>
> They will tear your mind away from contemplation
>
> All my loyal and my much-loved companions
>
> They approve of me and share my code
>
> Make the most of one last extra hour
>
> I practice a faith that's long-abandoned
>
> Who says I can't get heavenly aid?
>
> The suffering is unending
> Every nook and cranny has its tears.
>
> I'm not nursing any superfluous fears
>
> In the last outback at the world's end[19]

Each of these vitalizing lines, again calibrated by elisions and reversals, arise from *Tristia,* the *Amores,* and *Black Sea Letters.* Ovid famously was a skilled gardener—"Yet does not my heart still yearn for those long-lost meadows . . . those gardens set amid pine-clad hills," as he wrote in the first of the *Black Sea Letters.* So pervasive is his imprint on "Ain't Talkin'" that it is tempting to set the song in the abandoned gardens of his country villa. "There's no one here," Dylan sings, "the gardener is gone."[20]

From the dustup in the *Times*—after our paper of record found a middle-school teacher who branded Dylan "duplicitous," Suzanne Vega earnestly supposed that

Dylan probably had not filched the texts "on purpose"—you might not know we just lived through a century of Modernism. For Timrod and Ovid are just the tantalizing threshold into Dylan's vast memory palace of echoes. Besides Ovid and Timrod, for instance, *Modern Times* taps into the Bible (Genesis, Exodus, Samuel, John, Luke, among others), Tennyson, Robert Johnson, Memphis Minnie, Kokomo Arnold, Muddy Waters, Sonny Boy Williamson, Blind Lemon Jefferson, the Stanley Brothers, Merle Haggard, Hoagy Carmichael, Cole Porter, Jerome Kern, standards popularized by Jeanette MacDonald, Crosby, and Frank Sinatra, as well as vintage folk songs like "Wild Mountain Thyme," and "Frankie and Albert."

Still more astonishing, though, his prior two recordings *Time Out of Mind* and *"Love and Theft"* could be described as rearranging the entire American musical and literary landscape of the past 150 years, except the sources he adapts are not always American or so recent. Please forgive another Homeric catalog, but the scale and range of Dylan's allusive textures are vital to an appreciation of what he is after on his recent recordings. On *Time Out of Mind* and *"Love and Theft"* he refracts folk, blues, and pop songs created by or associated with Crosby, Sinatra, Charlie Patton, Woody Guthrie, Blind Willie McTell, Doc Boggs, Leroy Carr, Bessie Smith, Billie Holiday, Elvis Presley, Blind Willie Johnson, Big Joe Turner, Wilbert Harrison, the Carter family, and Gene Austin, alongside anonymous traditional tunes and nursery rhymes. But the revelation involves the cavalcade of film and literature fragments: W. C. Fields, the Marx brothers, assorted film noirs, *As You Like It*, *Othello*, Robert Burns, Lewis Carroll, *Huckleberry Finn*, the *Aeneid*, *The Great Gatsby*, Junichi Saga's *Confessions of a Yakuza*, Confederate General Nathan Bedford Forrest, and *Wise Blood*. So crafty are Dylan's reconstructions for *"Love and Theft"* that I would not be surprised if someday we learn every bit of speech—no matter how intimate, or Dylanesque—can be tailed back to another song, poem, movie, or novel.

One conventional approach to Dylan's songwriting references "folk process" and recognizes that he has always operated as a magpie, recovering and transforming hand-me-down materials, lyrics, tunes, even film dialogue (notably on his 1985 album *Empire Burlesque*). Folk process can readily map the associations linking "It Ain't Me Babe" and "Go 'Way from My Window," or tail his variations on traditional blues triplets on "Rollin' and Tumblin'." In his interview with Hilburn, Dylan illustrated his folk process, remarking that he "meditates" on a song. "I'll be playing Bob Nolan's 'Tumbling Tumbleweeds,' for instance, in my head constantly—while I'm driving a car or talking to a person or sitting around or whatever. People will think they are talking to me and I'm talking back, but I'm not. I'm listening to the song in my head. At a certain point, some of the words will change and I'll start writing a song."[21]

Yet what about Ovid and Timrod, or Twain, Fitzgerald, O'Connor, and *Confessions of a Yakuza*? It is no stretch to imagine a writer rehearsing Timrod's "A childish dream is now a deathless need," or Ovid's "I'm in the last outback at the world's end," on the way to a song. But the lyrics that draw on multiple Ovid and Timrod poems and shrewdly tweak the sources? That play Ovid against Timrod, or merge the two into a single verse? Might that require books, notes, other constellations of intention? Perhaps along the lines of what Dylan said of painter Norman Raeben and *Blood on the Tracks*—"He put my mind and my hand and my eye together, in a way that . . . did consciously what I used to do unconsciously"?[22] Folk process probably validates Dylan in his current designs, but if those allusive gestures are also folk process, then a folk process pursued with such intensity, scope, audacity, and verve eventually explodes into Modernism. Dylan seems galvanized by the ways folk process bumps up against Modernism, and the practices of the great blues songwriters intersect the intertextual dispositions of the classical poets. As far back as "Desolation Row," he sang of "Ezra Pound and T. S. Eliot / Fighting in the captain's tower / While calypso singers laugh at them / And fishermen hold flowers." His emphatic nods to the past on *Time Out of Mind*, *"Love and Theft,"* and *Modern Times* probably can best be apprehended as instances of Modernist collage.

If we think of Modernist collages as verbal echo chambers of harmonizing and clashing reverberations, then they tend to organize into two types: those collaged texts, like Pound's *Cantos* or Eliot's "The Waste Land," where we are meant to remark the discrepant tones and idioms of the original texts bumping up against one other; and those collaged texts, composed by poets as various as Kenneth Fearing, Lorine Niedecker, Frank Bidart, and John Ashbery, that aim for an apparently seamless surface. A model of the former is the ending to "The Waste Land":

> London Bridge is falling down falling down falling down
>
> *Poi s'ascose nel foco che gli affina*
> *Quando fiam ceu chelidon*—O swallow swallow
> *Le Prince d'Aquitaine à la tour abolie*
> These fragments I have shored against my ruins
> Why then Ile fit you. Hieronymo's mad againe.
> Datta. Dayadhvam. Damyata.
>
> Shantih shantih shantih[23]

The following passage by Bidart, from his poem "The Second Hour of the Night," proves as allusive as Eliot's, nearly every line rearranging elements assembled not only from Ovid, his main source for the Myrrha story, but also Plotinus and even Eliot. But instead of incessant fragmentation, we experience narrative sweep and urgency:

> As Myrrha is drawn down the dark corridor toward her father
>
> not free not to desire
>
> what draws her forward is neither COMPULSION nor FREEWILL:—
>
> or at least freedom, here *choice*, is not to be
> imagined as action upon
>
> preference: no creature is free to choose what
> allows it its most powerful, and most secret, release:

I fulfill it, because I contain it—
it prevails, because it is within me—

it is a heavy burden, setting up longing to enter that
realm to which I am called from within . . .

As Myrrha is drawn down the dark corridor toward her father

not free not to choose

she thinks, *To each soul its hour.*[24]

Dylan's songwriting inclines toward the cagier, deflected Bidart-Ashbery-Fearing-Niedecker Modernist mode. We would scarcely realize we are inside a collage unless someone told us, or we abruptly seized on a familiar locution. The wonder of the dozen or so nuggets Dylan sifted from *Confessions of a Yakuza* for *"Love and Theft"* is how casual and personal they sound dropped into his songs, a sentence once about a bookmaker reemerging as an aside on marriage in "Floater": "A good bookie makes all the difference in a gambling joint—it's up to him whether a session comes alive or falls flat."[25] Not one of those *"Love and Theft"* songs, of course, is remotely about a Yakuza, or gangster of any persuasion.

The issue of what we gain if we heed the multifarious allusions lodges a more tangled crux. For a long time I preferred to think of the phrases as curios of vernacular speech picked up from Dylan's listening or reading that slant his songs into something like collective, as against individual, utterances and only locally influence his designs. But after immersion in Ovid and Timrod, it is hard to miss both grand and specific calculations. Dylan manifestly is, for instance, fixated on the American Civil War. "The age that I was living in didn't resemble this age," as he wrote in *Chronicles*, "but it did in some mysterious and traditional way. Not just a little bit, but a lot. There was a broad spectrum and commonwealth that I was living upon, and the basic psychology of that life was every bit a part of it. If you turned the light towards it, you could see the full complexity of human nature. Back there, America was put on the cross, died, and was resurrected. There was nothing synthetic about it. The godawful truth of that would be the all-encompassing template behind everything I would write."[26]

His 2003 film *Masked and Anonymous* takes place against the backdrop of another interminable domestic war during an unspecified future. Dylan sees links between the Civil War and America now—the echoes from Timrod help him frame and sustain those links. Ovid, too, lived through the assassination of Julius Caesar, the violent Roman internal conflicts, and wrote at the start of the Pax Augusta. Even the tidbits of Yakuza oral history irradiate the terrain. On recordings steeped in empire, war, corruption, masks, moral failure, male power, and self-delusion, aren't Tokyo racketeers as apt as Charlie Patton or the Carter family? Ovid and Timrod (or Twain, O'Connor, and Fitzgerald) should not be mistaken for a high-brow alternative to the "old weird America" of Dock Boggs; they are an extension of it.

Exile, ghosts, romantic and spiritual abandonment, wary dawn departures, an abiding death in life—the devastated inflections of *Tristia* and *Black Sea Letters* offer the closest analogue in poetry I know to *Time Out of Mind*, particularly to "Love Sick," "Not Dark Yet," "Tryin' to Get to Heaven," and "Highlands." Ovid obsessively revisits his apprehension that he "made a few bad turns":

> . . . yet sick though my body is, my mind is sicker
>   from endless contemplation of its woes.
> Absent the city scene, absent my dear companions,
>   absent (none closer to my heart) my wife:
> what's here is a Scythian rabble, a mob of trousered Getae—
>   troubles seen and unseen both prey on my mind.
> One hope alone in all this brings me some consolation—
>   that my troubles may be soon cut short by death.[27]

The phantoms of Ovid and Timrod transform individual songs. Dylan's "Rollin' and Tumblin'" pushes past the eroticism—and erotic anger—of the Hambone Willie Newbern and Muddy Waters versions toward something like forgiveness: "Let's forgive each other, darlin', let's go down to the Greenwood Glen." The axle of that forgiveness is the sudden nod to mortality in the verse I quoted earlier about the "long dead souls" and their "crumbling tombs," out of Ovid. Yet isn't our alertness to mortality also deepened after we know that the prior repeated line that Dylan reshaped from Timrod, "Well, the night is filled with shadows, the years are filled with early doom," draws on "Our Willie," a heart-sore, self-accusing poem about the death of the poet's son?[28] Similarly, isn't the haunted and inconsolable refrain from "Nettie Moore"—"the world has gone black before my eyes"—still more haunted and inconsolable after we return the line to Ovid's nightmare vision about "the stain of adultery" in the *Amores*? In "Workingman's Blues #2" Dylan persistently roots his litany of the troubles of globalization in references to Ovid's exile from Rome, as though the poet (and his poems) were only the first victims of outsourcing among the "proletariat." "Ain't Talkin'," as submitted earlier, all but name checks Ovid's dark, bitter personal story, reclaiming his grief and anger, his vengeance and narratives of a "world gone wrong" as Dylan's own.

When Dylan lifts from Ovid and Timrod, the phrases often occur during passages where the original poets discuss their art. That "cheerful dance" and those "countless foes" are items in Ovid's reply to a friend who urged him to "divert these mournful days with writing."[29] As Dylan sings, "I practice a faith that's long abandoned," he glances at a section of *Tristia* where Ovid is reflecting on the quandaries of keeping his Latin alive amid the "barbaric" languages of Tomis:

> Yet, to prevent my voice being muted
>   in my native speech, lest I lose the common use
> of the Latin tongue, I converse with myself, I practice
>   terms long abandoned, retrace my sullen art's
> ill-fated sins. Thus I drag out my life and time, thus
>   tear my mind from the contemplation of my woes.
> Through writing I seek an anodyne to misery: if my studies
>   Win me such a reward, that is enough.[30]

Even when Ovid exclaimed, "I want to be with you any way I can," he was not addressing a lover but his audience back in Rome reading the new poems he was sending them from the Black Sea. Finally, Timrod's recurrently invoked "A Vision of Poesy" traces in fanciful, mythic guises the curious route that might guide a boy born of "humble parentage" in Charleston, South Carolina, say, or in Duluth, Minnesota, to poetry.

During his incisive entry on *Street Legal* for *The Bob Dylan Encyclopedia,* Michael Gray argues that "Every song deals with love's betrayal, with Dylan's being betrayed like Christ, and, head on, with the need to abandon woman's love."[31] On *Time Out of Mind,* and especially *"Love and Theft"* and *Modern Times,* art and tradition—I wish to propose—now seize the ground zero once occupied by love, and later God. Dylan always emphasized the traditional footing of his writing. "My songs, what makes them different is that there's a foundation to them," he told Jon Pareles. "They're standing on a strong foundation, and subliminally that's what people are hearing."[32] Yet the current intensification of his allusive scale is undeniable.

Without ever winking, Dylan proves canny and sophisticated about all this, though after a fashion that recalls Laurence Sterne's celebrated attack on plagiarism, itself plagiarized from *The Anatomy of Melancholy.* On "Summer Days" from *"Love and Theft"* Dylan sings:

> She's looking into my eyes, and she's a-holding my hand
> She looking into my eyes, she's holding my hand,
> She says, "You can't repeat the past," I say, "You can't? What do you mean you
>   can't? Of course, you can."

His puckish, snaky lines dramatize precisely how one can, in fact, "repeat the past," since the lyrics slyly reproduce a conversation from *The Great Gatsby.*[33] On *Modern Times,* Dylan veers from mediumistic—"I've been conjuring up these long dead souls from their crumblin' tombs"—to self-mocking: "I'm so hard pressed, my mind tied up in knots / I keep recycling the same old thoughts."

When asked what he believed by David Gates during a 1996 interview in *Newsweek,* Dylan replied, "I find the religiosity and philosophy in the music. I don't find it anywhere else. Songs like 'Let Me Rest on a Peaceful Mountain' or 'I Saw the Light'— that's my religion. I don't adhere to rabbis, preachers, evangelists, all of that. I've learned more from the songs than I've learned from any of this kind of entity. The songs are my lexicon. I believe the songs."[34] Let's presume that by "songs" Dylan now also must mean poems, such as Ovid's or Henry Timrod's, and novels, such as Fitzgerald's, along with traditional folk hymns and blues.

Speaking to his sixteenth-century Chinese listeners, Matteo Ricci affirmed the imperative of "good roots or foundation,"[35] and conceived the memory palace he offered them inside a Renaissance visionary architecture that "not only performs the office of conserving for us the things, words and acts which we confide to it . . . but also gives us true wisdom."[36]

• • • •

In *The Memory Palace of Matteo Ricci*, Spence quotes Augustine from the *Confessions:* "Perchance it might be properly said, 'there be three times; a present of things past, a present of things present, and a present of things future.'"[37] Dylan, too, as far back as his *Renaldo and Clara* pressed the eternizing powers of art. "The movie creates and holds the time," he told Jonathan Cott. "That's what it should do—it should hold that time, breathe in that time and stop time in doing that."[38] Or, as he again sketched *Blood on the Tracks,* "Everybody agrees that was pretty different, and what's different about it is that there's a code in the lyrics and also there's no sense of time. There's no respect for it: you've got yesterday, today and tomorrow all in the same room, and there's little that you can't imagine not happening."[39]

All in the same room. Dylan's "conjuring," as he might say, and as Ovid did say, of the dead on *Time Out of Mind,* *"Love and Theft,"* and *Modern Times* stands among the most daring, touching, and original signatures of his art. Who else—or who besides classical Roman poets—writes, has ever written, songs as layered and textured as these? Sheltering the dead among the living, his memory palace tips past into present, but conjurers inevitably summon also the shadows ahead. "Whatever music you love, it didn't come from nowhere," Dylan recently advanced on his radio show, and *Theme Time Radio Hour* is another wing of his memory palace. "It's always good to know what went down before you, because if you know the past, you can control the future."[40]

Notes

1. Jonathan D. Spence, *The Memory Palace of Matteo Ricci* (New York: Penguin, 1984), 1–2.
2. Bob Dylan, *Chronicles, Volume 1* (New York: Simon and Schuster, 2004), 86.
3. Spence, *The Memory Palace of Matteo Ricci,* 16.
4. Ibid., 22.
5. "Who's This Guy Dylan Who's Borrowing Lines from Henry Timrod?" *New York Times,* September 14, 2006; and Suzanne Vega, "The Ballad of Henry Timrod," *New York Times,* September 17, 2006.
6. All Timrod quotations are drawn from *Poems of Henry Timrod with Memoir and Portrait* (Richmond: B. F. Johnson Publishing Co., 1901; reprinted in facsimile by Kessinger Publishing). Also helpful is Walter Brian Cisco, *Henry Timrod: A Biography* (Madison, N.J.: Fairleigh Dickinson University Press, 2004).
7. For passages where there are even minor departures between Dylan and Timrod, and when I do not quote the Timrod source elsewhere in this essay, here are the relevant Timrod "originals": "How then, O weary one! Explain / The sources of that hidden pain?" ("Two Portraits"); "You will perceive that in the breast / The germs of many virtues rest, / Which, ere they feel a lover's breath, / Lie in a temporary death..." ("Two Portraits"); "Ah! Christ forgive us for the crime / Which drowned the memories of the time / In a merely mortal bliss!" ("Our Willie"); "And o'er the city sinks and swells / The chime of old St. Mary's bells..." ("Katie").
8. Jonathan Cott, ed., *Bob Dylan: The Essential Interviews* (New York: Wenner Books, 2006), 432.
9. Green's translations can be found in Ovid, *The Erotic Poems* (London: Penguin Books, 1982); and Ovid, *The Poems of Exile* (Berkeley: University of California Press, 2005). Dylan studied Latin for two years at Hibbing High School, but was Ovid among the authors he translated? During my own sophomore Latin class at Boston College High School, we read

the "Pyramis and Thisbe" story from Book IV of *The Metamorphoses*. It was also at BC High that I first encountered Matteo Ricci, a hero for the Jesuits who taught and resided there, and during a senior year Asian studies course we were assigned an early biography of the Jesuit missionary to China, Vincent Cronin, *The Wise Man from the West* (New York: EP Dutton, 1955). Any mention of "memory" in proximity to Dylan inevitably must also be indebted to Robert Cantwell's brilliant chapter on Harry Smith and Robert Fludd, "Smith's Memory Theater," in *When We Were Good* (Cambridge, Mass.: Harvard University Press, 1996). I also benefited from Francis A. Yates's *The Art of Memory* (Chicago: University of Chicago Press, 1966); and an anthology edited by Mary Carruthers and Jan M. Ziolkowski, *The Medieval Craft of Memory* (Philadelphia: University of Pennsylvania Press, 2002).

10. For two invaluable annotated Dylan Web sites, see http://republika.pl/bobdylan/mt/ and http://republika.pl/bobdylan/lat/.

11. Or as these lines and phrases appear in Green's translations: "The facts demand Censure, the face begs for love—and gets it..." (*Amores*, Bk. 3, section 11B); "May the gods grant that my complaint's unfounded / that I'm wrong in thinking you've forgotten me!" (*Tristia*, Bk. V, section 13); "Revulsion making you wish you'd never had a woman / And swear you won't touch one again for years..." ("Cures for Love," ll.416–17); "...wife dearer to me than myself, you yourself can see..." (*Tristia*, Bk. V, section 14); "This girl's got me hooked..." (*Amores*, Bk. 1, section 3); and *"I want to be with you any way I can..."* (*Tristia*, Bk. V, section 1).

12. Dylan, *Chronicles*, 36–37. By referencing "the scary horror tale" (not *tales*) might he be conflating Ovid *(Metamorphoses)* and Kafka *(The Metamorphosis)*? Is this mention of Ovid in *Chronicles* an early signal of his interest in the Roman poet for *Modern Times*?

13. Green, introduction to *The Poems of Exile*, xix.

14. Ovid, *Tristia*, Bk. II.

15. Dylan, *Chronicles*, 92–93.

16. Ovid, *Amores*, Bk. 1, section 9.

17. For the Ovid/Green sources: "Crumbling sepulchers," etc. from *Amores*, Bk. 1, section 8; "Houseboy," etc. from *Amores*, Bk. 1, section 8; "Barely enough skin," etc. from *Tristia*, Bk. IV, section 6 ("I lack my old strength and colour, / there's barely enough skin to cover my bones..."). "Driven from mine," etc. from *Tristia*, Bk. I, section 5.

18. For the Ovid/Green sources: "'...The bruise on her breast bears witness / To the stain of adultery.' There his interpretation ended. At those words the blood ran freezing / From my face, and the world went black before my eyes..." (*Amores*, Bk. 3, section 5). "Show mercy, I beg you, shelve your cruel weapons..." (*Tristia*, Bk. II). "You write that I should divert these mournful days with writing... Priam, you're saying, should have fun fresh from his son's funeral, / or Niobe, bereaved, lead off some cheerful dance..." (*Tristia*, Bk. V, section 12).

19. As these various lines appear in Ovid/Green: "Catch your opponents sleeping / And unarmed. Just slaughter them where they lie..." (*Amores*, Book 1, section 9). "I practice / terms long abandoned, retrace my sullen art's / ill-fated signs. Thus I drag out my life and time, thus / tear my mind from the contemplation of my woes..." (*Tristia*, Bk. V, section 7). "[L]oyal and much-loved companions, bonded in brotherhood... This may well be my final chance to embrace them—let me make the most of one last extra hour..." (*Tristia*, Bk. I, section 3). "...even here you're already familiar to the native tribesmen, / who approve, and share, your code..." (*Black Sea Letters*, Bk. 3, section 2). "Though I lack such heroic / stature, who says *I* can't get heavenly aid / when a god's angry with me?" (*Tristia*, Bk. I, section 2). "The whole house / mourned at my obsequies—men, women, even children, / every nook and corner had its tears..." (*Tristia*, Bk. I, section 3). "Of this I've no doubt—but the very dread of misfortune / often drives me to nurse superfluous fears..." (*Black Sea Letters*, Bk. II.

section 7). "Some places make exile / milder, but there's no more dismal land than this / beneath either pole. It helps to be near your country's borders: / I'm in the last outback, at the world's end..." (*Black Sea Letters*, Bk. II, section 7).

20. Ovid on his garden is from *Black Sea Letters*, Bk. I, section 8. But *Ovid's* garden in "Ain't Talkin'"? Or Tennyson's (via "Maud"), as Christopher Ricks proposes? The Garden of Eden? God (or Christ) appears often in the guise of a gardener in Renaissance poems. A case can also be made that the absent gardener at the finish is the singer himself, unconscious (perhaps even dead) after he was "hit from behind" in the opening verse, and presiding over the scene as a ghost.

21. Cott, *Bob Dylan*, 438.

22. Dylan quoted by Michael Gray in *The Bob Dylan Encyclopedia* (New York: Continuum, 2006) in his entry on Raeben, 561.

23. T. S. Eliot, "The Waste Land" (1922) in *Collected Poems 1909–1962* (New York: Harcourt, 1991), 69.

24. Frank Bidart, "The Second Hour of the Night," in *Desire* (New York: Farrar, Straus and Giroux), 46.

25. Junichi Saga, *Confessions of a Yakuza* (Tokyo: Kodansha International, 1991), 153–54. The Dylan lines, from "Floater (Too Much to Ask)," run: "Never seen him quarrel with my mother even once / Things come alive or they fall flat."

26. Dylan, *Chronicles*, 86.

27. Ovid, *Tristia*, Bk. IV, section 6.

28. Timrod, from "Our Willie": "By that sweet grave, in that dark room, / We may weave at will for each other's ear, / Of that life, and that love, and that early doom / The tale which is shadowed here..."

29. "...I'm barred from relaxation / in a place ringed by countless foes." (*Tristia*, Bk. V, section 12). Also see above, note 13.

30. Ovid, *Tristia*, Bk. V, section 7.

31. Gray, *The Bob Dylan Encyclopedia*, 643.

32. Cott, *Bob Dylan*, 396.

33. F. Scott Fitzgerald, *The Great Gatsby* (1925). As Nick says of Gatsby in chapter 6:

> He broke off and began to walk up and down a desolate path of fruit rinds and discarded favors and crushed flowers.
> "I wouldn't ask too much of her," I ventured. "You can't repeat the past."
> "Can't repeat the past?" he cried incredulously. "Why of course you can!"
> He looked around him wildly, as if the past were lurking here in the shadow of his house, just out of reach of his hand.

34. David Gates, "Dylan Revisited," reprinted in *Studio A: The Bob Dylan Reader*, ed. Benjamin Hedin (New York: Norton, 2004), 236.

35. Spence, *The Memory Palace of Matteo Ricci*, 146.

36. Ibid., 20. He is quoting Guilio Camillo (Delminio) on his sixteenth-century "memory theatre."

37. Spence, *The Memory Palace of Matteo Ricci*, 16.

38. Cott, *Bob Dylan*, 192.

39. Ibid., 260.

40. Dylan quoted in *MOJO*, April 2007, 34.

13. Among Schoolchildren:
Dylan's Forty Years in the Classroom
Kevin J. H. Dettmar

"Dylanology," the cynics call it, and if there is any doubt that the serious study of Bob Dylan's work and legacy continues at an astonishing pace, the publication of this volume more or less simultaneously with *The Cambridge Companion to Bob Dylan,* which I am editing, should put all doubts to rest. The *Companion* will be the first in Cambridge's venerable and long-running series devoted to a living popular culture figure. And the commissioning editor's logic is airtight: across the popular arts, Dylan is the figure most thoroughly entrenched in the undergraduate curriculum, and Cambridge University Press expects a "big uptake among undergraduate courses" for the book. Thus, the commissioning and publication of the *Cambridge Companion* serve as confirmation of the phenomenon I will explore in this essay: the sometimes uneasy accommodation of Bob Dylan by American universities, and to a far lesser extent of American universities by Bob Dylan (as evidenced by Dylan's nearly walking out when Princeton conferred an honorary degree upon him in 1970).

No other figure from the world of American popular music, of this or any other era, has attracted the volume and quality of critical attention that Dylan has; he has become the most carefully explicated figure in all of popular music, perhaps in all of popular culture. Just as significantly, no popular culture figure has ever been adopted into the curricula of college and university language and literature departments in the way Dylan has. By the late 1960s articles had started to appear in scholarly journals analyzing the songs of Dylan using, however loosely, the methodologies of literary studies. Perhaps more surprisingly *Scholastic Magazine,* with its audience of secondary-school students and teachers, featured an article on Dylan back in 1970, and even today an enterprising high school teacher can go online and download a lesson plan for teaching, for instance, a unit on Dylan and protest music. And by "today" I do mean today: less than a week before I typed this essay, the *Times* of London ran a piece by none other than the current British poet laureate, Andrew Motion, announcing that this year's National Poetry Day would focus on the work of Dylan, promoting "an online secondary-schools project 'to celebrate poetry through the lyrics of Bob Dylan's legendary songs.'"[1] It is quite a production, with the promotional muscle of Sony/BMG standing behind it: teachers can download lesson plans, songs, and video and can request a free eighteen-track sampler from the upcoming three-CD retrospective *Dylan;* students can win big prizes, including—wasn't it inevitable?—a limited-edition Dylan iPod.

Motion considers for a moment whether a more contemporary band—the Arctic Monkeys is his example—might better suggest a living poetic tradition in popular song for contemporary students, but he avers, somewhat surprisingly, that Dylan is in effect "canonical":

> Dylan is Dylan, and you don't have to be approximately of his age to see that his lyrics are simply better than those by most other songwriters—better because they are more concentrated, more allusive, more memorable (even without the melodies), more surprising, more risk-taking, more willing to engage with the whole range of human experience.[2]

Dylan biographer Clinton Heylin calls his oeuvre "the most important canon in rock music."[3] This praise may actually understate the case, for arguably Dylan's is the most important canon in all of twentieth-century American popular music (as Bobby Vee remarked repeatedly in his talk at the "Highway 61 Revisited" symposium, March 25–27, 2007, "He's Irving Berlin"). And Heylin's unembarrassed use of that politically charged term *canon,* implied as well in Motion's remarks, serves to suggest that Dylan has long since passed into the academy. Arriving on the scene when he did, Dylan seemed to be God's gift to English and other humanities departments.

College and university courses in the United States and Europe devoted to the study of Dylan's work are now so common as no longer to count as a curiosity. By far the majority of these courses are taught within departments of English or literature, for Dylan came to public prominence at precisely the moment that departments of English were seeking to break down traditional barriers between "high" and "low" culture, and his highly literate and literary popular songs provided the perfect texts for classroom use and scholarly analysis. Hundreds of schools from Ruskin College, Oxford, to Utah Valley State College, from Wofford to Harvard, from Brown to the Rhode Island School of Design to the Community College of Southern Nevada, now teach semester-long courses on Dylan; countless other courses examine Dylan's work within a larger literary, musical, or cultural context.

Thus, Dylan has the honor, but also bears the scars, of being one of the first popular performers to be introduced into high school and college classrooms in the wake of the student protests of the 1960s. A spoonful of Dylan, or so it was thought, would convince students of their teachers' hip credentials and go some way toward bridging the newly dubbed "generation gap" and making the curriculum "relevant." According to Alfred Aronowitz, "American colleges and universities began adding Contemporary Popular Music to their curricula, teaching it as if it were Business

Administration," in 1966.[4] In the context in which this claim appears, Aronowitz gives no evidence to support this precise dating, but he is pretty close to the mark. Certainly by 1966 the critical infrastructure for the university study of Dylan was taking shape. Paul William's landmark "Understanding Dylan," for instance, showed what was involved in taking this music seriously, and Peter Gzowski's "Dylan: An Explosion of Poetry," suggested the generic conventions through which Dylan would appear on syllabi.[5]

As the New Critical method of "close reading" came to dominate American English departments, hand in hand with the establishment of American studies programs—and as the political unrest of the civil rights movement and Vietnam War protests forced their way into college classrooms—just at the right moment, the well-wrought lyrics of Dylan's sophisticated pop songs presented themselves as a legitimate means for making the teaching of American literature and cultural history "relevant." Dylan's impressionistically suggestive, surrealistically charged songs proved wonderfully amenable to the close-reading techniques championed by the New Critics, and his self-conscious adoption of literary, and especially biblical, allusion suggested his genealogy from the great poets of the English-language and Western European literary traditions. A student coming to university in fall 1966 represented the leading edge of the post–World War II baby boom; it would have been possible for her to bring with her Dylan's first seven albums—not a bad set of texts, as it turns out, for exploring the range of what poetry can do. And Dylan not only repaid close reading but suggested in his own work the benefits of a careful literary apprenticeship. In the words of Gordon Ball's letter nominating Dylan for the Nobel Prize, "His words and music have helped restore the vital, time-honored link between poetry and music, and have so permeated the world as to alter its history."

But perhaps the most important reason for Dylan's migration into the classroom, and into the canon, has less to do with literary quality than with a quality that during the 1960s was universally known as "relevance."[6] Through the vehicle of the Port Huron Statement, the Students for a Democratic Society gave voice to a generation of college students dissatisfied with a college structure unresponsive to their needs and to the needs of the larger society. Addressing his colleagues at the annual Modern Language Association Convention in December 1969, in the waning days of the 1960s, professor and English department chair Stanton Millet was more candid than most, examining "the course of student unrest during the last few years and ... some of the assumptions about the nature of the university and the relationship among students, faculty, and administrators that provide the context for our student rebellion," and asserting that "until quite recently, the best model for describing the relationship of students to the university has been that of the medieval craft or guild. Students entered as apprentices...."[7] Millet dubbed this the "pre-revolutionary model," and it is a model whose utility he had over time come to question. He found it best exemplified in a speech by University of California-Berkeley Chancellor Roger Heynes on "The Nature of the Academic Community" delivered to the American Council of Education in October 1966:

The teacher, the faculty member is an expert, not only in the content of his discipline, but also in the conditions of learning. It is he who is expected to select the content, the approach, the experiences which are designed to make most efficient the student's effort to acquire the mastery of content and the acquisition of the necessary skills. Moreover, the faculty member sets the standards, he motivates, he evaluates. In these roles he and his students are not equal partners, but they are partners in learning nonetheless.[8]

The challenges starting to be registered against this traditional model were felt as a real shock in some quarters. Lewis Feuer, for example, writing in the *New York Times* on September 18, 1966, warned:

No matter how much responsible student self-government emerges, it still remains true that a modern university cannot be a republic of equals. It is an institution which tries to transmit the accumulated knowledge, wisdom, doubts and uncertainties of the past's scholars, artists, and scientists and to impart to the student a sense of probity and evidence so that he can carry on the unfinished work of civilization. It is based on one essential presupposition—that knowledge and wisdom are cross-generational, that the elders have something to transmit. This can be carried to an extreme of gerontocracy, where the elder generation thinks in its pride it has exhausted all experience. Far more real today, however, is the risk of juvenocracy, which strikes at the whole of wisdom.[9]

The authors of the Port Huron Statement, on the other hand, had a somewhat less sanguine view of this state of affairs: "With administrators ordering the institutions," they write, "and faculty the curriculum, the student learns by his isolation to accept elite rule within the university, which prepares him to accept later forms of minority control"; "academia includes a radical separation of student from the material of study. That which is studied, the social reality, is 'objectified' to sterility, dividing the student from life."[10] "Under these conditions," they continue, "university life loses all relevance to some. Four hundred thousand of our classmates leave college every year." Hence their insistence that the curriculum once again be made relevant at the document's conclusion, when they call for

national efforts at university reform by an alliance of students and faculty. They must wrest control of the educational process from the administrative bureaucracy. They must make fraternal and functional contact with allies in labor, civil rights, and other liberal forces outside the campus. They must import major public issues into the curriculum—research and teaching on problems of war and peace is an outstanding example. They must make debate and controversy, not dull pedantic cant, the common style for educational life.

Though it turns out to have been a somewhat shortsighted solution, inviting Dylan into college classrooms was one of the most popular solutions hit upon by a cohort of young teachers hoping to rise to the challenges issued by their students.

And when Dylan came to college—after, of course, having dropped out after four quarters at the University of Minnesota—he came as a poet. The 1960s were, for historical and cultural reasons too diverse to consider in detail here, the heyday for the study of poetry in English departments: the critical tools of the New Criticism were especially attuned to the textual complexity of poetry, and the lyrics of Dylan's songs were consequently accommodated and subjected to the close reading paradigm in which college teachers were training their students. The earliest traces of Dylan as a classroom subject were doubtless rather ephemeral ones: the playing of LPs, distribution of dittos. But before long the textbook publishers, sniffing out an opportunity, began to put Dylan between hard covers.

The foundational contribution in the area of classroom texts belongs to David R. Pichaske, whose *Beowulf to Beatles: Approaches to Poetry* (1972) was the first college textbook to subject rock lyrics to "the close examination literary critics lavish on poems."[11] Pichaske's goal was to add rock lyrics to the traditional classroom poetic canon, in the hope that the inclusion of popular song would demonstrate that "everything we designate as 'poetic' is to be found in rock lyrics"; as an added pedagogical bonus, "the college generation is most obviously 'into' rock."[12] For the poetic traditionalist, then, smuggling of rock into the poetry classroom may serve to demonstrate that the best contemporary lyrics hold up well under high poetic scrutiny; and for the students, broadening the category "poetry" to include rock should, apparently, open students up to a much wider range of (traditional) poetic expression.

Pichaske's books—the two editions of his classroom text *Beowulf to Beatles,* as well as the companion volume of sorts *The Poetry of Rock*—represent the most significant gesture in the movement to consider rock songwriting, and the work of Dylan in particular, as a kind of vernacular poetry. But they are very much part of a movement in curriculum reform and textbook publishing that was gathering momentum as the 1960s were coming to an end; the title of my favorite representative "hip" anthology of the period, *Grooving the Symbol* (1970), succinctly suggests the tenor of the times.[13] Perhaps the most symptomatic of these anthologies—a bit more artless, because intended primarily for a secondary-school audience—is the two-volume anthology assembled by Homer Hogan called *Poetry of Relevance,* also published in 1970. To a literary critical audience, Hogan's title was a tip of the hat to two landmark works of then-recent literary criticism, Robert Langbaum's *The Poetry of Experience* (1957), and J. Hillis Miller's *Poets of Reality* (1965). Both these titles describe a grouping of poets according to their subject; Hogan, on the other hand, explicitly picks his poets based on their intended audience and more particularly their relevance to that audience.

The rationale for Hogan's anthology is twofold: first, to provide relevance in college teaching, acknowledged in the Port Huron Statement and other manifestos of the time; and second, to give a boost to contemporary American poetry, the enthusiasm for which among students had all but dried up, no matter how popular it remained with teachers. Hogan writes in his preface, "To the Instructor":

> *Poetry of Relevance* invites students to find significant connections between poems of our literary heritage and songs that express contemporary interests and concerns. The table of contents makes clear the general strategy: each song lyric is

followed by one or more poems that develop the theme or poetic technique found in the lyric.

To take full advantage of this text, the instructor should be sure to play the recommended recording of the song preceding the poems he wishes to discuss. Once a mood is established by the recording, the ways of working from song to poem are limited only by the instructor's ingenuity. The special interest sparked by hearing the songs of such artists as John Lennon, Leonard Cohen, Paul Simon, and Joni Mitchell extends to the poetry itself.[14]

Among the units centered around the poetry of these rock songwriters, Hogan includes a cluster of poems called "Myth and *The Ballad of Frankie Lee and Judas Priest,*" opening, of course, with the lyrics to Dylan's song but then followed, according to a logic I am not able to parse, by Yvor Winters's "Sir Gawaine and the Green Knight," William Blake's "The Little Vagabond," Gerard Manley Hopkins's "Carrion Comfort," Bob Kaufman's "Song of the Broken Giraffe," Dunstan Thompson's "The Lay of the Battle of Tombland," Edward FitzGerald's "Rubiyat of Omar Khayyam," and Muriel Rukeyser's "Easter Eve."

Toward the end of his instructors' preface, Hogan finally comes to his defense of the then-controversial idea that rock lyrics could be profitably read and taught as poetry:

> We consider now the contents of this book, popular songs and poems. Popular song has always come in many varieties, though today it takes more shapes than ever before—folk, blues, rock, calypso, western, raga, jazz, straight pop, and all combinations thereof bearing labels like "urban," "rural," "cool," "heavy," "African," "acid," "funky," "put-down," "protest," and so on ad infinitum. For our purposes, however, one basic division is crucial; namely, that between what we shall call "authentic" and "inauthentic" popular song. The first kind attempts to do justice to the rhythms, joys, sorrows, and dreams of ordinary life. When it fails in this attempt, people call it "sincere" but bad. The second kind tries to dull us to ordinary life as it is by soothing us into accepting a glossy, synthetic substitute. It is merely commercial, escapist, and "phony." When it succeeds, those whom it does not fool may admit that it is good, but will insist that it is still just "slick merchandise."
>
> *Poetry of Relevance* includes only what we believe to be "authentic" popular song—that which tries, more or less successfully, to be *relevant* to everyday existence.[15]

This is a very rich passage, of course: Hogan's gloss on authenticity in popular music is priceless, reinscribing as he does the Frankfurt School condemnation of "mass" culture in defense of a pure and motiveless, truly "popular" art. For the student who chanced to read the instructor's preface, however—although if my own experience is any indication, students tend not to read around randomly and optionally in a textbook—Hogan's true colors do come out at the end of the preface:

[Poetry of Relevance] invites students to find connections between these songs and formal poems. One reason for the invitation is that we think students may discover many ways in which poems can be as relevant as popular songs to their present interests and in some cases, at least, even more so, since included in the interests of young people particularly is a desire for experience that is thoroughly extraordinary, a desire more likely to be satisfied by pure poetry than by songs.[16]

At the last minute Hogan reinstates a distinction between "rock" poetry and "pure poetry," severely compromising his project. I too am a textbook author and understand the pressures put on authors by large commercial publishers not to be too unsettling in their claims, but this caveat does, I think, suggest that in 1970 we were still a long way from the level playing field of all cultural texts envisioned by some cultural studies theorists and practitioners. Allowing Dylan into the curriculum as a "poet" required a somewhat broadened definition of poetry; many were not happy with that accommodation. But it did not require a fundamental rethinking of the grounds of literary study: that was to follow a decade or more later, in the guise of cultural studies.

The narrowly formalist reading of Dylan's work favored by the New Critics requires the suppression of its obvious, antiestablishment political message, and advocates of "cultural literacy" within the academy have too often approached Dylan's music blind to what Richard Goldstein calls their own "pop illiteracy," wresting the songs from the political, historical, and cultural contexts that are so integral to their functioning. Dylan has, of course, remained the privileged popular-culture subject of academic discourse to this day; as Benjamin Hedin shrewdly observes, "The excited teenagers and college students who stayed up all night hoping to decipher 'Maggie's Farm' became professors, journalists and other leaders of the educational hierarchy." The absorption of a popular-culture subject into university structures always involves both benefits and costs. Owing to his early adoption by English professors, Dylan's is the most carefully studied body of work in all of American popular music (and Dylan has repaid the favor, naming his penultimate studio album after a work of literary and cultural criticism). But this scholarly work must stay cognizant of what Goldstein has called the "Rolling Tenure Revue" and the discipline of "Ph.Dylanology": a warning not that Dylan's work does not hold up to careful scrutiny, but instead that his songs are not poems, not the "well-wrought urn" of New Criticism ideology, but rather songs forged in the crucible of personal, national, generational, racial, sexual change and can only be understood as such.

For the adoption of Dylan's music into American high school and college classrooms was the thin edge of the wedge, as cultural studies began to redefine the curriculum of literary studies. I remember being informed in a graduate school seminar twenty-five years ago that in ten years' time there would be no more departments of English, because they would all be replaced by departments of cultural studies. It turns out he was wrong, of course; the Centre for Contemporary Cultural Studies in Birmingham, founded in 1964 by Richard Hoggart, was far ahead of American developments. Rather than replacing English departments, however, the Birmingham center itself was closed in 2002. But certainly cultural studies has remade English departments in significant ways in this country, starting back in the mid-1960s.

As John Storey writes, "the cultural studies study of pop-music culture begins proper with the work of Stuart Hall and Paddy Whannel," in their 1964 book *The Popular Arts:*

> As they point out, "the picture of young people as innocents exploited" by the pop-music industry "is over-simplified." Against this, they argue that there is very often conflict between the use made of a text or practice by an audience, and the use intended by the producers. Significantly, they concede that although "this conflict is particularly marked in the field of teenage entertainment . . . it is to some extent common to the whole area of mass entertainment in a commercial setting." Pop-music culture—songs, magazines, concerts, festivals, comics, interviews with pop stars, films, etc.—helps to establish a sense of identity among youth.[17]

The slow adoption of at least some part of the cultural studies model in American universities is symbiotic, I think, with the universities' adoption of Dylan, but again, it is rather a long story. I can, however, quickly suggest a couple of important milestones along the way. The first would be the great-granddaddy of cultural studies, Roland Barthes's groundbreaking work *Mythologies,* published in 1957; Barthes's later advocacy of studying texts, broadly understood (in essays like "From Work to Text," 1971), has also been very influential. The notion of the "text" perhaps rescues Dylan from having to be sold in English departments as a poet, as texts, rather than the traditional literary genres, become the purview of literary studies. Next, I would mention again the Hall and Whannel book *The Popular Arts,* published in 1964. And finally in this brief litany, I want to mention Richard Poirier's 1967 *Partisan Review* essay, "Learning from the Beatles," an essay that bristles with the energies of a newly mobilized cultural studies understanding of the possibilities of textual, rather than narrowly literary, studies (though Poirier himself, now retired from Rutgers and director of the Library of America, never really made that shift).

Ultimately, of these two avenues into the curriculum (lyrics as poetry, on the one hand, and cultural studies' shift of emphasis to the text, on the other), the one tries to make rock and roll conform to the rules of literary studies, while the other tries to reform the rules of literary study in light of rock and roll and other popular and mass forms. This somewhat tendentious formulation perhaps gives you some idea whose side I am on.

I would like to close with just a couple of thoughts about how Dylan functions in our classrooms today. The first answer, of course, is that he is there as a poet, even if I would argue he is not most productively considered that way.[18] Though for a time he was being included in new editions of venerable anthologies, my very unscientific sampling suggests that this trend may now have come to an end. Dylan is not included in the *Oxford Book of American Poetry,* Cary Nelson's left-leaning *Oxford Anthology of Modern American Poetry,* or the 2,200-page *Norton Anthology of Modern and*

Contemporary Poetry; he is represented in the 2,000-page flagship *Norton Anthology of Poetry*, but by a single song, "Boots of Spanish Leather."

But if Dylan's stock as a poet has fallen in value lately, his stock as a writer has never been stronger. One way that Dylan has been significant on campuses of late, for instance, is as a great test case for our current understanding of plagiarism and intellectual property issues. I know this because I teach at a school where the chancellor was fired last year owing in part to allegations that he had plagiarized our strategic planning documents, and our system president is currently being investigated on charges that he plagiarized portions of his master's thesis and doctoral dissertation. Dylan's work is absolutely central to recent discussions of plagiarism, appropriation, and repurposing. A prime example is in Jonathan Lethem's essay "The Ecstasy of Influence," in the February 2007 issue of *Harper's*, in which he points out that

> Appropriation has always played a key role in Dylan's music. The songwriter has grabbed not only from a panoply of vintage Hollywood films but from Shakespeare and F. Scott Fitzgerald and Junichi Saga's *Confessions of a Yakuza*.... Dylan's art offers a paradox: while it famously urges us not to look back, it also encodes a knowledge of past sources that might otherwise have little home in contemporary culture, like the Civil War poetry of the Confederate bard Henry Timrod, resuscitated in lyrics on Dylan's newest record, *Modern Times*. Dylan's originality and his appropriations are as one.[19]

Lethem, coincidentally, interviewed Dylan for the cover of *Rolling Stone* in September 2006, on the release of *Modern Times*.

Dylan is in our classrooms today in large part because he is now part of a contemporary canon expanded by cultural studies. Dylan has gone from timely in 1966 to timeless in 2006: even a professional cynic like Dylan cannot have imagined, when he penned it forty-five years ago, that he would be singing "Masters of War" again, with new urgency, on tour today. There is both profit and loss in the transition from timely to timeless. Dylan's music certainly has not lost its timeliness, but there is a danger that we will lose it, or more to the point our students will lose it, as he goes from outlaw to establishment figure. "To live outside the law, you must be honest" (a line, as Lethem points out, that Dylan lifted from the 1958 film *The Lineup*), but once embraced by the establishment, as Dylan has been, there is a danger that one's ability to disrupt and challenge the status quo is neutralized. Tocqueville pointed this out about American society more than two hundred years ago: rather than putting down dissent, we simply pat our dissenters on the head and send them on their way. As I have argued elsewhere, this is in pedagogical terms perhaps the greatest danger in canonization: that we bring less critical rigor, less healthy skepticism to those texts that carry the imprimatur of the Great Tradition.[20]

Dylan first began to be taught in an effort to tap into our students' interests, but today he is taught more broadly than ever, more (I suspect) to cater to teachers' interests than those of our students. Which is not to say that Dylan is no longer of interest to our students: in fact, they are rather fascinated. But fascinated most often for reasons rather different than ours: I taught an honors rock-and-roll class last semester including a unit on Dylan, and my students, at least, are interested in him primarily not for historical reasons ("Masters of War" or "Maggie's Farm") but instead because of the (to them, seemingly disproportionate) attention he has received of late in the public sphere. In an era where music stars are imposed on a passive public with some regularity (the Britneys, Xtinas, and Clays), our students are fascinated by the cultural phenomenon of stardom and what Joni Mitchell called "the star-maker machinery behind the popular song." For them, Dylan suggests the triumph of commitment and passion and years of hard work: not all stars, after all, are undeserving of the attention the public lavishes on them. Indeed, the primary danger I see in my students is an overwillingness to turn Dylan into the avatar of rock authenticity, a concept any music educator should be dedicated to debunking at every turn. Dylan's stardom is of course the result of raw talent, good timing, and Dylan's own savvy (if embarrassed) gift for self-mythologizing and self-promotion. For my students, Dylan is famous for being famous, and they want to understand why. Any attempt to answer that query requires rehearsing the whole career, and not, of course, in purely formalist terms, for Dylan's career cannot be understood, never mind predicted, based on lyrics alone. No, my students want to know about how the interaction of musical, cultural, political, and historical forces combined to create this larger-than-life figure, Bob Dylan. How, for instance, can an eighteen-year-old understand that the solid, workmanlike—but really, hardly epochal—album *Modern Times* was named by *Rolling Stone* the best album of 2006?

Agreeing to teach Dylan back in the 1960s was, whether we recognized it at the time or not (and I think not, but I was still in grade school), agreeing to teach from a position of relative ignorance. Dylan is a Trojan horse: his work looked like a gift and was admitted as a gift, but it wrought real changes, unforeseen by the university. One of those changes, of course, is that many of us now teach courses in which our students, in one sense at least, know much more about the topic than we do. When I teach the work of James Joyce, the subject of my dissertation and first book, to undergraduate or graduate students, I have little fear of being punk'd: I *own* that material and am comfortably ahead of my students on that particular learning curve, even if they continue to bring me up short, forcing me to reappraise some of my comfortable opinions. When it comes to teaching the literary canon, I am confident that I possess the requisite cultural capital, even if I am somewhat suspicious of those categories. But teaching rock and roll requires some subcultural capital, and the means of acquiring that are still rather mysterious and much less available to a middle-aged college professor than to his students. For that reason, it scares the shit out of me; for that reason I, and many of us, teach it as often as we are allowed. "You know there's something and you don't know what it is, do you, Professor Jones?"

Thus, teaching rock and roll, unless we reduce it into mere history (because we, the profs, own history) requires us to enter into a mutually interdependent relationship with our students. When we teach John Donne, *we* know "the hidden meanings"; when we agree to teach Dylan—or rather, when high school and college teachers first agreed to teach Dylan in the mid-1960s—there was every reason to think that the students were in a better position to hear what Dylan was saying than the professors were. Dylan entered the curriculum, that is to say, "for the kids." He is still there—in the curriculum, that is. Funny thing, though, now he is there primarily for us, the teachers.

Notes

1. Andrew Motion, "Andrew Motion Explains Why Bob Dylan's Lyrics Should Be Studied in Schools," *The Times* (London), September 22, 2007; http://entertainment.timesonline.co.uk/tol/arts_and_entertainment/books/poetry/article2503109.ece (accessed September 26, 2007).

2. Ibid.

3. Clinton Heylin, *Bob Dylan: Behind the Shades Revisited* (New York: HarperCollins, 2001), 585.

4. Alfred G. Aronowitz, "A Family Album," in *The Age of Rock: Sounds of the American Cultural Revolution,* ed. Jonathan Eisen (New York: Random House, 1969), 195.

5. Paul Williams, "Understanding Dylan," *Crawdaddy,* August 1966; Peter Gzowski, "Dylan: An Explosion of Poetry," *Maclean's,* January 22, 1966.

6. The term *relevance* floats with a notorious lack of reference throughout the radical discourse of the 1960s. Stanton Millet gets as close as anyone to pinning it down: "I am not aware, as yet, of any really satisfactory definition of relevance either from the dissident students or from the faculty, but it appears to me that at least two kinds of relevance are possible for a course. What the student learns may, on the one hand, be applicable to some problem beyond the classroom walls, resulting in, let us say, effective community action to alleviate poverty or racial strife. Or the course content may, on the other hand, have an impact on the student's inner life, helping him to construct a workable system of values, or to understand himself, or perhaps only to enjoy more what he reads, hears, and sees"; Stanton Millet, "Student Militancy and the College Curriculum," *College English* 32, 3 (December 1970): 248.

7. Ibid., 243.

8. Roger Heynes, "The Nature of the Academic Community," quoted in Millet, "Student Militancy," 244.

9. Quoted in Millet, "Student Militancy," 245.

10. All citations from the Port Huron Statement are taken from the unpaginated electronic version available at Tom Hayden's Web site: http://www.tomhayden.com/porthuron.htm (accessed September 27, 2007).

11. David R. Pichaske, *The Poetry of Rock: The Golden Years* (Peoria, Ill.: Ellis Press, 1981), ix.

12. David R. Pichaske, *Beowulf to Beatles and Beyond: The Varieties of Poetry* (New York: Macmillan, 1981), xiv.

13. Richard W. Lid, ed., *Grooving the Symbol* (New York: Free Press, 1970). One wonders how the "groovy" kids such an anthology was designed to appeal to reacted to an editor named "lid." . . .

14. Homer Hogan, *Poetry of Relevance* (Toronto: Methuen, 1970), n.p.

15. Ibid.

16. Ibid.

17. John Storey, *Cultural Studies and the Study of Popular Culture: Theories and Methods* (Athens: University of Georgia Press, 1996), 99–100.

18. Though I have avoided invoking it for reasons of space, the classic statement of the position that rock lyrics are not poetry is Robert Christgau's "Rock Lyrics Are Poetry (Maybe?)," *Cheetah,* December 1967.

19. Jonathan Lethem, "The Ecstasy of Influence: A Plagiarism," *Harper's,* February 2007, 59, 60.

20. See Kevin J. H. Dettmar, "What's So Great about Great Books?" *Chronicle of Higher Education,* September 11, 1998, B6–7.

PART IV.   IN A VOICE WITHOUT RESTRAINT

14. Women Do Dylan:
The Aesthetics and Politics of Dylan Covers
Daphne Brooks and Gayle Wald

Our Modern Times

Any music wonk will tell you that Bob Dylan persists as a revered if surprisingly confounding racial trickster in popular music culture. His recordings must surely beckon thoughtful rereadings that take into account the politics of cultural appropriation and racial masquerade. Dylan would himself seem to be continuously beckoning this kind of scrutiny. Consider, for instance, his decision to call his 2001 album *"Love and Theft,"* what amounts to a not-so-oblique nod to Eric Lott's definitive study of blackface minstrelsy.[1] Dylan's self-conscious "love and theft" provocatively mirror the focus of Lott's book and find him churning out stark and stirring musical encounters with African-American bluesmen of the past.

> Big Joe Turner lookin' East and West
> From the dark room of his mind
> He made it to Kansas City
> Twelfth Street and Vine
> Nothing standing there
> High water everywhere.

So sings Dylan on a track titled "High Water," aptly dedicated to pioneering blues guitarist Charlie Patton. As Lott has noted of the song, "High Water...sounds the most like actual minstrel show music from the nineteenth century."[2] Such blackface mischief is certainly no fluke for Dylan. His most recent effort, 2006's much-lauded *Modern Times,* for instance, lifts huge swaths of arcane lyrics from Henry Timrod, aka "the poet laureate of the Confederacy," only to cut and mix it, as Greil Marcus has astutely pointed out, with the compositional aesthetics of multiple black bluesmen, men who were no doubt driven *to* the blues by the historical traumas that Timrod and his army sought to protect and perpetuate.[3]

Dylan's late-career "master works," as many critics often refer to his past three studio recordings, are no doubt rich, iconic examples of the kinds of electric spectacles of racial miscegenation and transgressive social encounters that, in part, shape and fuel dominant narratives in American studies performance history.[4] Love and Death. Love and Theft. The sexed-up, necrophilic dalliances of white (musical) masters and the (always) black (most often) men that they admire and desire, consume and cannibalize, continue to hold center stage in the critical imaginaries of performance studies and rock music histories alike. Huck and Jim on a raft. Clapton and Hendrix in a deadly embrace. Into the woods with Kurt and Leadbelly. These are the historical mythologies that dominate our narratives of racial appropriation and fetishization.

The Dylan blackface romance remains a synecdoche for a much broader passion in popular music performance histories that too often threaten to recycle the racial and gendered biases of cultural appropriation debates plaguing pop culture since the rise of minstrelsy. In particular, Dylan hagiography reminds us of the fact that when rock-and-roll criticism talks about cultural appropriation, these discussions far too often remain coded as homosocial affairs. Instead of awakening us to the kinds of cultural "thefts" that remain presently absent in rock memory, instead of forcing us to talk in more specific terms about the very gendered economy of the cultural appropriation wars, Dylan's musical borrowings have somehow managed to foreclose sustained conversations about the conservation of stable masculinities in these sorts of debates.

As an antidote to this phenomenon, we attempt here to talk differently about cultural appropriation in pop music performance culture. By shifting the fulcrum of our critical focus on "love and theft" (surely a terminology that beckons further interrogation), we offer examples of what we are calling multiple counter-narratives of love and theft. As we demonstrate, these rich and unexpected musical encounters demand greater attention in cultural criticism, for they challenge listeners to reconceptualize canonical popular music histories and the historical framework for (re)reading genealogies of racial performative encounters. Below we consider the roles that female artists—and particularly black female performers—have played in complicating and disturbing the romance of that history. We begin by thinking about the key ways in which Dylan himself has disturbed and complicated conventional "love and theft" narratives through what he refers to as the "strange craft" of radio.

Dylan on the Radio

Theme Time Radio Hour, Bob Dylan's XM satellite radio show, airs each Sunday morning at 8:00 on XM40, Deep Tracks, a channel dedicated to the celebration of arcane album rock. This time slot (one among several) is particularly appropriate, since on his show Dylan plays the role of the preacher man delivering a musical sermon. Broadcast from the make-believe Abernathy Building, which gives the show its trademark old-timey feel, *Theme Time*—literally, an hour of song related to a single theme, from "Weather" to "Telephones" to "Shoes"—finds Dylan playing a variety of sounds. Doo-wop and gospel quartets get their due, as do quirky country tunes and all manner of blues, R & B, and rock and roll. Our host has a soft spot for novelty songs, musical factoids, and performers that run the gamut from Louis Jordan, the Staple Singers, and the Swan Silvertones to the Clash, NRBQ, and Run-DMC.

Although hard numbers are impossible to come by, *Theme Time Radio Hour* has tens of thousands—perhaps hundreds of thousands—of listeners. Not too long ago, for example, Dylan sent thousands to YouTube to check out video clips of "the great Rosetta Tharpe," who Dylan guaranteed would "blow your mind." In the wake of this endorsement, film images from the 1960s that had garnered two thousand hits on the popular Internet site suddenly were attracting twenty thousand or more hits. Posting responses to the film footage, fans produced their own lively commentary, interweaving paeans to Dylan with paeans to Tharpe: "thank you sister rosetta for creating the rock n roll / amen!" and "You're THE SOURCE, Bob. WOW!" and "Bob guided me to rosetta, he didn't need any guide, he already knew the way," and "It's ironic that people are saying 'Bob, you're the source' when clearly Bob is saying to people, 'I'm not the source, THIS is THE source.'"[5]

Intimate communion with Bob Dylan's personal record collection is the compelling conceit of *Theme Time Radio Hour.* The pleasure comes from discovering What Bob Will Play Next. Occasionally, he reads letters on air. In March 2007, in the first installment on "Trains," a woman wrote with a specific request for a song she likes. He took her down a notch or two. "If you want to hear the music you already have, get your own radio show," he chided, not unkindly. "On *Theme Time Radio Hour* you won't hear the music that's usually played on the radio."[6]

While Dylan's eccentricity certainly has its own rhythms, this commitment to music you won't hear on the radio is both the charm and the genius of *Theme Time Radio Hour.* With notable exceptions, satellite radio has largely been a disappointment, not merely because its song selection depends on programmers rather than the tastes of individual deejays, but also because it remains so deeply invested in *genre,* continuing a widely lamented, forty-plus-year trend of radio narrowcasting. Sometimes, "genre" is defined as lifestyle, as on Starbucks XM Café (XM45); at times, as race music, as on "Soul Street," XM60, part of the network's "Urban Music" "neighborhood"; at still other times, as the "sounds" of a particular decade. On XM, the 1940s, 1950s, 1960s, 1970s, 1980s, and 1990s all have their channels.

To be sure, this is *not* the radio of Dylan's "Lost Land," which he chronicles so vividly for readers in his gripping memoir *Chronicles, Volume 1.*[7] There, radio is the landscape of magical, wide-screen dreaming, a place where densely intricate, diverse, and colorful narratives unfold in aural splendor, triggering a young Dylan's imagination, stimulating his storytelling impulses, summoning him to push forward into the big lush possibilities that the world had to offer. "I went out"—to borrow Greil Marcus's phrase he borrowed from Dylan—"I went out into the world of radio":[8]

> Radio shows had been a big part of my consciousness back in the Midwest, back when it seemed like I was living in perpetual youth. *Inner Sanctum, The Lone Ranger, This Is Your FBI, Fibber McGee and Molly, The Fat Man, The Shadow, Suspense. Suspense* always had a creaking door more horrible sounding than any door you

could imagine—nerve-wracking, stomach-turning tales week after week. *Inner Sanctum*, with its horror and humor all mixed up. *Lone Ranger,* with the sounds of buckboards and spurs clinking out of your radio. *The Shadow,* the man of wealth and student of science out to right the world's wrongs. *Dragnet* was a cop show with the musical theme that sounded like it was taken out of a Beethoven symphony. *The Colgate Comedy Hour* kept you in stitches.

There was no place too far. I could see it all. All I needed to know about San Francisco was that Paladin lived in a hotel there and that his gun was for hire. I knew that "stones" were jewels and that villains rode in convertibles and that if you wanted to hide a tree, hide it in the forest where nobody could find it. Was raised on that stuff, used to quiver with excitement listening to these shows. They gave me clues to how the world worked and they fueled my daydreams, made my imagination work overtime. Radio shows were a strange craft.[9]

Perhaps in homage to this medium that in childhood made him "quiver with excitement," on *Theme Time Radio Hour* Dylan revels in creating a sonic world where contemporary radio categories fade and dissolve. The best shows are exercises in canon de- and reformation, displaying rich possibilities for rethinking notions of genre, repertoire, and, perhaps above all, influence.

Returning to our questions about appropriation, we want to think about how women have themselves been influenced by Dylan, whose best material has an elasticity that enables it to stretch to accommodate different musical styles and sensibilities. "Quintessentially Dylan" songs, it so happens, also provide women musicians, especially black women, multiple points of entry. The spirituality that courses through his music (whether or not it is from his explicitly born-again phase) complements the work of someone like Mavis Staples, for example, while the sensuality of his love songs provides a "way in" for Maria Muldaur, who remembers Dylan from the early 1960s, when she was a self-described "young beatnik babe" in the Village. On the other hand, Dylan's ability to transform protest into richly philosophical and self-reflective compositions makes him valuable to the social activist aesthetics of Nina Simone and Odetta.

Just Like a Woman

In summer 1969 the eclectically minded musical troubadour Nina Simone granted an interview with *Ebony* magazine in which she expressed her disdain for contemporary rock artists who sonically mimed a putatively "colored" aesthetic. "Most of it is junk," she said of rock-and-roll counterculture, this despite the fact that Simone was clearly a fan of multiple forms of music—rock included. By the time of that interview she had, for instance, already successfully interpolated into her repertoire songs by burgeoning pop-rock lyricists and composers such as Randy Newman and Barry Gibb, and the year 1969 would find her putting her own spin on Pete Seeger's "Turn! Turn! Turn!" a tune transformed into a folk-rock hit by the Byrds. By the 1970s, Simone would take on songs by everyone from George Harrison to blue-eyed soulsters Hall and Oates, but, among all other rock-folk pioneers, her admiration would always run deepest for Dylan, an artist whose intrepid originality would clearly match her own. "[H]e has his own thing, and I respect him and I really admire him," Simone told *Ebony*. "Bob Dylan. The Man is his own man, has his own statement and makes it. He's a universal poet. He's not trying to be white or colored."[10]

Dylan's iconic artistic freedom would provide a lasting inspirational example for a singer and musician who sought her own freedom throughout her long career. No one critical apparatus can sustain a sufficient reading of Simone, an artist celebrated in part for having stylized a heterogeneous musical repertoire of songs for nearly four decades. A classically trained pianist who shifted into jazz, pop, cabaret, and folk, performing in the mid-1950s as a way to support her education and subsequently to shore up her income, Simone gained notoriety for having moved fluidly from playing the music hall chanteuse by covering Gershwin's "I Loves You Porgy" (inspired by Billie Holiday's interpretation) and the Norwegian folk lilt of "Black Is the Color of My True Lover's Hair" to "Duke Ellington compositions, Israeli folk songs, and songs by the Bee Gees."[11] She was the ultimate queen of popular music "crossover" in the most exhilarating and unconventional sense of the word.

Nina Simone frequently commented on the significance of her generic moves, often proclaiming, "It's always been my aim to stay outside any category." "That's my freedom," she insisted to one reporter. But it was a "freedom" that, according to biographer David Nathan, "drove industry pundits and the music press crazy as they tried to categorize her."[12]

Simone herself commented on this struggle to elude generic categorization, specifically as a black female performer. In her autobiography, *I Put a Spell on You*, she put it plainly about the obtuse ways in which black female musicians were often characterized: "saying what sort of music I played gave the critics problems because there was something from everything in there."[13] For Simone, the constant (and, in her mind, completely erroneous) comparisons to Billie Holiday were signs of the music press's inability to read the diversity of black female musical expression. People, she argues, "couldn't get past the fact we were both black. . . . Calling me a jazz singer was a way of ignoring my musical background because I didn't fit into white ideas of what a black performer should be."[14]

To be sure, Simone's comments open up ways to talk about the meaning of "freedom" in black female musical performance and the ways that Simone defied conventional and potentially limiting definitions of what it means to be "free" in song. As historian Ruth Feldstein has noted in her marvelous work on the artist's sociopolitical activism, on albums such as 1964's landmark *In Concert* collection, Simone "rejected any singular definition of African American womanhood," and this effort "remained central to Simone's participation in black activism" beyond the album itself.[15] Born Eunice Waymon in 1933 in Tryon, North Carolina, Simone began playing piano when she was three years old and went on to play hymns and gospel music at her mother's church. By the age of five and with the help of local community fund-raising, she was studying classical music. From high school she moved on to the Juilliard School in New York City before taking a detour into the world of Atlantic City nightclub performing as a way to pay the bills in the 1950s. She has often stated that it was this need to support herself that led her to begin singing in addition to playing the piano. From those nightclub beginnings in the 1950s on through her debut album, 1957's buoyant and eclectic *Little Girl Blue,* and into the 1960s, Simone cultivated a diverse repertoire. As music critic Adam Bernstein sees it, "a hallmark of [Simone's] recordings was her love for contrasting sounds and defying predictability. Her version of the pop staple 'Love Me or Leave Me,'" Bernstein continues, "plays a dazzling classical run with a throaty jazz vocal."[16]

Like Dylan, Simone cultivated a kind of musical style that pulled adventurously from unexpected corners of American culture. Dylan heard in folk music a "way to explore the universe" and a way to anatomize America in all its weird eccentricities. Folk allowed Dylan to musically dissect what Greil Marcus has famously called "old weird America": an "invisible republic" where the remnants of everything from "sea shanties" and "Civil War songs" to cowboy dirges and women's rights pamphlets resonate with histories that are "gone but not forgotten."[17] In her own way, Simone the faithful musical archivist and song interpreter used her repertoires to excavate American and, more broadly, African diasporic tales of repressed racial and gender histories. From her classic black feminist historical manifesto "Four Women" to the folkloric calypso chant of "See-Line Woman," Simone wove black women's quotidian work songs into her sets alongside Brecht and Weill epic theater classics like "Pirate Jenny," Gershwin numbers, and blues standards. She was in pursuit of what she called "black classical music," what we might think of as a vast and imposing sonic and lyrical tapestry that vertically and laterally referenced black social, material, visceral, and emotional conditions in the wake of slavery and emancipation in the Americas.[18]

The racial and cultural diversity of Simone's repertoire thus evoked the "invisible republic" that is black diasporic identity, a mélange of interracial encounters, migration narratives, and spiritual eruptions of consciousness and self-reckoning. In this regard, she continuously and beautifully executed the pure gifts that Dylan identified in folksingers, jazz singers, as well as classical musicians and their ability to make long-playing records with heaps of stories in the grooves—"they forged identities and tipped the scales, gave more of the big picture." Their music, he insists—and surely he would include himself as well as Simone—"transcended the immediate culture."[19]

No surprise, then, that Simone would cover a number of Dylan songs over the course of her career, from "The Times They Are A-Changin'" to "The Ballad of Hollis Brown." Simone's 1969 album *To Love Somebody* featured two Dylan covers, including a gospel and blues-inflected version of "I Shall Be Released." Simone's (re)arrangement of that anthem instilled the song's prison narrative with a post-(Martin Luther King Jr.) assassination clear-eyed, spiritual resignation. This is Simone moving her earthy vocals gracefully toward "the light" shining down and toward redemptive release. Doris Willingham's and Virdia Crawford's warm background vocals, Al Schackman's and Stuart Scharf's guitars, and Weldon Irvine's Sunday-morning organ envelop Simone on piano, creating an iridescent circle of musical intimacy that turns this version of "I Shall Be Released" into a radiant waltz toward freedom. It is late in the Movement, this quietly joyful cover suggests, but Simone remains ascendant in spirit.

That boundless spirit allows Simone to rehearse counterintuitive articulations of blackness. She was just as capable of rendering devastatingly sly interpretations of the classic blues ("I Want a Little Sugar in My Bowl," "Backlash Blues") as she was of performing Dylan's folk and blues hybrid number, the somber "Just Like Tom Thumb's Blues." Interpolating herself into a tale of quiet desolation and resignation, Simone the black female protagonist assumes the role of Dylan's narrator who reflects on being "lost in the rain in Juarez" at Easter time. Here redemption is worlds away, and our weak and nomadic singer spins observations about absent saints and "peasant goddesses" who seduce and "take your voice . . . leav[ing] you howling at the moon." No conventional blues diva here, Simone surrogates the role of the struggling artist from the vagabond white male folkie. She opens up the song and travels its picaresque back roads through "Housing Project Hill" and all the way back to New York City, having learned much about the ubiquity of corruption and emptiness in the contemporary world. Simone stretches Dylan's blues revisionism to evoke the complexities of black female subjectivity, which is itself on the move in this cover song.

Subjectivity dramatically transmogrifies in Simone's sublime reinterpretation of "Just Like a Woman" on 1971's *Here Comes the Sun* album. If Dylan's classic tale of romantic rootlessness and "beatnik, on-the-road mobility" still ultimately imagines women as "bookends to men's journeys of self-discovery," Simone revises the song so as to convey the multidimensionality of a woman's emotional inner life.[20] From her vivacious opening piano riffs, a mixture of signature jazz wit and playfulness mixed with round, thoughtful cadences, to her distinct (re)arrangements that foreground the chorus, this "Woman" attests to the "aches" and "breaks" and love-making of a female protagonist who rescinds "this pain in here." Excising the second stanza entirely (one in which Dylan takes up with "Queen Mary"), it is Simone's "woman" rather than her restless lover, in this version of the song, who declares that she "can't stay in here."[21] Her lyrical revisions provide a welcome antidote to the problems that pioneering feminist rock critic Ellen Willis has observed of Dylan's work. As Willis has famously recalled, she initially "did not question the idea that women were guardians of the oppressive conventional values" in Dylan's music since she understood "men's need to go on the road because I was, spiritually speaking, on the road myself. That, at least, was my fantasy."[22] Simone's version of "Just Like a Woman" brought female fantasy and an inner spiritual life of womanhood to the surface in song. Despair and desire, rich longing, and self-reflection swirl at the core of her gorgeous rendition of Dylan's classic, in turn transforming "rebel masculinity" into (black) feminist nonconformity,[23] a most dazzling protest anthem if ever there was one.

Odetta Sings Dylan

"The first thing that turned me on to folk singing was Odetta," Dylan has said of the folk, blues, spirituals, jazz, work, and protest-song singer and civil- and human-rights activist whose 1956 LP, *Odetta Sings Ballads and Blues,* he recalled listening to in a record store, "back when you could listen to records right there in the store." "Right then and there, I went out and traded my electric guitar and amplifier for an acoustical guitar, a flat-top Gibson." Odetta's sound was "just something vital and personal," he went on. "I learned all the songs on that record."[24] Dylan evoked the same experience of immediacy, of hearing something that clicks, in the Scorsese documentary *No Direction Home,* in which he tells essentially the same story. "She played that upstroke downstroke rhythm," he tells the filmmaker, referring, per-haps, to Odetta's trademark dramatic rendition of the prison song "Water Boy"—"almost Tex-Mex."[25]

On the original liner notes to *Odetta Sings Ballads and Blues,* producer Dean Git-ter calls her "electrifying"—a curious and noteworthy word to describe the sound of a woman with an acoustic guitar. Gitter, of course, is referring not to any tech-nology per se but to the accumulated effect of Odetta's performance: her powerful contralto, her rhythmic guitar playing, which made the instrument into a second voice, so that she often needed no accompaniment but her own, and, not least, her regal bearing.[26] The fact that she was perceived as "as tall as a man," like a twentieth-century Sojourner Truth, has always been a subject of fascination and, perhaps, fear. No wonder, then, that to Gitter she evoked African-American legends of yore—Ma Rainey, Bessie Smith, the young Leadbelly, Blind Lemon Jefferson—even as, at twenty-five years old, she embodied to him the "future" of folk music: "A magnifi-cent new voice is here," he announced, "to sing the old songs."[27]

Who knows whether Dylan has ever used Gitter's word for Odetta: "electrifying." "Vital" comes close; even if it doesn't conjure the elemental forces of nature, it still points to that unexpected bolt from the blue. Nevertheless, it is tantalizing to think through Gitter's term, one that has so much resonance in Dylan's career: here, at the moment when he abandons his electric guitar for an acoustic Gibson to pursue "folk" music; later, when he famously returns to an "electrified" sound.

Within ten years of Dylan's discovery of Odetta—that moment when he himself was struck by something like lightning—she would record an entire album of his songs. Despite Dylan's many achievements, by 1965, when *Odetta Sings Dylan* came out on RCA Records, it must have been a thrilling, even overwhelming moment for him. Although Odetta was only ten years older than Dylan, the decade between them was musically and culturally significant. She belonged to that revered "genera-tion" that produced Harry Belafonte and others. Odetta had been untouchable—as for so many other folksingers, especially white men, she had been a mythic and certainly erotic figure—and here she was paying tribute to *him.* If we think about singing as an embodied act—as air being pressed through the lungs or the diaphragm or the throat, and passing through the mouth and lips—we might think of the cover song as a kind of kiss. A kiss at some distance, to be sure, but a kiss nonetheless, and just as immediate, just as electrifying. Dylan's words on Odetta's tongue and in Odetta's mouth. His songs passing through her body with each exhalation.

Dylan, it is said, turned up at those RCA sessions to hear Odetta do his songs. As she has told the story, when she found out that Dylan was in the control room, she made a point of shooing him away. She was not going to do *his* material with him sitting there contemplating whether she was doing it right or doing it justice. So she booted him out, the better to complete his songs on her terms. Odetta's version of "Don't Think Twice" exemplifies what these "terms" amounted to. The song is the quintessential leaving-my-lover blues-ballad: another in a long list of bittersweet *by the time you wake up I'll be long gone* songs. There is the line, "We never did too much a-talkin' anyway"—which can feel gentle, even protective of the lover's feelings— and the more acid (even if sung tenderly) phrase, "You wasted my precious time." Listening to Odetta's version, it is not difficult to understand what made people think of Bessie Smith when they heard Odetta. It is not just the commanding voice, which at times hardly seems to need amplification, but the projection of a kind of female independence, of the *I've got the world in a bottle and the stopper in my hand* variety.

The tender resoluteness of the lyric still feels unusual in a woman's voice, perhaps especially today, when lots of young women are shouting out their determination to leave a bad man. There is something infinitely more commanding in the stance of the speaker of "Don't Think Twice," who leaves without acrimony, principally because she doesn't care anymore. She is traveling light, liberated of the burden of resentment or anger or even rage, even as she proclaims, in no uncertain terms, "You're the reason I'm traveling on." In Dylan's song, the speaker leaves his lover's bed; he is literally catching the next train out of town. This is indeed the story that so many of the classic women blues singers told, only in their versions, the train was often a more plaintive trope, bespeaking loss, than a symbol of liberation, of promised geographical or spiritual transport—to the North, to better jobs, to places where lynching and violent racial insult were not as commonplace. In Odetta's version, on the other hand, you can almost hear her telling Dylan to get the hell out of her recording studio.

What Mavis Knew

A couple of weeks before the release of *Modern Times,* music critic David Yaffe examined what he described as "a long line of black female singers who have besotted" Bob Dylan "since his youth."[28] The point Yaffe sought to make was that the seemingly random reference made to R & B artist Alicia Keys on "Thunder on the Mountain," the lead-off track on *Modern Times,* is part of a broader personal and professional story of Dylan's fascination with black female performers.

Yaffe's piece offers a variety of biographical tidbits, from revelations about the depth and complexity of Dylan's romantic involvement with Mavis Staples to the little known fact that in 1986 the artist secretly married African-American backup singer Carolyn Dennis, with whom he shares a child. It also outlines the provocative claims that Dylan "long worshipped at the shrine of the black female voice, a source of musical inspiration, erotic obsession, and even religious conversion."[29] Dylan's aesthetic "conversions" are no doubt apparent in his gospel phase. And surely now in hindsight, critics are in a better position to appreciate the kind of specifically black female musical innovations that the artist sought to emulate and celebrate during his "gotta serve somebody" streak of recording.

In a 1992 article Chris Heim of the *Chicago Tribune* observed that "a new interest in 'roots music' and a deepening understanding of the history of American popular music has revealed a more complex interaction between black and white, African and European based musical traditions. There is now a slowly dawning recognition that spirituals and gospel shaped not only R & B and soul, but also had a much larger influence on country and rock than has previously been acknowledged."[30]

Alternative folk musician Michelle Shocked reinforces this contention. Shocked, a white convert to Pentecostalism who attends a black church (and who has recently released an album of spiritual music, including tributes to Rosetta Tharpe), has cogently observed that she believes that "Pops Staples' music and what he represents on my album is the heart and soul of what our contemporary music is really about. . . . A lot of the myth of Elvis is that he was the first man to put together black and white music and a lot of people look to the blues as the source for that. But what's really remarkable," Shocked argues, "is that not only was Elvis far from being the first man to put together white and black music, but the influence he drew on more than anything was gospel. Gospel has been pretty much written out of the history of our contemporary culture and it feels like a very fragile thread, as fragile a thread as Pops [Staples's] guitar playing. But there's something strong in that fragility. Something that will stay alive until someone comes along and picks it up and carries it to its rightful place at the front of our understanding of our culture."[31]

Staples and Dylan's long overdue duet reinforces this powerful claim. Their 2002 recording, a cover of Dylan's "Gonna Change My Way of Thinking," includes a playful version of the routine "Jimmie Rodgers Visits the Carter Family," which is on *The Carter Family—Their Complete Victor Recordings—Sunshine in the Shadows, 1931–1932*. Here Staples and Dylan create mischief together out on the farm in a "down home" interlude that features the two legendary performers trading lines:

> BOB DYLAN: Why look, someone's coming up the road, boys.
> MAVIS STAPLES: Hey, hey, Bobby!
> DYLAN: Hey, it's Mavis Staples!
> STAPLES: My goodness, Bobby you got a nice place here.
> DYLAN: Welcome to California, Mavis.
> STAPLES: You got a nice view. . .
> DYLAN: Yeah it is. You can sit on this porch and look right straight into Hawaii. . .
> STAPLES: Yeah, I was over there in them foothills. . . . I'm kind of hungry now. Got anything to eat?
> DYLAN: Momma, we got anything to eat?
> THIRD VOICE: . . . We got plenty of chicken out there in the yard.
> DYLAN: We're going to go knock a few of 'em off and fry 'em up. . . . Now Mavis, I've had the blues.

STAPLES: Oh Bobby, don't tell me you got the blues.

DYLAN: Mmm, hmmm. I've been up all night laying in bed with insomnia, reading snoozeweek.

STAPLES: Oh snoozeweek! That ain't gonna get rid of no blues! Let's do some singing. Sing about it.

DYLAN: *(singing)* Gonna sit up at the table, I'm as hungry as a horse.

DYLAN AND STAPLES TOGETHER: So hungry I could eat a horse.

DYLAN: I'm gonna revitalize my way of thinking. I'm gonna let the Lord take His course.

TOGETHER: Jesus is coming. He's coming back to gather His jewels . . . [32]

Dylan here plays host to a traveling Staples, and the reunion between these two former lovers is punctuated by laughter and conviviality. While Dylan greets Staples on the porch and readies himself to prepare a chicken feast for his unexpected guest, it is Staples who offers the nourishment of song as a salve for Dylan's blues (presumably over the monotony of material world events covered in "Snoozeweek"). Breaking bread in chorus, the two are revitalized together singing way over yonder in the hills of California. As Yaffe sees and hears it, Dylan here sounds less like a "white Negro" and more like a "soul survivor," and he argues that on this track, Dylan's "intonation and phrasing" sound more like Staples's than at any other time in his career.[33]

Yaffe's observations suggest the extent to which Dylan has learned something from Staples and other female singers—Staples in particular—about the spiritual dimensions of "the Voice": the way that Staples can use the voice, as Simon Reynolds once put it (riffing on Roland Barthes), "the way she chews and twists language . . . not for any decipherable, expressive reason . . . , but for the gratuitous voluptuousness of utterance itself. In [Staples's voice—reverberating in Dylan's on this track as well] you can hear a surplus of form over content. . . . Of 'telling' over 'story.' "[34]

And so we might think about Jim Washburn's observation of Staples, that her "contralto sometimes swoops so low it drags gravel with it, and the intent of her vocal lines seems similarly down to earth, always ringing emotionally true rather than being mere vocal affectations."[35] And we might think too about the resonance of Staples's ability to mine the gender-bending lower registers of her vocals, how "on early recordings such as 'Uncloudy Day,' which turned the Stapleses into stars, she was often mistaken for a man or a much older woman, before audiences laid eyes on the diminutive teenager."[36] Staples's deep register symbolized and sonically embodied the transgression of conventional gender paradigms and likewise evoked a sagacity that characterized the vital coalition between her generation's youth movement and that of Pop Staples's generation, its elderly leadership, sacrifice, and vision. It was a voice with a bottom deep enough to include that much.

For Dylan, the very grain of Staples's voice perhaps showed him ways of cultivating the sacred within the secular world. Staples has often theorized the ways that the religious, the personal, and the political converged in her work with the Staple Singers. "They said we were doing the 'devil's music,' but I said, 'The devil doesn't have any music. All music is God's music.' Listen to the lyrics in our songs: 'I know a place, ain't nobody crying, ain't nobody worried'; 'If you're ready, come go with me' . . . These are songs about the world, but they're also about God being alive for us in the world." As she makes plain in the liner notes to her latest album, the stirringly urgent *We'll Never Turn Back*, a searing collection of "freedom songs" from the movement, she and the Staple Singers "drew on the spirituality and the strength from the church to help gain social justice and to try to achieve civil rights."[37] On their long and intimate journey in song (and life) together, Staples and Dylan used song to explore the secrets of the universe and to bring those secrets vividly and colorfully to life in the deep, opaque registers of the gospel voice unleashed in ecstasy.

To Love Somebody

Maria Muldaur's 2006 album *Heart of Mine: Maria Muldaur Sings the Love Songs of Bob Dylan*, which spent time at the top of the *Billboard* Blues chart in late 2006, is one of the more remarkable Dylan "tributes" to appear in a while. In 2007, at the annual Dylan Days celebration in Hibbing, Minnesota, Muldaur performed a special concert at the Hibbing High School Auditorium, the same stage where Bobby Zimmerman played in 1958. A poster advertising the 2007 Dylan Days identified Muldaur as the singer "known for her quirky 1974 hit 'Midnight at the Oasis.'" The song was originally penned by David Nichtern, the TV and film songwriter who played guitar on Muldaur's first album, and who once released a CD titled *From Here to Nichternity*. "Midnight at the Oasis" is an alternately loathed and beloved track, with its campy and sweetly naughty evocation of lovers pretending to make love in a tent in the desert—obviously a desert of the imagination, not a place either of the lovers has actually ever been. The lyrics feel especially dated in the post-9/11 era: "*You don't need to answer / There's no need to speak / I'll be your belly dancer, prancer, / And you can be my sheik.*" In 1974, Nichtern thought of "Midnight at the Oasis" as merely a "cute" song, not expecting it to do anything (let alone pay his bills for the next several decades), but it was Muldaur's winning performance, combining girlish insouciance with come-hither knowingness, that made it fun and made both it and her famous.

For those who have been keeping track, Muldaur (born Maria Grazia Rosa Domenica D'Amato in 1943) has cultivated one of the longest and most interesting careers in the business. She honed her craft by listening to many of the singers that Odetta, also a mentor, would evoke: Ma Rainey, Bessie Smith, Memphis Minnie, and Victoria Spivey (at whose feet she literally learned). Unlike Dylan, who had to find his way to Manhattan from Hibbing, Maria D'Amato had the great good fortune of being born and raised in Greenwich Village, so she had only to leave her parents' apartment to frequent the same after-hours Saturday night jam sessions that Dylan attended, sometimes playing side by side with him, in the early 1960s. Her journey took her not east but south, on field trips that spurred pilgrimages by members of the charmingly named Friends of Old Timey Music in search of legends such as Doc Watson, Bukka White, Skip James, and Mississippi John Hurt. Extended visits to Watson's North Carolina home, where she learned Appalachian music and picked up the fiddle, completed her musical "education."

Which is to say, that even though Muldaur came from a place that was unmistakably a "place"—as opposed to the "nowhere" from which Dylan hailed[38]—her formation was not unlike Dylan's. Unlike Odetta, who was Dylan's early idol and inspiration, Muldaur was a peer, finding "something vital and personal" in many of the same sounds, which were simultaneously temporally and culturally distant and yet electrifyingly immediate. Like others who were central players in that early folk-music scene, Muldaur has enjoyed an enormously productive, wide-ranging, and critically acclaimed career largely under the radar of the star system. How many other folk-blues-gospel singers can boast of having gotten their start in an all-girl rock-and-roll band (as Muldaur did in high school with the Cashmeres), having recorded three children's LPs, including one of songs popularized by Shirley Temple (*Animal Crackers in My Soup*), and having devoted an entire album, *A Woman Alone with the Blues*, to the underrated Peggy Lee?

Heart of Mine finds Muldaur in a similarly eclectic mode, doing twelve Dylan tunes, from old familiar songs to relatively recent pieces like "Make You Feel My Love," from *Time Out of Mind*. Among these is her slow, sultry, leisurely version of "Lay Lady Lay"—interestingly, a favorite among the many women who have covered Dylan. Like Odetta on "Don't Think Twice," Muldaur messes with the lyrics, changing "Lady" to "Baby" to suit her own needs. More than the switch in pronouns, what draws a listener into the song is Muldaur's revelatory approach to its come-hither, carpe diem lyrics. Muldaur sings the song likes she is tired after sharing a couple of bottles of wine with someone, her voice trailing off sleepily at the end of lines. But she is not so tired that she doesn't have energy to urge her lover to share her "big brass bed"—which here, as in Dylan's original, comes across as vaguely naughty (perhaps especially for a single woman). The promise of the night-to-be in "Lay Lady Lay" is sensual, but in an *I'm not going to spell it out for you* way, which is in an era of copious *Let me tell you exactly how I'm going to undress you and oil your body up* R & B songs. "Whatever colors you have in your mind / I'll show them to ya' and I'll make them shine." It is the come-on of the artist, a sort of sweetly bohemian sexual promise. What Village girl or boy back in the proverbial day could have resisted the siren song of sex as intellectual and creative awakening? Who wouldn't want to have the world "begin" in a single night? Or, perhaps better yet, "have her cake and eat it too"?

Not unlike *Theme Time Radio Hour*, Muldaur's *Heart of Mine* is an act of canon deformation. This time, lightning struck when Muldaur was listening to "Moonlight" on "*Love and Theft*." Her account of that moment recalls Dylan's discovery of Odetta, overlaid with a frank and overtly erotic description of what it feels like to fall in love with a song. "Each line was like an evocative, gorgeous, impressionistic painting set to one of the most beautiful chord progressions and melodies I'd ever heard. The song seemed to draw me into an idyllic bucolic landscape, where I fell into a sort of dreamy swoon. I played it over and over and over again, and when I next saw [Dylan], I told him he'd finally 'painted his masterpiece' and that I wanted to record it."[39]

"As I continued to be captivated by the song," she continues, "it occurred to me that while Dylan is mostly known for his scathing, perceptive, brutally honest, and insightful songs of social consciousness, he has, in fact, over the years, written many passionate, poignant love songs.... As I thought about it, I became inspired to record an album of Dylan's love songs ('*yet another* side of Bob Dylan,' if you will)."[40]

Muldaur's perceptive account of her own reinterpretation of Dylan's iconicity ("yet another side of Bob Dylan") attracts us for being both full of admiration for a friend and peer and yet detached enough from the myth of Dylan as untouchable genius and prophet of a generation that it is not afraid of working its own process of "love and theft" on the master himself. The spirit of affectionate engagement that animates *Heart of Mine* recalls what Greil Marcus has described as the "empathy" that animates Dylan's best work.[41] In Muldaur's "Lay Baby Lay," you can hear the hard-earned freedom of an unashamed woman mingling sympathetically with the friend who recalls a skinny, scraggly Dylan, dirty hair but clean hands, harmonica strapped to his neck, emulating his own idol, Odetta.

Play a Song for Me

Many of the artists that we have been discussing here articulate a compelling creative connection to Dylan in that they utilize the complexity of Dylan's lyrical narratives to affirm their own interiority as female artists. In particular, Abbey Lincoln's whimsical 1997 rendering of "Mr. Tambourine Man" provides a template for her to travel in lyric metaphysically through flights of fancy and somnolence, "sleeping" and "dreaming" and beckoning a pied-piper music man who plays an instrument that recalls the tambourine-hammer "keeping time" on her 1960s Max Roach collaboration "Driva Man," from the epic protest album *We Insist.*[42]

How fitting then that Lincoln's recent cover of Dylan has provided another creative flight and autonomy for an adventurous lyricist and composer now in her seventies. Jean-Philippe Allard and Jay Newland, the producers of Lincoln's new album *Abbey Sings Abbey* "trac[e] the concept for the album back at least a decade, to a recording Ms. Lincoln made of . . . 'Mr. Tambourine Man.' She's a singer-songwriter too, Mr. Newland recalled thinking at the time."[43] Lincoln's "Tambourine" cover thus sparked the metonymical resonance between her original artistry and Dylan's. It may likewise have helped to make the latent folk structures and aesthetics of Lincoln's vocal style and compositional arrangements more audible. As Nate Chinen observes, "Many of Ms. Lincoln's songs employ a verse-chorus structure more in line with folk songs than jazz standards; some, like 'The Music Is the Magic,' resemble nursery rhymes."[44]

Using Dylan's work as a cultural vestibule of sorts, Lincoln has harnessed new stylistic and performative depth in her latest folk-inspired recording. Like Simone, Odetta, Staples, and Muldaur, she has ironically found renewed inspiration in "singing her own song," in part from dabbling with a cover song that places her outside of conventional jazz paradigms. Her example resonates with the next generation, as is clear in an assessment made by Cassandra Wilson, herself a fearless troubadour of generic experimentation. Wilson attests to the fact that "I learned a lot about taking a different path from Abbey."[45] All of these women found ways of appropriating the rebellious road less traveled far beyond Highway 61.

Coda

Greil Marcus's *The Old, Weird America* opens with a description of Dylan backstage in Manchester contemplating Sister Rosetta Tharpe's midcentury hit "Strange Things Happening Every Day." There is a bit of poetic license in the passage, which puts us inside of Dylan's mind at an important turning point in his career, and yet it is one of those times, as Dylan himself might say, when fiction is truer than truth. "Strange Things Happening Every Day" was Tharpe's rollicking contribution to the genre Teresa L. Reed identifies as religious "jokelore."[46] The song is a call to hypocrites of all stripes, but especially to preachers and other religious folk who talk the talk but don't walk the walk. At the time of its release, however, listeners might also have detected the strains of a somewhat more subversive, political satire in the song.[47] In 1945, when it peaked on the charts,

> there were indeed strange things happening, some wonderful, some horrific. May saw the German surrender, laying the groundwork for the end of the war in Europe. August saw the dropping of an atomic bomb on Hiroshima, as well as the breakthrough talks that led to the signing of Jackie Robinson as America's first black major league baseball player. Which event was strange? "Strange" was a powerful word, a word like "Precious" from Dorsey's "Precious Lord, Take My Hand."[48]

"Strange" could mean foreign or it could mean new; it conjured unfamiliarity and discomfort—the "strange misshapen thing, far less human in form than an ape" that Prospero discovers in Caliban in *The Tempest*—as well as things astonishing or remarkable—as when Miranda, in the same play, discovers Ferdinand for the first time, or when Ariel sings of the "something rich and strange" at the bottom of the sea. "Strange" captures something of the complex network of *"Love and Theft"* across borders of space, time, race, place, and gender that we have been trying to get at here.

Notes

Thanks to Lindsay Reckson for her assistance researching Mavis Staples, to Greil Marcus for pointing us to the Staples-Dylan duet, and to Colleen Sheehy for encouraging and enabling this chapter.

1. Eric Lott, *Love and Theft: Blackface Minstrelsy and the American Working Class* (New York: Oxford University Press, 1995).

2. David McNair and Jayson Whitehead, "Love and Theft: Interview with Eric Lott," http://www.gadflyonline.com/12–10–01/book-ericlott.html.

3. Bob Dylan, *"Love and Theft,"* Sony, 2001. Greil Marcus, conversation with author Daphne Brooks, fall 2006. For more on the Timrod controversy, see Motoko Rich, "Who's This Guy Dylan Who's Borrowing Lines from Henry Timrod?" *New York Times,* September 14, 2006.

4. See Jonathan Lethem, "The Genius of Bob Dylan: An Intimate Conversation," *Rolling Stone,* September 7, 2006. For other relevant examples of cultural appropriation and racial politics, see Leslie Fiedler, *Love and Death in the American Novel* (Normal, Ill.: Dalkey Archive Press, 1998); W. T. Lhamon, *Raising Cain: Blackface Performance from Jim Crow to Hip Hop* (Cambridge, Mass.: Harvard University Press, 2000); and Robert Christgau, "In Search of Jim Crow: Why Postmodern Minstrelsy Studies Matter," *The Believer,* February 2004.

5. For examples, see www.youtube.com/watch?v=rXv4ksV26Uk.

6. *Theme Time Radio Hour* is unofficially archived by fans. See, for example, www.patrickcrosley.com, which contains "Trains 1," the show in question.

7. Bob Dylan, *Chronicles, Volume 1* (New York: Simon and Schuster, 2004), 49–50.

8. Greil Marcus, "Hibbing High School and 'the Mystery of Democracy,'" chapter 1, this volume.

9. Dylan, *Chronicles,* 49–50.

10. See Phyl Garland, "High Priestess of Soul," *Ebony Magazine,* August 1969. On Simone's 1960s-era repertoire, see Ben Edmonds, liner notes for Nina Simone, *Just Like a Woman: Nina Simone Sings Classic Songs of the '60s,* RCA, 2007.

11. Adam Bernstein, "Nina Simone, Eclectic Soul and Protest Singer, Dies," *Washington Post,* April 22, 2003, 1.

12. David Nathan, *The Soulful Divas* (New York: Watson-Guptill Publications, 1999), 49.

13. Nina Simone, with Stephen Cleary, *I Put a Spell on You: The Autobiography of Nina Simone* (New York: Da Capo, 1993), 68.

14. Ibid., 69.

15. Ruth Feldstein, "I Don't Trust You Anymore: Nina Simone, Culture, and Black Activism in the 1960s," *Journal of American History* 91, 4 (March 2005): 1349–79, 1360.

16. Bernstein, "Nina Simone."

17. Greil Marcus, *The Old, Weird America: The World of Bob Dylan's Basement Tapes* (New York: Picador, 2001).

18. Brantley Bardin, "Simone Says," *Details Magazine,* January 1997.

19. See Dylan, *Chronicles,* 18–19, 34, and 27. For more on histories that are "gone but not forgotten," see Joseph Roach, *Cities of the Dead: Circum-Atlantic Culture* (New York: Columbia University Press, 1996).

20. Simon Reynolds and Joy Press, *The Sex Revolts: Gender, Rebellion and Rock 'n Roll* (Cambridge, Mass.: Harvard University Press, 1995), 50.

21. Nina Simone, *To Love Somebody/Here Comes the Sun,* Raven Records, 2001.

22. Essay on Bob Dylan in Ellen Willis, *Beginning to See the Light: Pieces of a Decade* (New York: Alfred Knopf, 1981).

23. Reynolds and Press, *The Sex Revolts,* 8.

24. Dylan, *Chronicles.*

25. *No Direction Home,* directed by Martin Scorsese (Hollywood, Calif.: Paramount, 2005).

26. Dean Gitter, liner notes, Odetta, *Sings Ballads and Blues,* Empire Musicwerks, 2005.

27. Ibid.

28. David Yaffe, "Tangled Up in Keys," *Slate Magazine,* August 11, 2006, http://www.slate.com/id/2147487/.

29. Ibid.

30. Chris Heim, "A Sound Foundation: Gospel's the Heart and Soul of the Staples Family and the Family's at the Heart of American Music," *Chicago Tribune,* July 19, 1992, 14.

31. Ibid.

32. Bob Dylan and Mavis Staples, "Gonna Change My Way of Thinking," *Gotta Serve Somebody: The Gospel Songs of Bob Dylan,* Burning Rose Productions, 2003.

33. Yaffe, "Tangled Up in Keys."

34. Simon Reynolds, "Noise," in *Audio Culture: Readings in Modern Music,* ed. Christopher Cox and Daniel Warner, 55–58 (New York: Continuum, 2004), 58.

35. Jim Washburn, "Gospel Review: Staples Performs with Amazing Grace in Irvine," *Los Angeles Times,* February 8, 1999.

36. Greg Kot, "A Singer's Faith Bubbles Over," *Los Angeles Times,* August 6, 2004.

37. Ibid.

38. Marcus, *The Old, Weird America.*

39. Maria Muldaur, liner notes, *Heart of Mine,* Telarc, 2006.

40. Ibid.

41. Marcus, *The Old, Weird America.*

42. Farah Griffin, *If You Can't Be Free, Be a Mystery: In Search of Billie Holiday* (New York: Free Press, 2001), 171.

43. Nate Chinen, "Abbey Lincoln's Emancipation Proclamation," *New York Times,* May 20, 2007.

44. Ibid. It seems particularly serendipitous that the guitarist on Lincoln's new album, former Dylan guitarist Larry Campbell, was "tasked with paring down a number of Ms. Lincoln's other songs, in preparation for a recording session."

45. Ibid.

46. Teresa L. Reed, *The Holy Profane: Religion in Black Popular Music* (Lexington: University of Kentucky Press, 2003).

47. Gayle Wald, *Shout, Sister, Shout! The Untold Story of Rock-and-Roll Trailblazer Sister Rosetta Tharpe* (Boston: Beacon Press, 2007), 68.

48. Ibid., 68–69.

15. Crow Jane Approximately: Bob Dylan's Black Masque

Aldon Lynn Nielsen

> black betty, black bready blam de lam! bloody had a baby blam de
> lam! hire the handicapped blam de lam! put him on the wheel
> blam de lam! burn him in the coffee blam de lam! cut him with a
> fish knife blam de lam! send him off to college & pet him with a
> drumstick blam de lam! boil him in the cookbook blam de lam!
> fix him up an elephant blam de lam! sell him to the doctors blam
> de lam . . .
>
> —*Bob Dylan,* Tarantula

"Uncle Remus Can't Tell You"

"He speaks in your voice, American."[1] These are the opening words to Don DeLillo's novel *Underworld*. In sorting through these slippery pronouns, we soon learn that the "he" who speaks in our voice is a black adolescent. This might have been surprising to many in the Hibbing, Minnesota, of Dylan's youth, the time of the novel's opening, perhaps as surprising as the thought that young Robert Zimmerman would one day stand on the stage of New York's Gas Light Café singing "No More Auction Block for Me," or that rechristened as Bob Dylan, he would write words that would become inextricably a part of the common parlance of American; that by speaking so recognizably in our voice, American, he would change the register of our voice forever.

Time in the end brought both Leadbelly and Bob Dylan to Woody Guthrie's side. Where else might the road that leads from "Hudie Ledbetter" to "Leadbelly" and the lost highway that runs from "Robert Zimmerman" to "Bob Dylan" more likely intersect than here? Recordings of Leadbelly's work songs and blues must surely have been scarce along the edge of the Mesabi Range in the early 1950s, but an obliging relative presented a set of Leadbelly records to Dylan as a high school graduation present, and surely those recordings were well known in the Dinkytown haunts that drew Dylan away from the University of Minnesota. There Dylan copped chops from Tony Glover and swapped songs with John Koerner, two young men who knew the Leadbelly catalog intimately. Later, having become "Little Sun" Glover and "Spider" John Koerner, they joined with "Snaker" Dave Ray to record a series of widely circulated blues, rags, and hollers, many by Leadbelly.

We need to remind ourselves today that many of those recordings that Dylan was hearing in Dinkytown, and even more of those from which Koerner, Ray, and Glover learned the songs they shared with Dylan, were of more recent vintage than Dylan's "greatest hits" are for young listeners coming to them for the first time now. In a very real sense, those old songs that so thrilled Dylan then were his contemporaries. Leadbelly's Capitol recordings had been made in California shortly before the artist's death, and his version of "Black Betty" had been preserved by Alan Lomax's recording apparatus just a few years before Dylan was born. A number of the artists whose songs were studied so avidly by Dylan, Glover, Koerner, and their friends were still alive. People like Victoria Spivey, Josh White, Sonny Terry and Brownie McGhee, Sleepy John Estes, Jessie Fuller, Mississippi Joe Williams, Lonnie Johnson, and Jimmy Reed were all still performing as Dylan made his way to New York and to Woody Guthrie's bed at the Brooklyn State Hospital.

And then, in the streets surrounding Greenwich Village's cafés, Dylan walked into the revivifying remnants of America's interracial underground, the latest of a constantly denied succession of political and social vanguards stretching back to the abolitionists of the previous century and now stirring again in the convergence of music, poetry, and civil rights activism, a pure product of America that produced blinding rage from many Americans. Guthrie, Leadbelly, Josh White, Sonny Terry, and Brownie McGhee had all been part of the earlier café scenes, part of a previous decade's vortex of radical politics, folk music, and racial interchange. The bohemia that reached from Harlem to the Village in the midst of the cold war's social repressions followed a well-worn track that was the legacy of preceding generations, and they were listening to the beats of such different drummers as Max Roach and Tampa Red. Disengaged from the old Left politics of the *New Masses,* there were still those among the newer bohemians who gravitated toward such overtly political magazines as the *Liberator,* and those folk magazines that appeared in time, such as *Sing Out* and *Broadside,* continued the old Left's tendency to associate folk music with progressive politics. That association is only strengthened in *Blues People,* published by another name-changing artist, LeRoi Jones/Amiri Baraka, in 1963, the same year that Dylan recorded songs for *Freewheelin'* and *The Times They Are A-Changin'.*

In this atmosphere there was nothing unusual about Dylan's early proclivity for the music he was learning from Odetta and Lonnie Johnson. It would have been far more surprising had Dylan not tried his hand at performing black music. Still, the blues of his own "Obviously Five Believers" are as great a departure from the endless versions of "House of the Rising Sun" sung by young white people in the early 1960s as Dylan's removal from Hibbing to Bleecker Street must have appeared to his childhood friends. But Dylan was not traveling that route by himself.

Early Dylan lyrics and writings show an unmistakable affinity with the protest songs of preceding decades and with the deepest spiritual resources of black lyric. His "Playboys and Playgirls," for example, borrows the form of "Ain't Nobody Gonna Turn Me 'Round" in the lines "Your Jim Crow ground / Can't turn me around," and makes poetry of the increasingly evident links between red baiting and race baiting.[2] In his "Last Thoughts on Woody Guthrie," Dylan, who had by then spent so much time sounding like Guthrie that the idiom really had become his own, writes lines that match Guthrie's for earnestness and direct treatment of the issue at hand: "You need a Greyhound bus that don't bar no race / that won't laugh at your looks / your voice or your face."[3]

In Dylan's first recordings, though, we can locate in our listenings a crucial performative shift that prepares the way for his movement from such covers as "Fixing to Die" to compositions on the order of his "Leopard-Skin Pill-Box Hat." Some among Dylan's initial renderings of African-American folk material, despite their accomplished guitar work and evident sincerity, employ vocal clichés familiar to any who have audited a fair number of white artists' recordings of black songs of the era. Indeed, what was to mark a later artist like Paul Butterfield as such a refreshing break from cliché, in addition of course to Butterfield's incredible instrumental virtuosity, was the rejection of overt attempts in singing to sound "black." Dylan performances on the order of "Gospel Plow" too often sound affected, and the problem is that the affectations are not Dylan's own. They are not the idiosyncratic vocal inflections for which he has been alternately praised and damned; rather they seem drawn from a persistent repertoire of white stylings of blackness that were common currency on the folk circuit then. A real contrast is found in Dylan's handling of the song "No More Auction Block." Here Dylan's performance has a depth and sense of mystery largely lacking on his "Gospel Plow." The power of his performance on "No More Auction Block" does not, however, result, as John Bauldie would have it, from "a young white boy somehow conjuring the persona of the singer, the exhausted but newly liberated slave acknowledging his deliverance."[4] Instead, Dylan's success is the result of his having found within the song the art and resources left there by its first singers, according to Alan Lomax, former slaves who had fled to Canada.[5] Dylan does not try to play the role of the escaped slave. He sings with the conviction and voicing of one who has lived with the song and come to understand it, to inhabit its forms, and it is from that experience that he later draws his own "Blowin' in the Wind."

This same phenomenon is evident in most of those songs Dylan wrote in the early 1960s that came to be treasured as civil rights anthems. Dylan's approach to the racial politics of his day was poetic and narrative, making frequent use of the ballad form. In a song such as "The Death of Emmett Till" it is significant that the persona does not presume to speak on behalf of black suffering, displacing black people from their own narrative, as still occurs in travesties like *Mississippi Burning* and very nearly occurs in *Amistad*. Still, Dylan's song is written from the point of view of an implicated witness. In its fifth stanza the singer declares, "I saw the morning papers but I could not bear to see / the smiling brothers walkin' down the courthouse stairs."[6] These lines set the stage for Dylan's concluding jeremiad, linking the audience to the narrated events in a web of mutuality: "If you can't speak out against this kind of thing, a crime that's so unjust / Your eyes are filled with dead men's dirt, your mind is filled with dust."[7] This concluding note is echoed in "Oxford Town" and elsewhere, songs that carry on the ballad form's traditional editorializing, a mode mastered by Woody Guthrie.

At the same time that Dylan was writing these ballads, which in some ways resemble the civil rights–era ballads of poet Gwendolyn Brooks, he was already composing lyrics that operated much more elliptically, that pointed in the direction of the lyric rupture to come. "Only a Pawn in Their Game" is far more fatalistic than "The Death of Emmett Till," though no less tied to the news of the day. This lack of explicit moral lesson and imperative may account in some small part for the sense of disengagement evident among some of the civil rights workers shown listening to Dylan's tailgate performance of the song in a bit of film that was later edited into the landmark *Dont Look Back*. Clearly, though, one reason that "Blowin' in the Wind" and "Chimes of Freedom" have such a seemingly timeless quality is the combination of their still higher level of metaphoricity and their lack of local particularity; there is an unending openness in the interpretation of these songs that is also found in folk materials such as "Many Thousands Gone" and religious songs like "Amazing Grace."

These qualities were already in place in much of the music Dylan had heard throughout his apprenticeship in Minneapolis, Denver, Chicago, and New York. A newer element came into view as Dylan read the opening of Allen Ginsberg's "Howl": "I saw the best minds of my generation destroyed by madness, starving hysterical naked, / dragging themselves through the negro streets at dawn . . ."[8] There is entirely too much that needs to be said about the appearance of these hysterics in the Negro streets to begin the discussion here. Suffice it to say that in a time when Dylan was adapting "Ain't Nobody Gonna Turn Me 'Round" to include lines expelling "red baiters and race haters" from the invisible republic, the association of white bohemia with black people was taken as a self-evident sign of creeping communism by all too many Americans. Dylan's own version of the first moments of "Howl" is still very much in the Guthrie mode but seems to be largely free of the elements of exoticism and primitivism that mark so many similar moments in Ginsberg and Kerouac: "as my friend, Bobby Lee, / walks back an' forth / free now from his native Harlem / where his ma still sleeps at night / hearin' rats inside the sink / an' underneath her hardwood bed."[9] While this passage from "11 Outlined Epitaphs" is a little too much like 1930s agitprop in tone, its free verse form and its collaged relationship to the other outlined epitaphs promises a more experimental writing that is just around the corner in Dylan's work. For Bob Dylan was moving in the space of just a few years from roots in the folk ballad and acoustic blues, through a highly charged metaphorical lyric, to a nearly antisymbolist aesthetic most visible in works extending from the first side of *Bringing It All Back Home* through the last side of *Blonde on Blonde*.

Dylan would return to the moralizing mode of his youthful ballads in later years, as he would return to all the musical forms of his career from time to time, and songs like "Hurricane" and "George Jackson" are of a piece with "The Death of Emmett

Till" and "Who Killed Davey Moore." But that mode of narrative suasion somehow did not seem sufficient for an America poised between civil rights and Black Arts, an America with Martin Luther King on its television sets and Malcolm X as its trouble in mind, an America in which, as Sister Rosetta Tharpe had sung years before, there are "Strange Things Happening Every Day." That was an America whose face could be glimpsed barely through the joined hands of those singing "Blowin' in the Wind" from the stage of the Newport Folk Festival in 1963, an underground America that forced its way into public consciousness through impolitic ruptures but that had always been the shaping force of American culture.

This was what Uncle Remus could not tell us. Uncle Remus was another pure product of America's race dreams, a tale white folk told themselves so that they could continue to live with themselves and the history they had made. We would not be America without these narratives of innocence we tell ourselves, without the self-perpetuating act of earnest young white people darkening their voices into black simulacra, but the Dylan of the mid-1960s had an ear cocked to the undertones of that song. When, decades later, Dylan recorded "Stack A Lee," he insisted that the hero of that song "is not some egotistical dionysian idiot, neither does he represent any alternative lifestyle scam."[10] Stak A Lee was no Sidney Poitier (he wasn't even Lloyd Price's "Stagolee"), Leadbelly was certainly not Pat Boone, and if Uncle Remus couldn't tell us, then perhaps the ghost of electricity could. But first Dylan had to do this crazy thing.

"Gazing out the Window of the Saint James Hotel"

"The underground's gone deeper," Dylan writes in "11 Outlined Epitaphs," and that deeper underground railroad was electric. Lost in the legends of the crazy thing Dylan did to Newport in 1965 is the fact that his was not the only electric guitar to grace a Newport stage. The electric guitar, like everything else in the folk revival, had a rigorously assigned position in the hierarchies of authenticity. Somehow the folk audience could attend to an older black blues man playing an electric instrument without losing all equanimity. Dylan's electric band was playing blues patterns in 1965, but louder than they had ever before been heard at Newport, and Dylan's blues were no longer attired in their purist work shirt. They didn't bear the tribal colors of the folk revivalists, who policed their genre boundaries with all the intensity of a southern segregationist.

The problem with Dylan's new songs went much deeper than instrumentation and wattage. Though few that day in Newport could hear Dylan's words at all clearly, despite the heightened amplification, his lyrics had taken a turn that left the good folk at *Broadside* and *Sing Out* apoplectic. It was as if the metaphors themselves were blowing fuses. While the guardians of folk purity seemed to suffer no damaging cognitive dissonance at the sight of fresh-faced white kids straight out of the suburbs solemnly intoning "Joshua Fit the Battle of Jericho," they demanded a certain reverence toward the forms. What were such to make of Dylan's parodic advice in the aptly titled "Some Other Kinds of Songs," to "leave joshua / split / go fit your battle"?[11]

Dylan increasingly inhabited a different world, beyond the well-patrolled boundaries of revivalist nostalgia, a world gone wrong, where, as the Mississippi Sheiks underwrote Rosetta Tharpe, "Strange things are happening like never before." On the simplest level, Dylan's writing had soaked up influences far beyond Guthrie and Leadbelly. He had been reading Kerouac, Ginsberg, Burroughs, and Rechy. His writing began to invoke Eliot, Brecht, Behan, Yevtushenko, even Gertrude Stein. Yet Dylan's new lyric style was no simple matter of substituting Rimbaud for Tampa Red. If there was now more of Villon than there had been before, it was Villon as read through Pete Wheatstraw, the devil's son-in-law, who figures prominently in Amiri Baraka's writings as well. The poetics Dylan increasingly adopted during this period was a practice of radical transmutation. And in this, again, he was only the most public and visible part of a much larger interracial movement of writers whose experiments melded European and American literary modernism to vernacular American lyric forms, particularly African-American, all set to the transformative impulses of jazz and rock. Among the sounds explicitly invoked by Dylan in "11 Outlined Epitaphs" are not only the works of Ginsberg but the "jail songs of Ray Bremser."[12] Bremser, along with his prison poet friend, the black writer Harold Carrington, wrote a poetry close in spirit to the work that Dylan was doing. Bremser's "Drive Suite" and Carrington's "Lament" are poems that operate by the same radically associative aesthetic rooted in the rhythms of African-American music that animates so many of Dylan's mid-1960s compositions. Bremser's *Angel*, exactly the kind of jail song Dylan wrote of in "Epitaphs" (and close cousin to Bob Kaufman's jail poems), turns to the surreal imagery offered everywhere by America as a means of finding a way to negotiate the punishing sentences America exacts. When Bremser writes, "Somewhere back in the dawn of it, beyond these small newsy items, it occurred...the breach in the wall,"[13] he could easily be the Dylan of "Visions of Johanna" or "Drifter's Escape."

The closest analogue to what Dylan is doing in these works is neither Ginsberg nor Bremser but their colleague and publisher Amiri Baraka. Dylan could well be one of the folksingers who appear in a passage of Baraka's 1965 book *The System of Dante's Hell*, a passage written at almost the same time as Dylan's vision of Shakespeare in the alley. The landscape of Dylan's "Memphis Blues Again" shares its population with Baraka's hell, where "Shakespeare rattled drunkenly in the fog, folksingers, a thin Negro lying to his white girlfriend."[14] There is no possible mistaking of the source for one potent riff that appears in Baraka's subsequent novel, *6 Persons*: "Blowin in the wind is a form—who's to do it was our first question. Is there a change can come?"[15] Here Baraka brilliantly brings Dylan's lyric, which had been set to the music of former slaves, back home to its source in turn, melding Dylan's "The Times They Are A-Changin'" to the lyric broadcast to a popular audience by Sam Cooke, Otis Redding, and Aretha Franklin, "A Change Is Gonna Come." (Legend has it, indeed, that Cooke penned "A Change Is Gonna Come" in direct response to Dylan's "Blowin' in the Wind.") Readers of Dylan's *Tarantula* may recognize the character Crow Jane, who appears in the segment titled "Mouthful of Loving Choke," as a fugitive from a song by Mississippi Joe Williams. What needs to be more often remarked is this passage's relationship to one of Baraka's pivotal poetic sequences of the same period. Baraka at this time (and to this day, I believe) shared with Dylan that "personal empathy with Egypt and a Pop Art approach to Platonic Archtypes" that Ginsberg noted in Bremser's poetry in 1964.[16] In Baraka's poems, Crow Jane is a deathly muse of Western civilization, sister to the better-known Lula of Baraka's play *Dutchman*. Crow Jane is "Mama death," the "Dead virgin / of the mind's echo. Dead Lady / of thinking, back now, without / the creak of memory."[17] Dylan's Crow Jane functions similarly, but in the different racial context provided by *Tarantula* her multiplying significations speed quickly out of reach of the civil rights framework of the folk milieu. The characters Dylan parades before us here, including the "cracker boy" with his spike shoes, "crawl with the blues feeling." But Jane, a Remus-like projection of white desire for authenticity that will leave whiteness untouched, punctures the pretensions to blackness shared even by the book's narrator: "how come you so smart crow jane," she is asked, "& she say back 'how come you wanna talk so colored? & don't call me no crow jane!'"[18] Jane also deflates both Eliot and Cummings, two earlier American artists who had taken their turn at poetic blackface: "& i think i'm gonna do april or so is a cruel month & how you like your blue eyed boy NOW mr octopus?"[19] For both Baraka and Dylan, Crow Jane is a mocking phantasm of our own imaginings who won't, precisely because we can't imagine life without her, give up the ghost. Mississippi Joe Williams sang, "Crow Jane, Crow Jane, don't hold your head so high, / You realize, baby, you got to lay down and die." This is the rhetoric we hear in "Like a Rolling Stone" and "Positively Fourth Street." Dylan finds Crow Jane residing in a "beast nest" and writes at the end, "i touch jane on the inside & swallow."[20] Dylan was no longer likely to attempt to sing from the position of a black man, but he could reach to the inside of America's minstrel shadowings of blackness. When he declares in the liner notes to *Bringing It All Back Home*, "I happen to be one of the Supremes,"[21] the internal motive is an effort to evade identification with the commodification of the folk industry. He is responding to someone who insists he has seen Dylan at a hootenanny. But it is also a sign of Dylan's readiness to slip in and out of the racial masques America deploys as a politics of the popular. If Crow Jane cannot be finally exorcised, she can at least be read as a testament of our own racial imaginary rather than repackaged in new wrapping as authentic blackness for enthusiastic new generations of cracker jack impersonators.

Jacques Derrida once wrote, "A testament is read, offers itself to readings, but also ordains readership."[22] Seldom in the recent history of American letters has this been so evident as in the case of *Tarantula*, a book that was published in the end only because so many people were already reading it. The readership for the book that eventually appeared bound in stores to displace its illicit street simulacra appears as variously constituted as the book itself. Described by many originally as Dylan's novel, a more recent edition carries the word *poems* as a warning label on the cover. The individual sections are identified as fables, poems, even an opera. Though roughly half the book might be safely described as epistolary free verse, the whole is one of those genre-defying texts like Jean Toomer's *Cane*, Thoreau's *Walden*, Baraka's *The System of Dante's Hell*, or Lyn Hejinian's *My Life*. Among the teeming personalities that flicker through its pages are characters of no fixed race, slippery gender, and odd relationships to the putative "real" world of those readers supposedly living "outside" the text. In one segment we meet a rabbit seller, "call him White Man." There is a man whose "ears always bleed in heavy weather—call him Black Man." And then there is the glass-eyed hatcheck girl, "call her Audience."[23] Audience vanishes as quickly as she materializes; she doesn't seem to be around to witness the "blackface musician" from Two Women or the "negro medicine man from Denver, who plays folk songs for kicks & speaks french for a living."[24] There are passages that seem to arrive before their historic moment, as when the author wonders, "who ronald reagan talked to about the foreign situation."[25] Other passages manage, without benefit of Foucault or Barthes, to dispose of the presumptive author quite handily: "here lies bob dylan / murdered / from behind / by trembling flesh."[26] This is certainly unlikely to please any who might have turned to *Tarantula* out of some celebratory biographical curiosity. Old folkies were probably disturbed to read that "this land is your land & this land is my land—sure—but the world is run by those that never listen to music anyway,"[27] a passage that seemingly dispenses with the very motivation for protest music, a label Dylan had long distrusted anyway. And who among an eager later generation of retro-hipsters will take encouragement from the book's description of "Hefty Bore, a leftover horror from the beat generation"?[28]

At last, though, *Tarantula* ordains a certain form of audience, one that differs from itself, an audience constructed on the same paratactic principles by which a centuries-long tradition of folk song renews itself, the mode of Baraka's and Dylan's writing. *Tarantula*, like all books really, ordains an audience that ministers to its reading, that forms itself in the web of the text. If Dylan and his readership ultimately refuse to be any one thing, so does his book. Commenting upon the recent rolling thunder review presented by President Clinton's peripatetic advisory panel on race, Congressman Robert Matsui complained that "we really, unfortunately, aren't able to really talk about race because, again, it's like saying, let's talk about America."[29] But if Congressman Matsui would only listen to the likes of Don DeLillo or Dylan, he might learn that this is exactly why we can't stop speaking about race, why the American voice is the voice heard singing "Trouble in Mind." Which is simply to say that *Tarantula*, like *The System of Dante's Hell*, demands a reading of ourselves as racialized improvisation from the historical given, which, again, is how the blues happens, how Dylan and Baraka do their work.

Songs evolve like rumors from some strange neighborhood over the ridge, recombinant remnants becoming part of the already there and changing it utterly. In Dylan's own writing, "No More Auction Block" provides the chordal beginnings of "Blowin' in the Wind," Chuck Berry's "Too Much Monkey Business" offers itself up as a riff around which "Subterranean Homesick Blues" is wrapped, and his rendition of "I Want to Be Your Driver" is transmuted to become Dylan's "Obviously Five Believers." In *Tarantula*, Roger Miller's wildly successful novelty songs are wedded to a fallen gospel of irreverent ministry. The segment titled "Chug A Lug - Chug A Lug / Hear Me Holler Hi Dee Ho" begins: "he was propped in the crutch of an oak tree—looking down—singing 'there's a man going round taking names.' "[30] As the roots of rock are embedded in the amalgamated subsoil of country music and rhythm and blues, Dylan's writing grows out of the miscegenated soul of the American language. *Tarantula* gives onto a world where Mexican Maria is as "american as Howling Wolf," where among the very few things that "exist" are boogie-woogie and Nashville blues, where, in Gary, Indiana, a "colored man [is] shot twenty times thru the head" and "the coroner says cause of death is unknown."[31] This world gone wrong is our America, finally more real than the social realism of the hootenanny with its legions of white folk searching out innocence tricked out in their newly purchased overalls that no one yet had thought to market pre-stressed. *Tarantula*'s America is that invisible republic presided over by an Aretha who is not the hot commodity flipping through the faux diner of *The Blues Brothers* (eerily recalling the pancake flipping at the heart of *Imitation of Life*), but rather an Aretha of the "blues dunes," an Aretha who is a "menace to president as he was jokingly called,"[32] and her text, that same text sought out by Jes Grew in the pages of Ishmael Reed's *Mumbo Jumbo*, is "your black mongrel vagabond,"[33] and he speaks "in your voice, American."[34] While any number of white knights in denim were trying to sound black on the sound stage of America's folk revival, Dylan was sounding the depths of blackness in American consciousness. In lifting up new lyrics in old songs, he was, as he writes of the flowers in "11 Outlined Epitaphs," "liftin' lost voices of the ground's people,"[35] and where have all those flowers gone with the end of the twentieth century? As Dylan listened to the history that formed the choruses of "Many Thousands Gone," he found his own voice in the whirlwind of the song, already implicated in the interstices of abolitionist lyric. Later, black artists would answer in kind. Randy Crawford sings "Knockin' on Heaven's Door" like someone finding a station of the underground railroad in her flight to Canada. Roberta Flack answered Dylan's "Just Like a Woman" just by singing the song in the first person. (As Dylan sings in "Tangled Up in Blue," "We always did feel the same, / We just saw it from a different point of view.")[36] Her taking up the subject position in that song subjected its words to a new lyric analysis. Jimi Hendrix, in "Like a Rolling Stone," "All along the Watchtower," and the posthumously released "Drifter's Escape," became that "bolt of lightning" that "struck the courthouse out of shape."[37]

The audience ordained by Dylan's writing can never appear as a univocal mass; it won't wait. This is, as *Tarantula* tells us, "what makes people different than / signs."[38] It is an audience summoned by song, a black mongrel vagabond who appears, like Dylan himself at times, to be pursuing a never-ending tour of the lost highway that runs from its own past to some vanishing point in its own as yet unsung history. It is an audience that finds itself in listening to vaguely familiar choruses, endlessly improvising yet one more verse. Dylan once heard Leadbelly in the person of Black Betty's crazed baby, "standing in a window, blam de lam! hundred floors up, blam de lam! with his prayers and his pigfoot, blam de lam!"[39] Today you can hear Dylan through the lyric window of the Saint James Infirmary, and he speaks in the blackness of your voice, an American prayer: "See them big plantations burning, / Hear the cracking of the whips, / Smell that sweet magnolia blooming, / See the ghost of slavery's ships."[40]

Notes

1. Don DeLillo, *Underworld* (New York: Scribner, 1997), 11.
2. Bob Dylan, *Lyrics 1962–1985* (New York: Alfred A. Knopf, 1985), 160.
3. Ibid., 34.
4. John Bauldie, liner notes to Bob Dylan, *The Bootleg Series*, 1991, 8.
5. Quoted in ibid., 6.
6. Dylan, *Lyrics 1962–1985*, 20.
7. Ibid.
8. Allen Ginsberg, *Howl and Other Poems* (San Francisco: City Lights Books, 1956), 9.
9. Dylan, *Lyrics 1962–1985*, 111.
10. Bob Dylan, *World Gone Wrong*, Columbia 575901993, 4.
11. Dylan, *Lyrics 1962–1985*, 148.
12. Ibid., 115.
13. Ray Bremser, *Poems of Madness & Angel* (Sudbury, Mass.: Water Row Press, 1986), 50.
14. Amiri Baraka, *The Fiction of LeRoi Jones/Amiri Baraka* (Chicago: Lawrence Hill Books, 2000), 90.
15. Ibid., 373.
16. Allen Ginsberg, introduction to *Poems of Madness*, by Bremser, 1.
17. Amiri Baraka, *Transbluesency: Selected Poems 1961–1995*, ed. Paul Vangelisti (New York: Marsilio Publishers, 1995), 87, 88.
18. Bob Dylan, *Tarantula* (1971; New York: St. Martin's Press, 1994), 35.
19. Ibid., 35–36.
20. Ibid., 35, 37.
21. Ibid., 180.
22. Jacques Derrida, *Politics of Friendship*, trans. George Collins (London: Verso, 1997), 177.
23. Dylan, *Tarantula*, 56.
24. Ibid., 67, 85.
25. Ibid., 65.
26. Ibid., 118.
27. Ibid., 88
28. Ibid., 117.
29. Steven Holmes and James Bennet, "Renewed Sense of Purpose for Clinton Panel on Race," *New York Times,* January 14, 1998, A1.
30. Dylan, *Tarantula*, 82.
31. Ibid., 137, 127, and 125.
32. Ibid., 71.
33. Ibid., 62.
34. DeLillo, *Underworld*, 11.

35. Dylan, *Lyrics 1962–1985,* 116.

36. Ibid., 359.

37. Ibid., 258.

38. Dylan, *Tarantula,* 95.

39. Ibid., 12.

40. Bob Dylan, *Bob Dylan: The Bootleg Series Volumes 1–3 [rare & unreleased] 1961–1991,* 3 vols., Columbia 47382, 1991.

16. Not Dark Yet:
How Bob Dylan Got His Groove Back
David Yaffe

Bob Dylan's Harlem Incident

June 7, 2004, was not just another gig for Bob Dylan. Sandwiching a show between one-nighters in Atlantic City and Delaware, Dylan went uptown to play the Apollo Theater, the legendary venue where Ella Fitzgerald passed the audition for the Chick Webb orchestra, and where, on a 1962 live album, James Brown made a gig in Harlem a chart-topping soundtrack for the world. In black America, *Showtime* at the Apollo could make or break a career. It is the room where African-American discourse is taken to the people, and the response is either up or down. If you're a comedian and you don't get laughs, or if you're a singer and you do, it may be the moment to go back to your day job. "Went to the Apollo, should've seen them go-go-go," sang Lou Reed on his only hit single. In the 1965 liner notes for *Bringing It All Back Home,* Dylan wrote that "the fact that the white house is filled with leaders who have never been t'the apollo theater amazes me." The world had changed four decades later: the Manhattan headquarters for Bill Clinton, who had Dylan sing a half-hearted "Chimes of Freedom" at his 1993 inaugural, were right down the street.

Before Dylan's racial journey had dropped him off uptown, he had been the civil rights bard of the early 1960s, the racial fetishist and converso of the late 1970s, and the minstrelsy-obsessed allegorist of the twenty-first century. It was typical, after Elvis, for white American pop singers to find their voices through someone else's blues, but Dylan's relationship to race is unique. Just three years earlier, he had named his 2001 CD *"Love and Theft"* after Eric Lott's 1993 study of blackface minstrelsy, and in his film *Masked and Anonymous,* Dylan is taunted by the specter of a blacked-up, banjo-playing Ed Harris, taunting Dylan's character Jake Fate to remember the burnt cork origins of his musical identity. Rock and roll is filled with white imitators of black style, but none had contextualized the appropriation of black culture so deeply. When he opened his mouth to sing, he adopted many personae, but never that of the Minnesotan Jew. He was fond of Rimbaud's maxim "J'est un autre," literally translated as "I is someone else," which sounds like it could be a blues lyric.

In his voice, Hank Williams and Woody Guthrie drifted in from the white working class, and Leadbelly and Robert Johnson as African-American blues avatars. The former Robert Zimmerman spent a few years in Christianity but all of his adult life in a reckoning with blackness. "Nobody could sing the blues like Blind Willie McTell," he sang, but nobody sang about not being able to sing those blues like Dylan, which in turn made for compelling blues in its own way. What began as youthful imitation followed by impassioned activism was followed by racial transference. He saw through the fake appropriations and wanted to get to blackness as deeply as possible. In his journey from civil rights to minstrelsy, politics became sex, religion, and, finally, a way to come to terms with mortality and masks. The various personae fashioned by Dylan would not be possible without black America, and his work—blues, civil rights anthems, gospel songs, and more—repeatedly acknowledged this fact.

But did black America need Bob Dylan? Would he pass his audition for *Showtime* at the Apollo? He would perform for at a fund-raiser supporting Jazz at Lincoln Center, playing two songs with a septet led by Wynton Marsalis, the institution's artistic director, jazz's impassioned musical ambassador and biggest living celebrity. One of the music's most accomplished trumpet players and beguiling raconteurs, he was the first jazz composer to win a Pulitzer Prize. His detractors have called him a "neoconservative" for his rejection of most music after the middle period of John Coltrane—including all forms of rock and roll and anything with an amplifier— yet in the service of funding the orchestra's new headquarters, which would open that fall at Columbus Circle in Manhattan, he was collaborating with pop stars in performances with Stevie Wonder, Paul Simon, and, on this night, with Dylan. Dylan apparently acted like quite the rock star in rehearsals, filling the room with expensive guitars that he didn't even touch. But before the show, the audience could hear him backstage riffing on his harmonica, sounding like he could have been around the corner on Lenox Avenue playing for passing change.

Jazz was not completely unfamiliar territory for Dylan. The jazz bassist Art Davis sat in on "Rocks and Gravel," an unreleased track from the *Freewheelin' Bob Dylan* sessions in 1963, when he was also the bass player for the John Coltrane Quartet. In *Chronicles, Volume 1,* Dylan wrote of jamming with the avant-garde virtuoso Cecil Taylor ("Cecil could play regular piano if he wanted to"), as well as Don Cherry and Billy Higgins (in the years when they were blazing the new territory of free jazz alongside Ornette Coleman). In this remarkable passage from his memoir, he recalled crashing a rehearsal with Thelonious Monk: "I dropped in there once in the afternoon, just to listen—told him that I played folk music up the street. 'We all play folk music,' he said. Monk was in his own dynamic music even when he dawdled around."[1] This exchange resonated enough to wind up in Dylan's memoir more than four decades later, but even if he was curious enough to listen in, and even as he was hip to Monk's assertion that all music was folk music, Dylan also admitted, "I liked modern jazz a lot, liked to listen to it in the clubs ... but I didn't follow it and I wasn't caught up in it. There weren't ordinary words with specific meanings, and I needed to hear things plain and simple in the King's English, and folk songs are what spoke to me most directly."[2] "*We all play folk music*": what a rich description of two musical roads that diverged, yet are still fed by similar sources, still driven to transform vernacular material into something new and strange. A black genius in a porkpie hat sent a powerful message to the scruffy Jewish kid that day, something that Dylan had pondered for decades. In a scene from *Dont Look Back,* Dylan and Bob Neuwirth are facetiously snapping their fingers to a jazz recording, and while it may appear they are parodying the music, the pretentious hipsters are the real targets. In this passage, Dylan could admit his affection and curiosity while also pleading ignorance. Even if Dylan claimed to prefer "the King's English," his use of it was hardly plain and simple. The author of "my warehouse eyes / My Arabian drums" could be abstract, associative, and dense, but his musical world was simple: variations on folk forms and the twelve bar blues.

And the blues was the turf where Dylan and Marsalis could meet. Marsalis's jazz canon was centered on Duke Ellington, Louis Armstrong, and Charlie Parker (all of whom would surface on Dylan's XM Radio show), and the blues flowed through it all. It was Dylan's second gig at the Apollo that year. That April, he performed a rage against the dying of the light rendition of Sam Cooke's civil rights anthem "A Change Is Gonna Come," a song Cooke wrote after he heard "Blowin' in the Wind" and thought, "Geez. A white boy writing a song like that?" Cooke would be gunned down in his prime a year after recording the song, and Dylan sang it like he was fighting for his life, ripping up his larynx to get the story out. On this night, the circle closed even more. But before he could hit the stage, the comedian Cedric the Entertainer, who was emceeing the event reading patter from a teleprompter, had to give him a hazing, testing the waters uptown. This was not Dylan's crowd. The lyrics of Lou Reed would have resonated: "Hey, white boy. What you doin' uptown?" The moment before a performer appears onstage is always sensitive, and for Dylan, who, according to legend, inspired Robbie Robertson to write "Stage Fright," this is especially the case. "No man sees my face and lives," Dylan once wrote. Cedric the Entertainer's introduction was more like a celebrity roast:

> Now, when you think of jazz and you think of the Apollo theater, there is one man that instantly comes to mind: Bob Dylan. [This gets a big laugh.] I don't know about y'all, but it just adds up to me. Jazz-Apollo-Bob Dylan. Could be my fuzzy math. Okay, it might seem like a stretch. Aiight. But when it comes to compelling songs that resonate profoundly today, here's what comes to my mind: *How many cannonballs must fly before they are forever banned? The answer, my friend is blowin' in the wind.* Now, the artist that wrote that song *decades* ago is not known as a jazz artist, but his body of work reflects something akin to jazz: change and adaptability. How else would you describe someone whose work has spanned four decades and collaborations with everyone from Willie Nelson to Beatle George Harrison? And, of course, he's received Grammys and lifetime achievement awards galore, all richly deserved. That achievement began with the spirit of rebellion that filled the jazz and folk clubs of the fifties and sixties. Many artists have come a long way since then, but few have truly been trailblazers. Ladies and gentlemen, would you please welcome Mr. Bob Dylan?

There were waves of applause, some polite, some baffled, and some thunderous, especially from the Dylan fans among those paying for four-figure tickets or on press comps. The band began playing a B-flat blues at a snail's pace, complete with Ellingtonian splashes of brass and a lilting piano riff. It was a blues that sounded wounded yet wrapped in elegance. Then a low, gravelly voice ascended from the crypt: "Well I ride on a mail train, baby... Can't buy uh-ah thrill," Dylan rasped. The horns answered his call with taunts, and he would often turn around in a mixture of disbelief and simpatico bliss. *Highway 61 Revisited* and the brash young man who had initially delivered those lines had receded in the rearview mirror decades earlier. "Don't say I never warned you / When your train gets lost," he snarled, and he seemed in danger of getting lost himself, but the band managed to catch up with him, rushing to the next bar, only to be reined in by the band. The blues found him in the end. Marsalis was laying down the iron law of swing and did not work against Dylan, but pushed him into a groove where he had never gone. Raising his voice just above the cellar for emphasis, he rasped, "I tried to tell everybody, but I could not get across."

The next song, "Don't Think Twice, It's Alright" tried to get something else across. A devastating breakup tune dating back to *Freewheelin'*, Dylan stayed nestled in a few notes in the nether regions of what was left of his range. Marsalis's arrangement was so dense, it seemed impenetrable, but Dylan attempted to croon his way in anyway. Drummer Herlin Riley rumbled a Latin groove known as "The Big Four" (bomp-ca-bomp-ca-bom-CHA). Marsalis played lines behind Dylan, circling around the melody, finding rhythmic and harmonic counterpoints that strayed way beyond the song's simple origins. Dylan was so startled he lost his place in a song he had been singing since 1963, singing the line "on the dark side of the road" twice, but it hardly mattered. He was in sync, finally sitting in with a real jazz band, perhaps as he had wanted to when he crashed Monk's rehearsal all those years earlier. As the band slowly quieted down on the out chorus, Dylan's harmonica lines were fading out, too. Dylan seemed shaken up when he was over. He nearly tripped over his microphone. But he and Marsalis shook hands. For two songs, a musical draw was called.

When Blackness Was a Virtue

Dylan had reason to be disturbed. Not only were these musicians recognizing things in him that he seemed afraid yet exhilarated to find reflected back from musicians with intimidating authority, they were channeling a deeper identity narrative, one that Dylan was still playing out that summer night on 125th street. Dylan's racial journey had dropped him off uptown, after a four-decade run that included teenage appropriation, youthful activism, and the rest of a lifetime of finding his musical voice through someone else's blues. As a teenager, he traded in his electric guitar for an acoustic after an Odetta record stopped him dead in his tracks. After he soaked up her strumming and singing style, he performed for her during his brief stint as a student at the University of Minnesota, and her encouragement helped give him the confidence to make that fateful journey to New York City during that cold, auspicious winter of 1961. Soon after he arrived, he played harmonica with Harry Belafonte's version of "Midnight Special" for his first record date; the musicians on the session laughed at Dylan's nervous attempts to keep the rhythm by thudding his foot so loudly, it caused reverb throughout the studio.

Authenticity was the rage in a folk scene dominated by white college kids and dropouts affecting the voices of the Delta and the dust bowl. Rock and roll, of course, was also a white, adolescent affectation of the sounds of blackness and the working class, but the ethnic affectations of the Greenwich Village folk scene were not merely in the name of style or profit (although there would be plenty of that for a few of them), but political and social change. Soon, Dylan had a bohemian girl-friend, Suze Rotolo (she was on his arm for the *Freewheelin' Bob Dylan* cover), who got Dylan involved with CORE (Congress of Racial Equality), and he was writing songs about Emmett Till, Hattie Carroll, James Meredith, and writing words that would be belted out at the March on Washington by Peter, Paul and Mary: "How many years can some people exist until they're allowed to be free."

Yet while Dylan was in the trenches of the civil rights movement, there was a notable absence of the black musical influence he soaked up elsewhere. When he confronted the struggle face-to-face in civil rights demonstrations, he did not sing in the blues inflected drawl of his 1961 performances of Bukka White's "Fixin' to Die" or Blind Lemon Jefferson's "See That My Grave Is Kept Clean" (both featured on his first album, though not staples of his live sets at the time) but stuck to Okie affectations. Dylan also recorded two blues standards for the *Freewheelin'* sessions—Big Joe Williams's "Baby Please Don't Go" and Robert Johnson's "Milk Cow's Calf's Blues"—but left them off the final album. Even though he sang, in "With God on Our Side," "The country I come from is called the Midwest," his phrasing evoked an imaginary region inspired by his teenage readings of Guthrie's *Bound for Glory* or Steinbeck's *Grapes of Wrath*. That twang—not anything resembling his blues in-vocations—was on display in his two most memorable political appearances, both from the incendiary summer of 1963. In footage from his performance in a Green-wood, Mississippi, cotton field, Dylan, surrounded by black men in sunglasses, is sweating under a work shirt, belting out "Only a Pawn in Their Game," a screed about the assassination of Medgar Evers written weeks earlier:

> And the Negro's name
> Is used it is plain
> For the politician's gain
> As he rises to fame

Dylan sings these lines like he sprang right out of the dust bowl. The Negro's name may be used for the politician's gain, but the bluesman's cadences are noticeably absent from Dylan's delivery; he would not make these civil rights appearances as Mailer's White Negro. Dylan was not playing the hipster contemplating existential dread but looked like a humble singer-activist, earnestly intoning his finger-pointing invective in that sultry cotton field, and was not about to channel his own inner Robert Johnson while he was deep in the Delta. Theo Bikel, who brought Dylan down along with Pete Seeger, recalled, "Bob said that he hadn't met a colored person until he was nine years old and apologized that he had so little to offer."[3] Dylan also avoided racial appropriations at the March on Washington, where he sang "When the Ship Comes In" with Joan Baez, who dragged him to the event, warbling by his side, and, repeating his Greenwood, Mississippi, cotton field performance, "Only a Pawn in Their Game." Dylan was apparently inspired to write "When the Ship Comes In" after being denied a hotel room with Joan Baez and recalling a performance of Bertolt Brecht's "Pirate Jenny." The words he summoned, "The whole wide world is watchin'" were fortuitous. His performance was met with a dismissal in the *New York Times* and some ironic asides from comedian Dick Gregory, but he was singing into a momentous podium. He belted these anthems to a crowd of 250,000 as a warm-up act for Martin Luther King's "I Have a Dream" speech. This was during Dylan's brief (albeit glorious) period of political engagement. When Dylan was singing about lynchings and assassinations, he was joining the movement, but in this period and in these performances, he avoided phrasing out of African-American vernacular.

Just a few months later, on December 16, 1963, Dylan would make a drunken acceptance speech for the Tom Paine Award from the Emergency Civil Liberties Committee, in which he attempted to bite the hand that fed him, expressing sympathy for Lee Harvey Oswald weeks after the Kennedy assassination and saying this about his appearance on the Washington mall: "I was on the March on Washington up on the platform and I looked around at all the Negroes there and I didn't see any Negroes that looked like none of my friends. My friends don't wear *suits*. My friends don't have to wear any kind of thing to prove that they're respectable Negroes."[4] Dylan clearly felt ill at ease with what seemed like a bourgeois costume for a radical event. In the 2000 interview that appeared in Martin Scorsese's *No Direction Home*, Dylan would reflect that he was standing a few feet away from King when he made his speech, and it had "a profound effect on me to this day," but at the time he was pledging a political *non serviam*. Dylan had looked at blackness from the outside but clearly wanted in. When he was speaking irreverently about the march and spoke of his friends who wore more casual clothes, he was claiming a kinship of another kind. "I'm not part of no Movement," he told Nat Hentoff in 1964. "If I was, I wouldn't be able to do anything else but be in 'the Movement.' I just can't make it with any organization."[5]

On *Another Side of Bob Dylan,* recorded in one Beaujolais-soaked evening in 1964, Dylan bid fare thee well to politics. "I was so much older then, I'm younger than that now," he sang in a voice that no longer invoked Woody Guthrie. But his fixation on black culture—now removed from the label of "protest songs" that he always protested—turned more playful and, in the case of "Spanish Harlem Incident," erotic. The song is addressed to a "gypsy gal" with "pearly eyes" and "flashing diamond teeth," a reference to old-school bling, possibly to the blues singer "Diamond Teeth" Mary—certainly to her dental style and what its extravagance signified in African-American communities. This gypsy gal represents an ideal of sensuality, one that makes him disparage his own whiteness:

> The night is pitch black, come an' make my
> Pale face fit into place, ah, please!

When Dylan sings these lines, he is gazing longingly at blackness, but he does not attempt to imitate it. In these images, Dylan attempts, earnestly and somewhat awkwardly, to match the lover's dark skin with the night. At the song's end, he begs the gypsy gal to "surround" him so that he can determine whether he is "really real." After Dylan distanced himself from politics, in this song, he brought himself closer to interracial eros. A year later, in "From a Buick 6," he would playfully sing about a "soulful mama" who "keeps me hid," a lover who "walks like Bo Diddley / And she don't need no crutch," indicating that it takes a black rhythm and blues guitarist to truly walk the walk. The lover of "Spanish Harlem Incident" also needs no assistance. There were many associations swirling in Dylan's head during the songwriting binge that included "Spanish Harlem Incident" as a charming but minor track in a harvest that also included the far more monumental "To Ramona," "Chimes of Freedom," and "Mr. Tambourine Man" (which would not appear until *Bringing It All Back Home*). As the title suggested, *Another Side of Bob Dylan* meant to show that Dylan was revealing a new aspect of his complicated persona, embarking on a post-political identity, one that included sharing a momentous joint with the Beatles, a breakup with Suze Rotolo, and a halfhearted epilogue to his fling with Joan Baez. "It ain't me, babe," he sang on the album's closing track. But who was he? Never before had Dylan sounded so unaffected; the Guthrie-inspired twang was gone, and he sounded like he was itching for a rock-and-roll band behind him, which he would get soon enough. There were black musicians in Dylan's orbit, and he never believed, as he sang in "Chimes of Freedom," in the "lies that life [was] black and white." Dylan was working (without much satisfaction) with the producer Tom Wilson, the first black man to rise up in the world of pop production, who had previously produced Cecil Taylor's *Jazz Advance* (1955) and Sun Ra's *The Futuristic Sounds of Sun Ra* (1961), a jazz partisan who thought folk music was just for "dumb guys" until he heard Dylan's lyrics; "Mr. Tambourine Man" was inspired by the giant tambourine of the black guitarist Bruce Langhorne, who did not learn about the inspiration himself until he read Dylan's interview in the *Biograph* liner notes in 1985.[6] Stevie Wonder, Sam Cooke, and even Duke Ellington were all covering "Blowin' in the Wind." Dylan had distanced himself from politics in the year of the Freedom Summer, but in "Spanish Harlem Incident," he sang about his desire to become one with blackness in a different way.

Yet he was also aware of the price of artifice, and the anger that he would express about racial injustice would also be directed toward racial affectation in one of his greatest songs. When Dylan entered Columbia's Studio A on June 15, 1965, to record "Like a Rolling Stone," he gave the following order to the guitarist Mike Bloomfield: "I don't want you to play any of that B. B. King shit. I don't want you to play any of the fucking blues." This was a strange directive for a guitarist who had played with the Paul Butterfield Blues Band—someone who had played nothing *but* blues. That "something else" was a simple 1-4-5 riff, one that Dylan had said was inspired by Richie Valens's 1958 "La Bamba." "Like a Rolling Stone" is a jeremiad against artifice, lashing out at Miss Lonely, a female poseur who affects what Muddy Waters embodied for real. The song explodes with fury, but it is never been clear exactly who its target is. The speculations have ranged from Edie Sedgwick or Joan Baez in particular to his audience in general, with more than a modicum of misogyny in the former case, misanthropy in the latter.

"I'm a rollin' stone," intoned Waters, and Hank Williams was not ashamed of identifying himself that way either. (In D. A. Pennebaker's *Dont Look Back,* filmed shortly before the song was written, Dylan is caught backstage playing Williams's "Lost Highway" with its "I'm a rolling stone" lyric.) Miss Lonely graduated from "the finest school all right," but no one ever taught her how to "live out on the street." Like many a white college student in 1965, she might have fetishized an old bluesman like Waters—she may have listened to him at Newport or on a record in her dorm—but she probably would not have wanted to live like him. Yet what seems to make her truly beneath contempt, what makes her most worthy of his scorn, is not that she ignored all those warnings that this doll was bound to fall, but that she is a Dylan fan. "You used to be so amused / At Napoleon in rags and the language that he used"; "You said you'd never compromise / With the mystery tramp, but now you realize / He's not selling any alibis / As you stare into the vacuum of his eyes / And ask him do you want to make a deal?" Dylan is the mystery tramp, the Napoleon in rags who used language so cunningly, and he is berating Miss Lonely for following him so blindly while he also takes aim at himself. To be *like* a rolling stone is to be a pretender to the throne of Williams and Waters. How does it feel to affect the styles of those less privileged than you? How does it feel to be ersatz? The voice that snarls it triumphs in identifying a bohemian who has the style but not the credibility—who can't walk the walk. This masterpiece of bile continues to be a crowd pleaser. But is it in the voice of the Dylan who wants the gypsy gal of "Spanish Harlem Incident" to make him "really real," or does it revel in its artificiality, its invented persona of the mystery tramp? The mystery of the mystery tramp continued to confound.

There is a film of Waters performing "Rolling Stone" at the Newport Folk Festival from 1960, entrancing an interracial crowd a few years before Dylan became the festival's star (in 1963 and 1964) and Judas (in 1965, when he blew the eardrums off some purist listeners with a version of "Like a Rolling Stone" when it was brand-new). No one had any problems with Waters playing electric there, and the lyrics he sang intoned his vagabond status with pride. Being a rolling stone gave him strength, resilience, and would give him something to sing about:

> Well, my mother told my father,
> just before hmmm, I was born,
> "I got a boy child's comin',
> He's gonna be, he's gonna be a rollin' stone"

This is in the same song where men leave their heartbroken women behind and the singer wishes he were a catfish, just so fine-looking women could fish after him. All this would be insufferable bragging were it not for Waters's ingenious guitar playing, seductive singing, and devastating stage presence. Waters's refrain about himself, even in utero, was a destiny first uttered by his parents: "He's gonna be a rolling stone." It is blues stoicism, affirmation, and defiant self-possession. He will gather no moss, endure, and sing about it in a thrilling performance to the white college kids at Newport in 1960. "Nothin' in ramblin'," sang Memphis Minnie, but Waters's song made it sound so appealing. Dylan takes this trope of "Rolling Stone," twists it, and throws it in the face of Miss Lonely, who was schooled (in the finest school, all right) for other things. Dylan, sitting the civil rights movement out in 1965, looks toward Waters as the ultimate image of black masculinity and musical depth, an exemplar that Miss Lonely, in the voice of the song, could never attain. And yet there is something about the condition of identifying that phoniness that created a new hybrid genre: a six-minute pop song bursting at the seams with Beat poetry and surrealism, a song that made Dylan realize that he wanted to put aside his novel and eschew other literary ambitions, because he could channel the range of his ideas, and his ever-inspired revenge fantasies, into a song, a "piece of vomit," as he described it. (Bob Neuwirth said the original draft of the song went on for pages. It would have taken up the entire side of a record.) But Dylan recognized it was no mere regurgitation. "Like a Rolling Stone" had a life of its own. Waters—along with Hank, Cisco, Woody, and Leadbelly, too—receded further into the distance.

"Like a Rolling Stone" is still belted out at Dylan's encores about a hundred times a year; it has been a staple of Dylan's tours since 1965 and 1966 (when it was met with boos and jeers from folkie purists) and when he went back on the road after an eight-year sabbatical in 1974. Apart from the period when he eliminated all secular material from his set in 1979–80, he has continued to perform it. But there was one performance where he did not get the last word. In a 1992 performance for the tenth anniversary of the *David Letterman Show,* Dylan sang the song in a perfunctory nasal growl, and it is only in the final choruses when the gospel legend Mavis Staples, leading an all-star chorus of backup singers that also included Michelle Shocked, Rosanne Cash, Nanci Griffith, and Emmylou Harris, kicked new life into the song. "Tell me, ohhhh…how does it feeee-huuul…," she wailed, growing increasingly forceful with every verse. She flashed knowing looks to Dylan. The question "How does it feel?" gained a new authority as a spiritual invocation from a virtuoso gospel diva. The performance was a reminder of how Staples could powerfully steal the show from a rock star, as she did in the Staple Singers' incendiary duet on The Band's "The Weight" in Martin Scorsese's *The Last Waltz.*

Staples was the youngest daughter in the Staple Singers, a gospel dynasty that scored crossover hits with pop covers, including Dylan's "The Times They Are A-Changin'" and "Masters of War." "This was inspirational music," Staples said, and she made it sound that way, bringing out the blues, the melisma, and the sophisticated cadences of the gospel church, bringing the music all back home in a different way. When Dylan met the Staple Singers in 1962, they were unfamiliar with his work, but he knew theirs up and down. He quoted verses from "Sit Down Servant" to them, and demonstrating his deep knowledge of their recordings, said, "Pops, you have this velvet voice, and Mavis, you have this big, robust voice." Dylan was smitten with more than just Mavis's voice. His musical admiration was accompanied by an erotic fixation. "Pops, I want to marry Mavis," Dylan said on film, and contrary to his biographies, he wasn't joking. He actually did ask her to marry him, and according to Staples, "we courted for about seven years, and it was my fault that we didn't go on and get married." Staples said she believed that Dr. King wanted her to "stay black," and it was a decision she would go on to regret. Dylan and Staples did not go on to be the next Johnny Cash and June Carter, but the image of African-American women would haunt his writing. "Outlaw Blues": "I got a woman in Jackson, / I ain't gonna say her name / She's a brown-skin woman, but I love her just the same"; and in a lamentable image, "I Want You": "Well, I return to the Queen of Spades. . . ."

Around the time Dylan was writing about his return to the Queen of Spades, he was also typing out *Tarantula,* his only "novel," and while the book was abandoned and disowned by its author and its random, associative passages do not succeed as experimental prose, it does provide access to the stream-of-consciousness rambling inside Dylan's head in 1966. That was the year it all came crashing down, when his muse was operating at such a frenzied pace that what he couldn't document in the extraordinary songs on the fifteen-month binge of brilliance that produced *Bringing It All Back Home, Highway 61 Revisited,* and *Blonde on Blonde* ended up in prose effluvia under contract with Macmillan. While many jokes, riffs, and half-baked images float around the book, the most constant trope is his worshipful images of black women: "i am just a guitar player—with no absurd fears of her reputation, Black Gal co-exists with melody & I want to feel my evaporation like Black Gal feels her co-existence. . . ."[7] The narrator of *Tarantula,* like the singer of "Spanish Harlem Incident," merges sexual desire with an urge to get inside the meaning of the blues, through an erotic "co-existence." The book's opening line is "aretha / crystal jukebox of hymn and him." This is not "Aretha Franklin" the real person but a dreamlike, archetypal vision of the Queen of Soul, his idealized vision of what Miss Lonely of "Like a Rolling Stone" is not; "aretha" haunts the entire book. "My soulful mama, she keeps me hid," Dylan sang on "From a Buick 6," and the soulful mama of this book keeps the author shrouded as well. *Tarantula,* while never coherent, is consistent in its sexualized images of mixing it up: "aretha-golden sweet / whose nakedness is a piercing thing" (19), "in the winter a blackface musician announces he is from Two Women" (57), "aretha in the blues dunes" (61), "aretha faking her intestinal black soul across all the fertile bubbles & whims & flashy winos" (62). Near the end of the book, "bob dylan," a lowercase version of his own invented persona of the moment, is pronounced dead: "Here lies bob dylan / murdered / from behind / with trembling flesh" (101). But his plans for a black female soul goddess are just beginning as the book ends: "in new york she's known as just plain aretha . . . i shall play her as my trump card" (115). "The Queen of Spades" from "I Want You" is the Queen of Soul trump card of *Tarantula*.

Before Dylan would revisit his worship at the shrine of the black female voice, he would reenter the fray of political songs—a realm he otherwise had relinquished—for two scorching anthems in support of two black men in prison. He wasn't having anything to do with Woodstock Nation, but in 1971 a newspaper article about the shooting of Black Panther George Jackson, gunned down while trying to escape San Quentin, inspired a return to his protest mode of 1963. "Some of us are prisoners, the rest of us are guards," sang Dylan in the single "George Jackson," and he was clearly identifying with the former, aligning himself with a violent, controversial radical figure in a period when he seemed otherwise politically complacent. (The song would never be issued on an album or performed live.) Four years later, Dylan was among the celebrities sent copies of Hurricane Carter's prison memoir, *The Sixteenth Round,* which asserts that he had been framed by a racist judge and jury for a crime he claims he did not commit. There has been much debate and speculation about the veracity of Carter's claim, but Dylan put himself on a mission in the name of a kind of identification: "The first time I saw him, I left knowing one thing . . . I realized that the man's philosophy and my philosophy were running down the same road, and you don't meet too many people like that." In his film *Renaldo and Clara,* a sprawling, improvised account of the Rolling Thunder Revue, there is a section where Dylan is outside the Apollo Theater in Harlem, three decades before his duet with Wynton Marsalis. As an uptown roving reporter, he is seen asking a group of African-American locals on 125th street about the Carter case, and interspersed with a rehearsal take from the song, they all avow his innocence. (This is shown in contrast with a seventy-two-year-old white cop, who tells Dylan he is afraid to express his opinion.) The line is drawn, and Dylan, called a "white brother" by Carter, comes down on the side of the boxer. When Dylan played a benefit for Carter at Rahway Penitentiary in New Jersey, a photo op was staged for *People* magazine. Dylan was wearing whiteface, which he wore throughout the tour as part of the commedia dell'arte ambience. Carter is behind a cage (brought in for the shoot) in shadow, beaming in Dylan's presence. Dylan is looking in, fascinated, driven, a painted vision of artificial whiteness.

The Queens of Rhythm

The years that followed the triumphs of Rolling Thunder were difficult for Dylan. Once he washed off his whiteface makeup, he had to face a marriage that was in ruins. To subsidize his multimillion dollar divorce, he began what became known as his "alimony tour," barnstorming 110 cities in ten countries and commercializing his repertoire with disco arrangements and Neil Diamond–style jumpsuits. Some men get a sports car or a mistress while midlifing; Bob Dylan hired a group of African-American backup singers instead. He appreciated their glitz and decoration, but he also wanted to prove something to the world about his artistic and sexual prowess. "When I got divorced," Dylan said, "I really got divorced." Guitarist Billy Cross recalled that the costumes made the band look like "a large aggregation of pimps," and the singers, ostensibly hired for their gospel cadences, felt a little tarted up. Debi Dye-Gibson, part of the original lineup, recalled, "We looked like hookers. I felt a little stupid singing 'Blowin' in the Wind' with my boobs hanging out." On *Live at Budokan,* recorded near the beginning of the tour, the song "Oh, Sister," from 1975's *Desire,* is transformed from a foreshadowing of religious conversion to a funk-based session of traded moans and groans with his backup singers. "I happen to be one of the supremes," Dylan wrote in the liner notes to *Bringing It All Back Home,* and what seemed like a surrealist non sequitur in 1965 became fate by 1978.

Street Legal was the sonic result of what divorce proceedings, screeching, shouting, the coked-out Rolling Thunder Revue, and plumbing the muse could do to Dylan, who had done everything possible to make his voice sound heavier and more ravaged than his mere thirty-seven years would have otherwise deemed possible. Dylan had been writing songs (never released) with Helena Springs, one of his backup singers and new girlfriend. Robert Christgau would dub the singers "The Dylanettes," after Ray Charles's Raelettes, who secularized the call and response of the gospel church, a soulful mixture of blasphemy and musical genius that made it all the way to the top of the charts. A soulful female chorus accompanied Dylan on tracks from *New Morning* (1971), which came with a back cover of a baby-faced Dylan from 1961 standing shyly and reverentially next to the African-American blues singer Victoria Spivey, with whom he played harmonica on an early record date. But while "Father of Night" and "The Man in Me" were adorned with the oohs and aahs of a female trio, it was not until *Street Legal* and the tour that followed that Dylan finally realized all those obsessive references by having a chorus to talk back to him. "The Changing of the Guards" is cryptic even by Dylan's standards, but the Dylanettes respond to the end of every phrase, for emphasis, drama, a gospel echo chamber: "The captain waits above the celebration / Sending his thoughts to a beloved maid / Whose ebony face is beyond communication." As Dylan sings of a captain in love with an ebon-faced maid, the quartet of Dylanettes sing "ebony face" back at Dylan, adding clarity and emphasis to an opaque song, which ends with "a pale ghost retreating." Dylan is the captain of the tour and the record, but the dialectic gets reversed, an Echo and Narcissus that becomes call and response.

"New Pony," the second song, is more direct. On his way to religious conversion, Dylan is first having an immersion in a blues-based celebration of carnal pleasure, one that, in his version, is expressed in the call and response with a chorus that included his current girlfriend and future wife. "How much longer?" they would sing, repeatedly, like a gospel mantra, while Dylan, basing his blues on a Son House standard, is no longer standing at arm's length from his source material. He is not decorating it with surrealism or Beat poetry, French symbolism, Brecht, or modernism. The guards have changed. "I had a pony / Her name was Lucifer," he sang, foreshadowing the religious conversion to come, but celebrating raunchy, forbidden pleasures, an allusion and a familiar character in blues lyrics. There is the sound of conviction in his voice. Unlike when singing earlier blues, like "Pledging My Time" on *Blonde on Blonde,* he sounds less removed than ever from the genre he plunders. "You're so nasty and you're so bad / But I swear, I love you, yes I do," sings Dylan, goaded on by the chants of "how much longer?" By the end of his "alimony tour," the struggle that would begin as a sexual obsession and musical immersion ended up in religious conversion. By the time he had announced that he realized that "Christ is real," he was getting even further away from the Hibbing bar mitzvah boy he had tried to leave behind before. *Newsweek* caught him in 1963 lying about his name and his upbringing, and putting Abe and Beatty Zimmerman up in a hotel, filled with *nacchus* to see their Robert play at Carnegie Hall. "Never so utterly fake," pronounced Greil Marcus in his *Rolling Stone* review of *Street Legal,* but even under the murky production and Vegas staging, Dylan was trying to get away from the thing he railed against in "Like a Rolling Stone." Charlie Patton's lyrics to "Pony Blues" were already blatant, raw, and racialized: "Well saddle my pony, saddle up my black mare / Baby, saddle my pony, saddle up my black mare." In Dylan's arrangement, modeled on Son House's cover of Patton, he makes a similar entreaty: "Come over here, pony / I wanna ride one time up on you." Dylan is no longer raging against Miss Lonely, who could never be an actual rolling stone. He is fusing his sexual desire with his artistic and ethnic aspirations. On "New Pony," with Helena Springs in tow, he was trying to channel his inner Son House, attempting to find credibility through sex, drugs, racial appropriation, and, eventually, the Bible.

Although Dylan offered many explanations for why he became a Christian by the end of the alimony tour—including a cross thrown on stage by a fan and an encounter with Jesus in a Tucson hotel room—Springs pointed to a conversation with Dylan in which she asked him, "Do you ever pray?" He eventually did, producing a trio of Christian albums—*Slow Train Coming* (1979), *Saved* (1980), and *Shot of Love* (1981)—that preached the word of God with soul inflections. "You gotta serve somebody," he sang on his first Grammy Award–winning single, sounding a little like an adenoidal Al Green. The song would go down in the disco with a message for the prayer meeting, while he is goaded on by the chorus of Dylanettes repeating the line, "serve somebody." He was, he sang, property of Jesus, but his heart still belonged to backup muses. A line from the title track of *Slow Train Coming* suggested a spiritual sequel to "New Pony": "I had a woman down in Alabama, / She was a backwoods girl, but she sure was realistic," he sang in the Alabama recording studio. "Don't wanna be with nobody tonight / Veronica not here, Mavis just ain't right," sang Dylan on the title track of *Shot of Love* (1981). The shot of love was a spiritual injection, but his paradigm for fulfillment was still summed up with the name "Mavis."

By 1986, he had christened the chorus the Queens of Rhythm. One of his backup singers, Carolyn Dennis, became his secret wife and gave birth to a daughter, Desiree. Another, Madelyn Quebec, was his secret mother-in-law. Dylan would often jokingly introduce the singers as, "My ex-wife, my next wife, my girlfriend, and my fiancée." This was not mere hyperbole.

In the 1980s, his most erratic musical decade, Dylan was at his most inspired when guided by the muse of racial guilt. In "Blind Willie McTell," a song so powerful that Dylan perversely left it off *Infidels* in 1983, Dylan stood in deference to the blues master of the song's title, venerating McTell's authenticity in contrast to his glammed-up Queens of Rhythm, and, ultimately, his own artifice: "Them charcoal gypsy maidens / Can strut their feathers well / But nobody can sing the blues / Like Blind Willie McTell." Charcoal, like burnt cork, was commonly used by white minstrel performers blacking themselves up. Dylan's use of *charcoal* suggests that he is not only singing about actual black women wearing ruffled feathers but perhaps also minstrel singers with charcoal-smeared faces, imitating and appropriating the blues, which, in Dylan's hierarchical system, McTell does better than anyone else. He is surely aware that authenticity is a fetish, but like Judge Woosley's definition of pornography, he knows it when he hears it. "Blind Willie McTell" is a musical mea culpa like none other, one that saw the light of day only because it had been out on the street anyway. He had searched for salvation through African-American vernacular and was returning with a wearied response. On the song, he played "St. James Infirmary Blues" changes, but while he sang about being unworthy, he created a stunning portrait of plantations, whips, "the ghost of slavery ships," and the rock star's plundering. He was paying respect and laying down his own weary tune, a complicated story about how the blues can be translated all the way from New Orleans to Jerusalem and back again. The song is based on the haunting descending chords of "St. James Infirmary Blues," a song about eros, mourning, and melancholia, looking on a dead lover's corpse in an age of syphilis, inimitably rendered in Louis Armstrong's 1928 recording. "I'm staring out the window of the St. James Hotel / And I know no one can sing the blues like Blind Willie McTell," Dylan sang, cashing in his cultural debt. The St. James Hotel is a place where a rock star can hang his hat for the night before playing a stadium gig, a temporary resting place. McTell's blues are forever.

Three years later, in "Brownsville Girl," the Queens of Rhythm purr, croon, and map the dramatic action of a song in search of something real in a world gone wrong, or at least one where the stars had been torn down. "Now I know she ain't you but she's here and she's got that dark rhythm in her soul," he sang, essentializing the hell out of his clandestine betrothed while she provided soulful sustenance in the background. And yet he gives way to their voices. He sings, "Hang on to me, baby, and let's hope that the roof stays on," and they scream in response. The Queens of Rhythm helped him get righteous until he could strike through the mask himself, owning up to the racial hybrid he was striving to be all along. "Brownsville Girl" was a high point in an otherwise fallow period for Dylan. In *Chronicles*, he recalled taking a break from a listless rehearsal with the Grateful Dead in California in 1987, the year after "Brownsville Girl," and wandering off to a jazz dive, where an old black singer got under his skin. "The singer reminded me of Billy Eckstine," Dylan recalled. "He wasn't very forceful, but he didn't have to be; he was relaxed, but he sang with natural power. Suddenly and without warning, it was like the guy had an open window to my soul. It was like he was saying, 'You should do it this way.'" Dylan had a revelation that he didn't need to strain to hit notes coming from a younger man's angst long eviscerated by nicotine and howling. Later that year, his mystical encounters with black vocalists continued when he realized, on a foggy night in Switzerland, that he could deliver what the Queens of Rhythm had been providing for him: "It's almost like I heard a voice. It wasn't like it was even me thinking it. *I'm determined to stand whether God will deliver me or not.* And all of a sudden everything just exploded. It exploded every which way. And I noticed that all the people out there—I was used to them looking at the girl singers, they were good-looking girls, you know? And like I say, I had them up there so I wouldn't feel so bad. But when that happened, nobody was looking at the girls anymore. They were looking at the main mike. And that is when I sort of knew: I've got to go out and play these songs. That's just what I must do."[8] Once Dylan found his inner soul sister, the Queens of Rhythm lost a gig.

The High Muddy Waters

The older Dylan became, the more he lost the upper part of his vocal range, the more he would lean on blues inflections; age would make him the grizzled blues man he had aspired to be back when he was belting out Bukka White covers on those early busking days on Bleecker Street. Dylan told many tall tales to Nat Hentoff in the liner notes to *The Freewheelin' Bob Dylan,* but he was being sincere when he said, "I don't carry myself yet the way that Big Joe Williams, Woody Guthrie, Leadbelly and Lightnin' Hopkins have carried themselves. I hope to be able to someday, but they're older people." As the years went on, he would acknowledge his subjectivity while gaining authority at the same time. He named his 2001 album *"Love and Theft"* after Eric Lott's 1993 study of blackface minstrelsy, and he made it clear, in his way, why the subject of the book generated the response. "Every time you hear an expansive white man drop into his version of black English, you are witnessing minstrelsy's unconscious return," wrote Lott.[9] In Dylan's case, the return was as conscious as possible, and Dylan has made his audience more conscious of it as well; by the time he used the title, he had become one with the "charcoal gypsy maidens" strutting their feathers well. After he saturated his 2002 film *Masked and Anonymous* (based on a screenplay he cowrote, of course, under a pseudonym) with minstrel images (including a blacked-up Ed Harris who asks Dylan's character Jack Fate, "Do you remember me?"), he brought the mask of minstrelsy up to the surface, haunted by its history, fascinated by its legacy.

"I've been wading through the high muddy waters," Dylan sang on "Tryin' to Get to Heaven" in 1997. By then, he sounded like he had finally arrived; on his way, he shared a stage with Waters himself. The year was 1975, a decade after "Like a Rolling Stone" railed against Miss Lonely and her Waters pretensions. At New York's Bottom Line, Dylan, invited to play harmonica at a Waters show, was up on stage with the real thing. Flanked by a near-suicide Phil Ochs on one side and blues diva Victoria Spivey on the other, he was still cultivating the ad hoc club atmosphere that would become his Rolling Thunder Review. Waters knew someone important was backstage, pimping out the entourage and generating the buzz, but he didn't know who it was. Waters announced to the audience, "We have a special guest on harmonica. Please give a nice round of acclause (that's how Muddy pronounced applause and no one ever corrected him) for…JOHN DYLAN." A few people clapped politely until guitarist Bob Margolin staged whispered in Waters's ear, "His name is Bob, like my name—Bob Dylan." Waters then repeated, "Bob Dylan!" as if he had said it for the first time, inspiring pandemonium. Whether Waters was pulling a fast one on Dylan or not, Dylan probably wanted to get as far away from himself as he could at that moment. He was face-to-face with his metaphor, and his metaphor claimed not to know who he was. But Dylan knew fully well who Waters was, and was happy just to blow his harp in the background, trying to summon his inner rolling stone while he watched the man himself at work. After nearly half a century of imitating, protesting, loving, and thieving, he is still trying to earn his right to sing the blues. A lyric about mortality from 1997 could also apply to his transformation: He's not dark yet, but he's getting there.

Notes

1. Monk may have been intentionally echoing a statement made by Louis Armstrong: "All music is folk music."

2. Bob Dylan, *Chronicles, Volume 1* (New York: Simon and Schuster, 2004), 94–95.

3. Robert Shelton, *No Direction Home: The Life and Music of Bob Dylan* (New York: Da Capo, 2003), 179.

4. Ibid., 201.

5. Nat Hentoff, "The Crackin', Shakin', Breakin' Sounds," *The New Yorker,* October 24, 1964, in *Studio A: The Bob Dylan Reader,* ed. Benjamin Hedin (New York: Norton, 2004).

6. Wilson would eventually be replaced by Bob Johnston.

7. Bob Dylan, *Tarantula* (1971; New York: St. Martin's Press, 1994), 115; subsequent page references are given parenthetically in the text.

8. All quotations from Dylan, *Chronicles.*

9. Eric Lott, *Love and Theft: Blackface Minstrelsy and the American Working Class* (New York: Oxford University Press, 1995), 5.

17. "Nettie Moore":
Minstrelsy and the Cultural Economy of Race
in Bob Dylan's Late Albums
Robert Reginio

A particularly fascinating "controversy" surrounding Bob Dylan's 2006 album *Modern Times* was the discovery that Dylan has been since at least 2001's *"Love and Theft"* a concerted borrower from the poetry of Henry Timrod, the "Poet Laureate of the Confederacy."[1] In his 2003 film *Masked and Anonymous,* whose setting is a future America gripped by civil war, Dylan references a much more popular piece of Confederate culture by performing "Dixie" with his band. Ultimately, that Dylan is making reference—obscure or otherwise—to the American Civil War should not be surprising at this point. One of the more striking self-portraits Dylan draws in his recent memoir *Chronicles, Volume 1* is that of the young Bob Dylan supplementing his observation of various folk artists in New York City with what can be described as an obsessive study of the New York Public Library's archive of Civil War–era American newspapers. As he writes in *Chronicles,* during the Civil War "America was put on the cross, died, and was resurrected.... The godawful truth of that would be the all-encompassing template behind everything that I would write."[2] In this essay at least, I will take Dylan at his word.

I propose to read Dylan in his latest work as a self-critical historian. This means that rather than seeing his allusions to the culture of nineteenth-century America as a revision or retelling of American history, I will show how he is concerned with *how* the American past gets told and retold. And it is his song "Nettie Moore," from *Modern Times,* that will occupy my attention in this critical endeavor. "Nettie Moore" is an emotionally affecting and amazingly complex meditation on Dylan's own love and theft of American popular music. "Nettie Moore" borrows its title and its refrain from a song written by the minstrel performer and songwriter Marshall S. Pike, who served as a drum major in the Twenty-second Massachusetts Regiment during the Civil War.[3] Like Dylan's theft of Timrod's poetry, his reference to this obscure song—especially in the context of the song's other, more obvious references to folk and blues poetry—is, as Robert Polito has recently argued, "just the tantalizing threshold into Dylan's vast memory palace of echoes."[4] Polito's metaphor is apt here because

Dylan's use of fragments from the past does not add up to some unified vision of the past, but rather opens up a labyrinthine series of interpretive possibilities for the questioning listener. For so many to cry plagiarism in regard to Dylan's "use" of Timrod's work—since the poetry is so obscure—you might not guess, writes Polito, "that we've just lived through some two and a half decades of hip hop sampling, not only to mention a century of Modernism."[5] Dylan recognizes that the innovative, creative fire that fueled his songwriting in the 1960s is long past, and perhaps more importantly, he has come to grips with the fact that every lyric he writes will be squeezed to within an inch of its exegetical life for political, poetical, theological, or ethical meaning. Therefore, to sprinkle stray phrases from "the Poet Laureate of the Confederacy" across songs that often lilt and warble like Victorian parlor ballads is to play with his audience yet again, creating an allusive, textual trail of bread crumbs that leads not to Milton, nor Shakespeare, nor Robert Johnson—but to Henry Timrod's overwrought Romantic verse and its frequent, strident defense of the Confederacy and, necessarily, its oppressive, racial economy.

On the one hand this is funny—Timrod is no Milton or Robert Johnson ("That's what you get for your obsessive reading," Dylan might be saying). On the other hand, Dylan recognizes that American popular music is the story of white America's "love" of black culture, a culture shaped by manifold acts of thievery. A reference to Timrod plugs the reader/listener back into the stream of subterranean, yet ubiquitous, acts of racial "love and theft" that flow through American popular song. That Dylan achieves this through a set of metatextual gestures reveals his recognition of his position within contemporary culture and his uncanny ability to create great art despite the seeming claustrophobia of this prominent position.

What I will say about "Nettie Moore" and the way it references nineteenth- and early-twentieth-century music can be applied to the rest of *Modern Times, "Love and Theft,"* and even 1997's *Time Out of Mind*. In these albums, borrowing becomes something not only endemic to the songs' style, but frequently this borrowing is the thematic focus of the songs themselves. In "Nettie Moore," this self-consciousness resonates with America's vexed racial history. Instead of summarizing how Dylan's allusive late style comes to a boil on the album *"Love and Theft,"* I will quote someone more acquainted with minstrelsy and Dylan's "thieving" predilections. Eric Lott, the writer from whom Dylan "borrowed" the title for *"Love and Theft,"* has said of Dylan:

> He knows full well his musical indebtedness and is playing with it in the songs as well as the title of *"Love and Theft."* "High Water" sounds most like the actual minstrel show music from the 19th century, which is interesting not only since it's dedicated specifically to black blues singer Charley Patton but also because it's a song of high seriousness, as though ultimate truths are rooted in cultural plunder.[6]

The mixing of "low" subject matter and the tones of "high seriousness" is something Walt Whitman appreciated in the minstrel show. As Whitman wrote in the mid-1840s of a particular minstrel performance:

> Indeed, their "nigger" singing altogether proves how shiningly golden talent can be spread over a subject generally considered "low." "Nigger" singing with them is a subject from obscure life in the hands of a divine painter: rags, patches, and coarseness are imbued with the great genius of the artist, and there exists something really great about them.[7]

The difference, of course, between Dylan's combination of minstrelsy with "high seriousness" and Whitman's praise of this popular art form is the recognition of the suffering underwriting the "great genius" of the minstrel artist. The significance of minstrelsy (both its cultural significance and minstrelsy as a "sign" in American culture) lies in what Lott called minstrelsy's

> unstable or indeed contradictory power, linked to social and political conflicts, that issues from the weak, the uncanny, the outside. [T]he slippery political valences of the [minstrel] tradition . . . are instructive. For it was with precisely this slipperiness that the minstrel mask resonated: a derisive celebration of the power of blackness; blacks, for a moment, ambiguously, on top.[8]

For Whitman, authenticity is something achieved through the mastery of performance; for Dylan, performance is just that—a "performance" of authenticity that, of course, destabilizes the very notion of authenticity. As Lott argued at a conference on Dylan at Dartmouth College, authenticity is a "ridiculous" notion in thinking about Dylan's late work. Dylan is daring us to accuse him of theft by layering his explicit allusions above his series of more veiled pilfering.[9] In his late works, this daring points us to the love and theft that energizes American culture. Paradoxically, as Lott was quick to mention in his Dylan presentation, this energy also thrives on the oppressive systems that allowed (and allow today) these (crossings of) racial boundaries in the first place. If authenticity is a "ridiculous" notion, then Lott's provocative question—"When does minstrelsy end and original invention begin?"—is not to be resolved. "There is no transcending the paradoxes of minstrelsy by sheer force of will," he insisted.[10] Dylan's will, tempered by intimations of mortality and a lifetime spent in a memory palace of echoes, finds its inspiration now in the paradoxes that constitute American culture and the economies of race that define it.

Glimpses of this paradox emerge clearly in 1984's "Blind Willie McTell," a song inexplicably left off the album *Infidels* and a song Christopher Ricks inexplicably understands through the prism of "Envy" and "Gratitude." In Ricks's reading of the song, the distances of history and race are transcended by art.[11] "Blind Willie McTell" (the song, not the singer) is in fact, contra Ricks's reductive reading, an elegiac meditation on the paradoxical source of McTell's art. The third verse is a good example of the song's structure:

> See them big plantations burning,
> Hear the cracking of the whips;
> Smell that sweet magnolia blooming.
> See the ghosts of slavery ships.

> I can hear them tribes moaning,
> hear the undertaker's bell.
> And I know no one can sing the blues
> Like Blind Willie McTell.[12]

The song works by juxtaposing McTell's art and the violence that had a significant part in its creation; the summation that "no one can sing the blues like Blind Willie McTell"—repeated at the end of each verse—represents knowledge that is yet unable to account for the suffering toward which McTell's art continually draws the singer. With each repetition of the refrain, the singer becomes more and more bewildered by his implication in the economy of race, the way each act of love, appreciation, and perhaps even gratitude contains within them the shadow of theft. To be grateful for McTell's art—which one can be—is nevertheless to elide that art's history. And it is as a historian perplexed by this history that Dylan writes "Nettie Moore," a song that can be seen as a development of the theme and the form of "Blind Willie McTell."

But before turning exclusively to Dylan's "Nettie Moore," I want to return to Whitman's comments on minstrel performers I quoted above. Whitman's appreciation of minstrelsy was written specifically about a performance by the minstrel group the Harmoneons that took place at the Chatham Theater in lower Manhattan in the 1840s. Marshall S. Pike, a singer and performer with the group, wrote the lyrics for most of the songs in the Harmoneons' repertoire, and he wrote the lyrics to the original "Nettie Moore," also known as "The Little White Cottage." The song is sung from the perspective of a male African-American slave. The singer recalls listening to "the gentle voice of charming Nettie Moore" and how "on the Santee's dancing tide / Of a summer eve I'd launch my open boat; / [And] down the river we so merrily would float."[13] The crux of the song lies in what else the river enables:

> One sunny morn in autumn
> Ere the dew had left the lawn,
> Came a trader up from Louisiana-bay;
> Who gave to Master money
> And then shackl'd her with chains,
> Then he took her off to work her life away.[14]

Pike attempts to exploit the pathos of this inversion of the image of the river as a place of solitude, refuge, and escape. Dylan borrows, antiquated elision and all, the refrain of the original "Gentle Nettie Moore": "Oh, I miss you Nettie Moore, / And my happiness is o'er."[15] The refrain in Pike's song is the lament of a slave who is powerless to control the direction of his life, to keep safe the integrity of his family, and to find a public history in which this loss can be voiced. If Whitman heard this song performed at the Chatham Theater, this last point would have been clearly visible since the singer of Pike's song would have been "spoken for" by a white performer in blackface. When Dylan returns to, or recycles, or recovers, this song, he is thinking about the performance of grief and of loss in African-American culture, and how these performances—found most readily in the blues itself—were necessarily the product of the "theft" of African people and the erasure of their history.

The preface to *The Harmoneons' Casket of Songs and Glees* explains why the group felt impelled to publish their songs' lyrics (almost exclusively written by Pike) and not the music. The author of the preface writes that the songs' melodies were already well known in 1850 and that this in fact has spread the group's renown (we, too, seem to be more comfortable with a hip-hop producer lifting a James Brown beat break than we are with Dylan lifting lines from Timrod). Ironically, he explains, they have published this book of minstrel show lyrics because

> several of the Harmoneons' Songs and Glees have from time to time found their way, by stealth, into various books throughout the country without the publishers awarding to the rightful authors their just dues . . . and where, not in a few instances, the words have been transcribed from the correct printed copy-right sheet, without any attention whatever to grammar, rhythm, or originality; and also where, in one case certainly, if not more, plagiarism was committed by adopting a complete couplet, and claiming the whole theme, without reference or quotation.[16]

The irony in terms of Dylan's "theft" is self-evident, but it is telling that for Pike, his impersonation—in his writing and his performance—of "blackness" is something authentic, something that can be copied but is not a "copy" itself.[17] It seems utterly unambiguous to the author here (who is probably Marshall Pike himself) where original invention ends and where cultural plunder begins. One can read Dylan's "Nettie Moore" as a recovery and reanimation of the ambiguity that exists for us between the sentiments of Pike's preface and the sometimes crass, sometimes admiring stereotyping in the "black" songs contained within the volume. In other words, I see Dylan's "Nettie Moore" as a recovery of the history of Pike's "Gentle Nettie Moore." I do not want to suggest, however, that Dylan's "Nettie Moore" is some sort of compensation for, or an unproblematic recovery of, The Harmoneons' and Pike's theft of "blackness." Rather, Dylan's song is fully aware that it is difficult—if not impossible—to tell where loving recovery ends and cultural theft begins.

Dylan's lyrics are framed by a funereal, insistent drum beat that is overlaid with the song's melodic rise and fall; this rise and fall prepares our ears for the alternating, competing tones of the verses to follow, for the tension between a clear dramatic through-line (the drum beat), and the complexities of the song's intertextuality (the melody's rise and quizzical fall). Dylan begins by singing in a rising tone a line from the famous folk song "Lost John": "Lost John sittin' on a railroad track." Immediately, though, he sings "somethin's out of whack" with the perplexed falling portion of the verse's melody. It is as if the singer is well prepared to sit down with Lost John, the character, or to sing "Lost John" the song, but he is suddenly interrupted. Something is out of whack; something isn't quite right. The singer tries to sing another song from the folk and blues repertoire. He tries again to inhabit the past, this time singing an equally famous line from Robert Johnson: "Blues this mornin' fallin' down like hail." Again, the singer is interrupted; we get the non sequitur "Gonna leave a greasy trail."[18] In the song's title and first verse Dylan is flaunting the fact that he is writing from within the vast archive of American song. He is not engaged in the "folk process" as much as he is dramatizing it, commenting on it, questioning it, or—more compellingly—he feels forced to question this turn to the past.

The second verse suggests a more archetypal hero or antihero and his quest, but the third verse undercuts this sort of narrative and its implication of a single, unifying point of view. "I'm the oldest son of a crazy man," he sings, something a Faulknerian antihero might mutter. Faulkner, like Dylan in *Modern Times,* is a writer who weaves together the imagery of ornate antebellum Romanticism and the ironies attendant upon the modernist's contemplation of the problems of race. The next line, ("I'm in a cowboy band") sung with a wonderfully ironic—even bitter—deflation on the album, is like a splash of cold water in the face.[19] "I'm no Faulknerian hero," he seems to say, "I'm a 65-year-old guy wearing a big, white cowboy hat in 2006." A mask does not fall away; the contrivances of masks and masking become evident.

In the chorus, Pike's song is evoked but not like the echoes of "Lost John" or Robert Johnson, since Pike's song is much more obscure. It was not part of the 1960s folk revival repertoire,[20] and the song seems constructed to make the listener wonder who Nettie Moore is as Dylan sings that he misses her. Once the history of this song has been uncovered, things become more, not less, ambiguous: "Nettie Moore" as a character whose absence is mourned, like the African-Americans minstrelsy was supposed to "comprehend," is inaccessible through the history that speaks for her. The putative singer of Pike's song, the African Americans ambiguously figured as "the weak, the uncanny, the outside" through the traditions of minstrelsy, emerge fleetingly at the chorus's conclusion: "winter's gone / the river's on the rise." A rising river has ominous undertones, and the coming of spring cannot be connected to the cyclical turn of the seasons since these cycles have regenerative meaning only within a community. If anything, the singer of Dylan's song is utterly alone. Dylan sings, "I loved you then and ever shall" in a way that fractures the line with a pause between "then" and "and." With this line, the past is fractured from the future as well; the present moment is itself an empty gap. The last two lines of the chorus are also shaped by a fracturing pause: "But there's no one here left to tell / The world has gone black before my eyes."[21] The last line of the chorus, and thus the eventual last line of the song, is one of utter solitude; it is as close as Dylan gets to voicing something like the blues of Blind Willie McTell or something of the losses written into and implicated in Pike's song. It is a "telling" that is not—"there's no one here" for the singer to speak to, but there is also no witness to the darkness that has engulfed the singer (in other words, "There's no one here who can tell—who can intuit—that I'm gripped by this darkness"). The song's intertextuality lends this solitude special significance: Dylan is singing of the lost voices implied by but also occluded by the love and theft that generated American song.

The revelation that in America communication is contingent upon interpretive communities frequently defined by race is a version of the "double-consciousness" W. E. B. Du Bois described as a unique burden for African Americans. As Du Bois famously wrote,

> the Negro is a sort of seventh son, born with a veil, and gifted with second-sight in this American world—a world which yields him no true self-consciousness, but only lets him see himself through the revelation of the other world. It is peculiar sensation, this double-consciousness, this sense of always looking at one's self through the eyes of others.[22]

With this paradoxical way of seeing in mind, one can understand the singer in Dylan's song as partaking of both aspects of this perspective. The singer is both perceptive of the way identities are contingent in racialized America (he plays the vengeful pedagogue in one line: "I'm gonna make you come to grips with fate") and, like Du Bois's African American, is hidden behind a veil, something suggested by the chorus's insistence that "the world has gone black before my eyes," something that is difficult—if not impossible—to articulate to another ("there's no one here left to tell / the world has gone black before my eyes.")

The juxtapositions taking place from line to line in "Nettie Moore" and the juxtaposition between the ironies of the song's verses and the more direct plaintiveness of the chorus are versions of the juxtaposition between each verse and the refrain of "Blind Willie McTell." But unlike "Blind Willie McTell," which is itself a long crescendo of grief, "Nettie Moore" is a more ambiguous mix of "textual" indeterminacy and affecting emotion, something mirrored in the ruminative ascent and quizzical descent that structures the song's melody. The chorus of the song contrasts the grief of the past and the intractable confusion elicited by the seemingly irredeemable nature of that loss in the mind of the song's author. The singer is at once sitting by the little white cottage, pining for his wife who has been sold; he is recalling or citing Pike's attempt to wrest emotion from the forms of minstrelsy (which thus reveals that the slave pining for his lover in Pike's original is but a white figuration and exploitation of black grief); and the singer is thus ultimately left looking back through these "textual" layers and the great distances he perceives from the vantage point of "modern times." "Oh, I miss you Nettie Moore!" The grief in this refrain is layered; Dylan at once inhabits the longing of Pike's original song, but he also laments the fact that "Nettie Moore" (the object of longing in the refrain) is a cipher for those who had and have no voice. Dylan is able to find great emotion and pathos in the futility of searching through his American sources. He is dramatizing the most basic—and perhaps most unselfconsciously enacted—processes of American culture.

If Dylan is uncovering Pike's "Nettie Moore," then he uncovers that song's central, doubled vacancy: Nettie's absence after she is sold to another master and the absence upon which every representation in minstrelsy was founded. The way that the song opens a set of vacancies, like a Russian doll, comes out clearly in the next verse:

> Well, the world of research has gone berserk.
> Too much paperwork.
> Albert's in the graveyard, Frankie's raising hell.
> I'm beginning to believe what the scriptures tell.[23]

Here the singer is buried under leaves of texts: songs, newspapers, histories, and notes. There seems to be no end in sight. Frankie and Albert—a recognizable allusion—reenact the drama of their song; "scriptures" in this verse refers not only to biblical texts but to texts in general. Belief, in "Nettie Moore," is a willful ignorance of the theft that underlies each act of love in the racial economy of America's culture. To "believe" in Frankie and Albert—in Jesus, Lost John, or Nettie herself—is an essential part of this economy. In this verse, the singer retreats from textuality and its multiple indeterminacies and insists that "scriptures" of all sorts speak directly through the layers of history without any mediation.

> I'm goin' to where the Southern crosses the Yellow Dog.
> Get away from all these demagogues.
> And these bad luck women stick like glue.
> It's either one or the other or neither of the two.[24]

This following verse underscores the singer's trajectory: away from the present, entombed in texts and history, toward a less problematic past: the mythologized landscape of the blues tradition. Yet the singer also wants (perhaps quixotically) to be free of the "demagoguery" that obscures the complexities of history under a veil of crass emotionalism. The last line of the verse suggests a choice between the "scriptures" of society's demagogues and the "scriptures" of underground, fugitive culture and song (the blues trope of "bad luck women" countering the dominant strains of demagoguery).

Interestingly, the singer ultimately rejects refuge of any sort. In the next verse he cites (again) another scrap from the tradition of blues poetry (and references a song, "Moonshiner," Dylan played in his early years): "They say whisky'll kill you, but I don't think it will. / I'm ridin' with you to the top of the hill."[25] In a place of disbelief and doubt, the song does not rest, the insistent drum beat goes on, demagogues are feared, but the myths and tropes of the blues do not offer a place of timeless refuge. The singer seems to reject belief in "scriptures" and "texts" of all sorts.

Duplicity is rendered in terms familiar to the blues tradition in the next verse; the singer realizes his woman is dolling herself up for another man. He decides to swallow his pride and let it go, but it is tough to eat all of that duplicity in one sitting:

> Don't know why my baby never looked so good before.
> Don't have to wonder no more.
> She been cooking all day, gonna take me all night.
> I can't eat all that stuff in a single bite.[26]

And in this realm of disbelief and solitude the following verse's invocation of a judge is less significant than the ambivalent gesture that meets the appearance of this potential demagogue: "The judge is coming in, everybody rise. / Lift up your eyes."[27] Do we lift up our eyes in the hope that justice might finally be rendered, or is this a gesture of abject supplication? For a member of the dominant white culture, a black-robed judge is an emblem of justice, but for a black American, this emblem was (is?) a farcical presumption of justice. Is this an entreaty to join in a moment of communal hopefulness as the judge enters? Is this an imperative to offer up a requisite gesture of fealty to this figure of authority? Or is this a whispered bit of advice from a person who has been through the system before to another prisoner standing in the dock? Despite the different registers in which this gesture could be read (from the humble and respectful to the equivocal or counterfeit), the figure of the judge remains a powerfully ambiguous one. In the possible historical contexts of the song and in the context clearly established by its allusions to African-American culture, the biblical imagery taken up once again by Dylan here is neither apocalyptic nor positing a determinate judge, arbiter, or guiding force for history in this world or the next. In a historical continuum that is yet vacant of teleological structure and meaning, the singer goes as far to cancel out any "advice" his words might carry. In another, witty reference to one of his own songs, he asks his listener to think twice before speaking: "You can do what you please, you don't need my advice / 'Fore you call me any dirty names, you better think twice."[28] The hesitation of the song's first verses (where "Lost John," the song, just cannot get started) can be seen as an instance of the singer thinking twice, and it is the experience of this hesitation that is the only legacy the singer has to pass on to his listener.

The final verses of the song are powerful evocations of ambivalence, of hope cresting, dying off, and then vanishing, and they contain the dire vision of solitude that cuts through all of the song's many layers and intertexts:

> The bright spark of the steady lights
> Has dimmed my sights.
> When you're around me all my grief gives way.
> A lifetime with you is like some heavenly day.[29]

Lifetimes encompassed by single "heavenly" days seems to be something the singer does not quite believe. (It echoes the conclusion of Pike's "Gentle Nettie Moore: "But when weary life is past, / I shall meet you once again, / In Heaven—darling, up above the skies.")[30] The lines preceding this compress into them the ambivalence upon which the song is centered: "steady" lights that nevertheless "spark" up brightly could refer to a lighthouse and its intermittent illumination, but this line does not crystallize into a determinate image. Lights are flashing but are not fixed. Indeed, the singer's "sights" are dimmed by the alternating "spark" and darkness that briefly illuminates and then shadows his journey. It is getting too dark to see. "Grief" giving way compounds this verse's ambivalence. His grief seems to vanish, but it also slips out of his control, it "gives way," spilling out like the uncontainable, rising rivers that course through many of the songs on *Modern Times*.

"Everything I've ever known to be right has been proven wrong"; this is perhaps the most unadorned, and most affecting, line of the entire song. It speaks for the imagined singer of Pike's song, a slave whose God gave Moses the mantle and power of an earthly liberator, but who withholds his judgment in the present. It speaks for the singer/author of "Nettie Moore," a singer who is sustained by African-American culture, but whose journey through this culture's various texts uncovers—at every step—the unredeemed acts of theft that likewise shaped the culture. This is not "white guilt," but a profound expression of the way American history can never truly speak of or account for the amnesia forced upon (and the physical theft of) African Americans.

The singer of Pike's song and the historian/singer of Dylan's song speak together in the powerful last verse:

> Today I'll stand in faith and raise
> The voice of praise.
> The sun is strong, I'm standing in the light.
> I wish to God that it were night.[31]

Like eyes lifted to the judge, voices raised in praise must come down (again, the melody and the enjambment of the first two lines—rare in this song—brilliantly carry this terminal gravity across the song). Raising the voice of praise could be lip service, it could be a faithful, yet fruitless, gesture. The desire to hide, to find refuge—a central theme of the song—triumphs over belief. This could be the fugitive slave seeking the refuge of shadows, and it could be the desire of the sinner for shelter from God's wrathful storm. But another intertext emerges here that points us to the theme of racial oppression and the way religious or cultural myths are undermined by such oppression. In his *Songs of Innocence*, William Blake also paradoxically enfolded the desire for justice into the desire for refuge from justice. In "The Little Black Boy" a black mother tries to pass on not just spiritual knowledge to her son, but she attempts to help her son try and bear the burdens of racial oppression:

> And we are put on earth a little space
> That we may learn to bear the beams of love;
> And these black bodies and this sunburnt face
> Is but a cloud, and like a shady grove.
> For when our souls have learned the heat to bear
> The cloud will vanish, we shall hear his voice
> Saying: "Come out from the grove, my love and care,
> And round my golden tent like lambs rejoice!"[32]

As in Dylan's song, light—the most elemental of tropes, signifying wisdom, justice, and goodness—is a form of darkness. To be able to "raise the voice of praise" from within a very real system that denies one the most basic forms of justice is critiqued in Blake's and Dylan's songs. Light is a burden to bear, something to flee from—no alchemizing will turn the bitter light of "justice" into the idealized light of God's love, nor will the alchemizing art of the song and dance man (evident in songs like

Pike's "Gentle Nettie Moore," or "Frankie and Albert," or a song by Robert Johnson) transcend the theft that lies buried at the core of each American act of love that crosses racial and cultural lines. The most basic law of Dylan's "Nettie Moore" is that any upward-tending moment of transcendence ("Today I'll stand in faith and raise") must submit to the inexorable gravity of history (evident in the ironic way Dylan sings "—the voice of praise"). But the song's power comes in its chorus, where despite this gravity, Dylan sings, and sings without irony, the plaintive lament of a slave while understanding fully that this slave—and his object of desire—were fashioned by a white minstrel performer.

As a comment on Dylan's current method of composition, "Nettie Moore" lends ruminative and emotional weight to debates or arguments about sources and citation that unfortunately have tended to be rendered in the banality of legal terms, in cries of "plagiarism," and in responses that defend Dylan's "folk process"—neither of these responses is appropriate to this major work. In this song, Dylan accedes to the fact that in American culture, every moment of border crossing, every moment where the boundaries of race are transcended, is a moment that reinscribes those boundaries: every act of love an act of theft.

Notes

I would like to thank Andrew Muir and John Morris for editorial support and helpful suggestions while writing this piece.

1. Motoko Rich, "Who's This Guy Dylan Who's Borrowing Lines from Henry Timrod?" *New York Times,* September 14, 2006, E1.

2. Bob Dylan, *Chronicles, Volume 1* (New York: Simon and Schuster, 2004), 86.

3. Duke University Libraries, "Music Library Personal Papers and Research Collections," 2006, http://library.duke.edu/music/collections/personal.html (accessed September 3, 2007).

4. Robert Polito, "Henry Timrod Revisited," Poetry Foundation, 2006, http://www.poetryfoundation.org/archive/feature.html?id=178703 (accessed September 3, 2007).

5. Ibid.

6. David McNair and Jayson Whitehead, "Love and Theft," Gadfly Online, 2001, http://www.gadflyonline.com/12–10–01/book-ericlott.html (accessed September 3, 2007).

7. Walt Whitman, *Uncollected Poetry and Prose,* vol. 1 (New York: P. Smith, 1992), 236.

8. Eric Lott, *Love and Theft: Blackface Minstrelsy and the American Working Class* (New York: Oxford University Press, 1993), 29.

9. Eric Lott, "Love and Theft and 'Love and Theft': Just like Jack Frost Blues: Mask and Melancholia in 'Love and Theft,'" presentation made August 12, 2006, at the conference "Just a Series of Interpretations of Bob Dylan's Lyrical Works," Dartmouth College.

10. Ibid.

11. Although Ricks mentions the intertwining of suffering and art in Dylan's song, any historical suffering vanishes from the reader's mind since Ricks focuses on timeless virtues and vices and how art crosses the more quotidian boundaries of the historical. For example, he writes that "Blind Willie McTell's" refrain "endearingly combines the superlative and the highly individual, without having to enter competitively into the proportions of the one to the other. Perfectly judged, and determined to do justice to McTell. More, determined to see

and hear justice done at last to him" (74). Ricks's elision of the historical in his reading allows him to imply an equivalence between Dylan's judgment of McTell's art and the "justice" that can never quite be reached in the case of slavery in America. More evidently, Ricks's ahistorical reading is perplexingly deaf to the song's bleak tone, one that, as I argue, the repetition of the song's refrain underscores, the singer voicing his frustrated grief at the realization of the immense suffering that gave birth to the blues in general and McTell's art specifically; Christopher Ricks, *Dylan's Visions of Sin* (London: Viking 2003).

12. Bob Dylan, "Blind Willie McTell," 1983, Bob Dylan, http://bobdylan.com/moderntimes/songs/mctell.html (accessed September 3, 2007).

13. Marshall S. Pike, "The Little White Cottage or Gentle Nettie Moore," 1857, Public Domain Music, Benjamin Robert Tubb, http://www.pdmusic.org/1800s/57gnm.txt (accessed September 3, 2007).

14. Ibid.

15. Bob Dylan, "Nettie Moore," 2006, Bob Dylan, http://www.bobdylan.com/moderntimes/songs/nettiemoore.html (accessed September 3, 2007).

16. The Harmoneons, preface to *The Harmoneons' Casket of Songs and Glees: As Written and Sung by Them at Their Concerts in the United States and British Provinces, in Their Original Characters of Whites and Blacks. Organized in 1843* (Boston: Ordway, 1850).

17. Of course, despite the false histories attributed to the origins of minstrelsy by its contemporary advocates, minstrelsy was based on white imaginative figuration of "blackness" and not a study of African-American culture itself. Eric Lott's reading of minstrelsy as exposing white attraction to "blackness" (and, in fact, actual black bodies) established that this unequivocally racist cultural form is nevertheless a complex construction worthy of historical study.

18. Dylan, "Nettie Moore."

19. Ibid.

20. I would like to thank Ian Woodward immensely for his help in verifying this fact.

21. Dylan, "Nettie Moore."

22. W. E. B. Du Bois, *The Souls of Black Folk* (New York: Penguin, 1989), 5.

23. Dylan, "Nettie Moore."

24. Ibid.

25. Ibid.

26. Ibid.

27. Ibid.

28. Ibid.

29. Ibid.

30. Pike, "The Little White Cottage or Gentle Nettie Moore."

31. Dylan, "Nettie Moore."

32. William Blake, *Selected Poems* (London: J. M. Dent, 1993), 11–12.

18. "Somewhere down in the United States": The Art of Bob Dylan's Ventriloquism

Michael Cherlin and Sumanth Gopinath

That Bob Dylan has many voices will be an idea familiar to all readers who have followed his musical career. The wise country singer of the early recordings, the sneering hipster of the first electric phase, the weirdly rounded country voice after the "motorcycle accident," the gruff, dejected old man of recent years—these voices are inseparable from the many style shifts in Dylan's singing persona over the years. Yet there is another aspect of Dylan's many voices—the moment-to-moment changes in timbre, inflection, and accent that comprise the basis of his singing style. While one aspect of this essay will be to characterize Dylan's multiple and shifting identities, his cast of musical personae, our principal concern, focusing primarily on *The Freewheelin' Bob Dylan* (1963), will be the frequent changes in his voice within individual songs, the often subtle and mercurial inflections that embody his creative thought process. Dylan's changing voice serves multiple expressive functions, enacts shifts in poetic imagery, and highlights sonic associations among words.

Greenwich Village Ventriloquism, ca. 1963

Understood within the context of the aesthetic and cultural divides of the folk revival, Dylan's use of his voice would appear to be a dialectical response to the Greenwich Village scene that was rooted in the realities of post–World War II racial formation and mass culture in the United States and seems to have played a fundamental role in facilitating Dylan's own performances and songwriting.

When Dylan encountered the Greenwich Village folk revival in full swing in the early 1960s, the scene was divided into two streams: the college-campus and media-friendly "clean" tendency, in which the presumed universality of the folk song was reflected in an apparently neutral voice bespeaking a young, white, middle-class sensibility, and the ethnic particularist perspective, in which musicians attempted to re-create the sound of traditional music rather than abstracting it into some "purer" style.[1] If Peter, Paul and Mary were exemplars of the first group, Dylan's own mentors and influences, including Ramblin' Jack Elliott and Dave Van Ronk, might be

225

included in the second. Perhaps the distinguishing musical feature of these two tendencies was the use of the singing voice, in which clear tone and clear, regionally neutral speech were characteristic of the "clean" folk revival style, whereas an imitation of the gruff voices and unusual accents in singing styles of rural-vernacular music were the hallmark of ethnic particularism in the folk revival.

In Dylan's own self-conception, he would seem to have broken through this opposition, which resulted in a hardening of performance styles into atomized musical practices that prevented genre crossing and mixing. In his words, "Folk music was a strict and rigid establishment. If you sang Southern Mountain Blues, you didn't sing Southern Mountain Ballads and you didn't sing City Blues. If you sang Texas cowboy songs, you didn't play English ballads. It was really pathetic."[2] It could be argued that Dylan adopted the practice of genre crossing in a self-conscious manner, which originated in tentative and timid imitations of his favorite musicians, genres, and accents, like those of Jimmy Rogers, rockabilly singers, Woody Guthrie, the Everly Brothers, Scots-Irish ballads, and blues singers like Robert Johnson and Sleepy John Estes. But genre crossing might also find its determination in an imitation of the songster tradition, in which rural musicians developed a capacity for multi-hour performances and, in the process of developing repertoire, drew on a wide range of source genres.[3] And as a child of the post–World War II period and its new mass media and culture, Dylan's generic and vocal shifts evoke the switching of channels—on the radio and even the television—that facilitated an immediate access to a new sound or sensibility. Such switching is not only associated with a postwar, postmodern fragmentation of consciousness and identity but also recalls specific mass cultural forms frequently mediated through radio and television, particularly prewar comedy. The latter draws on ethnic comedy and theater traditions emerging from the second major wave of migration to the United States, from southern and eastern Europe around the turn of the century. As a theatrical form, comedy, which often involves vocal imitation (of stereotyped ethnic accents, particular individuals, etc.), plays into the distinction between acting and singing, in which musical acting, often self-evidently comic, gives the "performers" greater freedom to interpret musical texts by licensing "dramatic" readings that do not require the production of sonic beauty.[4] Comedy, of exactly this sort, was crucial for Dylan's creation of his stage persona. Susan Rotolo, Dylan's first girlfriend while in New York, likened him to Harpo Marx,[5] whereas folksinger Eric Von Schmidt compared him to Chaplin.[6]

As Dylan became more self-assured as a performer, he began to integrate his many voices—altering them in some cases, eliminating others from his repertoire—in the process assimilating them into the style that would come to be known as his "hillbilly sound."[7] And yet, in the early, folk music period Dylan never completely eschews appropriation. He abstracts vocal techniques, accents, and timbres into possible materials for use in the expression of distinct personae (exemplified in his song lyrics), from all of which the master creator/performer "Bob Dylan" maintains a certain distance. It is in this sense that Dylan is a ventriloquist of sorts, and through what appear to be often improvisatory shifts operating at multiple registers (technique, timbre, accent, lyrics), Dylan fashioned a mode of artistic production as a dialectic of simulation and assimilation that broke through the hardened antipodes of the folk revival.[8]

Theorizing the Unstable Voice

How should one speak about these vocal, often micro-vocal, shifts in Dylan's early music? At the risk of claiming a precision and expertise that we in no way possess, our approach is to break down the problem into a series of axes that intersect with one another, in an effort to open up and further the already rich dialogue on Dylan's voice. The four axes we emphasize are (1) the vocal techniques used by Dylan as a singer, (2) the specific spoken and sung timbres that Dylan adopts song by song and even moment to moment, (3) the linguistic accents used in the enunciation of words, whether spoken or sung, and (4) the dramatic personae conveyed by the texts of his songs in conjunction with vocal techniques, timbres, and accents. Examples of three of these axes are listed in the accompanying figure.

Because we have found identifying linguistic accents much more difficult in Dylan, we have left them off the chart, but we suspect that many English-language accents pervade Dylan's performed linguistic geography. Some of these include white rural southern accents of various types, quasi-Scottish accents that blend into the Appalachian variants of rural southern accents, African-American accents particularly in black blues contexts, western and southwestern accents (such as the Okie inflections borrowed from Guthrie), and "elevated" accents whose quasi-British quality may be vaguely New England-esque but can also serve as a mock upper-class marker. Although our lack of familiarity prevents its proper identification, we assume the presence of a north-Minnesotan accent in Dylan's vocalizations as well.

An exhaustive description of the techniques, timbres, and personae in the chart is not possible within the confines of this essay; however, a few examples may suffice to demonstrate some of the ways in which these elements combine. Consider the approach to the first chorus in "A Hard Rain's A-Gonna Fall," when Dylan sings, "I've been ten thousand miles in the mouth of a graveyard / And it's a hard, and it's a hard, it's a hard, it's a hard / It's a hard rain's a-gonna fall" (0:46–1:05). In this brief moment, we find a number of interesting factors at play. For one, Dylan's vocal timbre has a moderately scratchy and slightly choked or pinched quality, preternaturally aging his voice while keeping it within the orbit of his "default" voice of these years. (At other points in the song, as in "I've been out in front of a dozen dead oceans," Dylan allows his voice to waver, aging it further.) Also, Dylan declaims the text by exaggerating the voiced plosives in the word *hard* (/harda/), which reacts abruptly to the mellifluous alliteration of nasals (and effective assonance with the /aw/ vowel in /mahles/ in the /mahths/). And Dylan pronounces *hard* with a very closed and emphatic /ar/ sound, suggesting a Scottish accent, if perhaps filtered

Vocal Techniques
- clipping/sustaining/trailing off
- open throat/closed throat
- clarion call/holler
- yodel/interjected falsetto
- hoots/yells
- swooping
- hard (or soft) attack
- exaggeration of plosives, palatals, etc.
- singsong high/low alternation
- wavering, vibrato
- laughing
- singing/speaking (pitched/unpitched)

Timbres
- default voice: moderately open, slightly scratchy
- choked/open
- whisper/breathy

- nasal
- twang
- sneering

Personae
- prophet/visionary
- bard (Scots)–balladeer
- intimate/vulnerable
- country wise man
- country bluesman
- city hipster
- old man
- wanderer
- wiseass
- (drunk) fool
- post-Whitman-Emersonian listing and enumeration, filtered through the Beats, including Ginsberg
- Abe Lincoln filtered through Raymond Massey

Dylan's early vocal techniques, timbres, and personae.

through a southern (Appalachian?) accent.[9] The personae of the song generally would seem to evoke the Scottish bard—with the well-known Lord Randal reference in mind here—the wavering voice of an old man, and the visionary and prophetic tone found in the middle parts of the verses, which itself is created through the post-Whitman/Emersonian technique of emphatically expansive listing or cataloging. The effect here, when combined with the self-evident tone painting of a "rainfall" figure (the vocal descents, especially the 4-3-4-3-1 tag) and of the laborious ascent on the repeated word *hard,* is to convey the apocalyptic visions of the song through a subtly shifting persona in which the detached wisdom of the old seer then gives way to the emphatic Scottish bard (whose accent perhaps also signifies a working-class laborer, of an older time or remote geography) whose effort is used to depict the coming catastrophe.

Another example is found in the song "Bob Dylan's Blues," when Dylan sings "Oh you five and ten cent women with nothin' in your heads" (0:46–1:21). The rounded, open, even blustery, though slightly pinched quality of his voice can be clearly heard here. In combination with this timbre, Dylan belts out his voice in a somewhat higher register (between C♯4 and F♯4), granting it something of the quality of a holler. Although the vocal accent is not particularly striking, Dylan's affectation here does muffle his words somewhat—perhaps most extremely when he "swoops" his voice a little later, on the words *race track*. The persona here, rather different from those found in "Hard Rain," is one of an almost drunken fool who is calling out to all the women whom he imagines to be cheap and chasing after him. Interestingly, over the course of that verse, Dylan drops his "fool" voice as he begins to speak of his own love (especially at "Lord I'll love her till I'm dead") and then even laughs slightly on "my window," before speaking "right now" in a deadpan tone. Here, Dylan demonstrates the self-consciousness of his personified fool, making it clear that he is perfectly aware that women are not actually chasing after him—and then amusingly ending with a "right now" that reverses the laughter with a mock seriousness (almost as a kind of punch line—a technique very common in Dylan's talking blues songs, taken from Guthrie).[10]

Although there are not necessary relationships between particular techniques, timbres, personae, and accents, nonetheless these factors often join in semiconsistent ways that create consistent personae. The drunken fool, as described above, is one example of this. Others include an "intimate lover" voice, usually in a lower register and sung with an atypical breathiness; "Corrina, Corrina" and "Percy's Song" present this kind of voice. Yet another is the "sardonic wit" character, usually found when Dylan, in a somewhat lower register, adopts an incredibly nasal tone (as in "Oxford Town," as discussed below), though this vocal tone varies somewhat more than the previous two examples. It is, for example, blended with the intimate voice and a more "default" voice that combines with rural southern accents and clipped speech to represent a country wise man. Other types include the "young Abe Lincoln" voice, which is discussed below in "Blowin' in the Wind" and "Talkin' World War III Blues." Perhaps the most obvious voice is the black bluesman (or a white imitator of a black bluesman) found in "Down on the Highway" or "Milk Cow Blues"—a voice type from which Dylan seems to be distancing himself already at the time of *Freewheelin'*.[11] These personae seem to play the role of characters in Dylan's dramatizations of his texts. It is worth noting that Dylan consistently avoids the southern and eastern European accents from the turn-of-the-century migration that were both characteristic of Dylan's Jewish upbringing and a significant presence in popular culture in the postwar period (i.e., Italian American voices in gangster films, Jewish American voices in comedy, and the music of Tin Pan Alley). Dylan's focus on mostly white, rural voices gives his "hillbilly" persona a rooted, mythic character that creates the semblance of authenticity within the urban folk revival. Dylan avoids resorting either to the naked imitation of a single artist or even tradition (though his Guthrie-isms at times come close) or relying on white assumptions of black authenticity (as, say, Dave Van Ronk's very black-inflected singing style would).

Reading the Freewheelin' Bob Dylan

The opening song of *Freewheelin'* is "Blowin' in the Wind." Here Dylan composes a ballade for his generation, one several times removed from its ancestors in Scots ballades. The subject matter is the most obvious place of change. This ballade will not be about old times, or love lost, or any of the traditional narratives. Neither will it be topical, in the sense of being about a specific political/historical event. The text moralizes in ways later abandoned by Dylan, it has a biblical ring to it and a strong sense of social consciousness, and in its refrain we hear Dylan as prophet. The voice and message are not as hard-edged as in "Masters of War" or as bleak in their predictions as "A Hard Rain's A-Gonna Fall," the other two obvious examples of Dylan as prophet on *Freewheelin'*. The vocal persona of "Blowin' in the Wind" combines aspects of the bard with a kind of country wisdom that we hear in other early Dylan songs as well. We wonder if Dylan might have been influenced by Raymond Massey's portrayal of Lincoln in the film *Abe Lincoln in Illinois* (1940). The wisdom of the humble country boy prophesies an older man who is yet to become. The connection with Lincoln is made explicit in another song on the album— "Talkin' World War III Blues"—where Dylan parodies "You can fool all the people some of the time, and some of the people all the time, but you cannot fool all the people all the time," a comment attributed to Lincoln but evidently not to be located in any of his preserved speeches. In Dylan's version:

> Half of the people can be part right all of the time,
> Some of the people can be all right part of the time.
> But all the people can't be all right all the time
> I think Abraham Lincoln said that.
> "I'll let you be in my dreams if I can be in yours,"
> I said that.

In Dylan's *Freewheelin'* rendition of "Blowin' in the Wind," there is a tinge of sadness in his voice but no hint of crying. The restraint in the voice helps make the text all the more emphatic. Dylan's clear diction and his wonderful sense of timing make it easy to follow the words.

```
     5        6         5    3-(2) 1
     \     u u \      u   u\    \    \
  1. How many roads must a man walk down

     4 5      6    5 4   5
     u \ u    \   u u   \
  2. Before you call him a man?

     5        6        5    3-(2) 1
     \     u u \     u u \    \    \
  3. How many seas must a white dove sail

     x 5      4     3     2
     u \ u    \    u u    \
  4. Before she sleeps in the sand?

     5              6    5           3-(2) 1
     u   u    \ u u  \     u  u  \ u   u  \
  5. Yes and how many times must the cannonballs fly

     5            6 4    5
     u \      u    \ u u  \
  6. Before they're forever banned?
```

```
    4         3 2    4 3       3 2 1
    u  \ u   u   \    u \ u    uu  \
7.  The answer my friend is blowin' in the wind
```

```
    1     4    3  2   1 7    1
    u   \ u   u  \ u  uu   \
8.  The answer is blowin' in the wind.
```

The structure of the song and lyrics is well worth considering. All of the verse lines except for line 5, have varied poetic feet. For example, lines 2 and 4 open with two iambs u\u\ before expanding the foot to an anapest uu\. The irregularity of the accentual pulse stream forms one of several techniques that mimic blowing in the wind. All of the lines are end-stopped, and the music, especially Dylan's articulation of the words, intensifies this attribute. Accented syllables proliferate at the ends of lines 1 and 3, where we hear three consecutive accented syllables: "man walk down," "white dove sail." Line 5 adds the upbeat "Yes and" to the question of how many, opening up the line into a series of anapests—uu\ -, continuing through "must a cannon ball fly?"—to create the only unvaried line of poetic feet in the verse. The seventh and eighth lines form the refrain, which is echoed by the harmonica. The prosody of the refrain is particularly interesting to analyze. The words "the answer" and "is blowin'" in line 7 form a pattern of u\u, the foot called an amphibrach. When the words "my friend" are removed, to form line 8, the two amphibrachs are directly juxtaposed, before giving way to the uu\ pattern of "in the wind," right shifting the accent to fall at the end of the line. The parsing of line 8 into u\u u\u uu\ interacts with an expansion of consecutive weak syllables, u\ to uu\ to uuu\. The enigmatic answer blowing in the wind is hard to read.

The three questions that open each verse form a musical ABA structure: the "A" lines end on scale-degree 5 ("man," "banned"), whereas the "B" line ends with a descent to scale-degree 2 ("sand"). The refrain develops the B part of the music, completing the descent to the tonic, "blowin' in the wind," which is reaffirmed and embellished by the leading tone, "the answer is blowin' in the wind." The musical importance of the descent to tonic is very salient: the opening lines of each verse hover about scale-degree 5, tentatively touching on the tonic, but remaining without strong tonic closure. It is only in the refrain that Dylan sings what music theorists call a "structural descent," completing the scalar motion 4-3-2-1.

The pattern continues through three verses, each one containing three questions, followed by the answering refrain. The war imagery, which seems to pervade the whole, is actually made explicit only in the third questions of the first and third verse: "How many times must the cannonballs fly before they are forever banned" and "Yes and how many deaths will it take 'til he knows that too many people have died."

The use of plosives and palatals, mimetic of gusts of wind, plays a key role in this song; "walk down" and "cannonballs fly" are striking examples, as are some of the voicings of "blowin'." These are clipped, as opposed to the sustained timbres of the preceding words. The timbre of Dylan's voice changes, sometimes subtly and sometimes more emphatically as he voices the final words of musical phrases. The "answer" that is blowing in the wind, whatever that is, is something coming, and the song underscores this message through musical syntax (the descent to tonic, embellished by the leading tone), and through plosives concomitant with changes in voice that are placed at the ends of lines.

The harmonica's recapitulation of the refrain, appearing "early" if we were to assume a foursquare or quadratic syntax, seems to comment thoughtfully on the preceding music. In light of this, it is worth noting that Dylan is not a singer who merges the sound of his voice with the sound of his guitar. When applied to the relationship between instrument and voice, the African-diasporic technique of call-and-response recalls a manner we associate with Jimi Hendrix—among Dylan's contemporaries—and with Robert Johnson, Charlie Patton, and Blind Lemon Jefferson, among Dylan's precursors. Dylan's guitar is generally a rhythm instrument, laying out the harmonic rhythm, or sometimes a picking instrument, in the manner of bluegrass and other country musics. Dylan's "other voice" is his harmonica, although Dylan does not generally imitate the singing voice in the way that we hear, for example, in Sonny Terry and Brownie McGhee.[12]

In "Blowin' in the Wind," the thoughtful commentary of the harmonica, which repeats the structural descent described above, draws attention to the fundamental paradox of this classic protest song. Whereas the descent from 4 to 1 makes the chorus of the song very singable and memorable, even providing a sense of certainty, the lyrics and irregular poetic meter seem uncertain and vague, even if we might find the "true" answer in the gusts of plosives as described above. Mike Marqusee captures this contrast well, noting that the song "is filled with a sense that a long-awaited transformation is both imminent and frustratingly out of reach. The ambiguous refrain . . . gropes for the unnameable. . . . The 'answer' is here, and not here; it exists, a force felt all around us, but remains elusive."[13] The trope, blowing in the wind, is a new version of an old image, at least as old as Shelley's "Ode to the West Wind":

> from whose unseen presence the leaves dead
> Are driven, like ghosts from an enchanter fleeing . . .

In 1960, the prime minister of Great Britain, Harold Macmillan, had given a speech in South Africa speaking about the "winds of change," signaling a shift in British policy on apartheid. Dylan's "answer" that is blowing in the wind remains enigmatic and not linked to any one policy or event, but rather to something at once far more encompassing yet far less defined.

Two of the songs on *Freewheelin'*, "Girl from the North Country," and "Oxford Town," make use of the bifurcation of vocal registers, common in blues and country music traditions. The contrast in registers is sometimes articulated by moves back and forth from normal singing voice to falsetto, and sometimes by different vocal characteristics that distinguish the upper register from the lower, typically a more strained voice in the upper register, and a more open or sometimes growling voice in the lower. Dylan uses this technique, sometimes in vivid ways, but often more subtly. Tim Riley has noted how "his voice apes his harmonica in flights that shift between a thin, sandpapery baritone and a goosed falsetto, so that even on his static held notes his songs sound as if the meanings they toss off are in constant flux."[14]

The registral shifts are more striking and clear-cut in "Oxford Town," a song in which Dylan takes on the role as chronicler of his times. The bifurcation of the voice mimics the dichotomies of the song, the high and the low, the in and the out, the subjugators and the subjugated. With each shift, Dylan's voice moves from a somewhat choked upper register, with a hint of some sort of upper-crust accent— "Oxford Town, Oxford Town"—to a more sardonic inflection in the lower register. Through this disdainful commentary and tone painting, Dylan's song perhaps avoids being entirely "one-dimensional," as Marqusee argues.[15] In the transcription of some of the lyrics below, we use the alternation of normal and italicized text to notate the shifts in vocal timbre and register.

> Oxford Town, Oxford Town
> Ev'rybody's got *their heads bowed down*
> *The sun don't shine* above the ground
> Ain't a-goin' down to *Oxford Town*
>
> He went down to Oxford Town
> Guns and clubs *followed him down*
> *All because* his face was brown
> Better get away from *Oxford Town*

In contrast to "Oxford Town," "Girl from the North Country" is a personal song with a private history that is antecedent to its narrative, one that creates a mythic sense of place, set off by the bittersweet distance of remembering. The imagery approaches the sublime, with Dylan as bard rather than minstrel. The lower register tends toward the more personal statements, while the higher, more choked register is Dylan's "singing out" voice. The public bard is juxtaposed against the private person—an opposition that will continue through Dylan's career.

> If you're travelin' in the north country fair,
> Where the winds hit heavy on the borderline,
> Remember me *to one who lives there.*
> *She once was a true love of mine.*
>
> If you go when snowflakes storm,
> When the rivers freeze and summer ends,
> Please see if she has a *coat so warm,*
> *To keep her from the howlin' winds.*

Our final example, "Honey, Just Allow Me One More Chance," is Dylan's comic parody of the plaintive country song. The song as a whole is a play on the kinds of weepy country tunes made famous by Hank Williams and others. At the same time, the song is also a reworking of "Ragtime Texas," Henry Thomas's much slower and harmonically simpler original, which resembles Dylan's version only in the ending tag of the chorus, "Just a-one kind favor I ask you, 'low me just a-one more chance." Dylan's comic routine is almost like a vaudeville song, in the manner of Robert Johnson's "They're Red Hot," for example. The quick shifts of register and timbre serve a wide expressive palette ranging from drunken fool, to quick-witted comic, to sarcastic wise guy. We get to hear Dylan hoot and holler, as the comedic elements keep the sarcasm in check. No one song can contain the many voices of Dylan, but this one compresses a few of them into its small space.

> Honey, just allow me one more chance
> To get along with you.
> **Honey, just allow me one more chance,**
> **Ah'll do anything with you.**
> *Well, I'm a-walkin' down the road*
> *With my head in my hand,*
> *I'm lookin' for a woman*
> *Needs a worried man.*
> Just-a one kind favor **I ask-a you,**
> 'Low me just-a one more chance.
>
> Honey, just allow me one more **chance**
> To ride **your air**plane.
> Honey, just allow me one **more chance**
> To ride your passenger train.
> *Well, I've been lookin' all over*
> For a **girl like you,**
> I can't **find nobody**
> **So you'll have to do.**
> **Just-a one kind favor I ask-a you,**
> 'Low me just-a one more chance.

(Key: mildly nasal/sardonic voice as normal text, **fool voice as bold text,** *country bluesman as italicized text,* underlined text as extra sardonic/nasal emphasis.)

As one can see from our rendering of the song's text, Dylan moves deftly from a normative sardonic voice (one might call this one the "quick-witted comic") to his blustery fool voice and affected country bluesman voice (perhaps in dialogue here with Henry Thomas, while not imitating his slower, statelier enunciation), with nasal emphases injecting yet more sarcasm from time to time. Although many things can be said about Dylan's remarkable performance, one point worth considering is the fact that generally, over the course of the song, Dylan's voices begin to pare down in favor of a (relatively) more straightforward rendering of the text. Whereas the first verse seems at times to shift character from word to word, by the third verse Dylan restricts himself to his normative voice and the fool voice. (This shift is most noticeable in the first four lines, or both sentences beginning with "Honey just allow me one more chance," in which the performance mostly remains within his normative voice for the song.) By the end of the song, with the final lines "just-a one kind favor I ask-a you," Dylan begins to sing with a kind of field holler, emphasizing the high G (G4) or scale-degree 1 (or, rather, 8) — "ask-a you" the first time, "you" on the repetition — and even growls and gargles a bit on the repetition ("you, 'low"), all in the service of a more impassioned delivery than has appeared hitherto in the song. But after the repetition of "just-a one kind favor...," Dylan's final vocal utterance incorporates a little laugh and an interjection, which seems to undercut the relative earnestness of the third verse. The final joke in this absurd comedy routine, then, is revealed just as one begins to believe that the joking has ended.

Notes

1. Thanks to Michael Denning for his thoughts on this subject.

2. Quoted in Michael Gray, *Song and Dance Man III: The Art of Bob Dylan* (London: Continuum, 2000), 17.

3. Many blues musicians were part of this tradition, but owing to the racial rigidity of the early race records, few recordings of Delta blues singers singing white country, folk, or gospel songs exist. Black rural musicians who sang blues often performed within the "songster" tradition, in which the performance of many different song genres was typical. One well-known songster, Mance Lipscomb, was a key influence on Dylan according to Michael Gray in *The Bob Dylan Encyclopedia* (New York: Continuum, 2006), 416–17.

4. Gillian Rodger, a groundbreaking scholar of music, theater, gender, and transvestism in the United States, discussed this distinction between singing and acting with respect to recordings of songs in her talk "Contextualizing Cross-Dressed Performance in Nineteenth-Century Theater: Issues of Gender and Class," December 8, 2006, University of Minnesota, School of Music, Minneapolis.

5. Susan Rotolo, "Bob Dylan," in *Rock Wives*, cited in Elizabeth Thomson and David Gutman, *The Dylan Companion* (New York: Da Capo Press, 2001), 73.

6. This is discussed in Tim Riley, *Hard Rain: A Dylan Commentary*, updated ed. (New York: Da Capo, 1999 [1992]), 43.

7. Gray, *Song and Dance Man III*, 22.

8. By this, we refer to the relatively weak — not compelling, quickly forgotten, and often of a novelty or timely *(à clef)* quality — new song material written in the context of the folk revival. Indeed, this would seem to be the corollary of the folk revival's belief in a universal and universally accessible set of cultural texts (as songs) that could be shared and performed by all. See Robert Cantwell, "When We Were Good: Class and Culture in the Folk Revival," in *Transforming Tradition: Folk Music Revivals Examined*, ed. Neil Rosenberg (Urbana: University of Illinois Press, 1993), 35–60, esp. 37–38.

9. In a 1960 performance of "Johnny I Hardly Knew You," an Irish antiwar song that was later rewritten as "When Johnny Comes Marching Home," Dylan affects an explicit Irish (or maybe Scots-Irish) accent, making it clear that this kind of imitation was part of his vocal repertory. See Bob Dylan, "Minnesota Party Tape," recorded by Cleve Pettersen, 15th Ave. SE, Minneapolis, fall 1960, available at the Minnesota Historical Society library, St. Paul, Minnesota, Audiotape Call #203; for more information, see http://www.mnhs.org.

10. We can hear an example of this in Ramblin' Jack Elliott's version of "John Hardy," in a song in which Elliott himself seems to be drawing on Uncle Dave Macon and possibly others but creates an unhinged, fool persona. See Ramblin' Jack Elliott, *The Lost Topic Tapes: Isle of Wight 1957* (Live), HighTone Records 8176, 2004.

11. If one compares Dylan's much "blacker" "Milk Cow Blues," of the prior year, 1962, and notes the decline in blues songs before the electric blues numbers of his first electric period, we might read this as a move away from a vocal style being reclaimed as black within the civil rights and black liberation movements.

12. Here is, thus, another example of Dylan's distance from African-American musical practices.

13. Mike Marqusee, *Chimes of Freedom: The Politics of Bob Dylan's Art* (New York: New Press, 2003), 55.

14. Riley, *Hard Rain*, 53. Although Riley emphasizes falsetto here, it is worth noting that Dylan's registral bifurcations make less use of falsetto and instead highlight the strain created by singing in the higher register.

15. Marqusee, *Chimes of Freedom*, 62.

19. Dylan/Disabled:
Tolling for the Deaf and Blind
Alex Lubet

This contemplation of the work of Bob Dylan from the perspective of disability studies is not primarily a consideration of lyrics, though Dylan often references disability, freakery, and "old, weird" social outcasts.[1] It is not primarily biographical and certainly does not brand Dylan disabled, something rarely done in disability studies, which regards disability status as a form of minority status or otherness. Still, Dylan has had noteworthy encounters with disability, particularly in his formative early years.

Encounters

In *Chronicles, Volume 1,* Dylan writes of his father Abe's polio, a condition that kept him out of military service during World War II, while Dylan's numerous able-bodied uncles all served and survived.[2] The experience not only of having grown up with a father with a disability, but of one's father having been unable to serve in a popular war likely made a strong impression. The onus of a military deferment may have been compounded for a Jewish family in a substantially Jewish community like Hibbing, Minnesota.[3]

Dylan's pilgrimage to New York to visit his aging idol Woody Guthrie (arguably a musical father figure) is far better known, as is Guthrie's terminal illness of Huntington's disease during that time. Dylan's description of those visits in an interview with Sam Shepherd is illuminating.[4] Guthrie was in a hospital in New Jersey at the time, which was not easy to reach on public transportation. Yet, Dylan brought his guitar with him and serenaded his mentor with Guthrie's own compositions, as Guthrie requested of his young admirer. They spoke little.

Largely forgotten, Guthrie had few other visitors, and he was so infirm that real conversation was impossible. There was little for Dylan to do but perform for Guthrie his interpretations of his mentor's oeuvre, the requests of a dying man. These visits offer evidence of the kind of empathy that Greil Marcus observes in Dylan in his essay in this volume. That Dylan, still in his teens and surely consumed both with starting his career and basic survival in New York, would choose to spend that much time with Guthrie is a testament to Dylan's maturity and kindness. Most of his peers would likely have preferred to avoid the unpleasantness of staring the bad death of a beloved elder in the face. There is a temptation to interpret Dylan's good deed as a product of a solid Jewish upbringing in which visiting the sick is regarded as an important mitzvah (commandment).

Perhaps, though, the most famous and potentially influential of Dylan's brushes with disability was the first of his own two near-death experiences. In 1966, Dylan was in a serious motorcycle accident that took him out of commission for eighteen months. The precise influence of this experience on his work is not something the artist confirms explicitly, yet it is difficult to imagine an event that traumatic leaving no legacy. To be sure, the music of the period before the accident, which ended with *Blonde on Blonde,* and that which followed, beginning with *John Wesley Harding,* could hardly have been more vividly contrasting. In all likelihood, "something [was] happening," even if we "don't know what it is."[5]

Less known, likely because it occurred during a period of more limited public visibility, was the histoplasmosis, a serious heart infection, that Dylan experienced in 1997.[6] Although life-threatening and requiring a summer's hospitalization, he denies that the illness provided any sort of insights.[7]

A Body of Work: The Work of a Body
Voice

Sound is the focus of this study. Sonically, the meeting of Dylan and disability studies informs our understanding of both the artist and this relatively new (and new to Dylan scholarship) field. One can hear in Dylan a sense of woundedness that, to the good and as Greil Marcus writes earlier in this volume, promotes empathy. It is not only in lyrics that this generosity of spirit is conveyed; music also is a source.

The most forthright expression of musical wounding is in Dylan's malleable yet unmistakable voice. Those who have followed Dylan from the beginning recall him as a raspy voice, literally both from and in the wilderness, prior to the emergence of the numerous other transgressive popular musics whose aesthetics he inspired.[8] Old Dylan hands readily recall how strange and "off" his anything-but-nubile voice initially sounded to many listeners. This is, of course, why many fans of his songs preferred renditions by the Byrds, Joan Baez, or Peter, Paul and Mary.

Dylan's vocal timbre remains ravaged. Its impact is likely more potent to listeners unfamiliar with such diverse yet similarly rough-hewed Dylan influences as Robert Johnson, Woody Guthrie, and Bertolt Brecht and Kurt Weill. Except for some very early recordings such as the 1960 Hibbing home tape of the traditional "Rambler, Gambler" and the brief nonsmoking period around *Nashville Skyline,* Dylan's voice has always been thus.[9] At twenty, he already sounded "so much older then" and has yet to sound "younger than that now" for long.[10] Indeed, the opposite has occurred; his voice having roughened lately far beyond natural aging.

Gait

A woundedness less literally embodied than vocal timbre resides in Dylan's use of musical asymmetries. Scholars such as cognitive paleoanthropologist Steven Mithen observe that many species associate beauty and attraction with symmetry.[11] The political and cultural movements associated with disability studies posit that the ability to read beauty into the asymmetries of both aesthetic creations and actual disabled bodies constitutes human progress. In that context it is worth noting Dylan's various encomiums to Picasso, including some of his own visual artwork.[12]

Musical as well as visual asymmetries in Dylan might be regarded as ruptured symmetries, symmetrical relationships evoked and broken, even "disabled." They are both compositional and performative and evidenced in both local rhythms and larger formal units. To identify rhythm with the body is intuitive in idioms whose meters evoke walking, breathing, and heart function. Such simple folk time is rarely out of mind in Dylan. But it is often in play, in a gait that halts, trips, or is unsteady.

The Singular Case of Hattie Carroll

Dylan's rhythmic tool kit is exemplified by an early work, "The Lonesome Death of Hattie Carroll."[13] In both composition and performance, we hear Dylan increasingly hobbled by the emotion of the lyric, all the more effectively because the vocal is relatively restrained, even at times numbed.[14] The text's passion is carried by rhythm, though the apparent musical simplicity is only superficial. Some songs on *The Times They Are A-Changin'*, the album on which "Hattie Carroll" debuted, are truly folklike, being rhythmically regular and unambiguously strophic. The title song and "When the Ship Comes In" are exemplars, which contextualize, perhaps intentionally, more intricate pieces. "Hattie Carroll" uses that folk template as the basis for something more complex and searingly, if subliminally, passionate.

Those asymmetries defined here as "compositional" are inherent to works in a manner that transcends interpretation. In "Hattie Carroll," the asymmetry that is most forthright and overtly musical—rather than poetic—occurs in the song's refrain. A waltz-time composition, the refrain's opening "You, who" defines its meter as simply as possible on the downbeats. Its simplicity is deceptive, though, and musically striking, as Dylan rarely extends any syllable beyond diction's demands and never during the song's verses. Further, this song never truly rhymes until its refrain, which begins with this tight—and rare for Dylan—internal rhyme, heralding a shift from third to second person.

As Christopher Ricks observes, internal rhyme reappears in the third—"lay," "slain," and "cane"—and fourth—"spoke" and "cloak"—stanzas. "Spoke" and "cloak" are preceded by "cops" and "top" (Ricks does not register this latter pair).[15] As will be seen, these stanzas are, as entire musical units, more rhythmically fraught than the first half of the work, in accordance with the events related by the text. Internal rhymes of this kind, subtler and less strategically placed than the "You who" that opens the refrain, have the impact of percussive syncopations, a lexical drum set, common in the work of the Tin Pan Alley tunesmiths for whom Dylan has at times expressed admiration and keen understanding but also an awareness of their great aesthetic distance from his own art.[16]

In stark contrast, the next two words, "philosophize disgrace," struggle against the musical meter, displacing both its natural accent and the plainspokenness of the verses. The refrain's second couplet, "Take the rag away from your face / Now ain't the time for your tears," returns to solid folk ground, perfectly metered. The refrain's couplets provide "fears" and "tears" in alternating lines, the song's first instance of end rhyme, and the only such occurrence also lodged in the folk stability of symmetrical phrase structure.[17]

End rhyme will only appear again in the final, climactic fourth stanza. This most basic form of rhyme is prepared or foreshadowed by "almost rhyme" beginning in the third stanza: "kitchen" with "children," "table" (three times) with "level," and (three lines later) "gentle."[18]

In the fourth and final stanza, "gavel" almost rhymes with "level" (again),[19] followed by "persuaded" with "handled." These prepare at some length the first true end rhyme within any stanza, "caught 'em" with "bottom," an instance in which a colloquialism—"'em" instead of "them"—serves musical flow more than working-class allusion. (Americans, regardless of class or ethnicity, contract their words this way.) Three line endings of "almost rhyme"—"reason" with (the colloquial) "warnin'" and "distinguished," which harkens back to "persuaded" and "handled"—prepare more succinctly this second and final end rhyme at the very end of the stanza, the chillingly sacred, solemn, and slang-free "repentance" with "sentence."

A total absence of unambiguous rhyme would have taken that most familiar of poetic device's scarcity off the table as an issue, entirely beyond the work's poetic universe and thus unnoticed. Attention to rare rhyme is focused at another important juncture and by means of another rhyming technique. At the end of the third stanza, "Doomed and determined to destroy" is followed shortly by "never done nothin'." These constitute the text's most aggressive, rapid-fire use of alliteration, a poetic device that is likewise a Dylan rarity. Similarly, this is the lyric's most flagrant class-associated breach of grammar, another technique Dylan reserves for special impact.[20] In the relatively breezy refrain, "ain't," similar to "'em" in the third stanza, sounds more like an accommodation to the meter than a "walk on the wild side." In contrast, the words "never done nothin'" are performed with much attention, a slowing of tempo and a crescendo, the latter an element Dylan has always wielded with extraordinary virtuosity.

There are sprinklings of alliteration through "Hattie Carroll," mostly more spread out than these, seeming to prepare these climactic uses in the fourth stanza, which are calculated and potent. "Carroll," "cane," "cops," "called," and "custody" sporadically punctuate the first stanza, even linking sonically with "criticize" in the refrain. In the second stanza, "provide," "protect," and "politics," are succeeded by "swear," "sneering," and "snarling" in closer proximity. There is a respite from alliteration in the third stanza, where other forms of rhyme, internal and "almost" enter. It is as if the absence of assonance in the stanza clears the way for these other sonic devices.

The return of alliteration in the final stanza, this time alongside all the other rhyming devices in Dylan's arsenal, contributes to a veiled sense of syncopation, a tremulous, uneven gait, as they protrude from the lexical texture in an utterly aperiodic manner. The emotional intensity this creates is heightened by the apparent contradiction of Dylan's impassive delivery and the restraint, the choked anger, of the text itself, mixed signals that turn much of the responsibility for more overt grief to the listener to perform (the musical equivalent of "reader response"): "court-rooms" and "courts"; "pulled," persuaded," and "properly"; "cops" and "caught" (reprising the *c* sound); "ladder" and "law"; "who," "way," "without," and "warnin'"; and finally, "deep" and "distinguished," which grate ironically against "doomed," "determined," and "destroy" in the prior stanza. Along with all the other assonant devices of this stanza, these overwhelm the listener with additional layers of motivic sound distributed in utterly asymmetrical rhythm, whose tracking, consciously or not, simply demands even more of the listener than the horrific story alone, rendered with less sonic splendor, ever could.

To state that only in "Hattie Carroll" is Dylan "never limited by the rhyme scheme" is to make too little of Dylan's rhyming strategy.[21] Judiciously controlled rhyme in many forms, protruding from the lyrics in an utterly aperiodic manner and undermining any sense of regular gait, is an element that contributes much to the emotionally fraught state of one of his most compelling songs.

The other compositional ruptures of musical rhythm in "Hattie Carroll" might be better termed "poetic" than "musical." These are the numerous instances when text simply "just don't fit"[22] the poem's basic dactylic tetrameter.[23] There is a progression of metrical treatment in which the first stanza is nearly free of protuberances from the poetic meter, but things begin to fall apart in the second. The song is, as we shall hear, clearly divided into asymmetrical halves, and in the second half, strophes three and four, the original poetic meter is progressively more rent as the tableau of the text progresses to fever pitch without, however, a correspondence in the tone of Dylan's vocal performance. The opening couplet of the last stanza is particularly interesting:

> In the courtroom of honor, the judge pounded his gavel
> To show that all's equal and that the courts are on the level

This first of the paired lines nearly fits the norms of the meter, had only "the judge" been simply "judge." The almost rhyming line—"gavel" with "level"—starts in meter with "To show that all's equal" and then explodes the pacing entirely with "and that the courts are on the level." Dylan, as previously noted, does not always strategize meter—or rhyme—this way. It is only done when appropriate for expressive purposes. Here, it is a kind of cubist deformation of his still highly apparent folk model, kept simple in tonality, instrumentation, and waltz-time accompaniment, that gets at the horror of the situation portrayed as likely no other rendering could. His fidelity to poetic meter noticeably decreases with each strophe, but with no strophe purely metrical or ametrical. Ruptures in meter are always in close proximity to flowing meter and thus clearly exposed like open wounds and thus truly poignant.

A cognitive dissonance between Hattie Carroll's history and the song's poetic meter is noteworthy. Hattie Carroll actually had eleven children, not ten.[24] It seems the three syllables of "eleven" would have taxed the prosody of this line beyond even Dylan's liberal approach, so different from protocols of the uptown tunesmiths. While he is on record as refusing to yield to the demands of rhyme if it dilutes meaning, the same may at least occasionally not apply to meter.[25] The folk model can only sustain so much distortion while preserving recognition.

The harmonica solo is largely faithful to the melody until its end, when it briefly departs both the tune and the guitar's waltz timekeeping, the latter remarkable for Dylan's ability here and elsewhere to do two rhythmic things at once. Such instrumental metrical "breakdowns" often serve Dylan as cadence formulas. Other examples include the renditions of "Just Like a Woman" on *Blonde on Blonde* and "Visions of Johanna" from the 1966 Royal Albert Hall concert. Vocally and instrumentally, such metric irregularity is prominent in Dylan's work with bands, where the erratic wholesale shifts of tempo common in his solo performances would be difficult or impossible to achieve.

With this metrical strategy, Dylan deliberately distances himself from classic Tin Pan Alley's flawless prosody,[26] as well as that of his contemporaries in the Brill Building. He acknowledges this difference, while also having expressed admiration for these songwriters from the opposite end of town.[27]

Steady rhythmic gait is also overwhelmed at a deeper structural level. Extremely rare for a Dylan song and thus stunning in the context of his oeuvre, "Hattie Carroll" begins vocally without an instrumental introduction. The unequal halves of "Hattie Carroll" have different length strophes. The opening two strophes are six lines, the final two, eleven. The latter sound as plodding as their text is at first despondent and then evil. The odd number of lines deforms the earlier couplet structure, which was already compromised by the paucity of end rhyme and the asymmetrical distribution of other rhyme variants. Another example of this asymmetrical strophes technique, with shorter phrases and much rhyme, has quite a different effect in "Mr. Tambourine Man."

"Hattie Carroll," like its album companions "Masters of War" and "Restless Farewell," changes tempo extensively. The song's tempo holds mostly steady until the third refrain, which follows the strophe, where other rhythmic tremors, major ruptures of poetic meter, and the loss of couplet structure occur. The final strophe, which describes the trial, is completely unstable in its tempo. This strophe also exudes the characteristic Dylan rhythmic technique of varying the number of measures between verses and even lines. This occurs sporadically earlier in the song but quite noticeably here, particularly immediately prior to the refrain.

A cover of "Hattie Carroll" by Black Uhuru on the 2004 CD *Is It Rolling Bob: A Reggae Tribute to Bob Dylan* is rhythmically utterly recomposed. Though splendid in its own way, the jaggedness of Dylan's rhythms is smoothed into iambic pentameter and 4/4 time, restrategizing the expression of the text in a quite different style, one that would later influence Dylan greatly, particularly on the 1983 *Infidels* album.

Multiple Traumas

A variety of other expressions of musical woundedness are manifested in other facets of Dylan's music. These will only be introduced here. Numerous further examples deserve nuanced consideration.

Attenuated Limbs: Album *Structure*

One source of such ruptures is the asymmetry of entire albums, whose individual songs are much enriched when heard as elements of multimovement compositions. Put simply, most Dylan albums end in irresolution, seemingly purposefully denying the gratification of, say, the finale of a Beethoven symphony. Such musical question marks are both a modern and a postmodern nontriumphalist flourish.

Dylan discusses one such example, the choice of the solo acoustic "Dark Eyes" as a closer to *Empire Burlesque,* an otherwise thickly scored album.[28] That the song was freshly written during recording the sessions, extremely rare for Dylan, at the suggestion of producer Arthur Baker, does not alter our perceptions of its affect or its meaning in the context of Dylan's recorded oeuvre. Dylan has always been an extraordinary collaborator, who listens to producers (when he is not the producer himself) and provides plenty of opportunity for creativity to his accompanists.

Such album asymmetry is strategized by a dazzling variety of ingenious means. "Dark Eyes" represents but one obvious, if highly effective, possibility. For example, the second half of *Bringing It All Back Home* offers a more extreme form of the asymmetry of the ending of *Empire Burlesque* by receding from the electricity of its opening, going first acoustic and ultimately solo, the forces gradually thinning to Dylan at his most austere in "Gates of Eden" and "It's Alright, Ma," until the final "It's All Over Now, Baby Blue" slightly thickens to a duet and softens the still acoustic texture; it is too little closure, too late.

In marked contrast, *John Wesley Harding,* terse, consistently austere, formalist, grim, and replete with songs that end in bizarre anti-cadences, with only harmonica as a melody instrument, closes with two utterly out of character good-time country songs—foreshadowings of *Nashville Skyline?*—that add Pete Drake on pedal steel.

Finally, there is *Gotta Serve Somebody: The Gospel Songs of Bob Dylan,* an otherwise reverent Dylan gospel tribute album from 2000 (Columbia), long after Zimmy's born-again had died. (As if there were any doubt of this, Dylan's "Christian" period was ended with an album titled *Infidels.*) His only appearance on the album as performer, the closing duet with Mavis Staples, "Gonna Change My Way of Thinking," which begins with a hilarious spoken dialogue and whose hard-rocking groove starkly contrasts the old-school gospel blues feel of the rest of the album, makes his fall from grace, or even belief in the possibility of grace, perfectly clear.

Dylan Live: Busy Dying?

Finally, there is Dylan live in concert. Since his well-known epiphany concerning performing, during the Tom Petty and Grateful Dead tours, Dylan has associated live performance with survival and renewal, conflated it with struggle against illness and fatigue, and referenced it to mortality. He reports emerging from this epiphany with a new approach to performance, clearly heard in reinterpretations of his most canonic songs. He describes the technique as rhythmic. That is its clearest manifestation, although sometimes other "things have changed" as well. Most obviously, he radically transforms the rhythms of melodies of his most familiar songs, more even at times than Ella Fitzgerald at her most adventurous. With rhythm likely the most recognizable dimension of musical motifs, it can take some time and effort to even recognize such a recast Dylan song, no matter how familiar, especially in live acoustical spaces where text intelligibility is compromised.

Former Beatle and occasional Dylan sideman Ringo Starr describes a most extreme experience of this transformation in an interview in *Rolling Stone: The Fortieth Anniversary*. Starr lamented that at some Dylan performances he "couldn't find the songs." Invited backstage at a Dylan concert and asked to request a song, Starr asked for "Maggie's Farm." "And the band cracked up, because they'd done it already."[29]

It is possible on Dylan's live recordings to assess the difficulty of "find[ing] the songs." Several pieces on the 1995 *MTV Unplugged* set are paradigm, particularly "All along the Watchtower." This song, which he performs most often, lately as an encore at nearly every concert,[30] and is his most famous cover, especially by Jimi Hendrix but also by Dave Matthews Band and U2, is radically recomposed here. Listening, of course, demonstrates this far better than any verbal description.

Experiencing a canonic Dylan song this way is nothing like hearing Paul McCartney or the Stones rendering their oldies. When one is made to struggle with old, cherished memories in this fashion, comfortable nostalgia, the fantasy of youth, is impossible. But there is more. Not only have these pieces, for purely musical reasons—the words are only rarely changed—added the implicit subject weight of aging, they evoke a non-neurotypical experience. Without putting too fine a diagnostic point on this characterization, one cannot hear and identify a radical Dylan recomposition—common in his concerts—without simultaneously hearing the beloved and orienting canonic performance. To hear these simultaneous renditions—one folklike but imagined or remembered, the other surreal yet actual—is to both experience altered perception and to struggle with "what is real and what is not."[31] If this is not quite a disability simulation exercise, it is surely a call to empathy and self-awareness.

As elsewhere in Dylan, context matters. Only those works that are truly canonic are thus recomposed. Others in the *MTV Unplugged* set, the then-new songs "Shooting Star" and "Dignity" and the old but at that time rarely performed "John Brown," are played straight, an essential foil to his rhythmically erratic, performatively evolving canon.

The Moral of This Song

Nothing revealed here is either subtle or metaphorical. All of it is embodied, palpable, felt as much as heard or thought, not at all elusive. Dylan makes numerous, if sometimes subtle, references and allusions to all the phenomena I describe, about which my thinking is fueled by exposure to disability studies, Dylan's *Chronicles,* and various interviews.

When the perspectives of disability studies (or any other fresh methodological approach) are contemplated as a mode of inquiry into the music of Dylan (or any new topic), two complementary questions need be asked. What are the benefits to disability studies? How is knowledge of Dylan enhanced?

For disability studies, the benefit may be mostly a matter of prestige and prowess. Disability studies is likely the busiest methodological intersection of culture and embodiment. A disability studies perspective may be the only means of effectively unraveling the intricacies of Dylan's *music.*

The analyses here demonstrate a deeply embodied way of hearing what is typically understood as the least embodied of artistic media, at least with regard to music's lack of overt representation in the manner of the visual arts or the only slightly more covert renderings in literature. Dylan has surely always been appreciated on sonic terms, likely more than is realized, given the far larger energy devoted to encomiums for his formidable gift for words. Christopher Ricks refers to his monumental *Dylan's Visions of Sin* as "literary criticism" in contradistinction to "music criticism."[32] For all the brilliance of that work (and a few others like it), something still lies in waiting: the contemplation of the musical and more broadly sonic (that is, the sounds of words) elements, which Dylan himself continues to affirm in numerous ways to be of great importance.

And disability studies provides a remarkable way of hearing Dylan. Concerning poetry, Ricks quotes T. S. Eliot "that it 'is not always true that a person who knows a good poem when he sees it can tell us why it is a good poem.' "[33] This is even truer of music, whose aforementioned lack of representation sometimes evokes a sense of abstraction. The *only* apparent simplicity of Dylan's music, with its affinities to vernacular traditions in tonality, instrumentation, and some manifestations of rhythm, makes its sonic complexities more elusive to established methods of music analysis, especially those grounded in the Western canon.

Music is, when regarded in the realm of the senses, the *most* embodied of cultural expressions, by virtue of its power to evoke and inspire the corporeal. The "simplicity" in Dylan's music is only its sturdy folk template, which must, however, as we have learned, endure the complications of impairments in several forms:

bodily asymmetries, hobbling of gait, and the impact of age upon memory and orientation. In this, the American song man whose work is typically regarded as most surreal turns out to be most real, that is, human, fallible, and mortal. In one sense, that is hardly surprising and utterly apt, insofar as Dylan, among the greats of Anglo-American vernacular music, has always been among those least personally desired, least fantasized. If, per Ricks, "Hattie Carroll" is the perfect song, its poet/player is blessedly imperfect himself.[34] And the representation of bodily imperfections in sound drives the vehicle of the song's perfection. Only the disability perspective is capable of teaching us that.

The value of disability studies for Dylan is thus to enrich our hearing and to corporealize our understanding of music and, potentially, other forms of discourse and experience. Politically, the value of Dylan's perspective for disability is knowing that the woundedness that permeates his sound does indeed toll for deaf, blind, mute, and "everybody that was hanging out."[35]

Notes

1. Greil Marcus, *The Old, Weird America: The World of Bob Dylan's Basement Tapes* (New York: Picador, 2001). A comprehensive catalog of such references would overwhelm this essay. In addition to the title's reference to "Chimes of Freedom," the sensory impairments of "the blind and the deaf" are also summoned in "Ring Them Bells." Physical disability on the part of "the sick and the lame" appears in "Jokerman." Finally, mental illness is glossed as "Napoleon in rags" in Dylan's likely most famous song "Like a Rolling Stone."

2. Bob Dylan, *Chronicles, Volume 1* (New York: Simon and Schuster, 2004), 29, 230.

3. My father, the late Fred Lubet, was a World War II veteran who grew up in a predominantly Jewish neighborhood in Pittsburgh. The year he graduated high school, the yearbook listed the preferred branch of military service for each senior male. The social pressure to serve must have been great.

With regard to those young Jewish men whose disabilities rendered them unable to serve in the U.S. armed forces during World War II, University of Minnesota history professor emeritus Hy Berman provided the following: "All of my fellow draftees were Jewish. We were advanced students, so we were already sophomores in City College as we turned eighteen. Those of my classmates who were deferred because of physical disabilities were devastated because as Jews they were deprived of their right to fight Fascists and Nazis. Since most came from Immigrant homes whose families still had relatives in the 'old country' the feeling of failure was compounded by the belief that somehow they were betraying their obligation to defend their own."

For Jewish life in Hibbing and throughout the Minnesota Iron Range, see Marilyn Chiat's essay in this volume, "Jewish Homes on the Range, 1890–1960."

4. Sam Shepherd, "A Short Life of Trouble," *Esquire*, 1987, reprinted in *Bob Dylan: The Essential Interviews,* ed. Jonathan Cott, 347–65 (New York: Wenner Media, 2004), 355–56.

5. From Bob Dylan, "The Ballad of a Thin Man."

6. Murray Engleheart, interview, *Guitar World* and *Uncut,* March 1999, reprinted in *Bob Dylan,* ed. Cott, 408.

7. In an e-mail, October 23, 2007, this volume's coeditor Colleen Sheehy informed me that "Dylan had a near-death experience in Hibbing as a teenager, when he almost got hit by a train—escaping literally by inches, when crossing the tracks on his motorcycle. I have been

on the Dylan bus tour of Hibbing twice and they visit the spot and even re-enact the near fatal accident, as recounted by Leroy Hoikkala [drummer in Dylan's first band, the Golden Chords], who was there at the time." However, different from the other incidents described here, Dylan escaped unscathed and did not experience disability or incapacitating illness.

8. For example, Bruce Springsteen regards Dylan's influence as crucial to the work of U2, the Sex Pistols, and the most adventurous music of the Beatles and the Beach Boys; Engleheart, interview, 408–9.

9. The 1960 tape was made in Dylan's hometown of Hibbing, Minnesota, a fact for which I am indebted to this volume's coeditor Colleen Sheehy.

10. From Bob Dylan, "My Back Pages."

11. Steven Mithen, *The Singing Neanderthals: The Origins of Music, Language, Mind and Body* (London: Weidenfeld and Nicolson, 2005), 189–90.

12. For a verbal paean to Picasso, see Dylan, *Chronicles*, 55. More famous is Dylan's *Self-Portrait*, the painting that serves as both the cover and title of his controversial 1970 album. Legendary Canadian singer-songwriter Leonard Cohen called Dylan "the Picasso of song" in *Wanted Man: In Search of Bob Dylan*, ed. John Bauldie (New York: Citadel Underground, 1991), 155.

13. The complete lyrics for "The Lonesome Death of Hattie Carroll" can be found at Dylan's official Web site at http://search.bobdylan.com/moderntimes/lyricsearch/searchResults.jsp?doSearch=true&q=hattie&range=50.

14. See Christopher Ricks, *Dylan's Visions of Sin* (New York: Ecco, 2004), 15–18, 221–33. I hold this and several other observations in common with Ricks. My analysis was essentially (and purposely) complete prior to reading Ricks, except where he is expressly acknowledged.

15. Ibid., 224–25.

16. Dylan expresses his great admiration for Harold Arlen (49) and the Brill Building writers in *Chronicles*, 227.

While the idea of the lexical "drum set" is mine, it derives from the work of Philip Furia, one of the foremost scholars of the classic American song lyric.

17. Ricks's analysis (*Dylan's Visions of Sin*, 222–24, 226) is much grounded in feminine and masculine endings, which account for many word choices and help establish critical linkages between related themes, but which also transcend the musical framework, poetically stabilizing even at points of musically rhythmic rupture. Similarly, his analysis draws Dylan—appropriately—mostly into the tradition of the British literary canon and only occasionally into relation with Anglo-American folk musical idioms, the natural location of an analysis such as mine that primarily considers musical elements.

18. Ricks makes the same observation, adding "Carroll" at the very beginning of the stanza; *Dylan's Visions of Sin*, 225.

19. Ricks regards these *–l* endings as a continuation of their use in the previous stanza, rather than a return; *Dylan's Visions of Sin*, 225.

20. Ricks refers to this as "Black English," referencing a similar use in James Baldwin's *The Amen Corner; Dylan's Visions of Sin*, 229. I am hesitant to make this connection so explicitly, both because "Hattie Carroll" so famously avoids any overt mention of race and because this particular colloquialism is in fact class- rather than race-associated.

21. Oliver Trager, *Keys to the Rain: The Definitive Bob Dylan Encyclopedia* (New York: Billboard Books, 2004), 391.

22. From Bob Dylan, "Just Like a Woman."

23. Thanks to Professor Maria Damon, Department of Music, University of Minnesota, for her expertise in this matter.

24. Trager, *Keys to the Rain,* 391. Full disclosure demands that the possibility of a simple factual error on Dylan's part may be the culprit here, as it would not be the only such case. Ricks notes that Dylan refers to the villain of "Hattie Carroll" as "William Zanzinger," although it is properly "Zantzinger"; Ricks, *Dylan's Visions of Sin,* 222–23.

25. Robert Hilburn, interview, *Los Angeles Times,* April 4, 2004, reprinted in *Bob Dylan,* ed. Cott, 435.

26. For Dylan's ideas about rhyme, which seem to extend by inference to poetic meter as well, see Paul Zollo, interview, *Songtalk,* 1991, collected in Paul Zollo, *Songwriters on Songwriting* (Cambridge, Mass.: Da Capo Press, 2003); reprinted in *Bob Dylan,* ed. Cott, 367–89, 383; and Hilburn, interview, 435.

27. Dylan expresses his admiration for both Tin Pan Alley composer Harold Arlen (49) and the Brill Building composers and lyricists, especially singer-songwriter-pianist Neil Sedaka (227) in *Chronicles.* In a 1991 interview with Paul Zollo (370), Dylan contrasts himself as a "confessional" songwriter with "professionals," a category that by his description appears to include Tin Pan Alley, Brill Building, and Hollywood composers and lyricists. For a more mixed perspective on Broadway and Tin Pan Alley, see Hilburn, interview, 432–33.

28. Dylan, *Chronicles,* 209–11.

29. Anthony DeCurtis, "Ringo Starr," *Rolling Stone: The Fortieth Anniversary* 1025/1026: 33–7 (May 2007), 66–67.

30. The set lists of Dylan's live performances can be accessed almost immediately after the concerts at http://expectingrain.com/.

31. From Bob Dylan, "Gates of Eden."

32. Ricks, *Dylan's Visions of Sin,* 7.

33. Ibid., 8.

34. Ibid., 233.

35. From Bob Dylan, "Like a Rolling Stone."

20. Bob Dylan and the Beats:
Magpie Poetics, an Investigation and Memoir
Anne Waldman

"he taught me three chords,
so I got down to blues"

—*Allen Ginsberg*

I invoke "magpie poetics" in this investigative memoir as a way of understanding Bob Dylan's extraordinary creativity. He took what he needed from multiple places and sources—literary, musical, cultural—which included influences from and references to the Beat literary generation writers, particularly the works of Jack Kerouac and Allen Ginsberg. Dylan and Ginsberg were friends, and Dylan had an influence on Ginsberg's own songwriting and performing forays. He specifically told Allen to write and compose blues. Whatever Dylan gleaned from his association with the Beats—the sound and phrasing and movement of his language—his own work developed out of a fascinating amalgam of these influences into a highly original sound.

This is a rhizomic essay, invoking the influence of the Beat writers on the young Dylan. It includes a pastiche of quotation, unpublished correspondence with David Amram, and an unpublished transcript of a talk by Michael McClure delivered at the Jack Kerouac School of Disembodied Poetics at Naropa University. I also include a poem–memoir of my own from my travels with the Rolling Thunder Revue, the elucidating scholarship and insights of Greil Marcus and Michael Gray, and Allen Ginsberg's own observations on Dylan from *Spontaneous Mind,* a book of interviews. Dylan's recent *Chronicles, Volume 1* also indicates a fascination with, and consideration of, Beat tropes and a lifestyle peppered as it is with reference to the Beats. I will begin with my poem, written on the Rolling Thunder Revue tour, "Shaman Hisses You Slide Back into the Night":

> This is something about power taking off its clothes & laboring
>   & at the moment I did not know the value of knowledge
> to make sore by friction
>   Observe the structure of a group, each flickering detail
> surrounding shaman
>
>   this one lights, this one drives, this one makes you laugh,
> this one drums, that one's purely Byzantine
>   there's the Woman-Who-Manages

the Woman-Who-Sets-Up, the Money-Man, the Advance-Man
      the Man-Who-Collects-the-Bags

& clearly the pressure makes its imprint on the body turning me weak
it turns me weak it turns me weak it turns me weak
it turns me weak

I write to pass the time. Solo. Midnight. I spy the source
I am the frequent bystander. Molecular.

          A man-woman a woman-man a shaman

a man who makes a song to heal

                    elegance

   coercion

             diffidence

      Danbury, Connecticut, at the beginning

I ask for Dr. William Carlos Williams at the desk (Ginsberg's alias)
shirk all duty and keep the memory of the heart

     vicissitudes & finally, to vocalize

& shaman he swings a skinny leg to the sky
& shaman he desires you be there watching
shaman don't care about eating now
he's got his paint on he's ready for jive
& shaman's going to sway & gesture in space
& shaman's shouting yeah for you
& singing your sorrow
shaman's not faithful except to you
shaman does it for you you know all this
shaman's got his eyes on the violin
shaman's moving his eyeballs around
shaman's in Rome
shaman's going to finish what he started
shaman grows old & never changes
O shaman leave your dog outside
shaman makes no mistake
shaman lights a Gitane
shaman hisses you slide back into the night
shaman makes you disappear
cuts you out to include you
shaman's pacing & clocks your confusion
shaman makes you hungry to feed you
shaman in black & white
shaman a walking, talking kachina doll
shaman around five feet tall

shaman struts
shaman's brim casts a shadow
shaman points a toe
shaman wears a feather
shaman is reckless
shaman in whiteface
shaman barks a meter
shaman speaks occasionally
shaman dedicates this one to the great American writer
shaman appears on the right
shaman boots a compadre
shaman takes you west
shaman cuts the brush
shaman yawns & gazes out window
shaman gets gruff for you
      reaches the high notes
      has a family
      eats turkey
      swings his guitar like a baby
      is a baby
      is sometimes a woman
      is casting off
shaman is a centripetal force
shaman drives a hard bargain
shaman mixes it up
shaman is obvious o shaman so obvious
shaman won't be there
shaman takes liberties
shaman touches the ocean
shaman don't drown
shaman echoes himself
shaman bites down hard on the wind
you'd better well listen to shaman[1]

There is a wonderful "consociational" weave in Dylan's work, a syncretic, magpie amalgam of shared sources and proclivities as well as a kind of conversation or dialogue in the alliances and mutual interests of Dylan and the Beats. The Beats I refer to are Jack Kerouac and Allen Ginsberg, most referenced here, but also Gregory Corso, Michael McClure, Ray Bremser, Gary Snyder, Peter Orlovsky, Lawrence Ferlinghetti, Diane di Prima, Philip Whalen, Amiri Baraka (formerly LeRoi Jones), composer/musician David Amram, and William Burroughs.

Although I am nearly a generation younger than most of these figures, I participate in a lineage of poetics deemed "second generation" Beat/New York School/ Black Mountain, which is part of the New American Poetry. I participate in its attendant poetry cultures and its cultural interventions. Many of us, poets born in the 1940s and 1950s, are hybrids, and we have a bit of the magpie in us too, sorting through the glittering inheritance and precious detritus of the imaginations of many of our predecessors. We are the hybrid, the mongrel, the magpie. As a song-writer-lyricist, Dylan fed on his predecessors, including the genius work of black bluesmen. As poet, Dylan was introduced to the work of Kenneth Patchen by friends in Dinkytown in Minneapolis. Dylan also cites Gregory Corso's book *Gasoline* as an influence. He cites Lawrence Ferlinghetti. He cites Kerouac's *On the Road* and *Visions of Gerard* and quotes the opening lines of Ginsberg's "Howl":

> Minneapolis—. . . I came out of the wilderness and just naturally fell in with the beat scene . . . there were always a lot of poems recited; "Into the room people come and go talking of Michaelangelo. Measuring their lives in coffee spoons". . . "What I'd like to know is what do you think of your blue-eyed boy now, Mr Death." TS Eliot, e.e. cummings. It was sort of like that and it woke me up. Jack Kerouac, Ginsberg, Corso and Ferlinghetti – "Gasoline," "Coney Island of The Mind". . . oh man, I was wild—"I saw the best minds of my generation destroyed by madness," that said more to me than any of the stuff I'd been raised on . . . whatever was happening of any real value was sort of hidden from view.[2]

As David Amram wrote to me in a recent e-mail:

> I finally realized after many years that the reason why Dylan spent a lot of time with me and Allen was that we were the closest he could get to being with Jack, whom he really admired. Jack and I always said when walking around the village and Lower East Side at 4 a.m. that

> > #1 An artist must burn with a hard and gem-like flame (Walter Pater)
> > #2 By your works ye shall be known (Old Testament)
> > #3 A thing of beauty is a joy forever (either Keats or Shelley, since Gregory Corso insisted one of them stole it from the other, and could never decide which one thought of it first)

> These were our mantras. These three sayings certainly epitomize the prodigious output of Dylan, and in the time I spent with him, I always felt he was searching for way more than the industrial music scene ever has had to offer, and he transcended it and continues to do so, just as many of us refused to be hemmed in by the artificial walls we were told we were supposed to remain imprisoned by and stay behind.

> Dylan came out of a small town and grew up with big dreams of seeing the rest of the world, just as Jack did growing up in the mill town of Lowell, Massachusetts and as I did on a farm in Feasterville, Pennsylvania. We all felt outside the loop and had seemingly impossible dreams of becoming artists in families that didn't expect their sons to pursue such outrageous goals.[3]

There is a telling bit in *On the Road* that encapsulates Kerouac's poetics in a nutshell, a poetics that would influence the writing practice of many, including Ginsberg, and the young Dylan: "He watched over my shoulder as I wrote stories, yelling, 'Yes! That's right! Wow! Man!' And 'Phew' and wiped his face with a handkerchief. 'Man, wow, there's so many things to do, so many things to write. How to begin to even get it all down and without modified restraints and all hung-up on like literary inhibitions and grammatical fears . . .' "[4] Kerouac's an "ear poet" as is Dylan. Sound is the way we apprehend and empathize the movement of language. We get language's meaning from this subtle movement, and some poets hear subvocally in the head, in the process of the writing, as poet Clark Coolidge has noted in his critical studies of Kerouac.[5] I think Dylan picked up on Kerouac's sound in this way. Kerouac himself could hear what he was writing, and he wrote at a fantastic speed, one hundred words per minute is the official count.

In a letter to editor Donald Allen, Kerouac wrote, "The rhythm of how you decide to rush your statement determines the rhythm of the poem." If you rush your statement, you are also speeding up the words. Woody Guthrie did this, pushing on language and image. Long stretches of vocal energy. This quality of Kerouac had a monumental influence on Ginsberg and others, and one sees this subvocal energy in Dylan, albeit at a slower speed. Dylan's lyric is much less structurally, grammatically complex, and so much resides in the syntax and complexity of delivery. It is a different kind of mind grammar. As Dylan wrote, "Some plaintive woos in the twilight & throats ripping & laughing & fool's terror snapping like a tail & taking it in the ribs & bop music where south walls quivering & colliding bosoms & weigh the likes of maid marian's bandits & i repeat: two face minny/the army derelict/Christine, who's hung up on your forehead / steve canyon jones who looks like mae west in a closet. . . ."[6] Greil Marcus has suggested that "[T]he voice in Desolation Row [clearly a nod to Desolation Angels] is partly Kerouac's voice, in his narration for Robert Frank and Alfred Leslie's 1959 life-among-the-beatniks movie *Pull My Daisy.* 'Look at all those cars out there,' he says. 'Nothing there but a million screaming ninety-year-old men being run over by gasoline trucks. So throw a match on it.' From Kerouac you can go back more than half a century and hundreds of years from there, and find yourself in the same room."[7]

The roots for Dylan, and for much of the culture and my own generation and subsequent generations of poets, were in the 1950s, which is when the famous Six Gallery reading took place in San Francisco in October 1955, an occasion historically seen as the launch of the Beat movement and the poem "Howl." Michael McClure speaks of the political and cultural 1950s and the political setting in an unpublished talk from the Kerouac School at Naropa:

> The 50s were not the way people imagine them today, lovely and retro, very sentimental, they danced a certain way and television was just coming in. It was the time of the cold war, the time of the House on Un-American Activities committee, the time of Joe McCarthy, the time of the war in Korea, the beginning of our series of our massacres of people around the world, particularly in Asian countries. People were tremendously oppressed by their own need for conformity after having been through the Second World War and after having been through the educational machine of the propaganda system that was created by the Second World War. And everybody believed that being absolutely fucking miserable and

loveless and owning a Buick with a kind of ring on the nose with a torpedo through it and a tract home and feeling heartless, unloved, and unlovable was the way to go, as long as you had the right kitchen gadgets. It was a seriously ugly time, a seriously stressed time.[8]

That doesn't mean that some of the folks who were to change the frequency of the culture weren't *privileged* as well, yet still chomping at the bit, ready to let things rip. McClure goes on to speak of the "reservations" like North Beach in San Francisco, the reservation of Greenwich Village, enclaves of sanity and creativity and people "beginning to listen to black music, blues, so there's an enormous influence coming in of black music." We know Dylan had his sights on Greenwich Village, the New York nexus, where Pete Seeger and Woody Guthrie were based. Minneapolis was also an alternative enclave, as were many college campuses across the land that had alternative communities at the fringes of the academy, "temporary autonomous zones," so to speak, in the phrase of anarchist Hakim Bey.

As Greil Marcus observes in *Like a Rolling Stone*, "[I]n its headlong drive into the street, its insistence on saying everything because tomorrow it will be too late—to speak as a prophet, someone who, burdened with Knowledge he didn't want but, having received it, is forced to pass on—'Like a Rolling Stone' probably owes more to Allen Ginsberg's 1955 'Howl' than to any song."[9] The influence was mutual.

Ginsberg first met Dylan in 1963. Ginsberg was fifteen years Dylan's senior and thus a little too young to be the father figure many impute him to be, although there is that father-son, at least familial dynamic playing out, and sometimes in reverse, where Ginsberg seems the son anxious to please his elder, more powerful, more oracular Dylan-father-or-brother figure. In the liner notes of *Bringing It All Back Home* Dylan wrote:

> ....I have
> given up making any attempt at perfection/
> the fact that the white house is filled with
> leaders that've never been to the Apollo
> theatre amazes me. why allen ginsberg was
> not chosen t' read poetry at the inauguration
> boggles my mind/if someone thinks norman
> mailer is more important than hank williams
> that's fine.[10]

Ginsberg describes first meeting Dylan:

> I met him in 1963. I was in India for about a year and a half, and there was a welcome home party for us when we [Ginsberg and his companion Peter Orlovsky] got back. Al Aronowitz, the journalist who is a friend of Dylan's and whom I knew from the late fifties when he did a story on the Beat generation for the Post, came and brought Dylan. He was coming that night from his meeting with the Emergency Civil Liberties Committee's annual banquet, who had given him an award, Dylan had declared a sort of independence of any specific political

allegiance and that upset them a bit. So we talked about poetry and politics, how poetry was just a reflection of the mind, independent of politics. We made friends that night.[11]

There's the photo of Ginsberg embedded in the cover of *Bringing It All Back Home.*

Later Amram, famous for his score for *Pull My Daisy* (with narration by Jack Kerouac), brought Dylan to a reading at New York University, where Dylan heard Ginsberg improvising with Orlovsky. They talked afterwards, and Dylan came by and jammed with Ginsberg on harmonium on a song of Ginsberg's called "Going Down to Puerto Rico." Dylan said, "Why don't we go into the studio and record this?" Ginsberg called the Record Plant in New York the next day. I was at some of those sessions singing backup. Gregory Corso was making music with a child's toy. Dylan was extremely helpful to the gestalt of the situation, and I think Ginsberg felt he was getting Dylan's blessing for his musical/lyric explorations. The sessions were like a "dissipative structure," a lot of friends and musicians coming and going.

Ginsberg traveled with the Rolling Thunder Revue in the 1970s and assiduously studied Dylan's lyrics, his music, his performances. He often sat in the front row of the theaters and venues we would roll into. We joked that Ginsberg was Dylan's most dedicated groupie. It was a respectful, yet at times a complicated, relationship. Consequently Ginsberg, of all the Beat writers, has the most to say about Dylan. He championed him in his interviews and public commentary, and referred to him in his journals. He followed Dylan's exhilarating trajectory until his own death in April 1996. In many of my own conversations with Ginsberg he forged, even *pressed* (being the legend builder he was) the ongoing link of Dylan to the Beats. As he was dying, he regretted there was no opportunity to do an "Unplugged Ginsberg" session with Dylan, as he had hoped.

LeRoi Jones/Amiri Baraka has an early suite of poems, "Crow Jane," taking its title from the Mississippi Joe Williams's lyric, "Crow Jane, Crow Jane, don't hold your head so high, / You realize, baby, you got to lay down and die." There might also be an intentional nod from Baraka to William Butler Yeats's Crazy Jane poems. From the Baraka poems:

> Jane
> Wet lady of no image. We
> thought you had left us, Dark
> lady, of constant promise. We
> thought
> you had gone.
>
> Oh Jane (Her boats bumps at the/
> ragged
> shore. Soul of the ocean, go out,
> return
> Oh Jane, we thought you had gone.[12]

This last sounds to my ear a little like Dylan's "Sad Eyed Lady of the Lowlands." Dylan invokes Crow Jane in *Tarantula* in the piece titled "Mouthful of Loving Choke":

> Crow jane say come, hang out her limelight…there are green bullets in my throat / I walk sloppily on the sun feeling them turn into yellow keys—I touch jane on the inside & I swallow…[13]

There is a huge debt to black culture in the writing of the Beats and in Dylan's music and lyrics. But some mutual appreciation as well from black artists toward Dylan: "Blowin' in the Wind" inspired Sam Cooke's "A Change Is Gonna Come," and a version of "Like a Rolling Stone" was covered by Jimi Hendrix.

Consociational is a term I borrow from anthropologist Clifford Geertz, as it connotes the shared experience within a culture, although the ages and backgrounds of the participants may differ. For example, we are all consociates living in the aftermath of the events of September 11, 2001, although some denizens of this planet might have been born that very day or died a few weeks later or on that very day. Some might have been closer to the actual event than others, but many were affected by it and share in the aftermath or karma of that event. I share World War II and its aftermath with my father, who fought in Germany, although I was born in 1945.

I grew up on Macdougal Street in Manhattan, and although a few years younger than Dylan, I experienced a lot of the same alternative artistic Greenwich Village culture as he did. We share many of the same cultural reference points. I sat on Leadbelly's lap as a child. I first saw Amiri Baraka's *Dutchman* and *The Baptism* at the Cherry Lane Theatre, as Dylan did. I followed the work of artist Red Grooms (who was close to the poets Frank O'Hara and John Ashbery, whom I met early on), as Dylan did through his friendship with Susie Rotolo. I hung out at the clubs and coffee shops on Macdougal, as Dylan did. I even dated John Hammond Jr., who lived down the block and whose father ran Columbia Records and signed Dylan. I attended Pete Seeger's hootenannies in the neighborhood and played in Washington Square Park with his son. My older brother Mark was a dedicated folkie. And so on. I danced to "In the Still of the Night" and "Let the Good Times Roll," "Chantilly Lace." In 1962 at Bennington College I convinced my professor Stanley Edgar Hyman to allow me to write a paper on rock and roll and its African roots. I heard the Beatles coming on a scratchy radio station in Athens, Greece, in 1963, where I was friendly with country musician and producer Jim Rooney, who was studying there on a Fulbright. And Ginsberg (whom my father had met in the late 1950s) and I share a huge part of the past century together, just as many of us do, as Dylan and the rest of the Beats do. From the Gaslight, where he worked in the early 1960s, and a place I also spent some time in, Dylan writes, "You could sit on a bar stool and look out the windows to the snowy streets and see some heavy people going by, David Amram bundled up, Gregory Corso, Ted Joans, Fred Hellerman."[14]

At one point in *Chronicles* Dylan references the jukebox at the Gaslight:

[T]he jukebox in the place showed mostly jazz records. Zoot Simms (who Kerouac recorded with), Hampton Hawes, Stan Getz, and some rhythm-and-blues records—Bumble Bee Slim, Slim Galliard, Percy Mayfield. The Beats tolerated folk music, but they really didn't like it. They listened exclusively to modern jazz, bebop.[15]

I think this is a telling note. From the beginning, Dylan is comparing, measuring his proclivities to those of the Beats. He's a poet. A lone guy playing solo with his guitar and harmonica. He writes:

Within the first few months that I was in New York I'd lost my interest in the "hungry for kicks" hipster vision that Kerouac illustrates so well in his book *On the Road.* That book had been like a bible for me. Not anymore, though. I still loved the breathless, dynamic bop poetry phrases that flowed from Jack's pen, but now, that character Moriarity seemed out of place, purposeless—seemed like a character who inspired idiocy. He goes through life bumping and grinding with a bull on top of him.[16]

Witness Ginsberg in the recent Martin Scorsese documentary *No Direction Home,* where he weeps as he speaks about Dylan and "A Hard Rain's A-Gonna Fall," saying that the torch had been passed to a new generation.[17] He also speaks in this documentary of Dylan as a "column of wind." "Idiot Wind" was one of Ginsberg's favorite songs of Dylan's, and he would often quote the refrain.

I saw Bob Dylan in performance as the metaphoric shaman. His orality and imagination on stage were transforming. The conduit, the transformer, the "antennae of the race," in Ezra Pound's definition of the artist. He was at the center of the show, his pulse was the pulse of the entire entourage. If he was up, we were too. He and Ginsberg shared a charisma onstage but from different vantages. Ginsberg in his poetry or political zones was very much the center, the transformer, the word-worker, the conscience of the times. But Dylan was more amped up, and his stretch—through recordings—reached further into the public's psyche. Ginsberg's stretch is longer on the page. Ginsberg and Dylan visited Kerouac's gravesite in Lowell, Massachusetts, during the Rolling Thunder Revue period, which is documented in Dylan's epic movie *Renaldo and Clara.* When Ginsberg asked Dylan if he had ever read Kerouac, Dylan replies, "Yeah, when I was young in Minneapolis," saying further, "I didn't understand the words then, I understand them much better now, but it blew my mind." Ginsberg asked him why, and he responds, "It's the first poem that talked American language to me."[18]

Ginsberg discussed the reading of "Mexico City Blues," and they both proceeded to read various stanzas from this text at Kerouac's grave site: "like kissing my kitten in the belly, the softness of our reward." Ginsberg plays a character called the Father in *Renaldo and Clara.* We see him offering religious instruction to Dylan (as Renaldo). And there's a skewed irony with two Jewish poets. "What's with the Christian theology!" someone quips. And Ginsberg is a gay man, not a progenitor. Ginsberg guides a young David Mansfield to the brothel (it is one of the red velvet–walled suites in the Château Frontenac in Quebec City). I play one of the ladies of the night with red bra and red Tibetan Buddhist protection cord around my neck. What's it protecting you against? My own ego. "I'd rather be home reading a good book," I get to say. I make the most money I have ever made on a poem so far: Dylan pays me $2,000 for two minutes of my reading "Fast Speaking Woman" on the sound track.

What I notice during the tour is Ginsberg's yearning to be closer, to be able to get up on the stage. "Howl"—after the rehearsal with Jacques Levy in New York— had been cut from the show. Ginsberg is always up early in the morning. Soft-boiled egg. *New York Times,* when we can get it. Taking notes. Dylan says to Ginsberg (who relates to Dylan as his definitive music guru at one point), go sing your songs on street corners, don't wait to be recorded or discovered. There's a bit of taunt and tease in the relationship, whose intimacy I notice Ginsberg deeply enjoys. But he's on tenterhooks. Let the poet sing in the rain. I march into Dylan's dressing room. Let the poet sing in the rain! He had been promising Ginsberg the moon, that he could read on the rock-and-roll stage. We're in Colorado, Fort Collins. Hard Rain concert. I get a credit for headdresses in the documentary version, *Hard Rain.* I've been wearing a desert wrap looks like Joseph of Arimathea (which now resembles the mufti fashion of Osama bin Laden). Dylan, the guys in the band like the look. There's a break turning off the juice so no one gets electrocuted. Ginsberg comes out solo on stage and reads his elegiac long line haiku—

On Neal's Ashes
Delicate eyes that blinked blue Rockies all ash
Nipples, Ribs I touched w/my thumb are ash
Asshole anneale'd to silken skin all ashes, ashes all ashes again

We're in the Rockies, not far from Neal's hardscrabble back alleys of Denver. I conclude with lines from "Shaman Hisses You Slide Back into the Night":

shaman likes the cold
shaman is a harbor
shaman breathes across metal reeds
shaman makes you cleave to rocks
shaman blows you away
you'd better well go away
shaman heeds the percussion
shaman slows down
shaman dedicates this one to Brigham Young
shaman snaps another string
shaman's heels wear down
but shaman has timbrels in his voice
shaman has an ocean in his voice
shaman has a mean man in his voice
shaman has a chromium lover in his voice
shaman has disaster in his voice

shaman has all the creatures & especially a jaguar in his voice
shaman has carpets in his voice
shaman has icicles in his voice
shaman has pleasure in his voice
shaman leaves no ordinary trace
shaman imprinting on you
shaman is a victim for you
shaman is vagrant for you
shaman vindicates you
shaman is vigorous
shaman rides a horse
shaman loves a goddess
shaman says his thoughts vanish before they come
shaman still wandering
shaman lost his shadow
shaman don't need a shadow
shaman's shadow is scattered & walked upon in this dream[19]

Notes

1. Anne Waldman, *Shaman/Schamane* (Hannover, Germany: Apartment Editions, 1990), 49–51.

2. Michael Gray, *Song and Dance Man III: The Art of Bob Dylan* (London: Continuum, 2000).

3. David Amram, unpublished e-mail correspondence with the author, 2007.

4. Jack Kerouac, *On the Road*, rev. ed. (New York: Penguin, 1999), 4.

5. Clark Coolidge, unpublished transcript, "Kerouac's Sound," Jack Kerouac School of Disembodied Poetics Archive.

6. Bob Dylan, *Tarantula* (New York: Scribner, 2004), 35.

7. Greil Marcus, *Like a Rolling Stone: Bob Dylan at the Crossroads* (New York: PublicAffairs, 2006), 174.

8. Michael McClure, unpublished transcript, Jack Kerouac School of Disembodied Poetics Archive, 2007.

9. Marcus, *Like a Rolling Stone*, 123.

10. Bob Dylan, *Lyrics 1962–1985* (New York: Knopf, 1985), 180.

11. Allen Ginsberg, *Spontaneous Mind: Selected Interviews 1958–1996*, ed. David Carter (New York: Harper Collins, 2002), 431.

12. Amiri Baraka, "Crow Jane the Crook," in *The Beat Book*, ed. Anne Waldman (Boston: Shambhala Publications, 1999), 213.

13. Dylan, *Tarantula*, 37.

14. Bob Dylan, *Chronicles, Volume 1* (New York: Simon and Schuster, 2004), 48.

15. Ibid.

16. Ibid., 57–58.

17. *No Direction Home*, directed by Martin Scorsese (Hollywood, Calif.: Paramount, 2005).

18. Ginsberg, *Spontaneous Mind*, 505.

19. Waldman, *Shaman/Schamane*.

Acknowledgments

The editors thank Doug Armato, director of the University of Minnesota Press, who recognized the value of bringing this new work on Dylan to a wide readership after the March 2007 Dylan symposium at the University of Minnesota. Our editorial assistant, John Barner, was invaluable in keeping track of multiple versions of essays by multiple authors and adding his acute insights to our plans and his good humor to the process. The editors also thank Alicia Sellheim, Laura Westlund, Keir Keightley, and an anonymous reviewer for the University of Minnesota Press, who offered thoughtful suggestions for revising this book. Thomas Swiss especially thanks Cynthia, Jacob, and Alley—"If Not for You." Colleen Sheehy thanks Peter, Annie, and Brigid for understanding the value of this work and her many trips to Hibbing.

The essays collected here are based on the symposium "Highway 61 Revisited: Dylan's Road from Minnesota to the World," which took place on March 25 to 27, 2007. As a collaborative project led by Colleen Sheehy, director of education and a curator at the Weisman Art Museum at the University of Minnesota, the event coincided with the museum's presentation of *Bob Dylan's American Journey, 1955–65,* an exhibition organized by Experience Music Project (EMP) in Seattle.

We are grateful to the symposium advisory committee for their guidance and suggestions, most of whom are faculty at the University of Minnesota: Hyman Berman, Marilyn Chiat, Susan Clayton, Maria Damon, Alex Lubet, Todd Mahon, Lary May, Peter Mercer-Taylor, John Mowitt, Kevin Murphy, Riv-Ellen Prel, Paula Rabinowitz, Gilbert Rodman, Linda Schloff, Madelon Sprengnether, Ellen Stekert, and Paul Stone.

Other people at the University of Minnesota who deserve thanks are Lori Graven, Heather Dorr, Electra Sylva, Beth Gusenius, and Tim Tassone.

We deeply thank our Hibbing collaborators and friends: Bob and Linda Hocking, B. J. and Leona Rolfzen, Leroy Hoikkala, Dan Bergan, Greg French, Joe and Mary Keys, Roberta Maki, and Paul Aubin.

We are grateful for the contribution of Tunheim Partners, who worked on publicity for the symposium and helped us keep it visible, even earning a notice in *Time* magazine for their efforts. Kathy Tunheim, Sarah Shamala, and Emily Chapman were particularly involved from that firm.

The Weisman exhibition and symposium could not have occurred without the generous support of the Dylan project's major sponsor, Target, and of additional funds from Ameriprise Financial. The University of Minnesota's McKnight Fund for the Arts and Humanities, recognizing the scholarly importance of bringing together speakers on one of the university's own students (Dylan attended the university from fall 1959 to fall 1960), was a strong and generous supporter of the "Highway 61 Revisited" symposium. In-kind support for the symposium was provided by 89.3 The Current and Tunheim Partners. Anne Waldman's appearance was supported in part by the Morton Zabel Fund of the Department of English, the Institute for Advanced Study, and the departments of American Studies and Women's Studies at the University of Minnesota.

Dylan's business manager, Jeff Rosen, helped in many ways with this publication, especially with permissions to quote Dylan's lyrics and other published writings. Robert Zimmerman, Elston Gunnn, Bob Dylan, Jack Fate, and other incarnations joined us in spirit.

To all, we offer our deep gratitude.

Contributors

John Barner is a professional drummer and a graduate student at the University of Georgia. His research focuses on political sociology and culture, specifically the impact of popular media on the historical and contemporary growth and development of social and political movements.

Daphne Brooks is associate professor of English and African-American studies at Princeton University. She is author of *Bodies in Dissent: Spectacular Performances of Race and Freedom, 1850–1910* and *Jeff Buckley's Grace*.

Court Carney is assistant professor of history at Stephen F. Austin State University and is currently completing a book on the diffusion of jazz in the 1920s. His other projects include articles on Civil War memory, jazz in New Orleans, and the rock band Wilco.

Alessandro Carrera is professor of Italian studies at the University of Houston. He has published *La voce di Bob Dylan. Una spiegazione dell'America* and translated *Chronicles, Volume 1, Lyrics 1962–2001,* and (with Santo Pettinato) *Tarantula* into Italian. He has received the Montale Prize for Poetry (1993), the Loria Prize for Short Fiction (1998), and the Bertolucci Prize for Literary Criticism (2006), awarded by Academy Award–winning filmmaker Bernardo Bertolucci.

Michael Cherlin is professor of music theory and composition and founding director of the Interdisciplinary Program in Collaborative Arts at the University of Minnesota. He is a coeditor and contributor to *The Great Tradition: Dramatic and Musical Theater in Austria and Central Europe* as well as author of *Schoenberg's Musical Imagination.*

Marilyn J. Chiat received her Ph.D. in art history from the University of Minnesota. She has published four books and numerous articles on religious art and architecture.

As the director of the Project to Document Jewish Settlers in Minnesota, she conducted extensive research on Jewish settlers on Minnesota's Iron Range, particularly in the four communities with synagogues (Chisholm, Hibbing, Eveleth, and Virginia).

Susan Clayton is a Twin Cities art historian and critic who focuses on Minnesota artists and arts institutions. She is a former curator at the University of St. Thomas, St. Paul. She grew up in Hibbing, Minnesota, where she worked as assistant to the director of the Hibbing Historical Society.

Mick Cochrane was born and raised in St. Paul, Minnesota. He is the author of *The Girl Who Threw Butterflies, Flesh Wounds* (a finalist in Barnes and Noble's annual Discover Great New Writers competition), and *Sport* (Minnesota, 2003). He is professor of English and Lowery Writer-in-Residence at Canisius College in Buffalo, New York.

Thomas Crow is Rosalie Solow Professor of Modern Art at New York University's Institute of Fine Arts. He is contributing editor to *Artforum* and author of numerous books on art and art history, including *The Rise of the Sixties: American and European Art in the Era of Dissent*. He served as director of the Getty Research Institute from 2000 to 2007.

Kevin J. H. Dettmar is W. M. Keck Professor and Chair of English at Pomona College. He is author or editor of books on James Joyce and modernism and general editor of the classroom text *The Longman Anthology of British Literature*. In popular music studies, he coedited *Reading Rock & Roll* and published most recently *Is Rock Dead?* He is editor of the *Cambridge Companion to Bob Dylan*.

Sumanth Gopinath is assistant professor of music theory at the University of Minnesota. He is working on two book projects, one on issues of race and ethnicity in Steve Reich's music and another on the global ring tone industry.

Charles Hughes is a Ph.D. candidate in the history department of the University of Wisconsin-Madison. He is interested in intersections between race, politics, and musical culture in twentieth-century America. His research concerns the relationship between soul and country music in the American South, and his work has appeared in a variety of academic and journalistic publications. He is also a musician and songwriter.

C. P. Lee is a writer, musician, broadcaster, and academic based at the University of Salford, Manchester, England, where he teaches cultural studies in the School of Media, Music, and Performance. The author of several books on popular music and two on Bob Dylan in particular, he attended the infamous Manchester Free Trade Hall "Judas!" concert in 1966 and is still getting over it.

Alex Lubet is Morse Alumni/Graduate and Professional Distinguished Teaching Professor of Music, Jewish Studies, and American Studies at the University of Minnesota. He is also a composer, multi-instrumentalist, and theater artist, whose musical and dramatic works have received more than four hundred performances on six continents.

Greil Marcus is the author of *The Shape of Things to Come: Prophecy and the American Voice, Mystery Train, Lipstick Traces, Dead Elvis, In the Fascist Bathroom, The Dustbin of History, The Old, Weird America,* and *Like a Rolling Stone: Bob Dylan at the Crossroads.* In 2008 he taught the seminar The Old Weird America: The Commonplace Song as Democratic Speech at the University of Minnesota. He lives in Berkeley, California.

Aldon Lynn Nielsen is Kelly Professor of American Literature at Pennsylvania State University. His books of criticism include *Reading Race, Writing between the Lines, C. L. R. James: A Critical Introduction, Black Chant,* and *Integral Music.* Among his awards for literary criticism are the Kayden Prize, the SAMLA Studies prize, and the Josephine Miles Award. His poetry volumes include *Heat Strings, Evacuation Routes, Stepping Razor, Vext,* and *Mixage.*

Robert Polito is author of the poetry collection *Hollywood & God, The Complete Film Writings of Manny Farber, Doubles, A Reader's Guide to James Merrill's "The Changing Light at Sandover,"* and *Savage Art: A Biography of Jim Thompson,* which received the National Book Critics Circle Award in biography. He founded the Graduate Writing Program at The New School in New York City and continues to direct and teach there.

Robert Reginio is assistant professor of English at Alfred University in New York. His research interests include the study of Dylan and race.

Colleen J. Sheehy is director and CEO of the Plains Art Museum in Fargo, North Dakota. From 1993 to 2008, she was a curator and director of education at the Weisman Art Museum at the University of Minnesota, where she also taught art history and American studies. Her exhibition *Springsteen: Troubadour of the Highway* in 2002 was the first major exhibition on Bruce Springsteen and traveled nationally. In 2005, she curated *Musicapolis: Seen and Scene, 1965–2005* for the Minnesota Center for Photography. She was coordinating curator for *Bob Dylan's American Journey, 1955–1965* at the Weisman Art Museum and lead organizer of the symposium "Highway 61 Revisited: Dylan's Road from Minnesota to the World."

Heather Stur is assistant professor of history at the University of Southern Mississippi. She is author of a forthcoming book on gender and the Vietnam War.

Thomas Swiss is professor of culture and teaching at the University of Minnesota and editor or coeditor of several books, including *Key Concepts for Popular Music and*

Culture, Mapping the Beat, and *New Media Poetics.* His books of poetry include *Rough Cut* and *Measure.* He recently bought an old copy of *Rolling Stone* autographed by Courtney Love.

Mikiko Tachi is associate professor of American studies at the Division of International Languages and Cultures, Faculty of Letters, Chiba University, Japan. She holds a Ph.D. in American civilization from Brown University.

Gayle Wald is professor of English at George Washington University and author of *Shout, Sister, Shout: The Untold Story of Rock-and-Roll Trailblazer Sister Rosetta Tharpe.* She has published widely on music, performance, feminist theory and race theory, and American literature.

Anne Waldman is a poet, editor, performer, professor, and cultural activist. She has received a National Endowment for the Arts award and the Shelley prize for poetry. She cofounded the Jack Kerouac School of Disembodied Poetics with Allen Ginsberg at the Naropa University in 1974. She is a Distinguished Professor and chair of Naropa's Summer Writing Program, and is author or editor of more than forty books and small press editions of poetry. Her most recent book of poetry is *Manatee/Humanity,* and she is coeditor of *The Beats of Naropa* anthology.

David Yaffe is assistant professor of English at Syracuse University and author of *Fascinating Rhythm: Reading Jazz in American Writing.* His forthcoming projects include *The Many Roads of Bob Dylan* and *Reckless Daughter: A Portrait of Joni Mitchell.*

Index